GOD WITH US

Other Crossway Books by K. Scott Oliphint

Things That Cannot Be Shaken: Holding Fast to Your Faith in a Relativistic World
(with Rod Mays)

Christian Apologetics Past and Present: A Primary Source Reader

Volume 1, *To 1500* (coedited with William Edgar)

Volume 2, *From 1500* (coedited with William Edgar)

GOD WITH US

DIVINE CONDESCENSION

AND THE ATTRIBUTES OF GOD

K. SCOTT OLIPHINT

WHEATON, ILLINOIS

Cover design: John Hamilton Design
Cover photo: iStock
Interior design and typesetting: Lakeside Design Plus

First printing 2012
Printed in the United States of America

Unless otherwise indicated, Scripture quotations are from the ESV® Bible (*The Holy Bible, English Standard Version*®), copyright © 2001 by Crossway. Used by permission. All rights reserved.

Scripture quotations marked NASB are from *The New American Standard Bible*®. Copyright © The Lockman Foundation 1960, 1962, 1963, 1968, 1971, 1972, 1973, 1975, 1977, 1995. Used by permission.

Scripture quotations marked KJV are from the *King James Version* of the Bible.

All emphases in Scripture quotations have been added by the author.

Trade paperback ISBN:	978-1-4335-0902-5
ePub ISBN:	978-1-4335-2359-5
PDF ISBN:	978-1-4335-0903-2
Mobipocket ISBN:	978-1-4335-0904-9

Oliphint, K. Scott, 1955–
    God with us : divine condescension and the attributes of God / K. Scott Oliphint.
        p. cm.
    Includes bibliographical references (p.   ) and indexes.
    ISBN 978-1-4335-0902-5 (tp)
    1. God (Christianity) I. Title.
BT103.O39 2012
231'.4—dc23
                                            2011031379

Crossway is a publishing ministry of Good News Publishers.

VP	24	23	22	21	20	19	18	17	16	15	14	13	12
14	13	12	11	10	9	8	7	6	5	4	3	2	1

To

Larry and Mary Ellen Puls

And this is eternal life,
that they might know you, the only true God,
even the One whom you have sent, Jesus Christ.

JOHN 17:3 (MY TRANSLATION)

I believe that many who find that
"nothing happens" when they sit down,
or kneel down, to a book of devotion, would find
that the heart sings unbidden while they are working
their way through a tough bit of theology
with a pipe in their teeth and
a pencil in their hands.

C. S. LEWIS, "INTRODUCTION,"
ON THE INCARNATION BY ATHANASIUS

Contents

Introduction

> 'Tis mystery all: th' Immortal dies:
> Who can explore His strange design?
> In vain the firstborn seraph tries
> To sound the depths of love divine.
> 'Tis mercy all! Let earth adore,
> Let angel minds inquire no more.
> Amazing Love! How can it be
> that thou, my God, shouldst die for me?
>
> CHARLES WESLEY

The purpose of this book is to help us think biblically about who God is. More specifically, I hope to address some of the conundrums that arise when we attempt to think about God's character in light of the fact that he has created and has covenanted to redeem a people. Our focus, therefore, will be *first of all* on the character of God, in order then to focus on that character *given creation*. In order properly to understand the relationship of God to creation, it is necessary, in the first place, to understand who God is quite apart from his creation. As we will see, to begin with God-in-relationship (with creation) is to begin in the wrong place. We must first understand who the triune God is before we can begin to grasp who he is as he relates himself to creation. Thus, *God with Us* will explore God's character in order, first, to argue and reaffirm that he is independent *as the triune God*. Then we will begin to see what is involved when this independent God condescends to relate himself to his creation, as God *with us*.

So, this is not, in the first place, a book on the doctrine of God (what is sometimes referred to as theology proper).[1] Much that will be discussed in this book will have to be assumed, therefore, and not debated in these pages. Those debates are ongoing and important, and the lack of discussion with respect to them should not be understood as a lack of concern.

On the other hand, given certain biblical and historical truths with respect to the character, attributes, and properties of God, it is incumbent on the church to think about such things carefully in order more adequately to worship him.[2] The primary purpose of this book, therefore, is that the church might more biblically "think God's thoughts after him"—that we might understand better just who God is, what he has told us about himself, and how best to think about him. In that sense, the doctrine of God, or theology proper, will be the subject of every page.

As we will see, there is an inextricable link between the doctrine of God— his attributes and properties—and the biblical understanding of who Christ is. This should not be surprising. If indeed we know who God is by virtue of his revelation to us, the quintessential knowledge of God will naturally come by way of the quintessential revelation of God, which is given to the world in Jesus Christ. It would not be an overstatement to say that the way to a proper understanding of God and his character is given foremost in a proper understanding of the Son of God come in the flesh, Jesus Christ.[3]

---

[1] Anyone interested in the classical Christian doctrine of God, much of which will be presupposed rather than argued here, should consult Herman Bavinck, *Reformed Dogmatics*, vol. 2, *God and Creation*, ed. John Bolt, trans. John Vriend (Grand Rapids: Baker Academic, 2004); Francis Turretin, *Institutes of Elenctic Theology*, trans. George Musgrave Giger, ed. James T. Dennison Jr., vol. 1 (Phillipsburg, NJ: P&R, 1992); Richard A. Muller, *Post-Reformation Reformed Dogmatics: The Rise and Development of Reformed Orthodoxy, ca. 1520 to ca. 1725*, vol. 3, *The Divine Essence and Attributes*, 2nd ed. (Grand Rapids: Baker, 2003); Richard A. Muller, *Post-Reformation Reformed Dogmatics: The Rise and Development of Reformed Orthodoxy, ca. 1520 to ca. 1725*, vol. 4, *The Triunity of God*, 2nd ed. (Grand Rapids: Baker, 2003); John Calvin, *Institutes of the Christian Religion*, trans. Ford Lewis Battles, ed. John T. McNeill, 2 vols., The Library of Christian Classics (Philadelphia: Westminster Press, 1960). It seems nothing that is currently available, including this book, can take its place alongside these for rigorous, clear, biblical, and truthful exposition and explanation of classical Christian theism.
[2] Note, just to use one example, "The dogmatics of post-Reformation Protestantism did not develop in a vacuum and was not formulated simply for the sake of classroom exercises in speculative thinking—*it was churchly dogmatics*." Muller, *Post-Reformation Reformed Dogmatics*, 3:31–32, my emphasis.
[3] Readers will note that this statement is replete with covenant-historical connotations. There was, obviously, a time when Christ had not come in the flesh. I am not proposing that God, therefore, could not be known properly until that time. The Lord's people have always been responsible to know God according to his revelation in history, which itself is progressive. What I am proposing is that, given the climactic revelation of God in Christ, in history, it is from that time on incumbent on the church to know God by way of knowing Christ. This is true not simply for soteriology (salvation), but also for theology proper.

If we begin to think in this way—that the person of Christ gives us a proper way to think about who God is and how he relates himself to his creation—then we are more adequately equipped not only to think about God according to his own revelation, but also to meet some of the challenges that have arisen, historically and of late, with respect to God's character and attributes.

To mention just one example of those challenges: Clark Pinnock, commenting on the classical view of an immutable and impassible God, notes the following: "For most of us today, however, this immobility of God is by no means attractive. . . . I admit that modern culture has influenced me in this matter. The new emphasis upon human freedom requires that I think of God as self-limited in relation to the world."[4] This notion of God, sometimes called open theism (in that God is thought to be open to, and not in control of, the future), has gained a hearing and is even argued to be within the confines of evangelical thought. John Sanders, commenting on this view, emphasizes the newness of open theism: "Modern theology has witnessed a remarkable reexamination of the nature and attributes of God."[5] This reexamination, for open theists, includes the denial of virtually all of the classic, essential attributes of God.

In his helpful and poignant critique of open theism, John Frame gives a nice summary of some of the primary assertions argued by open theists, assertions that require them to reject classical Christian theism.[6]

1. Love is God's most important quality.
2. Love is not only care and commitment, but also being sensitive and responsive.
3. Creatures exert an influence on God.
4. God's will is not the ultimate explanation of everything. History is the combined result of what God and his creatures decide to do.
5. God does not know everything timelessly, but learns from events as they take place.
6. So God is dependent on the world in some ways.
7. Human beings are free in the libertarian sense.[7]

---

[4]Clark H. Pinnock, "Between Classical and Process Theism," in *Process Theology*, ed. Ronald H. Nash (Grand Rapids: Baker, 1987), 315, 317.

[5]John Sanders, "Historical Considerations," in Clark H. Pinnock et al., *The Openness of God: A Biblical Challenge to the Traditional Understanding of God* (Downers Grove, IL: InterVarsity, 1994), 91.

[6]When we mention the classic or orthodox doctrine of God, we are referencing the Reformed understanding of God.

[7]John M. Frame, *No Other God* (Phillipsburg, NJ: P&R, 2001), 23. Frame takes much of this summary from Richard Rice, "Biblical Support for a New Perspective," in Pinnock et al., *The Openness of God*.

As we will see later on, some of these tenets can be phrased in such a way that they can have a place in our overall understanding of who God is. But unless the place that they have is clearly and biblically set forth, these tenets can serve to override and undermine foundational and necessary aspects of God's essence as given to us in Scripture. Once that happens, any relationship with a biblical understanding of God, and with historic Christian theism, is lost. One holding an "open" view of God, as summarized above, is not within the pale of Christian orthodoxy and should not assume to be; intellectual honesty demands otherwise.

As we will see, the "remarkable reexamination" of which Sanders speaks is not altogether new (there's nothing new under the sun). It recapitulates much that has already been discussed and debated in the history of Christian thought. It is, however, destructive of any biblical notion of God. It undermines a proper understanding of his character (and thus of worship) and seeks to lessen, even eclipse, his glory while it raises high the glory and excellencies of sinful, finite humanity.

This should not be surprising, though it is tragic. It is the temptation par excellence for man to see himself as more exalted, or at least to desire such a thing, all the while seeking to place God on a par with his human creatures. The temptation, "You will be like God," was the undoing of humanity, and its infection continues to spread through human hearts in the course of history.

I hope to avoid that temptation in this book. Assumed throughout will be the bedrock truth of God's absolute independence. There is no point at which God's essential character intersects with ours. He is God, and we are not. He is God and there is no other. His ways are not our ways and his thoughts are not our thoughts (Isa. 55:9). His judgments are unsearchable and his ways inscrutable. No one has known the mind of the Lord, and no one has become his counselor. He is no man's debtor (Rom. 11:33–35).

He does, however, condescend to us. In that free act of his mercy he takes on characteristics that determine just how he will interact with us, and with creation generally. It will be useful for us to think carefully about those characteristics and attributes in order to see God in all of his resplendent glory and in light of his covenant faithfulness to all of creation.

A. About the Attributes

There will be in this book, therefore, a particular focus on God's character, attributes, and properties. Even so, the focus will not involve a delineation and determination of all or most of God's attributes as historically understood. As noted above, there are excellent resources available for such things. The focus, rather, will be on how best to think of God's attributes, given that he is God, in the first place, and that, as God, he has determined to relate himself to creation and to be "with us."

The first thing that is necessary to grasp about the attributes, properties, or perfections (which I use as synonyms) of God, therefore, is that a basic distinction must be maintained between God as he is and exists *in himself* and God as he *condescends*.[8] The theological (i.e., biblical) reason for this distinction is that it is obvious that before anything was created,[9] there was and has always been God. That is, God himself is not essentially subject to time; he does not, according to his essential character, live, move, and have his being in a temporal context. He has no beginning and will have no end. Not only so, but before there was anything created, there was *only* God. It is not as though things existed—ideas, concepts, properties, and so forth—alongside God prior to creation.[10] Before creation, there was nothing but God. To put it more starkly, before God created, there was not even nothing; there was God and only God.[11] The language of the Westminster Confession of Faith, chapter 7, "On God's Covenant with Man," section 1, is quite helpful in this regard.

> The distance between God and the creature is so great, that although reasonable creatures do owe obedience unto Him as their Creator, yet they could never have any fruition of Him as their blessedness and reward, but by some voluntary condescension on God's part, which he has been pleased to express by way of covenant.

The Confession, in this first section, is affirming a good bit in one paragraph. As a matter of fact, though all orthodox theology affirms God's con-

---

[8]If the problem I am addressing in this book can be summarily focused, it stems from a multitude of discussions and assumptions in which created properties are discussed relative to God's *essential* character (e.g., how can an *eternal* God speak at a *time* in history?), rather than to his covenantal, condescended character (e.g., he takes on temporal properties without in any way ceasing to be essentially eternal). As we will see, once God (the Son) takes on covenantal, created properties, discussing the relationship of creation to who he is (climactically, as the God-man) requires taking into account the assumption of those properties. This is rarely done in discussions of God's relationship to creation.

[9]We should note here that to speak in temporal terms in referring to a nontemporal state of affairs (i.e., the existence of God) is still wholly accurate, given that God himself, in his Word, does the same thing (see Eph. 1:4, 20). There is no other way for finite creatures to refer to such things, but neither is there a need for such.

[10]Thus, any notion, Platonic or otherwise, that there are eternal properties or verities that exist independent of God is erroneous. Whatever properties exist prior to God's condescension are themselves identical to God and exist only in that he exists.

[11]When Christians speak, therefore, of creation *ex nihilo*, what is actually meant is creation from nothing except God.

descension, the central thrust of this book will be that God's condescension, which is expressed by way of covenant, has not been taken seriously enough. It is just that condescension, I will argue, that should inform how we think about every passage dealing with God's character. I will elaborate on this point as we move along.

In this section of the Confession we should note, first, that the "distance" affirmed is not a spatial distance. There is no hint in Scripture or historically that God is absent or spatially distant from any part of his creation. The distance spoken of here is a distance of *being*; it is a distance determined by who God is *as God*, and who we are *as creatures*. There is a vast, even infinite, difference, thus a "distance," between God and everything else that exists.

That distance, the Confession notes, was so great that we as God's human ("reasonable") creatures could not even render the obedience due him, nor could we enjoy him as our Creator, unless he determined to be known and to be in a relationship with us. He did so determine, and that determination is helpfully set out in this section as "voluntary condescension." I will elaborate more on this as we go along, but I should affirm here that any relationship we have to God, and he has to us, we have only because of his free ("voluntary") choice to come down to us ("condescension")[12] and thus to establish a relationship with us. It is only by virtue of *God's* activity, therefore, and his initiation that we are able to be in a relationship with him.[13]

This understanding of God is, sadly, foreign to many who propose to discuss God's character. Philosophy of religion, for example, in the main, because of its anti-revelational bias with respect to matters philosophical, seems to be significantly wide of the mark when it comes to its understanding of who God is and of how he relates to his creation.[14] Virtually any article or book on the topic will conclude with some god who is (at best) far inferior to the triune God of Christian theism. The best one can hope for in current discussions concerning the character of God in philosophy of religion is a conclusion that

[12]More on God's voluntary condescension in chapter 3.
[13]In this first section of chapter 7, the Confession is not yet concerned with our sinful rebellion against God. It will begin to address that problem in section 3. We should keep in mind, therefore, that our relationship to God, *quite apart from sin*, depends on God's activity, not ours, given his absolute uniqueness and our inability as creatures to comprehend who he is. The problem of sin greatly complicates this inability, but it does not initiate it.
[14]See, for example, Michael L. Peterson, *Philosophy of Religion: Selected Readings* (Oxford: Oxford University Press, 1996); Louis P. Pojman, ed. *Philosophy of Religion: An Anthology* (Belmont, CA: Wadsworth, 1987); William L. Rowe, William J. Wainwright, eds. *Philosophy of Religion: Selected Readings*, 3rd ed. (Fort Worth, TX: Harcourt Brace, 1973).

will steer us toward a kind of super-man rather than the triune God. How should we begin to address this predicament?[15]

It should be said at the outset that, contrary to much confused language in some of the literature about whether one can know God's essence, orthodox theology has consistently held that God's essence can indeed be known as it is revealed to us, but it (he) cannot be known per se, that is, as it is known by God himself. Hence, Muller:

> As Turretin indicates, *the way in which God is what he is* in the simplicity of the divine essence cannot be known by the human mind, granting that the human mind knows things only by composition and composite attribution— nonetheless, we are given to know the divine attributes or *essential properties* by revelation and rational reflection on revelation in such a way that *God's nature is truly known* by means of the revealed attributes.[16]

Two historical points bolster our discussions here. First, the history of Christian thought is replete with discussions of the essential attributes, or the essence, of the triune God. Second, as Muller notes, though some might want to see Calvin's approach as decidedly anti-essentialist, Calvin "belongs as much to the theological tradition, with its interest in the divine essence and in its understanding of Scripture as containing references to the divine being, as any of the later Reformed writers."[17] What Calvin rightly opposed was not essentialist language, but abstract speculation with respect to the character of God.[18]

---

[15]This is true, as we have seen and will see, of much current-day discussion of the character of God in some theological circles. See, for example, Gregory A. Boyd, *God of the Possible: A Biblical Introduction to the Open View of God* (Grand Rapids: Baker, 2000); Clark H. Pinnock, *Most Moved Mover: A Theology of God's Openness*, Didsbury Lectures, 2000 (Grand Rapids: Baker Academic, 2001).

[16]Muller, *Post-Reformation Reformed Dogmatics*, 3:195–96, my emphases. For a discussion and defense of "essence language" among the Protestant orthodox, see ibid., 227–28. Note especially, "Thus, in answer to the question of 'What' or 'Who' God is, the orthodox set themselves first to describe the 'nature' or 'essence' of God" (232).

[17]Ibid., 250.

[18]According to Warfield, "The nature of this one God, [Calvin] conceives, can be known to us only as He manifests it in His works (I. v. 9); that is to say, only in His perfections. What we call the attributes of God thus become to Calvin the sum of our knowledge of Him. In these manifestations of His character we see not indeed what He is in Himself, but what He is to us (I. x. 2); but what we see Him to be thus to us, He truly is, and this is all we can know about Him. We might expect to find in the 'Institutes,' therefore, a comprehensive formal discussion of the attributes, by means of which what God is to us should be fully set before us. This, however, as we have already seen, we do not get. And much less do we get any metaphysical discussion of the nature of the attributes of God, their relation to one another, or to the divine essence of which they are determinations. We must not therefore suppose, however, that we get little or

How then do we construe God's essential attributes? One way, though admittedly not the only (or even perhaps the best) way, would be to take those attributes that are associated with *God as God*, that is, those attributes that God has quite apart from creation—attributes, we could say, that are related strictly to God—and affirm them to be of the essence of who he is. In other words, given that God is essentially *a se* (i.e., independent), we could begin to posit attributes or properties that are entailed by his essential independence, which would themselves, therefore, also be attributes that define who God *as God* is.

For example, is God essentially infinite? If we affirm that God is essentially a perfect Being (one who lacks nothing), if we affirm his character as *a se*, then it cannot be that he is in any way essentially limited by anything outside of himself, since to be limited would by definition be a lack; it would be a constraint placed on God by something else, be it space or time or human choices.[19] In other words, we can affirm, then, that God is essentially infinite. Entailed in his independence and his perfection is infinity itself.

On the other hand, is the property "Creator" of the essence of God? One way to answer that question is to ask whether it was *necessary* for God to create. Did God create the universe because *he had to*? Or, to put it another way, would it have been possible that God not create anything? The orthodox answer is, of course, that there was nothing in God, no necessity, that motivated him to create. He created by a free choice of his will. To answer otherwise would mean that God *had to* create the world, in which case the creation of the world would itself be a necessary property of God's. But then God would have a necessary property that (1) was not entailed by his independence (since the necessity of God's creative activity would entail a dependence on something outside of and besides God) and (2) implied some kind of lack in God (since the necessity of something outside of God, i.e., creation, would mean that God was in need of it in order to be who he essentially is). So "being Creator" is not an essential property that God has.

---

nothing of them, or little or nothing to the point. On the contrary, besides incidental allusions to them throughout the discussion, from which we may glean much of Calvin's conceptions of them, they are made the main subject of two whole chapters, the one of which discusses in considerable detail the revelation of the divine perfections in His works and deeds, the other the revelation made of them in His Word. We have already remarked upon the skill with which Calvin, at the opening of his discussion of the doctrine of God (chap. x.), manages, under color of pointing out the harmony of the description of God given in the Scriptures with the conception of Him we may draw from His works, to bring all he had to say of the divine attributes at once before the reader's eye." Benjamin B. Warfield, *The Works of Benjamin B. Warfield*, vol. 5, *Calvin and Calvinism* (Bellingham, WA: Logos Research Systems, 2008), 162.
[19]Note number 7 in Frame's list of open theist beliefs above. If one presupposes libertarian freedom for man, then God is essentially limited in some way or ways.

It would seem, then, that God has properties that are essential to him and others that are not essential to him. How should we delineate between these two? What is it that helps us to see God's essential properties as essential, and what is it that helps us to see God's other properties as nonessential? This will be a matter taken up in chapters below.

But so far I have simply delineated the *mode* of God's properties—God's essential attributes will certainly include any properties that are entailed by his aseity, his independence. But how are we to think of this aseity? Is it a biblical notion, or do we simply posit it because it suits our discussion?

I will argue that it is the divine name of God that gives us a way into his essential attributes, and any attribute that would be entailed by God's absolute essential independence would necessarily be included in God's essential attributes. This, we should note, is nothing new.

> The divine names present a biblical point of entry into the rather abstruse and necessarily metaphysical discussion of the essence and attributes—indeed, as far as the Protestant orthodox were concerned, the names of God, the biblical identifiers of who and what God is, provided the natural point of contact between the biblical language of God and a more strictly philosophical discussion.[20]

It is not possible for us comprehensively to understand what kind of being God is in himself. If we try to conjure up in our minds just what eternity—with its lack of time—might be, and how someone can actually *be*, and be without beginning or end, we soon reach our cognitive limits. We can affirm it, but we cannot conceive it. The best our minds can do is to try to project present existence backward until it can no longer be "seen" by our mind's eye. But surely God's eternity is of an entirely different character. Given that it is *God's* eternity, it simply *is* his existence; unlike time, it is not a context in which he exists, surrounding and engulfing him as time does creation. Rather, it just *is* him. Words cannot adequately express what *exactly* this is. More on this later.

Not only so, but God, since he is essentially infinite, is without boundaries—temporal *or* spatial. He is not "contained" by a context of space that surrounds him. Rather, his existence just *is*. It is not an existence *here* or *there*; it is simply existence.[21]

Not only is he "simply existence," but traditional Christian theism has always held that God is "simple existence." "Simple" here does not mean the

---

[20]Muller, *Post-Reformation Reformed Dogmatics*, 3:248.
[21]We should keep in mind here that we are thinking of God as he is in himself. As we will see later, Scripture is clear that there is a presence of God, but that presence presupposes his creation.

opposite of complex (what can be more complex than God?), but rather it affirms that God is not composed of any parts external to himself. Thus, any distinctions that we make with respect to God must themselves be identical to him. One way to illustrate this is by way of our understanding of God as triune. By "triune," we mean that God is one in three. He is one identical essence, and he is also three persons. But this does not in any way mean that God is composed of three parts—Father, Son, and Holy Spirit. Rather, it means that the three persons of the Trinity are each one and all together identical to God. They are, as the history of the church has taught us to say, one in essence, three in persons. So, we make distinctions—between Father, Son, and Holy Spirit—and the distinctions do actually tell us that the Father is not the Son, who is not the Spirit, who is not the Father. But those distinctions are in no way "parts" of God. The three *are* one and the same God.

So also, though not in an identical way, are the attributes of God. They are distinctions that we make with respect to God's character. But these distinctions with respect to who God is essentially are themselves not parts of God that come together to "compose" who he is. Rather, they just *are* God. Thus, when we say God is eternal, we do not mean that God partakes of that which is eternal and external to his existence. What we mean is that the eternity of God *is itself* God. To think otherwise is to make God dependent on something else—in this case eternity—in order to be who he is essentially.

And this brings us to an affirmation that should be seen as foundational to everything else we say about God: the *aseity* of God. This aseity, or independence, of God must be seen to be foundational because, in order to think and speak rightly about God, we cannot suppose at any point that God is essentially dependent. According to Herman Bavinck:

> Now when God ascribes this aseity to himself in Scripture, he makes himself known as absolute being, as the one who *is* in an absolute sense. By this perfection he is at once essentially and absolutely distinct from all creatures. Creatures, after all, do not derive their existence from themselves but from others and so have nothing from themselves; both in their origin and hence in their further development and life, they are absolutely dependent. But as is evident from the word "aseity," God is exclusively from himself, not in the sense of being self-caused but being from eternity to eternity who he is, being not becoming. God is absolute being, the fullness of being, and therefore also eternally and absolutely independent in his existence, in his perfections in all his works, the first and the last, the sole cause and final goal of all things. In this aseity of God, conceived not only as having being from himself but also as the fullness

of being, all the other perfections are included. They are given with the aseity itself and are the rich and multifaceted development of it.[22]

The aseity of God, therefore, must be the place on which we stand in order to assert anything else about him, given that anything else we say about him depends for its proper understanding and meaning on that aseity. Or, to put it a bit more succinctly, unless God is *a se* (of himself), he is not God, and no characterization of God that excludes aseity can be true of him. Any theology that denies or otherwise negates this aseity cannot be sustained as a true, biblical doctrine of God.[23] A god who is not *a se*, and thus who is essentially dependent, is a god who is unable to be god. In order for God to be who he is, he must be and remain essentially independent.[24]

B. Hermeneutics and Theology (Proper)

Before moving to some of our more specific concerns, it is necessary, in the interest of full disclosure, that I sketch at least some of the main interpretive principles that will be assumed throughout this study. These principles are particularly important and relevant when "theology proper," or a discussion of God (based on Scripture), is in view.

Perhaps one way to emphasize my (Reformed or Calvinistic) hermeneutic with respect to a biblical understanding of God's character is by way of contrast. Note, just to use one example, the way in which one current author seeks to deal with the character of God, given the particular hermeneutic he employs.[25] First, the biblical passage.

> When they came to the place of which God had told him, Abraham built the altar there and laid the wood in order and bound Isaac his son and laid him on the altar, on top of the wood. Then Abraham reached out his hand and took the knife to slaughter his son. But the angel of the LORD called to him from heaven and said, "Abraham, Abraham!" And he said, "Here am I." He said, "Do not lay your hand on the boy or do anything to him, *for now I know that you fear God*, seeing you have not withheld your son, your only son, from me." (Gen 22:9–12)

---

[22]Bavinck, *Reformed Dogmatics*, 2:152.
[23]This is not to say that there are no views of God that compromise or deny his aseity; only that such views are biblically unsustainable, as I hope to make clear.
[24]More on this later.
[25]I choose this particular example because of the obvious hermeneutic errors present. For a helpful discussion on the hermeneutic of open theism, see Frame, *No Other God*, 41–48.

In his book *Inspiration and Incarnation*, Peter Enns offers a hermeneutic that argues for the hegemony of the human in Scripture.[26] The main point of the book is that, given the humanness of the Bible, there are many and sundry passages that simply do not make coherent sense and cannot be brought together to affirm a coherent doctrine.[27] This hermeneutic is extended, in one section, to aspects of the biblical doctrine of God.

Under the section "Does God Change His Mind?," in the chapter "The Old Testament and Theological Diversity," Enns does indeed want to affirm a distinction between Creator and creature. The affirmation is given that God "is supreme over his creation" and that he "does not need creation in any way to be complete." Enns goes on to affirm that "God is in control" and that "no one can stop what he determines to do."[28] These affirmations are correct as far as they go. What is most troublesome in this section is the material that follows. Given that material, the best we are left with is that the Bible is confused in its descriptions and ascriptions of God. A couple of examples from the book should suffice to show this.

In the same section, a discussion of Genesis 22 ensues (Abraham's near sacrifice of Isaac).[29] Commenting on Genesis 22:12 ("Now I know that you fear God . . ."), Enns says: "It is clear that the purpose of the test was not to prove anything to Abraham but to God. For God to say 'Now I know' makes sense in this story only if the test was a real test; if something was at stake. . . . In this story, God did not know until after the test was passed."[30]

Without elaborating on various ways one might understand this passage, the obvious question, given the above, is just how the God of this story is related to the God who is supreme and self-complete. The answer given is simply that we cannot "allow either of these dimensions" of God's character "to override the other."[31] This answer is, at best, confused and should be seen as a direct result of the hermeneutic offered in the book (including a confused incarnational analogy). Not only so, but the indictment is issued that to try to

---

[26] To fully examine the hermeneutic method in this book is beyond the scope of our concerns here. For a more detailed and helpful overall analysis, see Gregory K. Beale, *The Erosion of Inerrancy in Evangelicalism: Responding to New Challenges to Biblical Authority* (Wheaton, IL: Crossway, 2008); also Bruce K. Waltke, "Revisiting Inspiration and Incarnation," *Westminster Theological Journal* 71, no. 1 (2009): 83–128.

[27] Coherence, for Enns, lies in a "Christotelic" understanding of biblical passages. Without detailing the problems in this view, I believe such an understanding is unable to make sense of the actual texts of Scripture, and thus contradictions and incoherence are to be expected.

[28] Peter Enns, *Inspiration and Incarnation* (Grand Rapids: Baker Academic, 2005).

[29] I will offer my own analysis of the passage later.

[30] Enns, *Inspiration and Incarnation*, 103.

[31] Ibid., 107.

reconcile different descriptions of God in Scripture is somehow to go beyond the Bible, to be interested in a God behind the scenes.[32] This too is a result of the hermeneutic method espoused, in which any attempt at bringing together passages that appear to be inconsistent is illegitimate, in that it does not do full justice to the "humanity" of Scripture.

To use another example, Enns provides some commentary on Genesis 6:5–8.[33]

> The LORD saw that the wickedness of man was great in the earth, and that every intention of the thoughts of his heart was only evil continually. And the LORD was sorry that he had made man on the earth, and it grieved him to his heart. So the LORD said, "I will blot out man whom I have created from the face of the land, man and animals and creeping things and birds of the heavens, for I am sorry that I have made them." But Noah found favor in the eyes of the LORD. (Gen. 6:5–8)

In this passage, Enns notes,

> The scene is straightforward: (1) God creates everything good; (2) wickedness and evil enter; (3) God *reacts* by intending to wipe out everything he made. Of course, it is possible to say that God already anticipated step 3 in step 1, that is, he knew what was going to happen, and so step 2 does not take him by surprise. That may be so, but that is only a guess that goes far beyond what we read. The story is told in such a way that steps 2 and 3 have an unexpected quality to them. Any attempt to force the God *of Genesis* 6 into a mold cast by certain theological commitments or to reconcile this description to other biblical passages simply amounts to reading past this story. I take it as a fundamental truth, however, that God did not put this story here so we could read past it.[34]

There are many questions that should be addressed in this regard. Not all of them can be pursued here. Is it really the case that the church should read these biblical passages as self-contained revelations of God, without access to any other characteristic or attribute of God? Is the proper method of interpretation simply to read the story on its own, to bracket it off as an independent piece of revelation, in order to understand *better* who God is? Such a suggestion can only misunderstand who God is and what his reve-

---

[32]See ibid., 106–7.
[33]We need not engage all the passages mentioned in this section of the book. The points made apply, more or less, to each example given.
[34]Ibid., 104, emphasis original.

lation is meant to communicate. Specifically, on what basis can the claim be supported that God's omniscience is "only a guess"? If the answer is that we must remain within the story line of Genesis 6, then the assumption is that the knowledge of God that those reading the story (or, *in* the story!) possess is gained exclusively and only from that story.

This answer is confused, at best, for at least two reasons: (1) It presumes that those reading the story have only that story in which to glean their knowledge of God. It would seem, however, that they have, at minimum, the fact of God as Creator in view as well, given the Genesis story up to chapter 6. And the truth of God as Creator cannot be divorced from the notion of God as sovereign and independent of his creation. (2) It assumes that no knowledge of God is present universally and clearly by virtue of God's natural revelation, such that his "invisible attributes, that is, his eternal power and divine nature" (Rom. 1:20) have *not* been clearly seen since creation (though Paul affirms that they have been). That is, "the story" comes to those who, by virtue of being created in God's image, already know him. There is not, nor can there be, any reading of any biblical passage from any other standpoint than the true and accurate knowledge of God given in and through creation. Here we need to see and affirm that no one comes to any passage of Scripture neutrally, or *de novo*, with respect to who God is.

Second, and specifically, just who is the "God of Genesis 6"? The answer seems to be that he is the God of the story, and that to import anything into the God of the story that is not given in the story is to misunderstand not just the story but who God is (or who the God of the story is). In other words, it is a "fundamental truth . . . that God did not put this story here so we could read past it."

This hermeneutic method begs a number of questions. Is it true that an affirmation of God as the sovereign, independent Creator of all, who himself is grieved by the sin of creation, is "reading past" the story? Is it really "reading past" the story to understand who God is from Genesis 1 to 6, attempting to see the character of God in all of his majestic glory, rather than simply a God who grieves? Can the hermeneutic Enns espouses possibly help evangelicals, or anyone else, in their attempt to know God better?[35] Hasn't this method,

---

[35]It should be noted here that to miss what this passage says about God is to miss the gospel itself. God condescends to his creation to deal definitively with wickedness. This judgment of wickedness is not tangential to this passage, but is at its heart. How a sovereign, omniscient, and independent God can stoop to grieve over the sin of his creation will be discussed in the rest of this book. It should be obvious, however, that the revelation of who God is in this passage is obscured, not aided, by the "human" emphasis and the hermeneutic proposed in *Inspiration and Incarnation*.

in its concern to highlight the humanity of Scripture, rendered a consistent knowledge of God impossible?

We should not miss, however, the clear intent of this section of *Inspiration and Incarnation*. Stated more than once, it is that the story, to be understood properly, must be "taken alone." Those who do not take the story alone "read past" the story and thus misconstrue its meaning. If the story is not taken alone, Enns argues, then the concern is for a God behind the scenes, rather than for the God of the story.

More generally, and related to the specific concerns noted above, why is it that "any attempt to force the God of Genesis 6 into a mold cast by certain theological commitments or to reconcile this description to other biblical passages simply amounts to reading past this story"? Presumably because any notion of systematizing with respect to who God is, as revealed in Scripture, is secondary at best and an outright foreign imposition on Scripture at worst.

While not wanting in any way to undermine the importance of textual exegesis, we should note here that the conclusions reached concerning this passage in Genesis 6 are given as a result of the hermeneutic, together with a (reassessed) doctrine of Scripture, proposed in *Inspiration and Incarnation*. The clear obstacle to this proposed hermeneutic method comes from those who would force the God of a certain text into a coherent or systematic teaching, a teaching that attempts to reconcile a biblical text that speaks of God with other texts that speak of him.

Enns's methodology seems to be in direct conflict with an understanding of Scripture that affirms one divine author (and therefore one truth), and with a hermeneutic that, for the sake of knowing God and his gospel better, seeks to bring the entire relevant teaching of Scripture to bear on a particular passage.[36] This is the reason, it seems, that Enns can state, quite erroneously, that whether or not prayer has "some effect on God" is "for God to know, not us."[37] Even though the book allows that there is a "ring of truth" to the notion of prayer's effect on God, Enns's discussion in this section, no matter the context or point being made, betrays a basic confusion with respect to knowledge of God and of his Word, rather than a proper hermeneutic.

---

[36]In Moisés Silva's words, "Our evangelical view of the unity of Scripture demands that we see the whole Bible as the context of any one part. . . . To the extent that we view the whole of Scripture as having come from one Author, therefore, to that extent a systematic understanding of the Bible contributes to the exegesis of individual passages." Moisés Silva, "The Case for Calvinistic Hermeneutics," in *Revelation and Reason: New Essays in Reformed Apologetics*, ed. K. Scott Oliphint and Lane G. Tipton (Phillipsburg, NJ: P&R, 2007), 87.
[37]Enns, *Inspiration and Incarnation*, 107.

Pursuing Enns's hermeneutic consistently would lead to a denial of the fundamental doctrines of the Christian faith.

Not only so, but it seems impossible to avoid the conclusion that those who are involved in working out (as the Westminster Confession of Faith 1.5 states) "the consent of all the parts, the scope of the whole (which is, to give all glory to God), the full discovery it makes of the only way of man's salvation" are in fact, if Enns's hermeneutic is applied, involved in obscuring the various texts of Scripture.

To his credit, Enns does attempt to bring his method into some conformity with a traditional understanding of God.

> I am not trying to drive a wedge between the Bible and God. Actually, and somewhat ironically, this is what I see others doing. I feel bound to talk about God in the way(s) the Bible does, even if I am not comfortable with it. The Bible really does have authority if we let it speak, and not when we—intentionally or unintentionally—suspend what the Bible says about God in some places while we work out our speculations about what God is "really" like, perhaps by accenting other portions of the Bible that are more amenable to our thinking. God gave us the Bible so we could read it, not so we can ferret our way behind it to see how things really are.[38]

However, it seems clear from this statement that those who in their exegetical work ascertain the unity of scriptural teaching on God or who bring the Bible's teaching to bear on a text (1) are denying the authority of Scripture by not letting God speak, (2) suspend what the Bible says about God in some places, (3) work out speculations about what God is "really" like, and (4) accent portions of the Bible that are more amenable to our thinking. This, however, seems to be by and large a false problem; it is a caricature both of evangelical theology and (especially) of Reformed theology. It cannot be shown, in either case and in the main, that "speculations" about God have superseded what passages of Scripture say about him.

It seems impossible to avoid the conclusion, given the above, that there is a great chasm fixed, impossible to bridge, between the hermeneutic espoused in *Inspiration and Incarnation* and the ascertaining of a biblical doctrine of God. It should be noted as well that this hermeneutic method is destructive of the Bible's organic unity. As John Murray put it:

---

[38]Ibid., 106.

The Bible is an organism; its unity is organic. It is not a compilation of isolated and unrelated divine oracles. Our knowledge of the Bible, if it is to be really adequate, must be knowledge of the Bible as it is, and must reflect this organic character, not knowledge of the piecemeal or block variety but knowledge of the vital organic unity that belongs to the Bible. We must understand that the whole Bible stands together and that the fibers of organic connection run through the whole Bible connecting one part with every other part and every one truth with every other truth.[39]

Not only so, but the hermeneutic proposed by Enns is detrimental to the basic tenets of a Reformed, Calvinistic hermeneutic. So, says Silva, "to put it in the most shocking way possible: my theological system should tell me how to exegete."[40] And further:

Indeed, the most serious argument against the view that exegesis should be done independently of systematic theology is that such a view is hopelessly naïve. . . . Exegetes who convince themselves that, through pure philological and historical techniques, they can understand the Bible directly—that is, without the mediation of prior exegetical, theological, and philosophical commitments—are less likely to perceive the real character of exegetical difficulties.[41]

The stark conclusion to this discussion is difficult to avoid. According to *Inspiration and Incarnation*, a hermeneutic method that attempts consistency and unity will inevitably skew the meaning of the various, diverse texts of Scripture. If this is the case, multiple problems persist. For example, practically speaking, students trained under this method cannot, as pastors, confidently stand in their pulpits and expound the truth of a given text in any coherent and consistent way week after week. The truth one week will be countered the next week.

Not only so, there is no hope for those whose theological commitments influence their exegesis. To put the matter squarely within a Reformed context, anyone allowing the "system of doctrine" taught in the Westminster Standards to influence his reading of particular texts of Scripture will inevitably misread and therefore misunderstand any given passage. And he will do this because he has failed adequately to grasp what seems to be the hegemonic, universal,

---

[39]John Murray, "The Study of the Bible," in *Collected Writings of John Murray*, vol. 1, *The Claims of Truth* (Carlisle, PA: Banner of Truth, 1976), 5.
[40]Moisés Silva, "The Case for Calvinistic Hermeneutics," 86.
[41]Ibid., 88.

and all-pervasive application of the messiness of Scripture's humanity as it is offered in *Inspiration and Incarnation*.[42]

On the other hand, the hermeneutical parameters marked out by Silva, along with the organic view of Scripture delineated by Murray (a view that Scripture itself demands), provides the ground on which the unity-in-diversity of Scripture can be faithfully articulated, and thus the ground on which the God of Scripture may be rightly and obediently understood. In other words, if we combine the assessments above (of Silva and Murray), we end up with a Reformed hermeneutic that follows the truth of the Westminster Confession of Faith 1.9: "The infallible rule of interpretation of Scripture is the Scripture itself: and therefore, when there is a question about the true and full sense of any Scripture (which is not manifold, but one), it must be searched and known by other places that speak more clearly."

The Proper and Protestant Principle

What basic hermeneutic principle, therefore, should we assume as we begin to think carefully about the character and attributes of God? It may help to note the principle in play, with respect to discussions of God's character and attributes, in the seventeenth century.

> The orthodox line of thought is guided not by a totally open or unbiased exegesis of texts, but by an *ontological conception* of the immutability of God: this guiding conception in turn leads to an interpretation of Scripture that gives priority to those texts stressing the unchangeability of God over those texts which indicate change, priority to those texts which stress God's otherness over those which indicate emotion, passion, or other kinship with humanity. But this is not a case of rationalism or metaphysical speculation overruling revelation: instead it is an example of one of the many instances in which theology must make a choice concerning its view of God, deciding which aspects of the scriptural view are governing concepts, anthropomorphisms or transcendence, the "repentance" of God or the divine constancy. And, in this case in particular, the Reformed orthodox stand not only in the line of the more philosophical argu-

---

[42]Readers should note that there seems to be a resurgence of evangelicals whose views are similar to the ones offered in Enns's work, views that will inevitably end up denying the full, inerrant authority of God's Word, and thus will confuse, if not deny, biblical truth as it is given in God's revelation. See, for example, Craig D. Allert, *A High View of Scripture? The Authority of the Bible and the Formation of the New Testament Canon*, Evangelical Ressourcement: Ancient Sources for the Church's Future (Grand Rapids: Baker Academic, 2007); A. T. B. McGowan, *The Divine Authenticity of Scripture: Retrieving an Evangelical Heritage* (Downers Grove, IL: IVP Academic, 2008); Kenton L. Sparks, *God's Word in Human Words: An Evangelical Appropriation of Critical Biblical Scholarship* (Grand Rapids: Baker Academic, 2008).

ments typical of scholastic theology but, together with the older scholasticism, in the line of the church's exegetical tradition—and indeed, in accord with the doctrinal statements and with the exegesis of the Reformers.[43]

Here Muller notes a basic hermeneutical principle. Contrary to what we have just noted, Scripture's unity must be given priority in our interpretation of the various texts of Scripture.[44] Muller denominates that priority as "ontological." He means that any and all texts of Scripture (and here we will confine our concerns to texts that deal with the character of God) that seek to tell us something of God's character must be prioritized on the basis of the fundamental aseity of God.

The reasons for this prioritization will be explored as we move along, but we should notice the initial motivation behind this method. To put it negatively, the motivation is *not* to impose an extrabiblical conception of God on the text so that it will say what we, in our preconceived assumptions, want it to say. Muller is not saying, nor is it the case, that the Reformed exegetes in the seventeenth century came to Scripture with their own preconceived idea about what God should be like (ideas gleaned from culture or philosophy or elsewhere) and then proceeded to prioritize the various texts of Scripture based on those ideas.

The point he is making is deeper and more radically biblical than that. This "ontological conception" with which the Reformed approached Scripture was itself based on the teaching of Holy Scripture. Perhaps it will help to think of it this way. There is embedded in the human constitution, by virtue of our being created in the image of God, an inherent understanding that God is and must be independent.[45] This can be seen most simply when we consider that creation itself is not eternal and that, prior to creation, God existed. His existence, therefore, does not in any way depend on the existence of creation.

---

[43]Muller, *Post-Reformation Reformed Dogmatics*, 4:451–52, my emphasis. This text appears in the context of a discussion of the divine will, but is applicable to the entire field of theology proper.

[44]This is the case, just to repeat, because God is the author of Scripture, and thus there is a unity to its (his) teachings, given that it has one author. This does not deny or in any way diminish the fact that God chose various men to write, and to write in various ways, but those considerations must take their place within the context of Scripture's inherent coherence and unity, since every human author of Scripture is writing that which God *breathes* (cf. 2 Tim. 3:16).

[45]In Rom. 1:18ff., the apostle Paul affirms that all people know God, and that what they know is "his invisible attributes, namely, his eternal power and divine nature." This knowledge includes the fact that God is in no way dependent on what he has made in order to be who he is (cf. Acts 17:24). Universal knowledge of God's independence is given to all human beings and is basic to who God is.

By "ontological conception," therefore, Muller is pointing to the fact of God's existence *as God*, apart from and prior to creation.

It is that existence, that "ontological conception," that must define, direct, and guide all other texts of Scripture that point us to the character of God. The natural and obvious question to ask when confronted with such texts (wherein God says, for example, "Now I know . . ." or "the LORD was sorry . . .") is just how we should relate those texts to the fact that the Lord himself is not dependent on creation in order to be who he is. This question has been asked in various ways throughout the history of the church and has been answered in different ways. We will look at some of those ways in later chapters. The point to be made here, however, is that it is right and proper to broach this kind of question at every turn. We should want to know precisely and clearly, as much as it lies within us, how it is that One who is altogether independent of his creation can, at the same time, "not know" (e.g., Gen. 3:9; 22:12) or "regret" (e.g., Ex. 32:14; Ps. 106:45).

But it is not only the image of God, entailing as it does a true knowledge of God, that causes us to ask such questions. As we noted above, it is also the fact that in our reading of Scripture we rightly, carefully, and routinely seek to bring what we read and know of Scripture to every other text, or set of texts, that we read. To put it in Silva's words, "My theological system tells me how to exegete" various other texts with which I am confronted. Given that my theological system may be errant, *even as my system guides my exegesis*, it is also the case that my exegesis may adjust my theological system.[46] But it is decidedly *not* the case that we come to the text of Scripture "on our own," independent of a prior knowledge of its teachings, and then seek to build up as we move along. Rather, we come *with* that knowledge of Scripture, applying it to specific passages and changing it as those passages inform our system. Nor do we simply take a text as a self-contained "story," as *Inspiration and Incarnation* seeks to do, because we will inevitably conclude with a confused and truncated view of God's character.[47] Instead, as Muller notes, the "ontological conception," that is, an understanding of God *as God*, must be our guiding principle as we attempt to understand, as much as possible, the Bible's teaching on God's character.

To put the matter differently, the way in which we read and interpret Scripture is that we let the clearer passages interpret the less clear. Given our

---

[46]Thus, the hermeneutical circle.

[47]A view, we should remember, that winds up asserting that we just don't know whether prayer has any effect on God. Such assertions can only hinder, not help, Christian growth.

concern over the attributes and character of God, the clearer passages are those passages in which God reveals to us his independent character. Passages, for example, in which God is revealed as the "I AM," in which he is declared to be from everlasting to everlasting, intuitively resonate with us, given that we as his image know his "eternal power and divine nature." Those passages are clearer because they articulate the "divine nature" of God; they tell us something of who he essentially is.

Passages that speak of God being sorry or ignorant of historical events or of our own commitment to him automatically demand questions. They cry out for resolution because we know enough about God's "Godness" (θειότης— Rom. 1:20) to know that he cannot be both independent and dependent in the same way. Yet there are passages that clearly note some level of dependence. Minimally, for example, if God swears by an oath to be faithful to his promises (Heb. 6:13), such an action depends on creation and God's working out of his plan in creation. More pointedly, if God is truly sorry that he created man, then that which takes place in creation—in this case, the extent of sin in the world—moves God to regret something he has done. We rightly question how such regret coheres with God's independence.

And now we come to the focus of our study. How do we, biblically, organize our thinking about God and his character, given the reality (1) of his independence and (2) of those texts in Scripture that indicate his dependence on creation? Before we address that question, a brief introduction to available responses may provide a helpful backdrop.

C. The Specific Concern

> For though God is said to change His determinations (so that in a tropical sense [*tropica*][48] the Holy Scripture says even that God repented), this is said with reference to man's expectation, or the order of natural causes, and not with reference to that which the Almighty had foreknown that He would do.[49]

As I have said, the more specific concern that will occupy us throughout this study has to do with the relationship of God's attributes as related, first, to him *only* and, second, to his creation.

The notion of some kind of lack in God, of God changing, or of God relenting or being sorry is rightly confusing on the face of it. As we noted

---

[48]"Tropical" here means relating to a trope, figurative.
[49]Augustine, *City of God*, trans. Marcus Dods, in *A Select Library of the Nicene and Post-Nicene Fathers of the Christian Church*, series 1, vol. 2 (Grand Rapids: Eerdmans, 1988), 437 (14.11).

above, it is confusing because basic to a biblical understanding of God is that he is independent. He existed prior to creation; his existence did not and does not lack anything. He did not create out of necessity. He did not need us for fellowship, in that, as triune, the Father, Son, and Holy Spirit had complete and perfect fellowship with each other as one God.

But the Bible clearly uses such language about God. As we have already seen, there are texts in Scripture that speak of God being sorry or of his discovering or knowing something that he might not have known previously. Scripture tells us that God becomes angry, that he has compassion, that he loves and hates. Because of these texts and our basic human tendency to exalt man at the expense of God, much of what goes under the name of theology or theism has been quick to place all or most of the emphasis on God's interaction with the world, to the exclusion or near exclusion of God's independence.

Our brief review of responses to this tension would therefore do well to begin with those whose affirmation of the absolute independence of God is unquestionable.

In his commentary on Genesis 6:6 ("And the LORD was sorry that he had made man on the earth . . ."), Calvin says:

> The repentance which is here ascribed to God does not properly belong to him, *but has reference to our understanding of him*. For since we cannot comprehend him as he is, it is necessary that, for our sakes he should, in a certain sense, transform himself. That repentance cannot take place in God, easily appears from this single consideration, that nothing happens which is by him unexpected or unforeseen. The same reasoning, and remark, applies to what follows, that God was affected with grief. *Certainly God is not sorrowful or sad*; but remains forever like himself in his celestial and happy repose: yet, because it could not otherwise be known how great is God's hatred and detestation of sin, therefore the Spirit accommodates himself to our capacity. . . . This figure, which represents God as transferring to himself what is peculiar to human nature, is called ἀνθροποπάθεια.[50]

This is standard fare in Reformed thinking. Henry Ainsworth, on the same passage, notes, "The scripture giveth to God, *joy, grief, anger,* &c. not as any passions or contrary affections, for he is most simple and unchangeable, James 1:17, but by a kind of proportion, because he doth of his immutable

[50] John Calvin, *The Comprehensive John Calvin Collection*, CD ed., The Ages Digital Library System, 2002.

nature and will, such things as men do with their passions and changes of affections."[51] Again, Calvin in his *Institutes* writes:

> Although he is beyond all disturbance of mind, yet he testifies that he is angry toward sinners. Therefore whenever we hear that God is angered, we ought not to imagine any emotion in him, but rather to consider that this expression has been taken from our own human experience; because God, whenever he is exercising judgment, *exhibits the appearance of one kindled and angered.*[52]

We will return to these analyses later on. It might be useful here, however, to note how one Calvin interpreter (commenting specifically on Calvin's comments on 2 Cor. 5:19) understands Calvin with respect to God's disposition in the transition from wrath to grace in history.

> So the truth about atonement, about reconciliation to God, has to be represented to us as if it implied a change in God, and so an inconsistency, an apparent contradiction, in his actions towards us. But in fact *there is no change in God*; he loves us from eternity. There is however *a change in us*, a change that occurs as by faith Christ's work is appropriated. The change is *not from wrath to grace*, but from *our belief* that we are under wrath to *our belief* that we are under grace.[53]

Is it accurate to say that God's dispositions of wrath toward sinners and of grace at the point of our union with Christ are simply a matter of what *we* believe about God? Admittedly, how God's eternal, electing purposes determine his disposition toward his elect in history before they are in Christ is a difficult matter. But it seems there must be a better way to articulate a biblical response than to shift the crux of the debate to our beliefs.

It is for this reason, among others, that (at least some) open theists understand the classic, Reformed understanding of God itself as disingenuous, as an attempt to play down or otherwise undermine biblical passages such as those cited above. So, for example, Greg Boyd says:

> My fundamental thesis is that the classical theological tradition became misguided when, under the influence of Hellenistic philosophy, it defined God's perfection in static, timeless terms. All change was considered an imperfection

---

[51]From Ainsworth's *Annotations upon Genesis* as quoted in Muller, *Post-Reformation Reformed Dogmatics*, 3:559.

[52]Calvin, *Institutes*, 1.17.13, my emphasis.

[53]Paul Helm, *John Calvin's Ideas* (Oxford: Oxford University Press, 2004), 395, my emphases.

and thus not applicable to God. Given this definition of divine perfection, there was no way to conceive of God as entertaining real possibilities.[54]

So also Clark Pinnock:

> According to Scripture, God moves with his people through time. He is even described as wondering what they are going to do next! God says "I thought, after she has done all this, she will return to me, but she did not return" (Jer. 3:7). God had thought he could bless his people but they proved unfaithful (Jer. 3:19–20). God had planted a pleasant vineyard and put a lot of effort into it but it yielded only wild grapes, and in Isaiah 5:1–4 he asks why. He had hope for things to happen which did not happen and he was disappointed. God existed before creation and before creaturely time but since then has related to the world within the structures of time. God is not thought of in terms of timelessness. He makes plans and carries them out; he anticipates the future and remembers the past. Since creation, divine life has been temporally ordered. God is participant, not onlooker; he enters the time of the world and is not just above the flow of history looking down, as it were, from some supra-temporal vantage point. God is inside not outside time, sharing in history—past, present, and future.[55]

Process theology, as well, has wrestled with the relationship of God to the world and has concluded that such a relationship is necessary for God to be who he is. As with open theism (as noted above), process theologians tend to view the love of God as central to his character.[56] One of the differences between them and open theists is that the latter locate this love of God, first, in his triunity, expressed in Father, Son, and Holy Spirit, whereas for process theologians the love of God requires creation in order to be properly expressed.[57]

---

[54]Boyd, *God of the Possible*, 17.

[55]Pinnock, *Most Moved Mover*, 97.

[56]According to Richard Rice, an open theist, "Both process thought and open theism place love at the center of the divine reality. Both believe that God's love comes to expression in God's relationship to the world, and both maintain that love involves genuine sensitivity to its objects. Consequently, both believe that ultimate reality is inherently social or relational. Love requires an 'other.'" Richard Rice, "Process Theism and the Open View of God," in *Searching for an Adequate God: A Dialogue Between Process and Free Will Theists*, ed. John B. Cobb and Clark H. Pinnock (Grand Rapids: Eerdmans, 2000), 195.

[57]It should be noted that there was a certain priority to the love of God in Arminius's theology as well, though it did not take the form now articulated in open theism. Says Arminius, "I know, indeed, that the love of God, referred to, is not in all respects equal towards all men and towards each individual, but I also deny that there is so much difference, in that divine love, towards men that He has determined to act towards some, only according to the rigor of His own law, but towards others according to His own mercy and grace in Christ, as set forth in his gospel" (James Arminius, *The Works of James Arminius*, 3 vols. [Christian Classics Ethereal Library], 2.186). Given what Arminius says here, the love of God takes precedence over God's eternal decree, and in that way is given a certain primacy.

Even with such differences, the result of both open theism and process theology is that God's independence is severely compromised. Even if God's independence is affirmed in some way, the reality is that in both systems God remains essentially dependent on the world in order to be who he is and to act.[58]

But it gets worse. Those with less acumen with respect to theology proper,[59] but who nevertheless involve themselves in such discussions, that is, philosophers of religion, are reticent at best to see how God's independence could be affirmed, given the creation of the world.[60] Many current-day philosophical discussions seem to ignore the (vast majority of the) historical discussion and thus to present God as in some ways fundamentally dependent on creation. Stephen Davis, to use one example, cannot make sense of God's eternity, given the existence of time. If God is eternal, says Davis, then the following sentences are either meaningless or necessarily false:

> God existed before Moses.
> God's power will soon triumph over evil.
> Last week God wrought a miracle.
> God will always be wiser than human beings.[61]

These statements are thought to be meaningless or necessarily false because, obviously, they postulate something time-conditioned of One presumed to be essentially independent of time.

But Davis's concerns run deeper than this. He is convinced that the traditional understanding of eternity, in which God is not subject to time, serves in the end to deny the existence of the Christian God. The following argument illustrates his point:

---

[58] I should state the obvious here, though I will not pursue it, given our more specific focus, and that is that these debates on the character of God go back to the beginning of church history. Most prominently, questions about God and his relationship to creation surround Augustine's debates with Pelagius, the ascendency of semi-Pelagianism, and the discussions of Arminianism from the seventeenth century to the present. I will mention these later on, but will not be able to engage the substance of those discussions directly. However, what I conclude in this study would have implications across the spectrum of these various debates.

[59] "Less acumen," we should note, owing to a neglect of biblical revelation.

[60] This is a general statement and there are glowing exceptions. With respect to theology proper, the exceptions in the main are the Roman Catholic philosophers who, for reasons that cannot be pursued here, seem to be more sympathetic to an appeal to God's revelation for a proper understanding of God, and who therefore use their skills in philosophy to better articulate those truths. Protestant philosophers, by and large, seem not to exhibit such sympathies.

[61] Stephen T. Davis, "Temporal Eternity," in *Philosophy of Religion: An Anthology*, ed. Louis P. Pojman (Belmont, CA: Wadsworth/Thomson Learning, 2003), 211.

1. God creates x.

2. X first exists at T.

3. Therefore, God creates x at T.[62]

Now 3 is ambiguous, notes Davis, between 3a and 3b:

3a. God, at T, creates x.

3b. God creates x, and x first exists at T.

The defender of divine eternity will opt for 3b as the proper understanding of 3.[63]

Given this argument, says Davis, a timeless God cannot create anything at all. He cannot create because we do not have a usable concept of atemporal causation (i.e., causation that would not itself be dependent on time) that would allow for 1 and 2 to be meaningful. "Therefore, we are within our rights in concluding that [1] and [2] entail that God is temporal, i.e. that a timeless being cannot be the creator of the universe."[64]

Furthermore, says Davis, the Christian God's existence must also be denied by the defender of divine eternity because of the ways in which Scripture speaks of God.

> He makes plans. He responds to what human beings do, e.g. their evil deeds or their acts of repentance. He seems to have temporal location and extension. The Bible does not hesitate to speak of God's years and days. . . . And God seems to act in temporal sequences—first he rescues the children of Israel from Egypt and later he gives them the Law.[65]

Davis is to be commended for his motive here. He wishes to do justice to the Christian view of God as presented to us in Scripture. He wants to argue for God as Creator and as one who interacts with his creation, but he just cannot make his way clear to do so if what must be affirmed is God's fundamental and essential independence and aseity with respect to time.

William Hasker, a philosopher of religion and proponent of open theism, has the same kinds of concerns.

---

[62]Ibid., 211, my numbering throughout.

[63]Ibid., 213.

[64]Ibid.

[65]Ibid.

The other main difficulty about divine timelessness is that it is very hard to make clear logical sense of the doctrine. If God is truly timeless, so that temporal determinations of "before" and "after" do not apply to him, then how can God act in time . . . ? How can he know what is occurring on the changing earthly scene? How can he respond when his children turn to him in prayer and obedience? And above all, if God is timeless and incapable of change, how can God be born, grow up, live with and among people, suffer and die, as we believe he did as incarnated in Jesus?[66]

But it gets even worse. There is an apologetic dimension to all of these discussions on the compatibility, or lack thereof, of God's character and attributes. These matters are not simply intramural debates among Christians; they are also used to argue against the existence of God. In the anthology *The Impossibility of God*, Theodore Drange marks out two primary categories of atheological arguments (arguments for the nonexistence of God). The first category consists of "incompatible-properties arguments," which seek to show that God is assumed to have properties that cannot reside in the same person. If Drange is right, then God—that is, a God who is thought to be both infinite and Creator—cannot exist. The second category consists of "God-vs.-world arguments," which contend that there is a serious incompatibility between the supposition of God's existence and the nature of the world such that we are compelled to conclude for the nonexistence of God.[67]

While Drange's categories might point to different nuances in certain atheological arguments, category 1, incompatible-properties arguments, is really just a subset of category 2, God-vs.-world arguments. For example, the first incompatible-properties argument that Drange gives is "The Perfection-vs.-Creation Argument," which proceeds as follows:

1. If God exists, then he is perfect.
2. If God exists, then he is the creator of the universe.
3. A perfect being can have no needs or wants.
4. If any being created the universe, then he must have had some need or want.
5. Therefore, it is impossible for a perfect being to be the creator of the universe (from 3 and 4).
6. Hence, it is impossible for God to exist (from 1, 2, and 5).[68]

---

[66] William Hasker, "A Philosophical Perspective," in Pinnock et al., *The Openness of God*, 128.
[67] Theodore M. Drange, "Incompatible-Properties Arguments: A Survey," in *The Impossibility of God*, ed. Michael Martin (Amherst, NY: Prometheus, 2003), 185.
[68] Ibid., 186.

Whatever the merits of this argument (and there seem to be none), it is strange for Drange to set this out as an "incompatible-properties argument" when clearly the problem here is the fact of God's creating activity. It is because God's creating comes into the equation that Drange sees conflict in God. Even stranger for Drange is that he doesn't seem to be aware of some of the most basic elements of Christian theology regarding the attributes of God. So, for example, he notes, "If the creation were accidental, then that in itself would imply that God is imperfect (since perfect beings do not have accidents), and that would be another basis for the Perfection-vs.-Creation Argument."[69]

We will discuss these arguments below. For now, the point to be kept in mind is that, as I have said, the problem is creation. More specifically, once God determines to bring into existence something that is contingent, finite, and of a different order than himself, the relationship of that existence to his own becomes a problem (for us, not for God). It is in response to that problem that we will seek to understand the character, attributes, or properties of God.

Antinomy and Paradox

At this point we need to be clear about some of the terminology that will be useful to us as we proceed. Whenever we discuss God, who is altogether different from creation and created things, which are essentially and fundamentally dependent, we will inevitably encounter *antinomies* and *paradoxes*.

As I will use the term here, any *antinomy* will refer to two or more entities that in some sense contain laws or operations that seem to be in conflict and resist reconciliation by us. I am using the notion of antinomy, therefore, in its more strictly etymological sense; it is a conflict of *laws*.

For example, as Cornelius Van Til notes:

We were in the nature of the case completely interpreted before we came into existence; the universal plan of God needed not to be supplemented by historical particulars and could not be supplemented in this way. The historical could not produce anything wholly new. This much we see clearly. God being what he is, it must be his counsel which acts as the indispensable and self-complete unity back of the finite one and many. The only alternative to saying this is to say that the historical produces the wholly new, and this would be to give up the basic idea of the Christian-theistic scheme, namely, the idea of God and of his creation and control of the universe. On the other hand the historical

---

[69]Ibid., 187.

must have genuine significance. Or else why should God have created it? Prayer must be answered or God would not be God. The universe must really glorify God; that is the purpose of its existence. So we seem to have on the one hand a bucket that is full of water and on the other hand we seem to add water to this bucket which we claim to be already full.[70]

The point I wish to make at this juncture is that *antinomy*, in the way that I will use it, has to do with a state of affairs, a circumstance *in the world*. Thus, it is more metaphysical than epistemological. That is, because the focus of an antinomy is on *laws* that are an essential aspect of certain entities, the primary concern has to do with the way things are. As Van Til notes, it has to do with the way God is—his character as *a se*, his unchangeable decree, etc.—on the one hand, and the way the universe or people in the universe are, on the other hand. This conflict of laws is something that obtains whether or not we believe it or are able to formulate it.

Paradox, in the way that I will use it, has to do with the articulation of antinomies, or the positing of things that seem contradictory. A paradox involves conflicting or seemingly contradictory *propositions* that themselves are presumed to be true. Again, taking *paradox* in its etymological sense, we are dealing with two (or more) *teachings* that conflict or that seem to be contradictory. Again, Van Til offers an example of a paradox.[71]

> Every knowledge transaction has in it somewhere a reference point to God. Now since God is not fully comprehensible to us we are bound to come into what seems to be contradiction in all our knowledge. Our knowledge is analogical and therefore must be paradoxical. We say that if there is to be any true knowledge at all there must be in God an absolute system of knowledge. We therefore insist that everything must be related to that absolute system of God. Yet we ourselves cannot fully understand that system. We may, in order to illustrate our meaning here, take one of the outstanding paradoxes of the Christian interpretation of things, namely, that of the relation of the counsel of God to our prayers. To put it pointedly: We say on the one hand that prayer changes things and on the other hand we say that everything happens in accordance with God's plan and God's plan is immutable.[72]

---

[70]Cornelius Van Til, *The Defense of the Faith*, 4th ed., ed. K. Scott Oliphint (Phillipsburg, NJ: P&R, 2008), 68. As in much of the literature that discusses *antinomy*, including Van Til's discussion, distinctions are not typically made between *antinomy* and *paradox*. For purposes of clarification, I would like to make just such a distinction.

[71]Van Til is actually discussing antinomies in this paragraph, but he uses the term *antinomy* interchangeably with *paradox* here. I am using the terms in a more distinctive way.

[72]Van Til, *The Defense of the Faith*, 67–68.

A paradox has to do with the expression, verbal or propositional, of an antinomy. Thus, we say (and know from Scripture) that prayer does change things; we also know that the change that prayer brings about was itself a part of God's immutable plan. This conflict has to do with the *antinomy* of prayer in relation to God's immutability, articulated paradoxically as (something like), "Prayer changes what would otherwise happen," and "God's plan is comprehensive and immutable."

It will be helpful to keep these terms, with their subtle distinction, in mind as we proceed. Because we will want to think about God's relationship to, and his dealings with, his creation, we can expect that antinomies and paradoxes will be a significant undercurrent in all of our discussion.

D. The Triune God

Before we begin the bulk of our discussion, I should make clear—though I will not be fleshing this out in detail—that we are always and everywhere discussing the attributes of the *triune* God. The history of discussions and developments in theology proper can sometimes leave the impression that an emphasis on the oneness of God excludes his three-ness. If it were to exclude his three-ness, it would be possible to understand the doctrine of God in some generic way that could easily transfer to Judaism or Islam, for example. But that is decidedly *not* the way I am proceeding in this study. However, because we will be focusing more specifically on the attributes and properties of *God*, and not, say, on the individual properties of the Father, Son, or Spirit, my emphasis in most of what I will say will be on attributes and properties that God *as triune* has—attributes and properties, in other words, that are applicable to each person of the Trinity in that they are essential to what it means for God to be God.[73]

A focus on the oneness of God with respect to his attributes may be one of the primary reasons that much of what we discuss in coming chapters has developed the way it has. The question could be posed, If we understand God's attributes in the context of his three-in-oneness, is it easier for us to see that God can remain who he is as *a se* and at the same time take on covenantal properties? So much of the discussion about the relationship of God's attributes vis-à-vis creation seems to miss the fundamental note of his

---

[73]Though, as we will see, our discussion presupposes that condescension is a *Trinitarian* act, with its focus in the Son. Though terminating in the Son, these properties will be applicable to God *as triune*.

triunity, and thus of his ability, as we will see in the incarnation, for example, to condescend, all the while remaining who he essentially is.

This point must be kept in mind throughout, especially given some of the modern-day criticisms lodged against an "abstract" consideration of God's essential nature prior to, or even apart from, a discussion of God's triunity. Karl Barth, for example, complains that,

> it is . . . hard to see how what is distinctive for this God can be made clear if, as has constantly happened in Roman Catholic and Protestant dogmatics both old and new, the question who God is, which it is the business of the doctrine of the Trinity to answer, is held in reserve, and the first question to be treated is that of the That and the What of God, as though these could be defined otherwise than on the presupposition of the Who.[74]

Barth expresses here a legitimate concern about a problem that must be avoided whenever Christians set out to think carefully about God and his character.[75] If what is discussed in any way obscures or undermines the truth of God's triunity, then to that extent the doctrine of God discussed is not the doctrine of the *Christian* God. But as Muller notes, Barth's concerns were misplaced, given the history of discussions and developments in theology proper after the Reformation.

> The order of the older dogmatics, in moving from proofs to essence and attributes and then to Trinity, was not a movement from "that" (or more properly, "whether"), to "what," to "who" . . . , but from "whether" . . . to "what" . . . to "what sort"—with the "whether" (Barth's "that") corresponding to the proofs; the "what" corresponding to the essence and essential properties (attributes of the "first order") and, in the arrangement of some of the orthodox writers, to the Trinity as well, not as Barth would seem to imply, to the essence and attributes generally; and the "what sort" referring to the relational attributes (attributes of the "second order") and, in other of the orthodox, to the Trinity. The *locus* [doctrine of God] does not segment Trinity off from the discussion of essence and attributes: the issue addressed by this order is not a movement from an extended philosophical or speculative discussion of "what" God is to a biblicistic, trinitarian definition of "who" God is, but the movement from a

---

[74]Karl Barth, *Church Dogmatics*, 2nd ed., ed. Thomas Forsyth Torrance, trans. G. W. Bromiley (Edinburgh: T&T Clark, 1975), 1.1.300–301, quoted in Muller, *Post-Reformation Reformed Dogmatics*, 3:155.
[75]We should be clear here that Barth's theology, including his doctrine of God, is unorthodox at every point. While his emphasis in the quote above is correct, the ways in which he sought to construe theology serves only to undermine and negate orthodoxy.

statement of "what" (or "who") the existent One is, namely, God, to a lengthy discussion in terms of attributes and Trinity, of precisely "what sort" of God has been revealed, namely, a triune God who is simple, infinite, omnipotent, gracious, merciful, and so forth.[76]

In other words, we should keep in the forefront of our minds that everything we say about God generally in our discussion applies to the *triune* God; it does not apply in abstraction, but to God as one in three.

We need, then, to remember that there are distinctions to be made between God's essential character—those properties that apply to God as God—and attributes that have in view the relationship that God as triune sustains to himself (and, secondarily, to the world). There are *personal* properties, therefore, that apply only to the respective persons of the Trinity (for example, filiation applies only to the Son, not the Spirit or Father), and not to the oneness of God. So also, there are essential properties that serve to highlight or emphasize God's essential relational character—properties such as the love of God (directed, in the first place, to the three persons). These characteristics of God are important and crucial, and our lack of direct attention to them in what follows should not be seen as a lack of importance.

As I said above, the problem (for us) is creation. This does not mean that creation per se is a problem. God saw all that he had made and it was very good. It means rather that the fact of creation, as well as its status as created, seems to be almost invariably what gets in the way of clear Christian thinking on these matters. Too many discussions about God and his relationship to creation conclude with a god who is in some way, like his creation, essentially needy. In order (supposedly) to safeguard intellectual respectability, the triune God of Scripture is given a back seat to a host of wants, needs, and aspirations as many philosophers and theologians choose to debate his nature and character. Is there any way to maintain the integrity of the revelation of the triune God in the midst of such a bleak and anemic context?

I will be arguing that God has essential attributes, properties that he has because of who he is quite apart from creation, and "covenantal" attributes, properties that God has, given creation. How, though, would this understanding of God be able to reckon with the fact that God is essentially triune—that is, that there is no way that he could be anything but triune? It is not possible

---

[76]Ibid., 156.

that the Godhead could consist of two persons in one, or four in one, or anything but three in one. How do we go about thinking of the three persons in relation to the one essential God?

This is a problem inherent in any discussion of God's characteristics, so it is not unique to those who affirm that God has essential attributes (and we will see that those attributes are not distinct from him). The best that one can do, it seems, is to affirm that there are essential properties of God, all of which apply to each of the persons, and that there are essential properties of each of the persons that are unique to each one. In line with historic Christianity (in this case, the Athanasian Creed), orthodox theology has historically affirmed that

> the Godhead of the Father, of the Son, and of the Holy Spirit is all one, the glory equal, the majesty coeternal. Such as the Father is, such is the Son, and such is the Holy Spirit. The Father Uncreate, the Son Uncreate, and the Holy Ghost Uncreate. The Father Incomprehensible, the Son Incomprehensible, and the Holy Ghost Incomprehensible. The Father Eternal, the Son Eternal, and the Holy Ghost Eternal and yet they are not Three Eternals but One Eternal. As also there are not Three Uncreated, nor Three Incomprehensibles, but One Uncreated, and One Incomprehensible. So likewise the Father is Almighty, the Son Almighty, and the Holy Ghost Almighty. And yet they are not Three Almighties but One Almighty. So the Father is God, the Son is God, and the Holy Ghost is God. And yet they are not Three Gods, but One God.

While affirming this truth, we must also affirm with the same creed that "the Father is made of none, neither created, nor begotten. The Son is of the Father alone; not made, nor created, but begotten. The Holy Ghost is of the Father, and of the Son neither made, nor created, nor begotten, but proceeding." Thus, while everything that God is, the Father, Son, and Holy Spirit are, there are properties of each of the three that do not apply to the one essential God *as one*. The one triune God, for example, is not from the Father; only the Son is from the Father.

Muller, in explicating the differences between the persons and the essence (and, in part, quoting Rijssen) explains:

> [The persons] differ from the divine Essence not realiter—that is to say, not *essentialiter, ut res & res*—but *modaliter, ut modus à re*: "the personal properties by which the persons are distinguished from the Essence, are modes of a sort, by which they are characterized, not formally and properly as in creatures who

are affected in certain ways by their properties, but eminently and analogically, rising beyond all imperfections."[77]

So, there are essential properties of each of the persons that do not apply to the one God, though the reverse is decidedly not the case.

One of the best ways, perhaps the only orthodox way, to distinguish these properties, as I suggested above, is with respect to the "essential properties" (*proprietates essentiales*) and personal properties (*proprietates personales*).[78] That is, the distinctions made between the persons and essence of God are personal rather than essential distinctions. Here, the word *essential* refers to the essence of God in distinction from the persons who are the Godhead. Thus, there are essential properties of the three persons—what have been called personal properties—and there are essential properties of the one God, applying as they do to each of the three persons equally and without dividing those properties in any way.

While there is no way for finite human beings completely to circumscribe the relationship of the one God who is the three persons, we may rest content, along with the history of the orthodox Christian tradition, with the fact of God's triunity and its evidence of God's utter incomprehensibility (Rom. 11:33f.).

Given God's essential, triune character, the crux of our concern is the way in which we are to think of God and his relationship to his creation in the context of theological and philosophical discussions. Or, to put the matter in the form of a question, why are theological and philosophical arguments routinely formulated such that they end up either (1) denying the (exegetically and historically) overwhelming evidence for the essential character of the triune God as *a se* or (2) denying the existence of God altogether? What kinds of principles are lurking in the background that seem to compel so many theologians and philosophers of religion who deal with theism to conclude with a less-than-Christian god?

E. Looking Ahead

As I have intimated throughout this introduction, the subject matter at hand is much too large to lay out in any detail. In the chapters ahead our focus

---

[77] Muller, *Post-Reformation Reformed Dogmatics*, 4:190.
[78] For an elaboration of this distinction, see ibid., 3:213ff. Muller notes: "As Alexander of Hales had argued, there cannot be any *distinctio realis* between the attributes—nor can there be such a "real distinction" between the divine persons and the divine essence—but the persons as identified by the *proprietates personales*, must be distinct from one another, indeed, really (*realiter*) distinct." See also ibid., 4:167–95.

will move from a consideration of God's character as he is in himself to a consideration of how we might think of God as God *and* as condescended, given his essential attributes and character.

In chapter 1, we will discuss God's revelation of himself as "I AM." I will stress how that revelation controls our affirmation of God as independent (*a se*). This is perhaps the most central and crucial chapter to understand, since everything else that I will say will presuppose what is said there. In sum, I will affirm the truths of a classic Reformed doctrine of God, in which his independence and the characteristics entailed therein are nonnegotiable. We will see how such characteristics are rooted in God's revelation of himself.

In chapter 2, I will begin to outline a way of thinking about God's voluntary condescension. This chapter will begin to introduce a relatively new approach to a discussion of God's character. Given God's essential independence, how do we think about God's relationship to the world? The central answer to that question, I will argue, is found in the free decision of God to condescend to us, which condescension finds its center climactically in the person of Jesus Christ. In this chapter I will set out the biblical and creedal truth of God's condescending love to his creation generally and to his people more specifically. Given those truths, it should be easier for us to think about how God relates to his creation since the time of creation and into eternity.

In chapter 3, having seen God's independence and that God's independence is in no way compromised as he condescends to come to us, I will begin to discuss exactly how biblically to construe the incarnation and other matters relative to the Son of God. This chapter will prove central to our understanding of God's covenantal attributes, and thus central to all that comes before and after it in this book. Any discussion of God's relationship to creation must reckon with his coming in the flesh. This chapter will foreshadow how the theological truths affirmed in an orthodox christology help us to flesh out a (hopefully) biblically accurate and more useful way to articulate theology proper.

In the next chapter I want to employ the christological paradigm for thinking about God's attributes. I will take those theological truths that have helped us express the biblical teaching on Christ's person and apply them, to a greater or lesser extent, to the reality of God's condescension throughout covenant history. In this chapter, I hope to show that our understanding of what is "compatible" with respect to God in creation should be controlled by how we think of the compatibility of Christ's two natures.

Finally, we will ask whether or not the *Eimi/eikon*, essential/covenantal paradigm for understanding theology proper is a way forward in helping us to understand the activities and actions of the condescended, covenant God.[79] We will discuss such matters as the power, knowledge, and will of God, as well as his decree and providence. These conundrums, it should be said at the outset, cannot be "resolved" in such a way that the mystery of God's working in the world is entirely comprehended. Without in any way compromising or denying the classic Reformed understanding of God's character, we will explore these kinds of questions by interacting with some of the philosophical theology that seeks to challenge the historic, orthodox notion of God. We will do that, in part, through the historic understanding that a biblical notion of compatibility (affirmed in christology) can provide a context in which we can take God's activity in relation to us and creation seriously while at the same time affirming the Reformed understanding of God's aseity. This last chapter will need to be much more philosophical in tone and vocabulary, given its subject matter. Readers less interested in such things may want to pass over this material.

In the end, my hope is that the glories of the gospel as expressed in God's free decision to come down and covenant with us, preeminently in Christ, will be teased out and highlighted throughout our discussion, so that the majesty of the sovereign God will stand out in bold relief, that all glory, laud, and honor will be given to him—for who he is and for what he has done. Even so, come quickly Lord Jesus.

---

[79] According to Roger Olson, the doctrine of God, theology proper, is the basis for the division between Calvinists and Arminians: "In spite of all the huffing and puffing of extremists on both sides who seem to believe adherents of the other theology exercising bad faith, people of equally good faith come down on different sides. Why? Because when they read the Bible, they find God identified one way or another. *At the bottom of these doctrinal differences lies a different perspective on the identity of God*, based on God's self-revelation in Jesus Christ and Scripture, that colors the rest of Scripture." Further, he says, "Contrary to popular belief, then, the true divide at the heart of the Calvinist-Arminian split is not predestination versus free will *but the guiding picture of God*: he is primarily viewed as either (1) majestic, powerful, and controlling or (2) loving, good, and merciful. Once the picture . . . is established, seemingly contrary aspects fade into the background, are set aside as 'obscure' or are artificially made to fit the system." Roger E. Olson, *Arminian Theology: Myths and Realities* (Downers Grove, IL: IVP Academic, 2006), 70, 73, my emphases.

I Am

The God of Abraham praise,
Who reigns enthroned above;
Ancient of everlasting days,
And God of love:
Jehovah! great I AM!
By earth and heav'n confessed;
I bow and bless the sacred name,
For ever blest.

THOMAS OLIVERS

A. God Revealed

(1) Introductory Matters

We have seen in the introduction that the proper, biblical way into a discussion of the characteristics and attributes of God is through his revelation, more specifically, his revelation of his names. Note again:

> A major mark of continuity between Reformation and orthodoxy in the development of the doctrine of God, moreover, is the emphasis on the biblical divine "names" as a point of departure for the discussion of the essence and attributes. . . . This pattern in the Reformed orthodox must be understood as an indication

of the importance of the text of Scripture and the interpretation of its original languages to theological formulation.[1]

It is crucial to keep in mind that the characteristics of God come from what *he* has said, and specifically what he has said with regard to his own *names*.

Any discussion of the names of God must be able to prioritize his names in a way that is consistent with Scripture. This may seem obvious to some, but owing to the reconstruction of theology proper that is currently underway (as discussed in the introduction), the groundwork for our study must be explicit. Two foundational principles bear repeating: (1) The Bible is, foremost, the word of God. It is God's revelation to his creatures, and his truth is communicated therein. Much more could and in other contexts should be said about the Bible. There are questions of interpretation, of textual variants, of idiomatic usage, of the New Testament's relationship to the Old, and so on. All of these are legitimate and necessary elements that pertain to the study of Scripture. They are not, however, the bedrock truth of what the Bible *is*. Rather, they presuppose what the Bible is. Unless one comes to Scripture with this full assurance, there is no adequate way to begin to address other, legitimate and perhaps pressing questions—about the Bible or anything else.[2] It was for this reason that the Westminster Confession of Faith, in setting out what things must be basic to our view of Scripture, noted regarding Scripture's *author* and its *authority*: "The authority of the Holy Scripture, for which it ought to be believed, and obeyed, dependeth not upon the testimony of any man, or church; but wholly upon God (who is truth itself) the author thereof: and therefore it is to be received, because it is the Word of God."[3] Any discussion of who God is and what he has done must begin with what he has said, generally, and by what names he is to be called, specifically.

(2) God's inerrant revelation is the only source from which we may begin to understand who God is. This, too, may be obvious to many, but it is not obvious to some. Much that passes for a discussion about the attributes of God

---

[1]Richard A. Muller, *Post-Reformation Reformed Dogmatics: The Rise and Development of Reformed Orthodoxy, ca. 1520 to ca. 1725*, vol. 3, *The Divine Essence and Attributes*, 2nd ed. (Grand Rapids: Baker Academic, 2003), 98–99.

[2]One of the fatal conceptual flaws in the book previously discussed, *Inspiration and Incarnation*, is that the author undermined what the Bible *is* by conflating what it *is* with how it functions and operates. Note, to use one example, "My aim is to allow the collective evidence to affect not just how we understand a biblical passage or story here and there within the parameters of earlier doctrinal formulations. Rather, I want to move beyond that by allowing the evidence to affect how we think about what Scripture as a whole *is*." Peter Enns, *Inspiration and Incarnation* (Grand Rapids: Baker Academic, 2005), 15.

[3]Westminster Confession of Faith 1.4.

is actually just more natural theology; it is an attempt to evaluate how things are in creation, and then to argue how God must fit in with that creation.[4] This methodology gets things backwards. To start with Scripture as God's revelation is to understand what God says, about himself and everything else, and then to work out, based on what God has said, how best to understand and articulate his relationship to everything else. The approach must be from the top down, not from the bottom up.

Given this truth, a word here should be said about our mode of reasoning with respect to the character of God (and of everything else, for that matter). In a discussion of a Reformed methodology for understanding Scripture, Richard Muller notes:

> The Reformed orthodox understood the text of Scripture as providing *principia* or *axiomata* [that is, foundational principles] from which conclusions could be deduced, as indicated in the hermeneutical principle of the Westminster Confession, "The whole counsel of God concerning all things necessary for His own glory, man's salvation, faith and life, is either expressly set down in Scripture, or *by good and necessary consequence* may be deduced from Scripture."[5]

This notion of "good and necessary consequence" is crucial; it is even an obvious and natural component of the way in which we rely on Scripture as our authority, but it may need a little explanation. Simply put, the "good and necessary" consequences by which we conclude what Scripture says and what it requires of us carry all of the authority of Scripture with them. Thus, they themselves are *scriptural* conclusions, in the fullest sense of that word. But what the divines had in mind, at least, is that the consequences of the truth of Scripture, in order to glorify God, must be both *good* and *necessary*. If a consequence is only good or only necessary, then it does not qualify as something that carries Scripture's mandate.

For example, a good consequence of the command to love your neighbor (e.g., Lev. 19:18; Matt. 5:43) may be that you decide to work weekly at the local mission. That is a good consequence, and you may be glorifying God in doing that. But because it is not something necessary for the Christian, it cannot be added to a list of things that are necessary for glorifying God. It may glorify God, but you may not, with scriptural authority, command your brothers and

---

[4]Examples of this abound. See, just to cite one example from an evangelical, William Lane Craig, *Time and Eternity: Exploring God's Relationship to Time* (Wheaton, IL: Crossway, 2001).
[5]Richard A. Muller, *After Calvin: Studies in the Development of a Theological Tradition* (Oxford: Oxford University Press, 2003), 76, my emphasis.

sisters to do such a thing. On the other hand, a necessary consequence of God's choosing his own people before the foundation of the world is that they will be saved. So you may conclude that the preaching of the gospel is something merely optional, given God's prior choice. But that consequence, though it might follow necessarily from the doctrine of election, is not a good one, primarily because Scripture does not agree with it. So, that too cannot be something that glorifies God.

A good and necessary consequence may be something like this: "If Scripture says, 'Everyone who calls on the name of the Lord will be saved' (Rom. 10:13), then since John Doe has called on the name of the Lord, he is saved." John's personal salvation, though not mentioned in Scripture, is a good and necessary consequence from what Scripture teaches. The Bible does not say that John is a Christian, any more than it says you and I are Christians. But by good and necessary consequence, it is true, and infallibly so, provided we have called upon the name of the Lord for salvation. Therefore, in order to glorify God, we hold such things to be true. In other words, the sufficiency of Scripture is meant to affirm that all that we need to glorify God in this life is explicitly or by good and necessary derivation set down in Scripture.

So, as we saw in the introduction:

> As Turretin indicates, the way in which God is what he is in the simplicity of the divine essence cannot be known by the human mind, granting that the human mind knows things only by composition and composite attribution— nonetheless, we are given to know the divine attributes or essential properties by revelation and rational reflection on revelation in such a way that God's nature is truly known by means of the revealed attributes.[6]

Ascertaining the attributes of God requires not simply that we stick with the parameters of the biblical text. It requires that we *begin with* that text; but it also requires that we derive conclusions from the truth of that text and thus affirm the truth of who God is.[7]

---

[6]Muller, *Post-Reformation Reformed Dogmatics*, 3:195–96. For a discussion and defense of "essence language" among the Protestant orthodox, see ibid., 227–28. Note especially, "Thus, in answer to the question of 'What' or 'Who' God is, the orthodox set themselves first to describe the 'nature' or 'essence' of God" (232).

[7]It is worth noting that, in the debates in the seventeenth century, and beyond, between the Socinians and the orthodox, it was the former who were insisting that the debate remain solely within the confines of the biblical text. Thus, the Socinians could deny the Trinity, given that the word itself never appears in Holy Scripture.

(2) *Speaking of Attributes*

There is a long and complex history of the problems that persist when finite creatures attempt to explore the infinite. Specifically, how can we who are limited grasp in any coherent way the One who is infinite and beyond all comprehension? God's essence is altogether above and beyond our ability fully to comprehend. Part of the answer to that question is given above—God has seen fit to condescend and reveal himself. He has given us a revelation, not only of his plan and purpose for history, but of himself, even of his essence. Thus, we can know him because, and only because, he has made himself known.

But coupled with the notion of God revealing himself is the sobering truth that he who reveals himself is, in his essence, beyond our categories of thinking. How, then, can we talk about him in a way that is faithful to who he is? This is the problem of theological predication. If we say something about God that is true, just how does the subject (God) "fit" with the predicate, that is, what is predicated of him (e.g., goodness)?[8]

To put the matter more squarely in the context of a discussion of God's attributes, there has historically been "the recognition that the idea of an 'attribute,' or 'predicate,' like the idea of a 'nature,' does not comport with the concept of God—at least not in precisely the same manner that attributes or predicates are spoken of finite things."[9] This is because whatever is predicated of the essence of God, as infinite and simple (i.e., not composed of parts), is identical to him; nothing can be attributed to the essence of God that is in any way different from or external to him. The problem of theological predication, then, revolves around the *fact* of attribution—that we do attribute certain things to God—and how what we attribute actually obtains in him. Does an attribute *actually* obtain *in* God, or are we simply speaking of attributes on a finite level that, on the level of the infinite God, do not obtain?

For this reason, it has been customary to distinguish between the notion of attribute and that of property with respect to God.

---

[8] For a more detailed discussion of the problem of theological predication, see K. Scott Oliphint, *Reasons for Faith: Philosophy in the Service of Theology* (Phillipsburg, NJ: P&R, 2006), 91–122. The basic idea here is that, unless we can say *something* determinate about the relationship of the subject to the predicate, we are handicapped with respect to the truth of the proposition. If the truth value has something to do with the relationship designated in the proposition, and if the term used in the proposition is used in an unspecified but different way, it seems impossible to determine the status of the proposition itself and thus, in this case, to say anything meaningful about God.

[9] Muller, *Post-Reformation Reformed Dogmatics*, 3:196.

In its most strict use, the term "attribute" very nearly avoids the problem of predication inasmuch as "attribution" is a logical task performed by a rational subject that does not raise the question of the actual properties of the object under consideration. The terms "property" and "perfection" do, however, indicate that the predicate in question actually belongs to the object under consideration.[10]

To pursue discussions of this kind could take us too far afield. Suffice it to say at this point that we will be concerned in what follows to work through how certain properties can rightfully be attributed to God, and how we should distinguish between those properties.[11] In the way that we will use the notion of God's properties and attributes, therefore, we should see them as virtually identical, unless otherwise indicated. That is, properties or attributes respecting God will be those aspects that inhere and obtain in him, though not in the same way in every case.[12] When we predicate something of God, therefore (e.g., that God is infinite), we will often be affirming and attributing something to him that is in some sense *in* him. We will not be concerned simply to predicate attributes of God that are mere "attributions" in that they do not inhere *in* him. Because God has spoken truly to reveal himself, we may predicate true things of him and then attempt to see how best to construe such properties, given the truth of his revelation.

B. The Significance of the Name

In the Old Testament and the New, the covenant community places emphasis on the significance of names. That principle continues today; we give our children names, not only as tags but to express something about them. So it is in Scripture.

Names are changed in Scripture as redemption redefines people: for example, God changes Abram's name to Abraham, since he would be the father of many nations (Gen. 17:5); Jacob's name is changed to Israel because Jacob strived with God (Gen. 32:28–29). So great is the biblical emphasis on names that the book of Revelation speaks of the saints receiving new names expressing the divine recognition of their specific character. Often the function of

---

[10]Ibid., 196–97.

[11]We must continually keep in mind, however, that any discussion of this kind (1) must conform to Scripture and (2) will never fully comprehend exactly *how* God is who he is, and how he does what he does.

[12]"Thus, the divine 'attributes' are not simply logical attributions, they are attributions or predicates that assume an intrinsic quality or property in God." Muller, *Post-Reformation Reformed Dogmatics*, 3:198–99.

giving names in Scripture expresses specific, changed character and destiny of individuals.

The calling of the human race is to express the likeness and image of God. Part of that expression was in Adam's responsibility to give other creatures names. This task is rooted in the principle that God himself provides us with names by which we may know him. Hence, particularly in the Old Testament, the importance of the divine name is stressed (see Ex. 33:19; Deut. 28:58).

We should not be surprised, therefore, that any discussion of the attributes—that is, of the character of God—must begin with his names. To think of and ascertain God's character by way of his names was a method revitalized during the time of the Reformation. God's name is to be revered because his name is glorious and awesome (cf. Ps. 8:1). The name of God is so integrally linked to the being and character of God that within the context of the divine-human relationship, God and his name are inseparable. Because, for example, the name is the medium by which we know who he is, the punishment for taking his name in vain is severe; it is tantamount to a crime against him (see Lev. 24:10–23).

The ability to pronounce the name of God, the care with which his name is to be used, and thus the ability to know God and who he is follow in Scripture the pattern of progressive revelation. God's revelation intensifies as he moves in history to redeem a people. The clarity of God's identity and character moves steadily onward as well. As is true with every aspect of divine revelation, there is a progressive and cumulative force through redemptive-historical revelation. This is no less true for the divine name(s). There is an intensification and accumulation in clarity expressed in such a way that the people of God are given more and more clues as to God's character and how God's name is to be properly pronounced.

(1) The Classification of the Names

In light of this, it may be helpful for us to understand something of the standard classification of the names of God. As Berkhof notes, Bavinck bases his division of the names of God on the threefold classification of *nomina propria* (proper names), *nomina essentialia* (essential names, or attributes), and *nomina personalia* (personal names, e.g., Father, Son, and Holy Spirit).[13] While these classifications are helpful, we should see that the development of the *nomina propria* in biblical history reach their culmination in the *nomina*

---

[13]Louis Berkhof, *Systematic Theology* (Grand Rapids: Eerdmans, 1953), 48.

personalia. The names, and *the* name, that God ascribes to himself in the Old Testament are developed and reach their redemptive-historical climax in the triune name of Father, Son, and Holy Spirit.

Note as well that at the end of the age, as Christ comes riding on the white horse, he is called Faithful and True (Rev. 19:11), and the Word of God (v. 13), and even though "on his robe and on his thigh he has a name written, King of kings and Lord of lords" (v. 16), there is nevertheless a name written on him that no one knows but he himself (v. 12). So, the revelation of the name of God is of central concern even to the end of the age and beyond, and we are reminded that, though we know something of his name, we are still unable to know him as he knows himself.

Finally, with respect to the name of God, it is crucially important that we understand God's name, or names, not simply as God's somewhat arbitrary ascription of who he is, but as identifying the true God of heaven and earth in a unique way. In other words, since we know God only as he reveals himself, it follows that we know God's name only as he reveals it. Given that, we should see that we do not have the option as his creatures to ascribe to him a new name. He is to be known rightly only as he reveals himself, and is to be addressed according to his name, not according to some ascription of our own invention.

We are not to address God by any other name than the name he has identified as his own. To attempt to tweak the name of God for purposes of cultural (or any other kind of) relevance is not to address God as he has revealed himself, but to address him according to how we want him to be, and thus is to come to him sinfully and in error. To put it in the most controversial way, it is not proper to address God in his *nomina personalia* as Mother. He has for good reason not identified himself in that way. That is not his name, and any attempt to stress that kind of address automatically calls into suspicion the authority of God to name himself and the authority of his revelation.

(2) The Name Yahweh

God said to Moses, "I AM WHO I AM." And he said, "Say this to the people of Israel, 'I AM has sent me to you.'" (Ex. 3:14)

Historically, then, Christian theology has derived the character and attributes of God, initially and primarily, from his names. Not only so, but those names have been prioritized according to the characteristics attached to them. So, says Turretin:

Yet because all our knowledge [of God] begins from a name, he assumes various names in Scripture to accommodate himself to us. Some are taken from might—as El Elohim; some from omnipotence and all-sufficiency—as Shaddai; some from loftiness (*exelsitate*)—as Elion; others from dominion—as Adonai. *But the first and principal name is Jehovah, which is derived from his essence or existence.*[14]

"All our knowledge begins from a name." We learn who God is, first of all, by virtue of the names that he gives himself. Supremely, we learn who he is by way of the name "Jehovah" or "Yahweh."[15] This name, as we will see below, tells us something of who God is essentially. Though it is God's covenant name, in that he reveals it in the process of establishing the Mosaic covenant, it nevertheless tells us things about who God is quite apart from his relationship with his people.

This explains his name Jehovah, and signifies, that he is self-existent; he has his being of himself, and has no dependence upon any other: the greatest and best man in the world must say, By the grace of God I am what I am; but God says absolutely—and it is more than any creature, man or angel, can say—I am that I am.[16]

This name of God, Yahweh, is used over five thousand times in Holy Scripture. So, though there are relatively few passages that speak of the Lord specifically as "I AM," the fact that his own name is taken from that ascription, and that it is used with such frequency, indicates that we are to think of the Lord as essentially *a se*. Each of the essential attributes of God is an expression of the inner significance of this great divine name, associated with God's revelation to Moses at the burning bush (Ex. 3:1–17; 6:2–8; 33:12–34:14). There is an inextricable link, therefore, between the *nomina propria, essentialia*, and *personalia*.

---

[14]Francis Turretin, *Institutes of Elenctic Theology*, trans. George Musgrave Giger, ed. James T. Dennison Jr., 3 vols. (Phillipsburg, NJ: P&R, 1992–1997), 1:184, my emphasis. See also Muller, *Post-Reformation Reformed Dogmatics*, 3:254ff.

[15]"Jehovah" is a name formed by adding the vowels of the Hebrew word for Lord—*Adonai*—with the consonants of the name of God given in Exodus 3—*YHWH*. One common theory is that, in the sixteenth century, Petrus Galatinus argued for the combination of the consonants with the vowels, thus forming *YeHoWaH*, which comes into English as *Jehovah*. This was not the common Hebrew pronunciation, which today is thought to be something akin to *Yahweh*. The two, however, are interchangeable, in that they both refer to this revealed name of God in Exodus 3.

[16]Matthew Henry, *Matthew Henry's Commentary on the Whole Bible: Complete and Unabridged in One Volume* (Peabody, MA: Hendrickson, 1996), on Ex. 3:14.

Before we look specifically at the text of Exodus 3, some general information may be helpful.[17] First, a brief analysis of the use of Elohim and Yahweh
(Yahweh Elohim—יְהֹוָה אֱלֹהִים) in Genesis 2:4–3:24. The use of the double name
occurs here twenty times and is rarely met with elsewhere (only in Ex. 9:30
in the Pentateuch). In every instance it is used to give prominence to the fact
that Yahweh is truly Elohim.

> For the constant use of the double name is not intended to teach that Elohim
> who created the world was Yahweh, but that Yahweh, who visited man in para-
> dise, who punished him for the transgression of his command, but gave him a
> promise of victory over the tempter, was Elohim, the same God, who created
> the heavens and the earth.[18]

In other words, the combination of the names is meant to reveal to us,
and to the original audience, that Yahweh is and was the Creator of the
world—the same God who is sovereign over all. With respect to the name
Yahweh itself, it

> was originally a proper name, and according to the explanation given by God
> Himself to Moses (Ex. iii. 14–15), was formed from the imperfect of the verb
> הָוָה = הָיָה. God calls Himself אֶהְיֶה אֲשֶׁר אֶהְיֶה [ehyeh aser ehyeh], then more
> briefly אֶהְיֶה [ehyeh] and then again, by changing the first person into the third,
> יהוה [Yahweh]. From the derivation of this name from the imperfect, it follows
> that it was likely either pronounced יַהְוַה [Yahwah] or יַהְוֶה [Yahweh], and had
> come down from the pre-Mosaic age.[19]

The custom, of Kethib/Qere (see/say), appears to have originated shortly after
the captivity, based on Leviticus 24:16. In the Apocrypha and Septuagint version, "the Lord" (ὁ Κύριος) is invariably substituted for Yahweh, a custom in
which the New Testament writers follow the Septuagint.[20]

According to Keil and Delitzsch,

> If we seek for the meaning of יהוה, the expression אהיה אשר אהיה, in Ex. iii. 14,
> is neither to be rendered ἔσομαι ὃς ἔσομαι . . . "I shall be that I shall be" (Luther),

---

[17]Most of what follows is taken from C. F. Keil, and F. Delitzsch, *Commentary on the Old
Testament in Ten Volumes*, vol. 1, *The Pentateuch*, trans. James Martin (Grand Rapids: Eerdmans,
1980), 73ff., 435ff. While there are more contemporary commentaries available, the discussion
here is quite concise and accurate and therefore most useful for our particular purposes.
[18]Ibid., 73.
[19]Ibid., 73–74.
[20]Ibid., 74.

nor "I shall be that which I will or am to be." . . . Nor does it mean, "He who will be because He is Himself, the God of the future" (*Hofmann*). For in names formed from the third person imperfect, the imperfect is not a future, but an aorist. According to the fundamental signification of the imperfect, names so formed point out a person as distinguished by a frequently or constantly manifested quality. In other words, they express a distinctive characteristic. . . . The Vulgate gives it correctly: *ego sum qui sum*, "I am who I am."[21]

Again, Keil and Delitzsch note, and this is a key point:

"The repetition of the verb in the same form, and connected only by the relative, signifies that the being or act of the subject expressed in the verb is determined only by the subject itself" (*Hofmann*). The verb הָיָה [*hayah*] signifies "to be, to happen, to become;" but as neither happening nor becoming is applicable to God, the unchangeable, since the pantheistic idea of a becoming God is altogether foreign to the Scriptures, we must retain the meaning *"to be;"* not forgetting, however, that as the Divine Being is not a resting, or, so to speak, a dead being, but is essentially living, displaying [him] self as living, working upon creation, and moving in the world, the formation of יהוה from the imperfect precludes the idea of abstract existence, and points out the Divine Being as moving, pervading history, and manifesting Himself in the world. So far then as the words אהיה אשר אהיה [I Am who I Am, Ex. 3:14] are condensed into a proper name in יהוה [Yahweh], . . . God, therefore, "is He who is."[22]

In this regard, in his commentary on Exodus 3:14 and with respect to the revelation of God's name, Calvin notes, "Therefore, immediately afterwards, contrary to grammatical usage, he used the same verb in the first person as a substantive, annexing it to a verb in the third person; *that our minds may be filled with admiration as often as his incomprehensible essence is mentioned.*"[23] "As often as his incomprehensible essence is mentioned"— and as we have noted, it is mentioned over five thousand times in Scripture. Clearly the Lord was jealous that his people see him for who he essentially is on every page of his written revelation. To think this name to be obscure or otherwise marginalized in Scripture is to miss entirely the meaning of his name.

---

[21]Ibid.
[22]Ibid., 74–75.
[23]John Calvin, *The Comprehensive John Calvin Collection*, CD ed., The Ages Digital Library System, 2002.

(3) *Exodus*

Given what I have said about the name Yahweh, it will be useful to look briefly at this key passage in Exodus.

> Now Moses was keeping the flock of his father-in-law, Jethro, the priest of Midian, and he led his flock to the west side of the wilderness and came to Horeb, the mountain of God. And the angel of the LORD appeared to him in a flame of fire out of the midst of a bush. He looked, and behold, the bush was burning, yet it was not consumed. And Moses said, "I will turn aside to see this great sight, why the bush is not burned." When the LORD saw that he turned aside to see, God called to him out of the bush, "Moses, Moses!" And he said, "Here I am." Then he said, "Do not come near; take your sandals off your feet, for the place on which you are standing is holy ground." And he said, "I am the God of your father, the God of Abraham, the God of Isaac, and the God of Jacob." And Moses hid his face, for he was afraid to look at God.
>
> Then the LORD said, "I have surely seen the affliction of my people who are in Egypt and have heard their cry because of their taskmasters. I know their sufferings, and I have come down to deliver them out of the hand of the Egyptians and to bring them up out of that land to a good and broad land, a land flowing with milk and honey, to the place of the Canaanites, the Hittites, the Amorites, the Perizzites, the Hivites, and the Jebusites. And now, behold, the cry of the people of Israel has come to me, and I have also seen the oppression with which the Egyptians oppress them. Come, I will send you to Pharaoh that you may bring my people, the children of Israel, out of Egypt." But Moses said to God, "Who am I that I should go to Pharaoh and bring the children of Israel out of Egypt?" He said, "But I will be with you, and this shall be the sign for you, that I have sent you: when you have brought the people out of Egypt, you shall serve God on this mountain."
>
> Then Moses said to God, "If I come to the people of Israel and say to them, 'The God of your fathers has sent me to you,' and they ask me, 'What is his name?' what shall I say to them?" God said to Moses, "I AM WHO I AM." And he said, "Say this to the people of Israel, 'I AM has sent me to you.'" (Ex. 3:1–14)

There is much that could be discussed in this passage, but we will focus on matters relating more directly to the name of God. Notice, for example, that it is the "angel of the LORD" that appears to Moses, and that this angel, as it turns out, is "the LORD," Yahweh himself (compare v. 2 with vv. 4–6). This will be more significant later on, but we should not miss the fact that Yahweh *is* the angel of Yahweh. Notice, too, that when Yahweh appears to Moses, he identifies himself as the God of "your father," the God of Abraham, Isaac,

and Jacob. God is identifying himself as the covenant God, the God who is
for his people, including Moses.

But the designation given to Moses by God—the God of your fathers, of
Abraham, Isaac, and Jacob—is not sufficient for Moses; he wants a name. He
wants Yahweh to identify himself in such a way as to confirm the announcement Moses has now been commissioned to give. So Yahweh accedes to
Moses's request and says that his name is "I AM."

There is so much written about this name that we can only be (highly)
selective here.[24] The first thing that needs clarification concerning this revelation of God's name is the phenomenon of the "unburning" bush. One
commentator thinks that "the most important function of the Burning Bush
is to signal a change in God's interaction with Creation. . . . And Yahweh's
first intervention in nature should be modest, in preparation for the greater
wonders to follow, and in proportion to the size of his audience."[25] Another
commentator sees the bush as "an overwhelming demonstration of God's
power who commissions and equips his prophet for a divine purpose."[26]

There is, however, a much richer, deeper, and more adequate interpretation of God's miraculous action here. There is something uniquely revelatory
about the name of God as presented to Moses in the unburning bush. God
not only *says* who he is; he also *shows* who he is. Thus, we have word revelation tied to deed revelation.[27] There is something modeled for Moses in
this event of divine revelation. It is not an insignificant detail that what draws
Moses into God's presence is an analogy for who God himself is. There is no

---

[24]For a helpful bibliography on this aspect of God's name, see John I. Durham, *Word Biblical Commentary*, vol. 3, *Exodus* (Nashville: Thomas Nelson, 1987), 34.

[25]William H. C. Propp, *Exodus 1–18*, The Anchor Yale Bible Commentaries (New Haven, CT: Yale University Press, 1999), 222.

[26]Brevard S. Childs, *The Book of Exodus: A Critical Theological Commentary*, Old Testament Library (Philadelphia: Westminster Press, 1974), 74.

[27]The relationship of word revelation and deed revelation is expressed well by Geerhardus Vos: "Besides making use of words, God has also employed acts to reveal great principles of truth. It is not so much the prophetic visions or miracles in the narrower sense that we think of in this connection. We refer more specially to those great, supernatural, history-making acts of which we have examples in the redemption of the covenant-people from Egypt, or in the crucifixion and resurrection of Christ. In these cases, the history itself forms a part of revelation. There is a self-disclosure of God in such acts. They would speak even if left to speak for themselves. . . . These miraculous interferences of God to which we ascribe a revealing character, furnish the great joints and ligaments by which the whole framework of sacred history is held together, and its entire structure determined. God's saving deeds mark the critical epochs of history, and as such, have continued to shape its course for centuries after their occurrence." Geerhardus Vos, "The Idea of Biblical Theology," in *Redemptive History and Biblical Interpretation: The Shorter Writings of Geerhardus Vos*, ed. Richard B. Gaffin Jr. (Phillipsburg, NJ: Presbyterian and Reformed, 1980), 9.

analogy in the creation for the independent and uncreated. So God creates an analogy in the bush. Two aspects of God's name and character are given in this revelatory act.

First, the fire, which itself represents God (as it does often in Scripture, for example, in Deuteronomy 4 and 5; 1 Kings 18; Ps. 50:3; Ezek. 22:31; Heb. 12:29), is *in* and *with* the bush.[28] It could have easily hovered above the bush or beside it. It could have had no obvious relation to the bush at all. The significance of its presence *in* the bush is that it is meant to signify Yahweh's presence with his people. It shows that God is a covenant God; he is the God of Moses, of Abraham, Isaac, and Jacob. This is the way Yahweh first announces himself to Moses; he first announces and promises his sacred presence with Moses and with his people ("I am the God of your father, the God of Abraham, the God of Isaac, and the God of Jacob," Ex. 3:6).

Second, the fire, which is *in* the bush, does not derive its burning from the context in which it burns. It is self-generated, contradicting all rules of creation. The bush is on fire, but the fire is not dependent on the bush; it possesses its own energy. There is, it seems, a deliberate miracle given by God to unveil the significance of the divine name, "I AM WHO I AM." It stresses the absolute independence of God's being, that he possesses being in and of himself in a manner that is uncaused. It is ontological. It is the ultimate fact about God that makes the human mind stagger and reel because we have no categories to describe or understand this element of the existence of God—that he simply is.

Generally speaking, the medieval view of this passage is that God is revealing himself here as the self-existent one. This is now criticized by many Old Testament scholars on the grounds that issues like the aseity of God would not have crossed the mind of an ancient Israelite. But this critical assumption certainly cannot be the case, given the history of God's dealings with his people. Such criticism may speak more about the influence of Immanuel Kant on current understandings of the Old Testament than about the text itself. It is interesting that those who claim such things may themselves have a view of metaphysics absent from historical considerations or from everyday experience.

It seems clear here that God is declaring his self-existence; his encounter with Moses is not concerned simply with engaging history as the God of Abraham, Isaac, and Jacob, though that is how he wants Moses initially to

---

[28]"This fire was a type or declaration of the presence of God in the person of the Son. For with respect unto the Father he is called an Angel, the Angel of the covenant; but absolutely in himself, he was Jehovah, the 'God of Abraham,' etc." John Owen, *The Works of John Owen*, ed. W. H. Gould, Ages Digital Library CD ed., 16 vols. (Edinburgh: Banner of Truth, 1977), 1:401.

understand who he is. Rather, he announces himself as the God who is also above history.

At the other end of the spectrum, seen in various forms, "I AM WHO I AM" is to be exegeted in terms of who God is in history, in what Moses is about to encounter. One reason that the commentators are confused about what God is saying here is their fascination with the etymological (i.e., grammatical and syntactic) aspect of the name, to the neglect of the redemptive-historical.

Just as the name of God was made known as the God of Abraham, Isaac, and Jacob in terms of what God proved to be to them, so also the significance of the divine name is to be understood, not from etymological considerations alone or apart from what God is doing in time and history, but particularly from redemptive-historical considerations.

Rather than isolating the pronouncing of the divine name from the context in which it is revealed, we find the context to be a help for understanding the name. Yahweh does indeed reveal his divine independence. In the context of the Exodus narrative (which, we should note, is the quintessential picture of salvation in the Old Testament), he proves himself to be unlimited by temporal distinctions. "I AM WHO I AM" indicates that by contrast, for example, with Moses, who had a beginning and an end in human history, God possesses his existence without beginning, without end, and without explanation beyond himself.[29] This is the ultimate fact of divine revelation, that God is who he is, without cause, without beginning or end.

Both the name and the act (of the unburning bush) imply the immanence of this God. They picture and look forward to the ideal of Emmanuel, God with us. This is demonstrated in the symbol of the unburning bush with its manifestation of God's being. The fire, like God, is in need of nothing in order to be what it is. It transcends the earthly. This transcendent One is nevertheless not a prisoner of his own transcendence, but in his transcendence is able to dwell among his people. Here we have in miniature an extraordinary illustration of that undying biblical principle that God's ultimate purpose in

---

[29]It is worth noting in this regard that, historically, the name of God in Ex. 3:14 is linked with Rev. 1:4 ("Grace to you and peace from him *who is and who was and who is to come . . .*"). According to Muller, "It is . . . this text in Revelation, more than the Septuagint rendering of Exodus 3:14, that sanctioned the traditional essentialist understanding of the text" (Muller, *Post-Reformation Reformed Dogmatics*, 3:259). Another helpful and fascinating study of the tetragrammaton can be found in John L. Ronning, *The Jewish Targums and John's Logos Theology* (Peabody, MS: Hendrickson, 2009), 72–77. In that section, Ronning makes the case for a (more or less) nonessentialist understanding of the name. He concludes that it would best be rendered as "'I will be who I have been,' that is, 'I am the same, past, present and future,'" (74). Assuming this is correct, however, the name would still point directly to God's immutability, and thus to his aseity. It seems to me that both interpretations could easily be in view.

creation, though remaining all the while God, is to dwell with his people. This is the Emmanuel principle that runs from the garden of Eden to the closing chapters of Revelation. Throughout all Scripture, God creates holy space in order to dwell with his people to manifest his transcendence-in-immanence until the consummation, when there is no temple, for in that place everything will be holy space and holy time—the ultimate manifestation of what we see in the unburning bush. The exegesis of the words "I AM" implies that who God is may be seen from the covenantal redemptive activities that surround the exodus.

This truth is given in a number of ways, for example, in the continuity that is stressed between the covenant revelation given to the patriarchs and the new revelation in and through Moses. Yahweh is the God of Abraham, Isaac, and Jacob. Exodus 3 and 6 make it clear that what is to take place in Exodus does so in the light of the specifics of the covenant made with Abraham, Isaac, and Jacob. Indeed, we see this in the significance of the words in Exodus 6:2–6.

> God spoke to Moses and said to him, "I am the LORD. I appeared to Abraham, to Isaac, and to Jacob, as God Almighty, but by my name the LORD I did not make myself known to them. I also established my covenant with them to give them the land of Canaan, the land in which they lived as sojourners. Moreover, I have heard the groaning of the people of Israel whom the Egyptians hold as slaves, and I have remembered my covenant. Say therefore to the people of Israel, 'I am the LORD, and I will bring you out from under the burdens of the Egyptians, and I will deliver you from slavery to them, and I will redeem you with an outstretched arm and with great acts of judgment.'"

The notion that what we have in Exodus is God's interpretation of his essential name has caused some discussion, since the divine name appears earlier than this (e.g., in Genesis). However, the end result is that there is continuity in what God is saying to the patriarchs and in this covenant made with Moses, both of which have a distinctively redemptive character. Each revelation expresses the redeeming power and the gracious mercy of Yahweh.

We see here an emphasis on the absolute sovereignty of God and his extreme mercy. Central here is the expression of covenantal bonding: "I will take you as my own people. And I will be your God." This is a definitive mark of what "covenant" means in the Old Testament (Jer. 7:23; 11:4; 30:22; Ezek. 36:28), into the New (2 Cor. 6:16; Heb. 8:10), and all the way into eternity future in the new heavens and the new earth (Rev. 21:3).

So if it is true that word and deed revelation are linked—the deeds exegete the words and the word illumines the deeds—then the revelation of the unburning bush expresses God's absolute independence, that in his essential character he is capable of condescension, and that as the One who condescends he reveals himself as the covenant-making Redeemer.

This revelation of the name of God, together with his covenant relationship to us, becomes obscured by sin in redemptive history, even as it does in our present time. Note, for example, Psalm 50:21. The Lord comes to rebuke his people because they do not understand who he is. He says, for example, in verses 12–13:

> If I were hungry, I would not tell you,
>   for the world and its fullness are mine.
> Do I eat the flesh of bulls
>   or drink the blood of goats?

The children of Israel have fundamentally misunderstood who God is; they have let the culture surrounding them dictate what kind of God is to be worshiped. The height of their condemnation comes in verse 21:

> These things you have done, and I have been silent;
>   you thought that I was one like yourself.
> But now I rebuke you and lay the charge before you.

This verse, as some translations note, could also be translated "you thought that the I AM was one like you."[30] As in Israel, so also today, the condescension of God, in which he freely purposes to be with us, is all too often mistaken for a lack of, or his giving up, his essential character, or a denial of (at least some of) his essential attributes. To put it in the context of the unburning bush, the fire *with* the bush is highlighted all too often, to the point of obscuring or even obliterating the *fact* that the bush remains unharmed and does not burn; the independence of the fire, though with the bush, is seldom affirmed. To be *with* us, it is sometimes argued, means to give up being independent.

But this revelation in Exodus tells us the opposite. Yahweh is *a se*. He is the "I AM." He depends on nothing to be who he is. Not only so, but his name attaches to his character in such a way that there is no possible way that he could be anyone else, or that he could give up who and what he is. To do

---
[30] דְּמִיתָ הֱיוֹת־אֶהְיֶה

that would be to give up his very name; it would be to move from being the
"I AM" to being dependent on something else. If the Lord had announced
his name to Moses, for example, as "I AM YOUR GOD" or as "I AM LOVE" or
something other than himself, then his character would be such that it would
depend on something other than himself to be what it is. God would then be
essentially dependent.

It is in the exodus that we see the character of God represented in all its
fullness and glory. This shouldn't surprise us. The exodus in the Old Testament
is the quintessential picture of the salvation of the Lord's people. It is in the
exodus that we have the most vivid picture of what God is doing and will do
to carry out his promises.

Not only so, but in this revelation to Moses, we have God's name given to
us *by God himself*. That is, while certainly all of Scripture is given by God
himself, what we have given to Moses on that mountain is God himself speaking to Moses in order to reveal exactly *who* is calling Moses and promising
to deliver Israel.

Given God's absolute independence, there are attributes, properties, and
characteristics that define and develop what it means for God to be *a se*. It
will help us to see, albeit briefly, just what some of those properties are.

C. Essential Characteristics

As we begin to think about God's character, we need to explain how we will
categorize his properties. The first category of God's attributes, those that
further define what it means for God to be independent, we will call *essential*
properties, attributes, or characteristics. Without rehearsing the long history of
discussions regarding "essences," we can understand "essence" and "essential"
here as those properties without which God would not be who he is. As I have
already mentioned, we will want to distinguish God's essential properties from
those that are covenantal. At this point, however, all we need to remember is
that if we were to deny or take away any of the properties discussed below,
God would not be God. Essential properties, therefore, are properties that
relate to God *as God*, or to God's "Godness." They are properties that help
us see who he is quite apart from his relationship to anything outside him.

These characteristics are sometimes referred to under the heading "apophatic theology," which means that our discussion of God here is characterized by its negation (*apophatic* is from the Greek word meaning "deny"). In
other words, the best way that we have to describe these characteristics is by
discussing them in terms of what God is *not*. Some have wanted to conclude

that in discussing God's characteristics in this way we are admitting that we can have no knowledge of God's essence. That, of course, as we have already seen, is not the case. It is better to say that we can have knowledge of the essence of God, but that our knowledge is delimited by all the qualifications of human knowledge—it is analogical, limited, perhaps marred by sin, and so on.

So, we know God as he is in himself, but that knowledge is dependent on his revealing it to us and is always characterized by human limitations. And while we cannot conceive of what these characteristics *actually* are in all their fullness in God, we can understand certain things about them. We can see, for example, that as the exact opposites of things in the created world they are inherently "other" than anything we know or could ourselves experience. In that way, we can affirm that of which we cannot conceive.

(1) Simplicity

The essential and apophatic characteristic that we should begin with is God's simplicity. As we do, and given that we have discussed the Trinity, we should think of these characteristics as applying to each person of the Trinity as God, rather than as applying to only the Father or as applying only to the unity of God, as if the persons did not have such characteristics. In other words, if God is eternal, then we are saying that the Father is eternal, the Son is eternal, and the Holy Spirit is eternal. So also, as God is simple, the Father is simple, the Son is simple, and the Holy Spirit is simple. Just how this works out is ultimately incomprehensible to us.

In discussions of the unity of God, distinctions are sometimes made between the *unitas singularitatis* and the *unitas simplicitatis*. The *unitas singularitatis* is the fact that God is one God and not three or multiple gods. The *unitas simplicitatis*, our concern here, is the fact that God's being is a unity; it is "simple." That is, the basic idea of simplicity with respect to God is that he is not composed of parts. The Westminster Confession of Faith 2.1 says that God is "without body, parts or passions." One of the reasons to affirm such a thing is stated by Turretin: "For all composition infers mutation by which a thing becomes part of a whole, which it was not before."[31]

The doctrine of God's simplicity says that the characteristics of God are not *parts* of God that come together to make him what he is, but rather identical with his essence, and thus with him. The simplicity of God not only affirms that whatever God essentially is, he is necessarily, but it asserts even more

---

[31]Turretin, *Institutes*, 1:192.

than that. The simplicity of God holds that God's attributes are not characteristics or properties that exist (in the same way that he exists) in any way
outside of God, such that his having such a characteristic or property entails
his participation in something other than himself. God is his characteristics
and his characteristics are identical to him.

Perhaps we can think of it by way of the contrary. What if God *were* composed of parts, or of a part? Imagine goodness as a part of God's character
such that it is not identical to him, but in some way actually composes his
character. What, now, must be true of this goodness? Since it is not identical
to God, it must be something *other* than him. If it is something other than
him, then it must be *outside* him, at least initially. Not only so, but if God is
essentially good, and goodness is not identical to him, then he depends on
goodness to be who he is essentially. Thus, God is dependent on something
besides himself in order to be who he is essentially. Were that the case, God
would not be *a se*; he could not be independent.

The fact that God is good, therefore, according to the Christian tradition,
does not mean that God participates in a property of goodness that lies in
eternity or exists eternally with or alongside him. Rather, as God, he simply
is good, and the goodness that he is just *is* himself. As good, God does not
partake of a universal goodness in a maximal way, such that he has the most
of it, or all of its eternal manifestation, or anything of the sort. Rather, God's
goodness is God himself; to separate him from that goodness would, *per
impossibile*, destroy him entirely.

Not only so, but when we think of the simplicity of God, we are also
committed to the notion that God's attribute of goodness and all of his
other essential attributes themselves are, since they are God's, attributed to
him essentially and thus are his essence. God's truth is a good truth, and his
goodness is true goodness, just because (in God) the one is included in and
identical with the other.

Perhaps the best way to think about the simplicity of God is that it demands
a denial of any composition of parts in God. In this denial there is an equally
important affirmation. The affirmative aspect of simplicity says that whatever attributes, qualities, or properties inhere essentially in God, they are all
identical with his essence. Notice in this denial and affirmation that there
is no denial of distinctions in God. The doctrine of simplicity, in its best
formulations, has never affirmed that God is some sort of Being in which
no distinctions do or can reside. That kind of "simplicity" is more akin to
philosophical speculation than to biblical truth. Rather, the distinctions that
reside in God, because they accrue to his essence, are identical with that

essence and thus are not parts of God, serving to make up the whole of who he is. Affirming the simplicity of God does not, then, deny distinctions; both must be true. According to Van Til:

> It is, of course, true that we must distinguish between God's knowledge and his being. This is as true as that we must distinguish between the various attributes of God. But if these distinctions are really to be maintained in their full significance, they must be maintained as correlative to a principle of identity that is as basic as they are themselves. To avoid the blank identity of pantheism, *we must insist on an identity that is exhaustively correlative to the differentiations within the Godhead*. So also to avoid the abstract differentiations and equivocations of deism, we need a differentiation that is exhaustively correlative to the principle of identity in the Godhead.[32]

Simplicity, therefore, is a characteristic with many distinctions, and one that applies to the essence of God.

An important aspect of this doctrine of God's simplicity is that these distinctions in God are not thought to exist as real "things" in God. That is, they should not be thought of as things at all, so that the Godhead is a composition of "thing upon thing." Rather, the distinctions of characteristics in the Godhead, because identical with his essence, are sometimes called formal or modal distinctions, describing for us the *forms* or *ways* in which the essence of God exists. Thus, for example, the three persons in the Godhead are not essential distinctions in God, but rather are the ways in which the essence of God exists personally.[33]

One can begin to see why objections have been raised against this notion of simplicity. We have no creaturely example of such a thing. It does not seem to fit anything else with which we are familiar, neither can we lay out exactly what kind of attributes these are, which both describe and entail, are distinct and are identical to, God's existence. But limitations of this sort need not arouse an immediate charge of irrationality or demand a call for a radical

---

[32]Cornelius Van Til, *An Introduction to Systematic Theology*, 2nd ed., ed. William Edgar (Phillipsburg, NJ: P&R, 2007), 372–73, my emphasis.
[33]Calvin's affirmations of the simplicity of God take place, for the most part in the *Institutes*, in the context of his discussion of the Trinity. Note, for example, "Indeed, if we hold fast to what has been sufficiently shown above from Scripture—that the essence of the one God is simple and undivided, and that it belongs to the Father, the Son, and the Spirit; and on the other hand that by a certain characteristic the Father differs from the Son, and the Son from the Spirit—the gate will be closed not only to Arius and Sabellius but to other ancient authors of errors." John Calvin, *Institutes of the Christian Religion*, trans. Ford Lewis Battles, ed. John T. McNeill, 2 vols., The Library of Christian Classics (Philadelphia: Westminster Press, 1960), 1.13.22.

revision of God's attributes as we understand them. As might be expected, however, some have called for just that.[34] But to deny simplicity is, at least by implication, to make God essentially dependent; it is to deny his character as "I AM." For this reason, orthodox theology has historically affirmed the necessity of simplicity with respect to God.[35]

So, the notion of simplicity is a direct implication of God's independence. God is sovereign over all. He is subject to nothing. Prior to anything else, all that existed was God and him alone. The notion of simplicity, in other words, follows, for example, from the essential character of God in which "he is what he is." In being what he is, he is not one whose existence depends on anything outside himself in order to be.

As you might expect, serious criticism has come from many over this doctrine. Seeking to do justice to our speaking of God, Thomas made a distinction between the way of signification (*modus significandi*) with respect to the attributes of God, and the thing signified (*res significata*). When we say that "God is good," goodness as a thing signified belongs to God; it is not a metaphor but is used of him literally. But our way of signifying it, according to Thomas, is itself improper. No subject-predicate proposition can be proper regarding God since he is one. So, we never signify anything of God properly.

These are deep and complex issues that we cannot get into here.[36] But we should note two things: (1) Had Thomas begun with God's revelation of himself rather than with creation, he might have been able to affirm a proper "way of signification"; (2) Thomas's preferring the oneness of God (by virtue of his understanding of natural theology) over the three-ness led him to affirm things of God that can easily go astray—for example, that any predication of subject/object is improper with respect to God. So, despite his helpfulness, some aspects of Thomas need revision here.

Since the medieval discussion some have wanted to deny simplicity altogether. Because the notion of simplicity is so contrary to our natural intuitions, many have sought to affirm the fullness of God's deity while rejecting simplicity. Robert Dabney, for example, claims that we must make a distinc-

---

[34] As a matter of fact, it would be difficult to find an evangelical theologian who has written on these matters and who affirms the doctrine of simplicity.

[35] "From Irenaeus to the era of Protestant orthodoxy, the fundamental assumption was merely that God, as ultimate Spirit is not compounded or composite being. It is also the case that, from the time of the fathers onward, divine simplicity was understood as a support of the doctrine of the Trinity and as necessarily defined in such a manner as to argue the 'manifold' as well as the non-composite character of God." Muller, *Post-Reformation Reformed Dogmatics*, 3:276.

[36] For a discussion of Aquinas's notion of God's simplicity and the problem of theological predication, see Oliphint, *Reasons for Faith*, 89–121.

tion in God between substance and attributes, and in that sense there is no difference between God and other finite spirits.

Perhaps one of the most significant challenges to this notion has come of late from Alvin Plantinga. In 1980 Plantinga gave the Thomas Aquinas lecture at Marquette University, which was entitled *Does God Have a Nature?*[37] This, of course, is a provocative question. Plantinga notes that the answer historically has been yes. However, a yes answer could very well deny the doctrine of divine simplicity. Divine simplicity affirms not that God *has* a nature but that God *is* his nature. Plantinga wants to answer yes and to argue that God's nature is not identical with who he is. Because Plantinga's lecture gives the most serious and rigorous challenge to this doctrine, we should at least be aware of its contents and of possible responses to it.

Plantinga first notes that the doctrine of divine simplicity is "a dark saying indeed."[38] To his credit, he thinks it is a dark saying because if one believes it, one is forced to affirm all kinds of notions that imply the rejection of the Christian God—that God is personal, for example. So, his reason for seeing simplicity as "dark" is the threat he sees it posing to (aspects of) traditional Christianity.

Plantinga's first argument can be stated fairly simply. If God is identical with his properties—his goodness, wisdom, and holiness, for example—then each of the properties is identical with the other. And if all of the properties are identical, then there is only one property. And if God is identical with that property, then God is a property. This is Plantinga's first problem, since he does not want to affirm that God is a property; he wants to affirm God as a person, or a personality. I will respond to this shortly.

Plantinga's second problem is a complex web of arguments centering on what he calls the "sovereignty-aseity intuition (SAI)."[39] The SAI basically affirms that God is sovereign over all things and is dependent on nothing at all. Plantinga then goes on to argue that, while the redness of a rose, for example, may be within God's control, the proposition "whatever is red is colored" is not. This latter proposition is a necessary truth, and necessary truths, according to Plantinga, are not up to God; they are true by virtue of what they are. If they were within God's control, according to Plantinga, then it must be that God could cause them to be false (in other words, they

[37]For a detailed analysis and critique of Plantinga's view of simplicity, see Frederik Gerrit Immink, *Divine Simplicity = De Eenvoud Gods* (Kampen: Kok, 1987).
[38]Alvin Plantinga, "Does God Have a Nature?," in *The Analytic Theist: An Alvin Plantinga Reader*, ed. James F. Sennett (Grand Rapids: Eerdmans, 1998), 228.
[39]Ibid., 249ff.

must be contingent truths). But God could not cause such things to be false, since they are true necessarily.

What does this have to do with simplicity? Simplicity affirms that there is nothing on which God is essentially dependent. If there were, then God would only be "potential" with respect to what he is, rather than essentially actual. In other words, he would not be who he is unless other things were true and applied to him; he would be "potentially" something or someone else. If it can be shown that there are some things on which God is dependent necessarily, then it should not be difficult for us to affirm that there are other things, things that compose who God is, on which he is dependent as well. So (to oversimplify), Plantinga's argument here is that God is dependent on a number of things, so we should have no problem rejecting the notion of simplicity (note how Plantinga rightly sees that God's independence entails his simplicity).[40]

There are other, much more detailed arguments offered by Plantinga, but this will have to do for now. In response to his discussion, first, is it really the case that if God is identical with his properties, then there is only one property, and God is in fact a property? Perhaps that follows logically, but there are other ways to construe the relationship.

We should remember here that we are discussing apophatic theology. As such, we are focusing on what God is not. In other words, we are arguing that there are certain ways in which we are not to think of God. One such way is as One who has a number of parts that make up who he is. So, in arguments for simplicity, we are not saying that God is *unqualifiedly* identical with his attributes. Rather, the argument for simplicity is in some ways similar to the arguments for the Trinity. While we affirm the oneness of God, we at the same time note real distinctions in him that are not in any way different from who he essentially is, though they are, nevertheless, legitimate distinctions that must be made. So, goodness is not a property of God's that we deem identical with him; goodness is who God, the personal God, *is*. So also for the other attributes.

We should also see that, to construe the argument differently, if God is identical with his properties, it may be (and in fact is the case) that, rather

---

[40]We should remember here that the rejection of simplicity is common fare among evangelical theologians. Since they affirm that God gives up his sovereignty in order for us to be truly free, it is a very short step to a dependent (open?) God. Plantinga, generally, falls into this category. His free-will defense cashes out, theologically, as Arminian, so he should have no problem rejecting simplicity on the same grounds. For a summary and analysis of Plantinga's free-will defense, see K. Scott Oliphint, *Reasons for Faith*, part 4.

than God being a property, the "property" is first of all a person, or personal, and only afterward a property. The main reason Plantinga wants to force the identity in the direction of properties is that he is convinced that (at least some) properties are necessarily what they are whether or not God exists. So, (at least) conceptual priority is given to properties, rather than God, at the outset. This priority, however, gets things backwards. If we begin our reasoning with God as *a se*, then we should recognize that, before God created, there was only God. There were no necessities along with God that were not themselves identical to him. Thus, for example, there were no necessary propositions that had to obtain. There was only God—Father, Son, and Holy Spirit—the one God. There was no "2 + 2 = 4," no "all things red are colored"; there was God and his triune, essential character—nothing else.

This brings us to the second response, a response to the SAI. Is it really the case that, since the proposition "whatever is red is colored" is a necessary truth, God has no control over it? Or, to use a more abstract example, is it the case that since two plus two equals four necessarily, God has no control over it? Must it be that to acknowledge God's control over it means that it must be possible that God make it false? These questions are integrally related to current discussions of possible worlds and of modal logic and cannot be dealt with in depth here. We can say, however, that the answers to these questions have everything to do with how we think of the modal notions of necessity and possibility.

How do we know, for example, that two plus two necessarily equals four? One way is to look at the meaning of the terms. Four consists necessarily of two and two. So, it simply could not be four unless two and two were included in it (in some way). But what kind of necessity is this? Is it the same necessity that we apply to God's existence? It cannot be the case that God and creation, including the necessary laws of creation, are subject to the same necessity.

What seems to be a better, more biblical affirmation is that necessity and possibility are all determined by God himself.[41] This means that there is no such thing as a possible world in which God does not exist. Nothing else can partake of this kind of necessity. Regarding the notion of necessity, therefore, we must maintain a distinction between God and everything else.

This means that, in order to think correctly of necessity, we should see it as defined in one way for the creature and in another way for the Creator. Whatever is necessary for us is such because God has so ordered and determined the world in that way. He might have determined it in that way because

---

[41]I will argue this in more detail in chapter 5.

that more closely reflects something of who he is. So, just to use one example, the reason God cannot square a circle is not that he is subject to some necessity outside himself or in some way constraining his character, but because he created a circle to be a certain way, and a square to be a certain way, and thus their necessity lies in his creative hand, not in something abstract and above God.

So, must we affirm that if God is in control of something, it must be possible for it to be false? There seem to be no indications that we must. God is in control of, for example, the proposition that everyone who calls on the name of the Lord will be saved, but that does not mean that God can make it false that everyone who calls on the name of the Lord will be saved. The book of Hebrews reminds us that God swore by himself that he would be true to his promises. The necessity of this truth (and others) lies in his faithful character, and not in some abstract modal notion to which he must be subject. The same is true of all he created. Some things may be changeable, but his creation reflects necessary elements all of which are the way they are because of his sovereign activity, and not because of some ultimate, metaphysical reality that he had to conform to in order to create.

This necessity, a created necessity, is what the Reformed have called "hypothetical necessity." Turretin explains it this way, in the context of God's will:

> On the state of the question observe: (1) that necessity is twofold; one absolute, which simply and by itself and its own nature cannot be otherwise, as that God is good, just, etc. The other hypothetical, which is not so of itself and simply such but that it could be otherwise, but yet on the position of something it necessarily follows and could not be otherwise; as for example, if you posit that God predestinated Jacob to salvation, it is necessary that Jacob should be saved, namely on the hypothesis of the decree. Otherwise he could have been not predestinated and not saved. When, therefore, the question is asked whether God wills some things necessarily, but others freely I refer not only to the hypothetical necessity (for thus those things which God wills freely, the decree being posited, he no more not wills), but concerning the absolute necessity.[42]

That which is necessary, therefore, must take its place either in terms of God's character, in which case it is absolutely necessary, or in terms of creation, in which case the necessity is based on a prior contingency (i.e., God's free act to create).

---

[42] Turretin, *Institutes*, 1:218–19.

It is no counter to simplicity, therefore, that God is sovereign and *a se*. Plantinga rightly sees these terms as interdependent, but it is incumbent on us to grasp the most crucial and foundational Christian distinction that must be initially affirmed—that of God *as God*, and of creation as God has intended it to be.

(2) Infinity

Given God's independence, it follows that he is not limited by anything, nor is he bound to abide by the boundaries of creation. One way to articulate this truth is to affirm that God is infinite. In line with traditional terminology, we can discuss God's infinity under two primary headings: eternity and immensity. God's infinity with respect to time is his eternity, and with respect to space is his immensity. Before discussing those two characteristics specifically, however, a brief note about infinity is needed.

Like the other characteristics we are dealing with here, infinity is another piece of apophatic theology—it is a negative attribute. What it says is that something—in this case, God—is *not* finite. We should be aware, however, (as Charles Hodge reminds us[43]) that even with negative theology, we are saying something positive about God as well. We are saying that he is not limited by anything created; he transcends all that he has made; we cannot decide or contemplate how we want God to be and then make him that way. So, in saying that God is infinite, we are also saying that he is transcendent—above and beyond any created mode of being with which we are familiar.[44]

This brings us to perhaps the most important aspect to remember in our discussion of God. One of the things most difficult for us to grasp, and even more difficult to apply, is the Creator/creature distinction. We all as Christians affirm this; it is no intellectual stretch to realize that God is different from us. But when it comes to the actual application of it in our thinking, at least historically, we are oftentimes negligent.

What the Creator/creature distinction maintains, first of all, is that God is of a completely different—*qualitatively* different—order and kind than we are. This means, as we shall see, that God's eternity is not centrally an environment in which God operates—one that is set over against time.

---

[43]Charles Hodge, *Systematic Theology*, 3 vols. (London: James Clarke, 1960), 1:381. See also Muller, *Post-Reformation Reformed Dogmatics*, 3:328.
[44]We are concerned here with the notion of God's infinity *ad intra*, i.e., with respect to him alone. There are aspects of infinity (and eternity and immensity) *ad extra* that I will not develop here. See *Post-Reformation Reformed Dogmatics*, 3:325ff.

God's eternity, whatever it is, is just what God is in all of his being. He is eternal. In this way, God's eternity is of a completely different kind than, for example, our eternity with him in the new heavens and the new earth.

This also means that, however we might conceive of infinity in the created realm, God's infinity is of a completely different kind. Suppose we tried to conceive of an end to space. What would an end to space look like? What would be there if space was not? It is impossible for us to say. But we hold that prior to creation there was no space as we know it. There was only God. But "where" was God when he was all that there was? In one sense, that is the wrong question. Since he was all that there was, there was no "where" relative to his existence. He just was.

So, though we often speak of an infinite regress, or the infinity of number, we should recognize that all of that kind of talk presupposes creation itself (assuming numbers and the numerical system, which themselves were created). Just because for every number we can imagine adding one more to it, *ad infinitum*, we should not assume that God's infinity is the same kind as that.[45] God's infinity is just who he is; it does not mean that he stretches over all of space (in his omnipresence), but rather that he is unlimited in his being.[46] Exactly what that means is not always easily construed.

For example, a standard premise in most cosmological arguments is that an infinite regress of causes is impossible. Perhaps it is and perhaps it isn't. Whatever the case with such a regress, it presupposes the creation of things, like causes, to regress. Just how or whether one can get from the created mode to a mode of existence and being that transcends creation, and is of its own kind, is never argued in the proof; it is merely assumed. On that line of argument, there seems to be no real move in the argument from creation to Creator, and no way of seeing how such could be done. So, we must keep the Creator/creature[47] distinction in mind all along. As trite as that might sound, neglecting that fundamental concept is perhaps the reason why so many cannot accept much of who God is and what he claims to do.

---

[45] As Muller notes, "The infinity of God is a transcendence of all 'categories,' whether mathematical, metaphysical, or physical" (ibid., 3:329). This is just one more affirmation of the fact that there are no, and never were, eternal, Platonic properties that are *ad extra* with respect to God.

[46] The concept of infinity is, according to some, simply a description of *all* the divine attributes and thus is sometimes seen to be identical to God's aseity. See ibid., 3:325–27.

[47] My preference is to refer to this distinction as the *Eimi/eikon* distinction, for reasons that will be discussed later.

(a) Eternity

The infinitude of God relatively to space, is his immensity or omnipresence; relatively to duration, it is his eternity. As He is free from all the limitations of space, so He is exalted above all the limitations of time. As He is not more in one place than in another, but is everywhere equally present, so He does not exist during one period of duration more than another. With Him there is no distinction between the present, past, and future; but all things are equally and always present to Him. With Him duration is an eternal now. This is the popular and the Scriptural view of God's eternity. "Before the mountains were brought forth, or ever thou hadst formed the earth and the world, even from everlasting to everlasting thou art God." (Ps. xc. 2.) "Of old hast thou laid the foundation of the earth: and the heavens are the work of thy hands. They shall perish, but thou shalt endure: yea, all of them shall wax old like a garment; as a vesture shalt thou change them, and they shall be changed: but thou art the same, and thy years shall have no end." (Ps. cii. 25–27.) He is "The high and lofty One that inhabiteth eternity." (Is. lvii. 15.) "I am the first and I am the last; and besides me there is no God." (Is. xliv. 6.) "A thousand years in thy sight are but as yesterday when it is past." (Ps. xc. 4.) "One day is with the Lord as a thousand years, and a thousand years as one day." (2 Pet. iii. 8.) He is "the same yesterday, and to-day, and forever." (Heb. xiii. 8.) God is He "which is [ever is], and which was, and which is to come." (Rev. i. 4.) Throughout the Bible He is called the eternal or everlasting God; who only hath immortality. *The primal revelation of Himself to his covenant people was as the "I am."*[48]

Note, as Hodge points out, that an understanding of eternity is inextricably linked to God's name as "I AM." As we will see below, it is in connection with that name that we can best understand, as far as is possible with us, what eternity is relative to God.

The classic notion of the eternity of God has—like most of the classic, essential characteristics of God—fallen on hard times of late. Virtually every Protestant philosopher and a good number of theologians now insist that our classic notion of eternity simply cannot be applied to God. To do so, they tell us, results in incoherence (see the introduction for examples of this).

The biblical references to God's eternity are important; much of the discussion about eternity is an effort to define properly what is meant when God is said to be eternal, and how we reconcile that notion with other truths of Scripture. In dispute is how we might think of God's eternity, especially given creation. Our concern here will be to understand what eternity is, and

---

[48]Hodge, *Systematic Theology*, 1:385–86.

then we will deal in coming chapters with how God can be eternal and also related to time.[49]

The classic definition of God's eternity is found in Boethius's *Consolation of Philosophy*, where he says that it is "the whole, simultaneous and perfect possession of boundless life" (*Aeternitatis igitur est interminabilis vitae tota simul et perfecta possessio*).[50] You will readily notice from this description that it is virtually impossible, in describing eternity, to avoid using temporal terminology. That is because eternity, like simplicity, is an apophatic characteristic—the best we can do is to say what it is *not*, since we have no experience of what it *is*. So, it is something, according to Boethius, that is simultaneous; it happens at the same "time" (whatever that might mean).[51]

The burden behind the classic view of eternity was the same burden behind the classic view of simplicity. Thomas Aquinas saw the notion of eternity as entailed by his view of simplicity, since simplicity was intended to affirm that God, being without parts, was also without parts with respect to moments—his existence cannot be measured by a division of moments.[52] That burden is what has driven our understanding of eternity. If God is to be *a se* and if he is to be One, then there cannot be other things in which God's essence participates—things like thoughts or actions—that can be parceled out or divided up in any way.

Since our main concern in this book is not with the attributes per se, but rather with how we might best think about and consider them, it may be helpful to note briefly the discussion of eternity in the recent book entitled *God and Time*.[53] This book represents four common and modern views on the subject.

Before we get to those views, it is important to understand the discussions concerning time itself with which contemporary philosophers deal. To oversimplify, there are two general categories of theories about time, with nuances in each category that we need not discuss here. The two categories are "time as a process," sometimes called the A-theory of time, and "time as 'stasis'" (standing), sometimes called the B-theory.

---

[49]Another aspect of eternity, which I will not mention here, is discussed in chapter 5, section D (2).
[50]Boethius, *Tractates, De consolatione philosophiae*, trans. H. F. Stewart, E. K. Rand, and S. J. Tester, Loeb Classical Library (Cambridge, MA: Harvard University Press, 1978), 423 (5.6).
[51]For those interested in an elaboration of what simultaneity might mean with respect to eternity, a helpful analysis appears in Eleonore Stump, *Aquinas* (New York: Routledge, 2003), 136–44.
[52]Aquinas was in agreement with the Boethian definition of eternity. For a helpful analysis of Thomas's view of eternity, see ibid., 131–58.
[53]Gregory E. Ganssle and David M. Woodruff, eds., *God and Time: Essays on the Divine Nature* (Oxford: Oxford University Press, 2002).

Take an event that necessarily occurs at a particular time. On the process view (A-theory), the event is not "real" until that time. It is real only at that particular time; it is past after it and future before it. On the stasis view (B-theory), the event is always real, though its existence is dependent on the particular time in which it occurs. The time in which it occurs is an instance of the event, which itself is always real. It endures through time, though it occurs only at a particular time.[54]

The first view of eternity that we will note is typically called the view of "Divine Atemporality."[55] One of the representatives of this view is Paul Helm. In his argument for an unqualified eternity, Helm rightly wants to maintain the transcendence of God with respect to creation. He wishes to guard against so anthropomorphizing God that he is thought to be merely a super-man. So, Helm's argument is for an unqualified timelessness in God.

However, in order for God's timelessness to be unqualified, Helm proceeds to support something like a notion of eternal creation. In other words, since God's eternity is not qualified by anything temporal, his dealings with creation are themselves eternal dealings. The priority of God's eternity over creation, according to Helm, is not a temporal one, but is rather like the priority of the queen over the prime minister—there is a logical relationship there, but no temporal one. Helm goes further in his support of this idea, setting out the notion that the incarnation itself is eternal. To quote Helm:

> The point is . . . there is no preexistent Christ with a life history independent of and prior to the incarnation. There was no time when the eternal God was not Jesus of Nazareth. There is no other life story . . . of God than the incarnation. There was no time when the Son of God was not willing himself to be incarnate in our history.[56]

What are we to make of this view of the incarnation? If we parse the words a certain way, perhaps we can affirm most of it. "There was no time when the Son of God was not willing himself to be incarnate in our history" could mean that the second person of the Trinity was always willing to be incarnate. That seems true enough. "There was no time when the eternal God was not Jesus of Nazareth" may be a stretch for us to affirm. Was the eternal Son of God also Jesus of Nazareth prior to creation? Perhaps the response would

[54]As far as I can tell, the stasis view of time, or something close to it, is found in the view of God as atemporal. The others in this book who discuss the relation of time to eternity hold to some version of the process theory of time.
[55]Ganssle and Woodruff, God and Time, 28–60.
[56]Ibid., 54.

be no, since there was no time prior to creation. But was the eternal God Jesus of Nazareth at the time of creation? This doesn't seem to be biblically defensible. The point Helm is (rightly) making is that there is no temporal succession *in* God, that is, in his essential character.[57] But perhaps there is a better way to make the same point.

The same kind of delineation of the relationship of the incarnation to eternity is presented by Eleonore Stump.

> The divine nature of the second person of the Trinity . . . cannot become tempo-
> ral; nor could the second person at some time acquire a human nature he does
> not eternally have. Instead, *the second person eternally has two natures*; and at
> some temporal instants, all of which are ET-simultaneous[58] with the existence
> of each of these natures in their entirety, the human nature of the second person
> has been temporally actual. At those times and only in that nature, the second
> person directly participates in temporal events.[59]

It seems to me that Helm (and perhaps Stump) is forced to go too far in his understanding of eternity. He has at least two strikes against his view. The first is that, while he should be commended for his appeal to Scripture in support of God's eternity, there seems to be no scriptural warrant, either by the express teaching of Scripture, or by good and necessary consequence of that teaching, for his view of the incarnation. While Scripture does represent God in human form throughout history, the best understanding of those "incarnations," as we will see in coming chapters, is that they were looking forward to the incarnation of the Son of God. There seems, biblically, to be something wholly unique about Christ's incarnation—something wholly humiliating about it—that would make its essential existence within the Godhead something repugnant. Helm would not affirm a necessity to the incarnation, but his view is not sufficiently clear to avoid such an interpretation. The second strike is that there is no view in classical Christianity, Roman or Protestant, that supports this view of the relationship of eternity to the incarnation.

It would seem then that Helm has attempted, perhaps, to defend the right view, but has given to that view specific qualities not supported by the biblical

---

[57] Though there is a non-successive duration. See chapter 5, D (2).

[58] Stump's notion of ET-simultaneity is complex, and to spell it out here would muddy the waters. Suffice to say at this point that, even if ET-simultaneity exonerates Stump's notion of the incarnation in the abstract (i.e., abstracted from biblical criteria), to affirm that the two natures of Christ are eternal and that only his human nature participates in temporal events is troublesome at best.

[59] Stump, *Aquinas*, 142.

data or by the orthodox tradition. One of the questions that should be asked in this regard is why the orthodox tradition did not see the need to posit such things as eternal creation or eternal incarnation. It is likely not because they did not sense the same pressures that Helm senses. There were other reasons (that I'll mention later) why such notions were not set forth.

The second view of eternity is proposed by William Craig, among others. He thinks of God in terms of "timelessness and omnitemporality."[60] His basic thesis is that when there was no creation, God was timeless, but having created, God became temporal (i.e., omnitemporal). His reasons for asserting the omnitemporality of God are primarily two. First, he argues that a timeless God could not have a relationship with a temporal world. To have such a relationship would require God acting at one point, but not at another, speaking in a succession of words, and so forth. Second, Craig sees the notion of omniscience as entailing time. That is, if God knows that Moses will set the children of Israel free, he must know of that event relative to the time when it happened, the time before it happened, and the time after it happened, all of which, according to Craig, entail a relationship to temporality.

In his book *Time and Eternity*, Craig seeks to set forth the relationship of God to time. In spite of the title, Craig devotes only the last twenty pages to "God, Time, and Creation." Here Craig notes that tensed facts and temporal becoming are real. According to him, therefore, it follows from God's creative activity and omniscience that, given the existence of a temporal world, God is also temporal. God quite literally exists now.[61]

One brief point must be made regarding Craig's view, and then a more substantial point later. It should be noted here that Craig's concerns have little to do with the substance of the discussion, but more to do with the discussion's impetus, its method of approach, including its starting point. First, Craig is resolute that the solution to the problem of the relationship of time to eternity is found in analytic philosophy.[62] This is a worrisome assumption.

It is also worth noting that Craig sets time over against a particular attribute of God's without seeming to notice the apples-to-oranges comparison. A distinction must be made in these discussions between a *context* of existence and an *essential attribute* of existence. Craig compares one of God's essential attributes, his eternity, with a context of existence in creation, time. This seems to be an obvious confusion of categories. He begins his analysis by insisting that an understanding of God's attributes is found

---

[60]Ganssle and Woodruff, *God and Time*, 129–60.
[61]Craig, *Time and Eternity*, 217.
[62]Ibid., 11.

in the writings not of Christian theologians but of Christian philosophers. Christian theologians are ill-prepared to discuss matters of such "depth," according to Craig, because they are ill-trained for such. He notes that, contrary to the present situation, in the Middle Ages "students were not allowed to study theology until they had mastered all the other disciplines at the university."[63]

The third position is offered by Nicholas Wolterstorff and is sometimes called the temporal-eternity view, or the everlastingness of God. Wolterstorff writes of "Unqualified Divine Temporality."[64] On Wolterstorff's view God must be temporal because (1) the A-theory of time is true and thus (2) God must know what is happening now (remember on the A-theory whatever is happening now was not real previously). God must also be temporal because of the unfolding plan of God in history. God does not speak to Moses and to Jesus at the same time, but he speaks to Moses before he speaks to Jesus. Thus, he must be in time. It doesn't seem to enter the realm of possibility for Wolterstorff that God could be both in time and transcend time.

The fourth view is the most creative. In this view Alan Padgett sees eternity as "relative timelessness."[65] He argues, against the temporal view of God, that since creation and time had a beginning, they are both dependent on God and therefore God must, at least in this sense, transcend time. He argues, second, that an atemporal view of God can be true only if the B-theory of time, the stasis theory, is true. Since Padgett believes the A-theory to be true, he also believes that God must be *in* time in some sense. So, he argues for relative timelessness.

On this view, there are two kinds of time: there is time as we know it, created and passing moment by moment, and there is what Padgett calls "metaphysical time." The latter is, to put it simply, God's time, in which there is duration but no change. After affirming that God creates the space-time world that we know, Padgett notes:

> Because God really does change in order to sustain a dynamic changing world . . . , there must be some sense in which God is temporal. But I reject the phrase "God is in time," because of its negative theological connotations. Rather, I want to argue that God is the metaphysical precondition for the existence of eternity. . . . Our time, created time, exists within the pure duration of God's time, which is relatively timeless. And God's time exists because God exists (not

[63]Ibid.
[64]Ganssle and Woodruff, *God and Time*, 187–213.
[65]Ibid., 92–110.

the other way around). What many people seem to imply by "God is in time" is that God exists only if time exists—and this is what I deny.[66]

There are a number of things we could say about these four views and about God's eternity generally, but I will only hint at a possible response.[67] First, it seems to me awkward that in virtually all of the discussions about time and eternity it never seems to cross the minds of those engaged in the discussions that their comparisons and contrasts are apples and oranges. That is, the discussion is automatically set up as a contrast between time and eternity. When God enters the discussion, the arguments center on God's environment as one either of eternity or of time.

The problem with this kind of approach is that it fails to see that what we are discussing is one of God's essential characteristics, and not his environment. We should be clear about the fact that, as essentially God, the environment for God is none other than God himself. So, this is not a question, first of all, about God's context of existence, his atmosphere, as it were. It is a discussion about who he essentially is. And none of the authors we have discussed want to say that God is essentially time. They want to say that he is *in* time, or temporal, but this again is to talk of God's environment and not of God as he is in himself. This crucial distinction must be made at the outset, but is not made in much of the contemporary discussion of God's eternity.[68]

We will reserve further discussion of the core problems until later. The problems mentioned above, therefore, should be kept in mind as we move along.

(b) Immensity

"Immensity" can be understood as the characteristic of the divine essence according to which God is "omnipresent," with omnipresence strictly identifying the repletive presence of God in relation to finite creatures, who have a definitive or circumscriptive presence. Taken as a whole, this set of terms [*magnitudo, omnipraesentia* and *immensitas*] identifies a distinction between the infinity of God's essence and nature *in se* and absolutely considered, as indicated in his name and power, and the divine infinity considered in *ad extra* relation to God's works, and authority, as evidenced in the exceeding greatness of his acts,

---

[66]Ibid., 106.
[67]More on eternity in chapter 5.
[68]It may be that all of these authors are simply presupposing a discussion of *ad extra* eternity with respect to God. If so, they should say so clearly. My concern here is first to affirm that God's existence, when there was no creation, had no beginning or end or succession, though it did have duration. That duration, which is simply God's life and existence, is God's eternity.

judgments, and counsels, a distinction between divine infinity "intrinsically considered" and divine infinity "extrinsically considered."[69]

In terms of God's relationship to space, *immensity* is a good word to use. It comes from the Latin *immensus*, which means immeasurable. This is the best way to think about God's "where-ness." As a matter of fact, most of what I have said about God's eternity relative to time can be transferred to the notion of God's immensity relative to space. Paul Helm, as we have seen, wants to argue for God's atemporality; he also uses as part of his argument the entailment of God's relationship to time with his relationship to space. According to Helm, God is to time as he is to space. This carries some weight because many who want God to be temporal in some way nevertheless want to think of God as somehow transcending space.[70]

The first thing we should be clear about is the difference between immensity as of the essence of who God is, and omnipresence. Though we sometimes use the ideas interchangeably, we should recognize that immensity characterizes God as intrinsically immeasurable, as the "I AM" who existed prior to creation. Omnipresence refers to God relative to space; and space, we should note, like time, is a part of the created order. It is also worth noting that the Athanasian Creed says, literally, that the Father is immense, the Son is immense, and the Spirit is immense (*Immensus Pater, immensus Filius, immensus Spiritus Sancti*).[71] So, there is a long history of the affirmation of the immensity of God in orthodox theology.

Traditionally, in speaking of God's omnipresence with respect to his immensity three modes of presence in space are noted: (1) Bodies are in space circumscriptively (which means they are bound, necessarily, by space). (2) Spirits are in space definitively (which means, as Hodge says, they have an *ubi*, a "where-ness"). (3) God, however, is in space repletively (which means he fills it all). "In other words," says Charles Hodge,

> the limitations of space have no reference to him. He is not absent from any portion of space, nor more present in one portion than in another. This of course is not to be understood of extension or diffusion. Extension is a property of matter, and cannot be predicated of God. If extended, he would be capable of division and separation; and part of God would be here, and part elsewhere.[72]

[69] Muller, *Post-Reformation Reformed Dogmatics*, 3:328.
[70] See Paul Helm, "God and Spacelessness," in *Contemporary Philosophy of Religion*, ed. Stephen M. Cahn and David Shatz (New York: Oxford University Press, 1982).
[71] The translation usually renders the Latin *immensus* as "incomprehensible."
[72] Hodge, *Systematic Theology*, 1:383–84.

As Augustine reminds us, regarding immensity relative to creation, we are not to think of God as we do of air or light.[73] Air and light are diffused through vast amounts of space, but only parts of it are present in different places. God is not like that. There is no part of God present in some place. He is completely present everywhere. There is, therefore, a ubiquity of God's essence in which he is always and everywhere wholly and completely present.[74]

Now this should again remind us that the where-ness of God is of a wholly different character than any other where-ness with which we are familiar. Prior to creation, there was no where-ness; there was only God, and he was not anywhere; he simply was. So, it should not surprise us that we cannot envision how someone can be always and fully everywhere. The best we can do is to picture something vast covering everything else. But that is exactly what God is not. If he were, then only parts of God would be present in different places, with all of him present over everything. But all of God is present in every place. And even though we can show that, in one given place, there is no "room" in space for anything else to occupy that place, God is still wholly there.[75]

It should be mentioned here, in order to avoid misunderstanding, that the immensity of God does not rule out the biblical emphasis on God's special presence with his people. Remember Moses's request:

> Now therefore, if I have found favor in your sight, please show me now your
> ways, that I may know you in order to find favor in your sight. Consider too
> that this nation is your people." And he said, "My presence will go with you,

---

[73] Note in ibid., 1:384: "The older and later theologians agree in this view of the divine immensity and omnipresence. Augustine says God is not to be regarded as everywhere diffused, as the air or the light: '*Sed in solo cœlo totus, et in sola terra totus, et in cœlo et in terra totus, et nullo contentus loco, sed in seipso ubique totus.*'"

[74] Some biblical passages that speak to this are, Jer. 23:23–24: "Am I a God at hand, declares the LORD, and not a God afar off? Can a man hide himself in secret places so that I cannot see him? declares the LORD. Do I not fill heaven and earth? declares the LORD"; Ps. 139:7–12: "Where shall I go from your Spirit? / Or where shall I flee from your presence? / If I ascend to heaven, you are there! / If I make my bed in Sheol, you are there! / If I take the wings of the morning / and dwell in the uttermost parts of the sea, / even there your hand shall lead me, / and your right hand shall hold me. / If I say, 'Surely the darkness shall cover me, / and the light about me be night,' / even the darkness is not dark to you; / the night is bright as the day, / for darkness is as light with you"; Acts 17:28: "In him we live and move and have our being"; Eph. 1:22–23: "And he put all things under his feet and gave him as head over all things to the church, which is his body, the fullness of him who fills all in all."

[75] The antinomy that is brought about by God's omnipresence is instructive to us for the rest of God's relationship to creation. Given that we cannot envision how God can be wholly present in a place in which there is no more space to occupy, we should not be surprised when other matters, matters that can threaten us, are themselves replete with antinomy. More on this in coming chapters.

and I will give you rest." And he said to him, "If your presence will not go with me, do not bring us up from here. For how shall it be known that I have found favor in your sight, I and your people? Is it not in your going with us, so that we are distinct, I and your people, from every other people on the face of the earth?" (Ex. 33:13–16)

It is the special presence of God that distinguishes the Lord's people from all the others on the face of the earth. That kind of presence, we find out most fully in the New Testament, is the presence of God the Holy Spirit taking up residence in his people because of the work of redemption accomplished by Christ. That presence is a presence of salvation and of sanctification. The immensity of God is foundational, but not identical, to his special presence with us.

The apologetic significance of this should not be missed either. Remember that Paul says that God's "invisible attributes, namely, his eternal power and divine nature (ἥ τε ἀΐδιος αὐτοῦ δύναμις καὶ θειότης) have been clearly perceived, ever since the creation of the world" (Rom. 1:20). Part of what that means is that God himself, because of the universal pervasiveness of his revelation, is always and everywhere present to everyone, revealing himself through what he has made. And Paul goes on to point out that it is because of that revelation, clearly seen and understood, that we all stand before God without excuse (ἀναπολογήτους). In other words, it is the presence of God in all places everywhere, a presence made clear and understood by us all, that renders us all inexcusable before God. All of us, therefore, live our lives *coram Deo*.

(3) Immutability

Thomas Aquinas affirms the immutability of God by way of the potentiality/ actuality schema of Greek philosophy:

> On the contrary, It is written, "I am the Lord, and I change not" (Malachi 3:6).
> I answer that, From what precedes, it is shown that God is altogether immutable. First, because it was shown above that there is some first being, whom we call God; and that this first being must be pure act, without the admixture of any potentiality, for the reason that, absolutely, potentiality is posterior to act. Now everything which is in any way changed, is in some way in potentiality. Hence it is evident that it is impossible for God to be in any way changeable.[76]

---

[76]Thomas Aquinas, *Summa theologica*, trans. Fathers of the English Dominican Province, 1.9.1.

This way of describing immutability, though not familiar to most moderns, is helpful. If we assume God to be perfect, in that he lacks nothing, any change in God would have to be a change from perfect to less than perfect. So, as Aquinas puts it, since God is pure act (i.e., he lacks nothing and is not in need of anything), there is no way in which there can be any potentiality in him (in that potentiality would entail a lack of actuality). Not only so, but potentiality is posterior to act, which would mean that if God were mutable, he would change from actuality to potentiality. But then God would not be pure actuality; he would be one who is less than perfect and who would seek to attain to perfection.

Turretin's definition is more concise: "Immutability is an incommunicable attribute of God by which is denied of him not only all change, but also the possibility of change, as much with respect to existence as to will."[77] In other words, and this point will become significant for us, immutability is understood as an essential aspect of God's character, such that not only does he *not* change essentially, but the very possibility of essential change is denied.[78] This is not to affirm some outside force constraining God. Rather, it is to affirm that God is who he is, and he cannot be otherwise. He is constrained, in other words, by his own essential nature.[79]

There are two very strong motivations behind the notion of God's immutability. The first is our now familiar "good and necessary consequence." Given all that I have said about God thus far, it stands to reason that, if it were the case that God essentially changed, he would either be moving from some kind of potentiality to an actuality or be reduced from pure actuality to potentiality. In other words, change must be either from worse to better or from better to worse. Now, if God is perfect, not only in the moral but also in the metaphysical sense, then it is impossible that he can change. Any change, whether from better to worse or from worse to better, would *ipso facto* (by virtue of the fact itself) be a move from absolute perfection to something less than that. So, the motivation behind affirming God's immutability has been to preserve what many consider to be one of the chief characteristics of his "Godness."

---

[77]Turretin, *Institutes*, 1:204.

[78]This denial of change in God pertains, first, as we have said, to his essential character, but it also lies behind the fact that his covenant with his people will not change. Contra Barth and Barthians, it is not the case that God could, for example, bring Judas to heaven and send Christ's mother, Mary, to hell.

[79]This point has ramifications for libertarian free will that we cannot pursue here. Suffice to say that, since God is constrained by his nature, in that he does not have the power of contrary choice in all matters, so also with those made in his image. In other words, the notion of free will advocated by libertarianism is an idol; it exists neither in God nor in his human creatures.

But the motivation has not been only, or primarily, logical; there is strong scriptural support for God's immutability as well. I'll just mention a few passages.

> Of old you laid the foundation of the earth,
>   and the heavens are the work of your hands.
> They will perish, but you will remain;
>   they will all wear out like a garment.
> You will change them like a robe, and they will pass away,
>   but you are the same, and your years have no end. (Ps. 102:25–27)

For I the LORD do not change; therefore you, O children of Jacob, are not consumed. (Mal. 3:6)

> God is not man, that he should lie,
>   or a son of man, that he should change his mind.
> Has he said, and will he not do it?
>   Or has he spoken, and will he not fulfill it? (Num. 23:19)

And also the Glory of Israel will not lie or have regret, for he is not a man, that he should have regret. (1 Sam. 15:29)

We should note a couple of things here. First, we should not allow a subtle Greek notion of immutability to creep into our understanding of who God is. The Greek philosopher Parmenides tried to demonstrate immutability from the notion that any change whatsoever would necessarily be a change to nonbeing, or to nothing, so that all that is, is only being itself. His view of being was of a static, removed, and aloof "something" that could necessarily have no contact with (what he called) the "common way," which was the way of everyday life.

The biblical view of God is in no way like that. Although it does proceed, as we saw, from a notion of absolute perfection, such that any change in his being would necessarily be from perfection to something less, Scripture does not in any way fear or avoid the idea of God's real and personal interaction with himself, in the first place, as Father, Son, and Holy Spirit, and then with creation. In fact, all of Scripture presupposes such interaction.

The immutability of God, as the Westminster Shorter Catechism says, applies to his being, wisdom, power, holiness, justice, goodness, and truth. In other words, the immutability of God describes his essence, who he essentially is. He is unchangeable essentially, because to change his essence would be to change from God to something or someone else. So, in spite of much discussion about how God's relationship to creation might change him, the reality is that, in relating to creation, he remains unalterably wise, powerful, holy, just, good, and true. Philosophers themselves make distinctions between essential properties of a thing and what they sometimes call "mere Cambridge properties," which are properties whose acquisition or loss leave something or someone substantially unchanged. Without going into that discussion, we do well to remember the distinction between who God is in himself and who he is relative to creation. As we will see, christology can help us understand this distinction.

When the immutability of God is applied to creation, it becomes, in one sense, a show of God's faithfulness to his purposes in creation. So, says James, "Every good gift and every perfect gift is from above, coming down from the Father of lights with whom there is no variation or shadow due to change" (1:17). Also, the psalmist in Psalm 100:5 says,

> For the LORD is good;
>> his steadfast love endures forever,
>> and his faithfulness to all generations.

And in Psalm 117:2,

> For great is his steadfast love toward us,
>> and the faithfulness of the LORD endures forever.
> Praise the LORD!

Yahweh does not and cannot lie because that would imply change, and also moral decay. In connection with his care for us, his purposes for our lives, God remains ever the same. This is the central focus in the scriptural doctrine of divine immutability: the issue is not simply a metaphysical construct, but is God's unchanging faithfulness to his own being and, therefore, to us. At the heart of this relationship lies the notion that in both blessing and cursing, God remains the same. He remains faithful to the fullness of his being, expressed in the covenant.

God's immutability is not that of a statue, which never decays and never smiles, but the changelessness of a Father whose faithfulness discloses the fullness of his being. The changelessness of God, of which Scripture speaks, arises out of the manifoldness of his character expressed in his relationship to himself and, secondarily, his faithfulness to man.

Impassibility

In this regard there has been a good bit of discussion of late concerning God's impassibility.[80] As we have noted, the Westminster Confession of Faith says that God is "without body, parts or *passions*." Is God truly without passions? Again, how do we reconcile such a statement with passages in Scripture that indicate that God does have passions?[81] Take, just to use one example, the prophet Isaiah's recounting of the exodus:

> For he said, "Surely they are my people,
>> children who will not deal falsely."
> And he became their Savior.
> In all their affliction he was afflicted,
>> and the angel of his presence saved them;
> in his love and in his pity he redeemed them;
>> he lifted them up and carried them all the days of old. (Isa. 63:8–9)

What does it mean that God was afflicted in Israel's suffering? How can a God without passions be afflicted? How can an impassible God love and pity? These can be intensely personal questions. Nicholas Wolterstorff, who argues against the notion of impassibility, does so, at least in part, because of the death of his son. If God is impassible, he reasons, he would not care one whit about such a tragedy. So how does an impassible God understand such a death? Can he really be passionless with respect to such tragedies? Here there are at least two things to remember.

First, we should get straight the way in which the notion of passions has been historically understood. In the notion of causality, it was generally held that the action and the patient were to be *mutually dependent*.

The common scholastic adage—*Actio est in passo*—notes that a transeunt action (an action that has effects outside the agent, rather than merely internal to it) exists in the patient. The relation of causal dependence is signified by the

---

[80]For a more detailed, philosophical discussion of God's impassibility, see Oliphint, *Reasons for Faith*, 216–23.

[81]One way this has traditionally been reconciled is given in Anselm, "For, in sparing the wicked, thou art as just, according to thy nature, but not according to ours, *as thou art compassionate, according to our nature, and not according to thine*" (Anselm, *Proslogium; Monologium; an Appendix, in Behalf of the Fool, by Gaunilon; and Cur Deus Homo*, trans. Sidney Norton Deane [Bellingham, WA: Logos Research Systems, 2009], 17, my emphasis). Note also, "*To sorrow, therefore, over the misery of others belongs not to God*; but it does most properly belong to Him to dispel that misery, whatever be the defect we call by that name" (Aquinas, *Summa theologica* 1.21.3, my emphasis).

term 'action' or 'acting' on the one hand and by the term 'passion' or 'being acted upon' on the other.[82]

A passion, therefore, in scholastic terminology, is that which is causally dependent on an external acting agent, and it affects the subject intrinsically.

So, when the Confession denotes God to be "without passions," what it is saying is that, however and whatever God "feels," he does so according to his own sovereign plan and not because he is dependent or because something independent of him caused him to *re*-act to something outside himself.

Second, we should remember that the second person of the Trinity underwent what has been called in the orthodox tradition "the passion." This will be central and paramount in our discussions as we proceed. Christ, the Son of God in the flesh, suffered; he died, and he did that as the God-man, the quintessential covenant person. Since that is true, there must be some real and fundamental sense in which God *can* have or experience passions. Note B. B. Warfield's words in his sermon on Philippians 2:5–8:

> We have a God who is capable of self-sacrifice for us. It was although He was in the form of God, that Christ Jesus did not consider His being on an equality with God so precious a possession that He could not lay it aside, but rather made no account of Himself. . . . Now herein is a wonderful thing. Men tell us that God is, by very necessity of his nature, incapable of passion, incapable of being moved by inducement from without; that he dwells in holy calm and unchangeable blessedness, untouched by human sufferings or human sorrows for ever,—haunting . . .
>
> Let us bless our God that it is not true. God can feel; God does love. We have Scriptural warrant for believing, as it has been perhaps somewhat inadequately but not misleadingly phrased, that moral heroism has a place within the sphere of the divine nature: we have Scriptural warrant for believing that, like the hero of Zurich, God has reached out loving arms and gathered to his own bosom that forest of spears which otherwise had pierced ours. *But is not this gross anthropomorphism? We are careless of names: it is the truth of God.* And we decline to yield up the God of the Bible and the God of our hearts to any philosophical abstraction. We have and we must have an ethical God; a God whom we can love, in whom we can trust.[83]

---

[82]Alfred J. Freddoso, "God's General Concurrence with Secondary Causes: Why Conservation Is Not Enough," *Philosophical Perspectives* 5 (1991): 570.

[83]Benjamin Breckinridge Warfield, "Imitating the Incarnation," in *The Person and Work of Christ*, ed. Samuel G. Craig (Philadelphia: Presbyterian and Reformed, 1950), 570–71, my emphasis.

This is a fitting place to conclude our discussion of God's essential character. It is worth remembering that Warfield declares this in a sermon on the attitude of Christ in the incarnation.[84] As I will argue later, a christological hermeneutical methodology gives us at one and the same time a God who is sovereign—not surprised or reacting to new things that independently come to him—and also a God who suffers, and who ultimately suffers for us. So, like all of God's essential attributes, impassibility has to be understood from the perspective of the character of God *as God*, first of all, but then also from the context of the person and work of Christ himself.

---

[84]It should be noted here that John Murray thinks Warfield to be mistaken in some key points of this sermon. In my opinion, Murray overstates and overreads Warfield's sermon; given Warfield's fine exposition (with which Murray agrees) of Phil. 2:5ff. in B. B. Warfield, "The Person of Christ According to the New Testament," in *The Person and Work of Christ* (Philadelphia: Presbyterian and Reformed , 1950), it seems rather that what is given in the sermon is rhetorical flourish that would not have been expressed in the same way in his exegetical/doctrinal exposition. See John Murray, "Reviews: The Person and Work of Christ. By Benjamin Breckenridge Warfield," in *Collected Writings of John Murray*, vol. 3, *Life of John Murray, Sermons and Reviews* (Carlisle, PA: Banner of Truth, 1982).

CHAPTER 2

I Am . . . Your God

O come, O come, Thou Lord of might,
Who to Thy tribes, on Sinai's height,
In ancient times did'st give the Law,
In cloud, and majesty and awe.
Rejoice! Rejoice! Emmanuel
Shall come to thee, O Israel.

UNKNOWN

We have seen that God is who he is. He is the one, the *only* one, who is altogether independent. He alone is *a se*. He dwells in unapproachable light (1 Tim. 6:16). He alone possesses existence in and of himself. This is who God is, and any notion that denies or contravenes this basic identity of God fundamentally misunderstands his essential character and thus wreaks havoc on his glory.

A. The *Eimi/Eikon* Distinction

God's essential existence, knowledge, character, and such simply are. That is, to move no further than the etymological sense of the phrase "I AM,"[1] all that

---

[1]As we saw in chapter 1, in the Hebrew this phrase is a word—אֶהְיֶה (or, in New Testament Greek, εἰμί)—translated "I AM."

God is, he is as the only genuine, essential, fundamental one. In the classical construction, God is the Archetype.[2] God, and God alone, is original. He is the "I AM." Because this is such a central and nonnegotiable aspect of God's character, we can say that God, and God alone, is *Eimi*.[3]

The reason it is important to designate God as *Eimi* is, in the first place, that it is how he reveals himself.[4] Because we come to our knowledge of God, at least substantially and initially, by way of his names, we need to keep before us the name of Yahweh. The "I AM" is utterly transcendent, beyond all categories of creation. He alone can be named "I AM."

Even as God revealed himself to Moses using the "I AM" designation, we also will use that designation to highlight and emphasize this fundamental attribute, or collection of attributes. While we in no way want to undermine, forget, or ignore God's personal name as Father, Son, and Holy Spirit, we nevertheless need to place in the forefront the independent character of the triune God; Father, Son, and Spirit are all *a se*. The one God—as three persons—is "I AM."[5]

We, on the other hand, are completely and exhaustively God's *image*; we (and we could add here, though with qualifications, everything else except God) are *eikonic*.[6] All that we are, think, do, become, and so on is derivative, coming from or out of something else; we depend on, as well as mirror, the real, the Original, the *Eimi*. In classical terminology, we are *ectypal*. The kinds or types of people that we are, of knowledge that we have, of thoughts that we think, and of things that we do are always and everywhere copies, patterns, impressions, images, taking their metaphysical and epistemological cues from the only One who truly is, that is, God himself.

A person is, in the deepest sense of the word, an image, an *eikon*, made according to the pattern of the Original, the triune God. This means that

---

[2] For an excellent discussion of the archetypal/ectypal distinction in theology, see Willem J. van Asselt, "The Fundamental Meaning of Theology: Archetypal and Ectypal Theology in Seventeenth-Century Reformed Thought," *Westminster Theological Journal* 64, no. 2 (2002): 319–36.

[3] This is the transliteration of ἐγὼ εἰμί, the Septuagint version of the Hebrew אֶהְיֶה.

[4] Note Aquinas's emphasis: "'The One who Is' is more appropriate than 'God' because of what makes us use the name in the first place, that is, his existence, because of the unrestricted way in which it signifies him. . . . Even more appropriate is the Tetragrammaton which is used to signify the incommunicable and, if we could say such a thing, the individual substance of God." Brian Leftow and Brian Davies, eds., *Aquinas: Summa Theologiae, Questions on God*, Cambridge Texts in the History of Philosophy (Cambridge: Cambridge University Press, 2006), 164; from *Summa theologica* 1.13.11.

[5] There will be more specific qualifications to this designation as we develop this discussion below.

[6] Taken from the Greek word for image (εἰκών), transliterated as *eikon*.

whatever we are, think, and do, we are, think, and do as image. As image, we will never become, at any time and in any way, original.

It may be helpful to think of a photograph as an illustration of this. Just what is that image in the photograph? It is a picture looking much like the original, but without the context, the dimensions, the "substance" of the original. No matter how accurately a photograph reflects the original, it will never be, nor should it ever be confused with, that original itself. It has, embedded within it as image, necessary and essential limitations. The photograph would be nothing, literally, except for the original that it copies. It is entirely dependent for its meaning and its interpretation on that from which it came.

So it is with people. We would be literally nothing without God, the Original, and all that we are depends on him each and every second (Heb. 1:3). The meaning of what we are as image can be understood only in the light of who he is as the Original.

Not only so, but the world, though not created in God's image in the way that people are, is itself an *eikon*. It declares God's glory; it displays his attributes. In that way, the universe too shows forth the characteristics of God. It "images" God in that it is created after the original pattern that always exists in the mind of God, and in that it reveals, as creation, something of its Creator.

This puts a different light on the way in which we think about the world and about ourselves and our activities. Instead of thinking about the subject of the nature of ultimate reality as the "study of being *qua* being," as Aristotle and Aquinas would have it, we think of metaphysics and epistemology (not to mention all of life itself) in the context of the relationship of things created (*eikons*) to the *Eimi*.

We must begin, then, it seems to me, with this basic and fundamental distinction—the *Eimi/eikon* distinction—the distinction of the "I AM" and his image.[7] If we begin in that way, then all of our discussion about who God is and his relationship to his creation has that distinction as its context and as its defining character.[8]

---

[7] I am avoiding the language of Creator and creature here simply because, as we will see, being Creator is not of the essence of who God is and thus could serve to confuse our discussion of God's essence.

[8] What is meant by "begin" with this distinction is, in part, described by Alvin Plantinga. What he says about philosophers holds true, *a fortiori*, for theologians and Christians as well: "My point is that the Christian philosopher has a right (I should say a duty) to work at his own projects—projects set by the beliefs of the Christian community of which he is a part. The Christian philosophical community must work out the answers to its questions; and both the questions and the appropriate ways of working out their answers may presuppose beliefs rejected at most of the leading centers of philosophy. But the Christian is proceeding quite properly in starting from these beliefs, even if they are so rejected. He is under no obligation to confine his

So, to repeat what I said above, while the Christian is to image God in his thoughts or to think God's thoughts after him, the actual thoughts of God cannot be thought by us. God's thoughts are always thoughts of the One who is *Eimi*. As such they are eternal, infinite, exhaustive thoughts; archetypal and original with him; always and only true; exhaustively and eternally independent; not gleaned over time; and so on.

The thoughts that we think, even when in conformity with God's, are still at root *eikonic*. They are patterned after his thoughts; they are formulated in the context of his image; they depend on and necessarily relate to him as the Original; but they are never identical to his thoughts, nor could they be. That would necessitate *Eimic* thoughts, of which creatures by definition, as *eikons*, are incapable. So, we think God's thoughts, but only after him.

The only way in which we have the thoughts of God available to us is by way of his revelation. And that revelation—because it comes from the true God and because it conforms to, though does not exhaust, his true character—is truth itself, but on a created (*eikonic*) level. God's revelation to us is not on the level of his archtypal knowledge. It is ectypal.

This, then, is the *Eimi/eikon* relationship. It is the relationship of the "I AM" to the image. That relationship will have a surfeit of implications as we continue to think about God and his relationship to the world.

There is more to God's character than his essential aseity. Even as *a se*, he has chosen to create. Not only so, but he has chosen to come down and relate himself to us, and he has chosen that freely. He has voluntarily condescended to us.

As we noted in the introduction, the Westminster Confession states that if it weren't for God's voluntary condescension, we as creatures made in his image could have no "fruition" of him. To repeat,

> The distance between God and the creature is so great, that although reasonable creatures do owe obedience unto Him as their Creator, yet they could never have any fruition of Him as their blessedness and reward, but by some voluntary condescension on God's part, which he has been pleased to express by way of covenant.

It is important to keep in mind that the Confession first delineates the notion of covenant simply as a *relationship* that God's "reasonable creatures" (i.e.,

---

research projects to those pursued at those centers, or to pursue his own projects on the basis of the assumptions that prevail there. Alvin Plantinga, "Advice to Christian Philosophers," *Faith and Philosophy* 1, no. 3 (1984): 263.

human beings) have to him. When we speak of covenant, therefore, in the context of God's character and activity, we are thinking primarily of the fact that God has chosen to relate himself to man.[9] The scope and depth of this insight may not be immediately obvious.

In order to flesh out the implications of this covenantal affirmation in the Confession, we need to think about two of the key terms presented there. The first is "voluntary"; the second is "condescension."

B. God Willing

To understand the nature of God's voluntary decision to condescend, we need to think more generally about God's will. It may be helpful in that regard to provide a brief discussion of distinctions that need to be made and kept in mind, first with regard to God's knowledge, in order better to understand the will of God.[10]

We have already seen that creatures know as creatures are. God, on the other hand, with respect to his essential character, has nothing essentially creaturely about him. He exists as a noncreature, thinks as a noncreature, knows as a noncreature, and so on. All that he essentially is and does, he is and does as One who is not in any way, nor could be, essentially creaturely.

The implications of this are many, and we will need to spell out some of the significant ones below, but here we note just one initially that is significant. God knows things. As a matter of fact, God knows everything, and knows everything exhaustively.[11] But just how is it that this One who is perfect and complete, who has always existed, and who has no external constraints on his essential being, knows?

Different answers have been offered. Alvin Plantinga, for example, asks how God can know such difficult propositions as future contingents and counterfactuals of freedom. After an illuminating discussion of such matters, Plantinga says: "By way of conclusion, it is indeed true that we don't see how God knows or could know such propositions. . . . For we don't see how God

---

[9]In the context of covenant/redemptive history, all people are either in Adam or in Christ. There are no other covenantal options available.

[10]So Muller: "As in their discussions of the divine will, the Reformed orthodox offer a series of distinctions concerning the divine knowledge" (Richard A. Muller, *Post-Reformation Reformed Dogmatics: The Rise and Development of Reformed Orthodoxy, ca. 1520 to ca. 1725*, vol. 3, *The Divine Essence and Attributes*, 2nd ed. [Grand Rapids: Baker Academic, 2003], 406). I will have more to say about God's knowledge and will in chapter 5.

[11]This highlights the knotty problem of God's omniscience, anything but accepted in much of theology today. At this point, like the church for over two thousand years, I will simply affirm it.

knows any of the things he knows; all we know is that necessarily, for any proposition p, p is true if and only if God believes it."[12]

Compare this discussion with that of George Mavrodes. Mavrodes, too, is concerned to ascertain how God knows what he knows. His argument, contra Plantinga, is that God knows by way of inference. Says Mavrodes:

> The proposal to be explored is that God knows everything that He knows by inference. More explicitly the thesis at hand is
>
> (T) For every proposition that God knows, He knows that proposition by inferring it from one or more other propositions that He knows.
>
> This thesis really is intended here to apply to everything that God knows—including, for example, his knowledge of his own essence, his will, and so on.[13]

So, which is it? Does God know everything by inference, or do we affirm that we do not know how he knows, but that truth follows necessarily from God's beliefs?

Both discussions seem significantly wide of the mark (though Mavrodes's discussion is wider than Plantinga's), given what we can infer from a knowledge of God's character. That is, instead of starting from the bottom up by attempting to flesh out how God can fit into the kind of knowledge that creatures must have *as creatures*, more (and more biblically accurate) analysis

---

[12]Alvin Plantinga, "Divine Knowledge," in *Christian Perspectives on Religious Knowledge*, ed. C. Stephen Evans and Merold Westphal (Grand Rapids: Eerdmans, 1993), 65. The question of whether God has beliefs cannot be discussed here in any detail. Suffice it to say that there seems to be no reason to assume that he does, especially since the holding of beliefs would entail some kind of noetic lack or privation. The view that God has beliefs seems to be an erroneous corollary of the view that God knows by way of propositions. This way of thinking has historically been denied in Christianity, since to know by way of propositions is to know by way of a process of reasoning. Pictet explains: "Concerning the manner (*modus*) in which God knows all things, we must speak cautiously and not attribute anything unbecoming or unworthy to the ultimate majesty. . . . Now we must not at all imagine that God knows things in the same manner as men, who understand one thing in one way, and another thing in another way, and the same thing sometimes obscurely and at other times more clearly, and who, from things known proceed to things unknown. The divine knowledge is of such a mode, as not to admit of any discursive imperfection, or investigative labor, or recollective obscurity, or difficulty of application. God comprehends all things by one single act, observes them as by a single consideration, and sees them distinctly, certainly, and therefore perfectly" (quoted in Muller, *Post-Reformation Reformed Dogmatics*, 3:413). See also Aquinas, *Summa theologica* 1.14.4.

[13]George I. Mavrodes, "How Does God Know the Things He Knows?," in *Divine and Human Action: Essays in the Metaphysics of Theism*, ed. Thomas V. Morris (Ithaca, NY: Cornell University Press, 1988). Mavrodes says explicitly what Plantinga's position may imply, i.e., that God's knowledge is propositional.

could take place if our inferences began with what we know about God and his character as given to us in his revelation.

The primary distinction concerning the knowledge of God (and, as we will see, the will of God) can be ascertained if we think of that knowledge in relation to the object known.[14] In the first place is God's *necessary* knowledge. This is knowledge that God has of himself and of his activity within himself (*ad intra*), including all possibilities that are themselves possible by virtue of his essential character.[15] This necessary knowledge that God has may also be dubbed a natural knowledge in that God has it by virtue of his own nature. As a triune-personal God, he necessarily and exhaustively knows himself. There are no surprises to God concerning his character; nothing comes to him out of the blue (thus an exhaustive knowledge of the possible is included). God is not in the process of learning more and more about himself. He knows himself exhaustively, infinitely, and eternally; his knowledge, like his essential character, is unchangeable. Whatever "happens" with respect to God's necessary knowledge of himself adds nothing to that knowledge.[16]

In other words, given what I have said in the previous chapter about God—given his character as *a se* and given the fact that God cannot be composed of parts—entailed in who God is essentially is the fact that his necessary knowledge is identical to his character. As Van Til puts it:

It should be noted that it is only if we hold to the cotermineity of the being and the consciousness of God that we can avoid pantheism. If knowledge and being are not identical in God, as pertaining to himself, he is made dependent upon something that exists beside himself. In that case the consciousness of God is made to depend upon temporal reality and then the being of God in turn is made dependent upon temporal reality. . . . We do not hesitate to emphasize therefore that God has and is complete internal coherence. As far as God's own person is concerned the subject is the object of knowledge. His knowledge of himself

[14] There are actually two aspects of God's knowledge that are traditionally emphasized—the *mode* and the *object*. I will mention something of the mode below, but it should be said here that God "knows all things intuitively and noetically, not discursively and dianoetically (by ratiocination and by inferring one thing from another)" (Francis Turretin, *Institutes of Elenctic Theology*, trans. George Musgrave Giger, ed. James T. Dennison Jr., 3 vols. [Phillipsburg, NJ: P&R, 1992–1997], 1:207). In other words, God does not know by way of discursive reasoning, nor are the objects of his knowledge propositions.
[15] In this section, I will set forth fairly standard notions with respect to God's knowledge and will. In chapter 5, we will seek to understand, with modifications, these notions within the context of the essential/covenantal distinction.
[16] This is, of course, a mystery to us. Because God is tri-personal, he does have eternal and infinite fellowship with himself. Just how that can be when all things are exhaustively known is beyond our ability to comprehend.

is therefore entirely analytical. By that we do not suggest that God had to go
through a process of looking into himself and finding information with respect
to himself. It is impossible for us as creatures to get away from the temporal
associations that come with all the words we use. But the term analytic has
come to mean in the field of philosophy the idea of self-dependence. Analytical
knowledge, in distinction from synthetic knowledge, means knowledge that
is not gained by reference to something that exists without the knower. God
knows himself not by comparing and contrasting himself with anything, not
even non-being, outside himself. He knows himself by one simple eternal act
of vision. In God therefore the real is the rational and the rational is the real.[17]

God's necessary knowledge, then, is identical with who he is. He did not
acquire it, nor is it in some way added to who he is as God. For this reason
and in line with God's character, this necessary knowledge that God has is
sometimes called his simple knowledge; like God, it is not composed of parts.

That which is not necessary but is known and willed to be contingent
(i.e., possible *to be or not to be*) as an object of God's knowledge is related
to God's *free knowledge*. In this category we begin to see more explicitly the
relationship between God's knowledge and God's will. In fact, oftentimes
the free knowledge of God and the free will of God have been thought to be
coterminous: "The knowledge that God must have is a necessary knowledge
but it is also natural, inasmuch as God has it by nature rather than by imposition from without—*the knowledge that God freely has is a knowledge that
coincides with his will* for the being or existence of all things *ad extra*."[18]

One of the main reasons that both knowledge and will have been set out
coincidentally should be obvious. If God freely knows something, that which
he freely knows (to put it negatively) cannot coincide with himself, since he
himself is necessary (and the character of knowledge is linked to the character of the object[s] known). Not only so, but God's exhaustive knowledge
of all possibilities is itself inextricably linked with his essential character. He
knows exhaustively both who he is and what he is able to do. In that sense,
the objects of his knowledge are who he is. Since everything except God is *not*

---

[17]Cornelius Van Til, *The Defense of the Faith*, 4th ed., ed. K. Scott Oliphint (Phillipsburg, NJ:
P&R, 2008), 60. "The real is the rational and the rational is the real" is, perhaps, the most famous
statement from Georg W. F. Hegel (1770–1831). In his *Phenomenology of Spirit*, Hegel argues
that the absolute, itself in the process of self-development, is, as absolute mind (*Geist*), real
and all that is real since it is itself the climax of the dialectical process of consciousness. Van
Til's point here is necessarily antithetical to Hegel's and the idealism that Hegel incorporated.
Rather, Van Til is saying that since God is fully self-conscious, in that he lacks nothing, in him
the real is identical with the rational. In other words, God is what he thinks and thinks what he is.
[18]Muller, *Post-Reformation Reformed Dogmatics*, 3:406–7.

necessary, whatever he knows that is *not* God is *by definition* contingently willed and known; it does not *have to* exist at all. Its existence, whether in the mind of God or in an objective context (created by him), is dependent on God's free determination.[19]

In our discussion of these things, we need to remember that, as Plantinga says above, "we don't see how God knows any of the things he knows." We cannot comprehend how One who is necessary and triune can have anything but necessary knowledge.[20]

But now consider God's free knowledge. How does this knowledge come about? Since it is God's, it does not come about by addition—i.e., by adding to his necessary knowledge. If it did, then God would be dependent on something else in order to know freely. Nor does it come about by God's necessary knowledge, in that such knowledge *must* be the case.[21] Rather, it is a knowledge that has something *ad extra*, something outside of God, as its object, even when nothing yet exists outside of him. Since God is a necessary Being, it would seem that such knowledge itself, given that it is *God's* knowledge first of all, must itself be necessary.

But this cannot be the case. Given that God's knowledge is characterized at least in part by its object, if God's free knowledge were necessary knowledge, then the object of that knowledge would be necessary, in which case something outside of God would be necessary and God would not be independent. So, though we are unable to know how God knows—either by necessity or freely—we acknowledge by good and necessary consequence that he does.

The necessary knowledge of God is, though utterly mysterious and incomprehensible to us, perhaps more easily grasped. If God is necessary, any knowledge that he has of himself is necessary as well. Not only so, but included in the necessary knowledge of God are all of the possibilities that could obtain, given who God is. Thus, God's necessary knowledge includes more than his own essential nature; it includes all things that could exist according to that nature. Just what those things are is impossible to tell, given that their sole rationale for being is in God's essential character and not in creation.[22] In

---

[19]This does not mean that God acquired knowledge by virtue of his free determination; however knowledge exists in the mind of God, the notion of free knowledge simply affirms that we must make a distinction, given God's character, between what he knows *necessarily* and what he *freely* determines to know.

[20]See note 12.

[21]In the case of God's necessary knowledge of all possibilities, the possibilities *must* be the case *as possible*, in that God could make them actual. It is not the case, however, that those possibilities *must be* actual.

[22]That is, creation's rationale for being is also in the character of God, but is also tied to his free will to create.

order, however, to take account of God's knowledge as exhaustive, it must include things that God himself could think and do, and that did not include, strictly speaking, himself as object.

It is the free knowledge of God that becomes more difficult for us to reconcile with God's character, especially as we think of God as independent of anything outside himself.[23] Thus, when we think of God's free knowledge, we are *not* thinking of all things possible to God—only he knows those things—but we are thinking of things that are possible *and determined to be actual*. Thus, in distinguishing between God's necessary and free knowledge, Pictet notes that we

> attribute to God a twofold knowledge: the one, by which he knows things that are possible, called by the scholastics the knowledge of natural and simple understanding (*scientia naturalis et simplicis intelligentiae*); the other, by which he knows things that *will be* (*res futuras*), called by them free and visionary knowledge (*scientia libera et visionis*). The first kind of knowledge is founded on the power of God (*ipsa Dei potentia*), the second has for its foundation the decree of God (*ipsum Dei decretum*), inasmuch as God knows things that will be because he has decreed that they will be.[24]

We begin to see, therefore, why the will of God with respect to things created, along with God's knowledge of such things, is distinguished from the knowledge of God that is necessary (and includes all possibilities).

Thus, three things need to be emphasized in this context (and will become important later on) relative to God's free knowledge and will, two positive and one negative.

First, the free knowledge and will of God have their focus in what God *determines*. That which God determines is surely something that he knows (for how could God determine the unknown; and what, in God, *could be* unknown?). That which God knows and determines, he carries out. To put it simply, there is no free knowledge of God that is not also a free determination, or will, of God. So, according to Turretin:

> Among the communicable and positive attributes (which affirm some perfection of God), there are three principal ones by which his immortal and perfectly happy life is active: intellect, will and power. The first belongs to the principle as directing, the second as enjoining, the third as executing.[25]

[23]I will deal with a specific argument to this effect in chapter 5.
[24]Quoted in Muller, *Post-Reformation Reformed Dogmatics*, 3:413, and also found in Benedict Pictet, *Christian Theology*, trans. Frederick Reyroux (Oxford: Oxford University Press, 1834), 80.
[25]Turretin, *Institutes*, 1:206.

God's knowledge is a directing knowledge; it has an object in view. His will enjoins (some of) what he knows, and his power executes what his will enjoins. When discussing God's free will, therefore, what he freely knows is what he freely wills. We can see now that we have moved from a discussion of his essential nature to a discussion of those properties of his that can, in some ways, be mirrored in man. Not only so, but we have moved from a discussion of God's essential nature to a discussion of his free activity.[26]

Second, the free will of God is tied to his eternal decree. This is important for a number of reasons, not the least of which is that it reminds us that God's free will does not simply and only coincide with his activity of creation, but is itself eternal. His free will *includes* the activity in and through creation, but is not limited to that activity. God's free determination is an activity of the triune God, even before the foundation of the world.

(1) A Third Way?

Another reason that it is important to get straight the relationship of God's free knowledge to his free determination has to do with so-called middle knowledge or *scientia media*. Since this is not meant to be a full exposition of the knowledge and will of God, we will not engage that debate in any exhaustive way here. However, I do need to distinguish the view I will set forth from any view that affirms a third category of knowledge in God.

The two aspects of God's knowledge and will that are most significant in the discussions about middle knowledge are (1) that it posits, with respect to the free knowledge of God, a discontinuity (rather than, as we noted above, a coincidence) between God's *knowledge* of what will be and his *determination* of what will be, and (2) that the foundation, ground, or *principium* on which middle knowledge depends is the libertarian free will of the creature.

Inherent in the traditional view of middle knowledge, therefore, is the supposition of the free will of the creature—so-called libertarianism.[27] Given this supposition, God is not able to determine the character of his human

---

[26]As Muller notes, "The movement from the divine simplicity, immutability, eternity, and like attributes to the attributes of the divine life (*vita Dei*) is variously described by the Reformed orthodox as a movement from the discussion of the essence or nature of God to a discussion of its operations, from the question *quid sit?* (what is it?) to the question *qualis sit?* (of what sort is it?), from the incommunicable to the communicable attributes, or from a primary to a secondary order of attributes. For many of the Reformed, the *vita Dei* is also the basic category which then divides into the two fundamental 'faculties' or 'internal activities,' intellect and will." Muller, *Post-Reformation Reformed Dogmatics*, 3:365.
[27]The "traditional view" of middle knowledge to which I refer is the view that was propagated

creatures unless he first considers all things possible regarding them and then creates based on his (middle) knowledge of such possibilities.

We can begin to see, therefore, why such knowledge is thought to be "middle" knowledge. It does not have reference to God's necessary knowledge, in that it does not refer to God himself or to his knowledge of all possibilities. Neither does it have reference to God's free knowledge in that it does not refer to God's determination to create or actualize the world. Rather, it is knowledge that God has of how one (and all) might choose in every possible set of circumstances. And it is knowledge that cannot include God's determination, but rather must be the secondary basis[28] for that determination.

To say it another way, God's middle knowledge is not the knowledge that he has of all possibilities, nor is it knowledge that coincides with his determination to decree "whatsoever comes to pass."[29] Rather, it is knowledge of conditional activity, which itself is determined by man's free will, *upon which* God's determination to decree is based. Perhaps the denial of this kind of knowledge, as we have it in the Westminster Confession of Faith 3.2, will help to clarify its impetus: "Although God knows whatsoever may or can come to pass upon all supposed conditions, yet hath He not decreed anything because He foresaw it as future, or as that which would come to pass upon such conditions."

Two things, therefore, are at work in the positing of middle knowledge: (1) There is the separation of the free knowledge of God from his free determination, since, in order to decree, God must first consult his middle knowledge, then decree *on the basis* of that knowledge. And (2) there is the foundational notion that man is inherently free, which freedom determines what God can or will do with respect to his human creatures.[30] There is, then, in the notion

---

primarily by Luis de Molina in the sixteenth century, which Arminius himself, as well as many of his followers, adopted and affirmed.

[28]"Secondary basis," because the primary basis for God's knowledge and determination is *the creature's* free choice and will.

[29]Unless otherwise indicated, whenever this or like phrases are used, they should be read to include as well that God's exhaustive sovereignty is both unconditional and effective. In other words, in using such phrases (from the Westminster Confession), I include the theology of the Confession from which they come.

[30]Recall from the introduction: "Contrary to popular belief, then, the true divide at the heart of the Calvinist-Arminian split is not predestination versus free will *but the guiding picture of God*: he is primarily viewed as either (1) majestic, powerful, and controlling or (2) loving, good, and merciful. Once the picture . . . is established, seemingly contrary aspects fade into the background, are set aside as 'obscure' or are artificially made to fit the system" (Roger E. Olson, *Arminian Theology: Myths and Realities* [Downers Grove, IL: IVP Academic, 2006], 70, 73, my emphasis). However, it should also be noted that Richard Muller sees the crux of the Arminian problem as the primacy of the (human) intellect in Arminius's understanding (Richard A. Muller, "The Priority of the Intellect in the Soteriology of Jacob Arminius," *Westminster Theological Journal* 55, no. 1

of middle knowledge, a constraint placed on God's character such that he cannot be sovereign, in the classic sense of that word (i.e., unconditionally *all*-controlling).

Arminians freely admit such constraints, but see them as natural and normal for God and his essential character. For example, according to William Craig:

> Middle knowledge is prior to the divine will, its content is independent of the divine will and, hence, outside the pale of God's omnipotence. Just as God's knowledge of logical truths is outside his control and is simply given, so, too, his knowledge of what would be the free decisions of created wills under certain circumstances is simply given and outside his control.[31]

Thus, Craig can easily affirm a constraint on God's character, specifically a constraint on his ability to control all things, given that God is constrained as well by logical truths. However, it seems Craig takes as a given that "God's knowledge of logical truths is outside his control," something that is far from clear and certainly not given as it stands. Logical truths presuppose creation, such that God, apart from creation, is constrained only by his own essential character. Not only so, but there are necessary truths of creation, *which themselves are necessary precisely because God is in control of them* and has determined their necessity. So, the link that Craig sees between our free constraint of God's will and God's own constraints is far from obvious. This notion of creation constraining God's essential character, we should note, has been consistently rejected by Reformed theology.

One more interpretation of the notion of middle knowledge should at least be mentioned here, especially since it attempts to differ from the historic understanding and, at the same time, falls under (some of) the same historic criticisms. In his article "Why Calvinists Should Believe in Divine Middle Knowledge, Although They Reject Molinism,"[32] Terrance Tiessen argues for a kind of middle knowledge in God that does not presuppose human libertar-

---

[1993]: 55–72). It seems to me impossible to delineate which of these two is primary, given that they are two sides of the same coin. Perhaps this is the Arminian version of Calvin's insight—in knowing (the Arminian) God, you at the same time know (the Arminian) self, and vice versa.

[31] William L. Craig, "Middle Knowledge, A Calvinist-Arminian Rapprochement?," in *The Grace of God, the Will of Man,* ed. Clark H. Pinnock (Grand Rapids: Academie, 1989), 148.

[32] Terrance L. Tiessen, "Why Calvinists Should Believe in Divine Middle Knowledge, Although They Reject Molinism," *Westminster Theological Journal* 69, no. 2 (2007): 345–66. We should note that as of the writing of this book, Tiessen has decided to reject middle knowledge as a category. That is a welcome change, but does not detract from the main point to be made here, i.e., that there can be no free knowledge of God apart from his will. It is also instructive to note the inconsistencies that have to be maintained for anyone who would seek to posit such a category.

ian freedom. Without looking at the specifics of his argument, we can note here that, while Tiessen does seek to eliminate the notion of synergism in salvation (given that man is not libertarianly free, according to Tiessen), he nevertheless also affirms a separation between God's free knowledge and his will. Thus, Tiessen concludes:

> God's knowledge of what particular kinds of creatures would do in particular possible circumstances is not dependent upon God's decree; nor is it something inherent in God's knowledge of himself and of all that could possibly be consistent with himself (i.e., his necessary or natural knowledge). This is something that God would only contemplate if he were to deliberate about creating a world distinct from but dependent upon himself. Thus, we do best to distinguish this as a distinct logical moment in God's knowing which is still prior to his deciding upon the history of the world. Once God decided that he would create a world, the kind of knowledge which Molinists have described is essential to God's wise planning.[33]

In arguing for a Calvinist version (or at least a Calvinist-compatible version) of middle knowledge, however, Tiessen, in a discussion of "future hypotheticals" (which are the objects of God's middle knowledge), says the following:

> They are, in the strict sense, *all* counterfactuals, until God decides which ones will be factuals and which will be (strictly speaking) *counter*factuals. Prior to the decree these objects of God's knowledge do not have actuality. They become actual truths only if God actualizes them, but prior to his decision they are truths of a particularly significant kind.[34]

The point Tiessen makes here is that *everything* is a counterfactual until and unless God determines that it will be factual. After affirming this, however, Tiessen notes:

> Thus, this middle knowledge of God does not "represent an indeterminacy and uncertainty in God himself," [quoting Muller] as though there were a deficiency in the being of God. The uncertainty exists precisely because, at this point, God has not decided what will be certain. *He has not yet determined whether this will be a factual or a counterfactual* (in the strict sense), *so it is indeterminate*

---

[33]Ibid., 366.
[34]Ibid., 362. We leave aside here the question of what kind of "truths of a particularly significant kind" these might be, particularly if they are *all counter*factuals. For one analysis of the lack of truth value for any and every counterfactual, see James F. Sennett, "Why Think There Are Any True Counterfactuals of Freedom?," *Philosophy of Religion* 32 (1992): 105–16.

until he does so. God's uncertainty at this point, concerning which of these hypothetical contingents will become actual, simply derives from the fact that God has not yet decided what world he will create and govern.[35]

Note that Tiessen seems to say, on the one hand, that *everything* is a counterfactual prior to God's determination to actualize, but then, on the other hand, that prior to his determination God "has not yet determined whether this will be a factual or a counterfactual (in the strict sense)."

Perhaps Tiessen means to equivocate on the notion of counterfactual here, but it should be pointed out that the apparent confusion goes to the heart of one of the chief Reformed objections to middle knowledge.[36] That concern centered on the status of things neither possible (with respect to God's necessary knowledge) nor actual (with respect to God's free knowledge and determination). What *are* these things known by God? Regarding the status of middle knowledge (and here it is *not* the notion of man's libertarian freedom that is central, but rather the notion of the status of what God knows "in the middle," given that it is an object included in neither God's necessary knowledge nor his free knowledge), Muller notes:

> For Molina's concept to function, the conditions standing prior to the contingent event must be understood as not merely possible, but as having some sort of actuality or quasi-actuality apart from the divine willing[37]—inasmuch as the point is not that God knows various and sundry possible contingencies and knows what would result on condition of their occurrence (viz., given their actualization by him). That would, once again, press back into the divine necessary knowledge. Nor is the point that God knows certain conditions within the realm of actuality that he has willed and also knows what will result from them. That would point toward the divine voluntary knowledge. Rather the point is that God knows what will occur contingently upon certain conditions lying outside of his will: these conditions are not mere possibility nor divinely willed actuality, but foreknown conditions, *foreknown as actual apart from the decree*, at least for the sake of stating the contingency. Once again, the Reformed deny that there can be such knowledge: "there can be no *scientia media*," Cocceius wrote, "because there can be no being independent of the divine will."[38]

[35]Tiessen, "Why Calvinists Should Believe," 362, my emphases.
[36]For Tiessen's retraction of middle knowledge, see Paul Helm and Terrance L. Tiessen, "Does Calvinism Have Room for Middle Knowledge? A Conversation," *Westminster Theological Journal* 71, no. 2 (2009): 437–54.
[37]Note that Tiessen is aware of this objection and is responding to it in the quotations given above.
[38]Muller, *Post-Reformation Reformed Dogmatics*, 3:421, my emphasis.

This problem—the problem that something (relative to God's free knowledge and determination) can be actual (or counterfactual) apart from the divine decree—was a significant part of the Reformed criticism against middle knowledge and is a problem that seems to plague Tiessen's view as well. This may be why he affirms that *everything* is counterfactual, but then argues that, prior to God's decree, things are neither factual nor counterfactual, but indeterminate. That which is indeterminate is, by definition, apart from the will of God. If so, how can it be "more than," or other than, mere possibility?

The problem of the actual existence (or counterfactuality) of the indeterminate (with respect to God's knowledge and will) turns the affirmation of middle knowledge to the question of ontology, or existence itself. If there are "things" (concepts, ideas, knowledge, counterfactuals) that are not determined by God's will, the question must be asked, "What kind of thing can exist quite apart from God's determining that it will exist?"[39]

If the answer given is that such a thing exists by virtue of God's determination, on this all will agree. The question to be asked is as to the basis of this determination of God. Tiessen wants to maintain that the basis for God's determination is *not* a middle knowledge that presupposes libertarian freedom, but rather is a middle knowledge that presupposes all counterfactual scenarios. However, counterfactuals are dependent not on possibilities in the abstract, but on *factuals* in which a determination has already been made. To count something that is indeterminate with respect to God's decree as something between the possible (God's necessary knowledge) and the actual (God's free knowledge and will) is to pretend that nothing is something.[40] There are no categories available to Reformed theology that allow for such an idea, and there are no advantages to its affirmation. All that is needed

---

[39]This was one of the problems that William Twisse had with Francis Suárez's affirmation of middle knowledge. "As Twisse pointed out, the status of middle knowledge, between the knowledge of all possibility and knowledge of all willed actuality, whether necessary or contingent, rests on one's ability to maintain a distinction between known future contingents . . . and apparently indeterminate future contingencies that are not capable of being known 'as a thing to come' any more than they can be known 'as a thing not to come.' The falsity of a notion of middle knowledge and the inability to sustain such a distinction appear, according to Twisse, when it is asked, not how such a contingent can be known, but rather how 'such a contingent shall exist'" (ibid., 422–23).

[40]As Muller notes, with respect to future contingencies that are indeterminate, "it remains the case that truly unknowable things cannot be known at all, whether by man or by God" (ibid., 423). It should be said here that a "truly unknowable thing" with respect to God is, quite literally, nothing. Given that God exhaustively knows all possibilities and he exhaustively knows all that he freely determines, there is nothing left for him to know. Indeterminate future conditionals, therefore, do not exist.

for God's activity and his relationship to the world are the two categories of necessary knowledge and free knowledge and will.[41]

(2) Deciding to Decree

There is a point, therefore—call it "before the foundation of the world"[42]—when God determines to condescend and to create. This takes place initially in eternity. The act of God's creation includes the triune God—Father, Son, and Holy Spirit—taking counsel with himself in order to confirm and establish a covenant relationship with his creation, especially his human creatures. At that point when God determines to decree "whatsoever comes to pass," there is condescension. Because, in order to decree all things, it is necessary for the object(s) of God's knowledge to be *ad extra*—outside himself—there must be condescension. Any object of God's knowledge that is *not* God is, by definition, less than God. It requires, then, that God "stoop" in order to determine and effect what is outside of himself.[43] This is what God does as he voluntarily condescends to be with his creation, including his human creatures.

As we have seen, the "voluntary" aspect of God's condescension relates to his free knowledge and will. That which is free with respect to God's knowledge is that which he *wills* or *determines* will be decreed and created. God, as it were, sets his sights on actualizing what does not yet exist. Specifically, he decides to bring into existence something outside of himself, something that is *not* existing. When he sets his sights on what is (determined to be) external to him, he at the same time freely determines to bring it about.

In this regard it may help us to focus our attention on what God does in eternity "before the foundation of the world." Specifically, we should note the

---

[41] Thus, as we will see in chapter 5, there may be something to James Ross's contention that actuality is not something that is added to possibility. Prior to creation, possibility, impossibility, and necessity were simply nonexistent (in a covenantal sense; they may have existed in God, but would have then been identical to him in some way). Thus, says Ross, "God creates the kinds, the natures of things, along with things. And he settles what-might-have-been insofar as it is a consequence of what exists." James F. Ross, "God, Creator of Kinds and Possibilities: Requiescant Universalia Ante Res," in *Rationality, Religious Belief, and Moral Commitment*, ed. Robert Audi and William J. Wainwright (Ithaca, NY: Cornell University Press, 1986), 319.

[42] We should remember that "time language" with respect to eternity is necessary not only for us as creatures; it is the language that God himself uses in Holy Scripture to indicate things that take place in eternity. See John 17:24; Eph. 1:4; 1 Pet. 1:20; Rev. 13:8.

[43] To anticipate a possible objection in this regard: the exhaustive knowledge of possibilities that is a part of God's necessary knowledge has, as its object, God's own power, thus God himself. God's knowing what he is *able* to do entails his knowing what things are possible (but see chapter 5 for further qualifiers). It should be obvious in discussions of this sort that we are attempting to articulate accurately what cannot be in any way comprehended.

character of what is sometimes called the *pactum salutis*, or the covenant of peace.[44] This *pactum* is an agreement between Father, Son, and Holy Spirit in which the triune God freely determines to redeem a people for himself.[45] Even more specifically, the *pactum* is not identical with God's predestinating purposes, though it certainly includes them. It is, rather, the free agreement that Father, Son, and Holy Spirit effect in order to carry out God's plan for history and, more centrally, to bring glory to himself.

A few points need emphasis relative to the *pactum* as we think about God's activity in eternity.[46] First, as Vos notes, this covenant of redemption between Father, Son, and Holy Spirit, is at the heart of and forms the foundation of God's entire covenantal relationship with creation.

> The covenant of redemption is nothing other than proof for the fact that even the work of redemption, though it springs from God's sovereign will, finds its execution in free deeds performed in a covenantal way. . . . Instead

---

[44] The *pactum salutis* has, of late, not sustained the emphasis it deserves in covenant theology. There are numerous reasons for this, among which would be, as Vos reminds us, that those who look askance at the covenant of works will likewise remain skeptical about the *pactum*. See Geerhardus Vos, "The Doctrine of the Covenant in Reformed Theology," in *Redemptive History and Biblical Interpretation: The Shorter Writings of Geerhardus Vos*, ed. Richard B. Gaffin Jr. (Phillipsburg, NJ: Presbyterian and Reformed, 1980), 245. Related to this would be the influence of Karl Barth in his aversion to all things orthodox, especially the covenant of works.

[45] Worth noting here is Robert Letham's strong aversion to the notion of a covenant of redemption: "The doctrine of the Trinity should have provided a barrier against the idea of the covenant of redemption. That salvation rests upon the pretemporal plan or counsel of God is evident from WCF 3. This counsel is Trinitarian, as is clear from that chapter and the preceding one on the Trinity. However, to describe the relations of the three persons in the Trinity as a covenant, or to affirm that there was a need for them to enter into covenantal—even contractual—arrangements is to open the door to heresy. The will of the Trinity is one; the works of the Trinity are indivisible. For all the good intentions of those who proposed it, the construal of the relations of the three persons of the Trinity in covenantal terms is a departure from classic Trinitarian orthodoxy. In two generations that was precisely what occurred in English Presbyterianism. Some other language should have been used" (Robert Letham, *The Westminster Assembly: Reading Its Theology in Historical Context* [Phillipsburg, NJ: P&R, 2009], 236). Then, in footnote 34, he says, "My point is that the covenant of redemption opened the door to Trinitarian heresy. Some went through the door, others did not. John Owen . . . recognized the dangers, acknowledging that the will of God is indivisible, and wrote of the will of God in its particular manifestation in the Father, in the Son, and in the Holy Spirit."

[46] We will not deal here with the exegetical foundation of this covenant of peace. Charles Hodge, while directing the reader to a few passages, among which are Luke 2:49; John 17:4, 18; and Heb. 10:10, notes as well that "in order to prove that there is a covenant between the Father and the Son, formed in eternity, and revealed in time, it is not necessary that we should adduce passages of the Scriptures in which this truth is expressly asserted. There are indeed passages which are equivalent to such direct assertions. This is implied in the frequently recurring statements of the Scripture that the plan of God respecting the salvation of men was of the nature of a covenant, and was formed in eternity." Charles Hodge, *Systematic Theology*, 3 vols. (London: James Clarke, 1960), 2:359.

of the covenant idea being presented here in a forced way, one must much rather say that only here does it fully come to its own. For it is only in the triune Being that that perfect freedom dominates which the covenant idea appears to demand.[47]

The covenant idea "appears to demand" the perfect freedom of the triune Being because, as we have seen, it presupposes God's determination freely to condescend and to act—to create and relate to that creation. Therefore, as Vos says, the covenant idea "comes to its own"; it finds its impetus and source in this eternal counsel of the triune God.

As might be expected, given that the *pactum* forms the foundation for all of God's dealings with creation, and especially for his relationship to his own people, it also highlights the monergistic character of salvation and thus has its focus in the aseity and glory of God. Again, as Vos argues, the Reformed emphasis on the *pactum*, as over against the Lutherans, was calculated to bring to the fore the *soli Deo gloria* aspect of Reformed theology. If God alone is to receive the glory in salvation, then it has to be his work alone, not his work plus our work, that accomplishes it.

> In the clear light of eternity, where God alone dwells, the economy of salvation is drawn up for us with pure outlines and not darkened by the assistance of any human hand. In the dogma of the counsel of peace, then, the doctrine of the covenant has found its genuinely theological rest point. Only when it becomes plain how it is rooted, not in something that did not come into existence until creation, but in God's being itself, only then has this rest point been reached and only then can the covenant idea be thought of theologically.[48]

Thus, the doctrine of the covenant of peace was emphasized, in a Reformed context, in part to argue against the Arminianism that was ascending in the seventeenth century and beyond.[49] Because its truth focuses on what God himself, *as God*, does prior to "the assistance of any human hand," it is a teaching that has its home only in Reformed thought.[50]

The other point that needs to be said with regard to the *pactum*—a point that will become more important in coming chapters—is that it has its focus

---

[47] Vos, "Covenant in Reformed Theology," 245–46. Vos also notes, as we have already seen, that the *pactum* is not to be confused with predestination.

[48] Ibid., 247.

[49] See, for example, ibid., 250.

[50] Because the *pactum* is not *directly* concerned with the doctrine of predestination, the notion of *scientia media*, discussed above, even if it were true, does not apply to it.

in the office and task of the Son of God as Mediator.[51] The truth contained
in this triune covenant concerning the Son of God is that his status and work
as Mediator of the covenant that God makes with creation are a status and
a work that commence from the point of creation into eternity future. As
Bavinck reminds us:

> All the grace that is extended to the creation after the fall comes to it from the
> Father, through the Son, in the Holy Spirit. *The Son appeared immediately after
> the fall, as Mediator, as the second and final Adam who occupies the place of
> the first*, restores what the latter corrupted, and accomplishes what he failed to
> do. And the Holy Spirit immediately acted as the Paraclete, the one applying
> the salvation acquired by Christ.[52]

The work of the Son of God as Mediator, Bavinck notes, includes his appearance "immediately after the fall." It was he who appeared as Mediator to
Adam and Eve; it was he who covered their nakedness, that their shame might
be hidden behind his gracious provision.[53]

The point that Bavinck makes is one that we will need to keep in mind as we
move along. The incarnation of the Son of God was not his first appearance
in creation. It was without question his first appearance *as Christ* in creation.
We should not in any way undermine the *sui generis* aspect of the incarnation of the Word. By the same token, we should not suppose that there was
no mediation between God and man prior to the incarnation. We know that
there was; this is what the covenant highlights for us. Since there was such
mediation, it had its focus and accomplishment in the One who covenanted
with the Father, in eternity, to be the Mediator. As Bavinck notes:

> Still, this relation between Father and Son, though most clearly manifest during
> Christ's sojourn on earth, *was not first initiated at the time of the incarna-
> tion, for the incarnation itself is already included in the execution of the work
> assigned to the Son, but occurs in eternity and therefore also existed already*

---

[51]So, says Owen, "Hence, from the moment of it (I speak not of time), there is a new habitude
of will in the Father and Son towards each other that is not in them essentially; I call it new, as
being in God freely, not naturally. And hence was the salvation of men before the incarnation, by
the undertaking, mediation, and death of Christ." John Owen, *The Works of John Owen*, ed.
W. H. Gould, Ages Digital Library CD ed., 16 vols. (Edinburgh: Banner of Truth, 1977), 12:627.
[52]Herman Bavinck, *Reformed Dogmatics*, vol. 3, *Sin and Salvation in Christ*, ed. John Bolt,
trans. John Vriend (Grand Rapids: Baker Academic, 2006), 215, my emphasis.
[53]Bavinck has in mind here that the immediate appearance of the Mediator is motivated by
the entrance of sin. We would maintain, as well, that it was the Mediator who appeared to
Adam and Eve prior to their act of disobedience. As Mediator, and the vehicle through which
revelation is given, it was he who communicated to and had fellowship with our first parents.

during the time of the Old Testament. Scripture also clearly attests this fact
when it attributes the leadership of Israel to the Angel of Yahweh (Exod. 3:2f.;
13:21; 14:19; 23:20–23; 32:34; 33:2; Num. 20:16; Isa. 63:8–9), and sees Christ
also functioning officially already in the days of the Old Testament (John 8:56;
1 Cor. 10:4, 9; 1 Pet. 1:11; 3:19). For there is but one Mediator between God
and [man] (John 14:6; Acts 4:12; 1 Tim. 2:5), who is the same yesterday and
today and forever (Heb. 13:8), who was chosen as Mediator from eternity (Isa.
42:1; 43:10; Matt. 12:18; Luke 24:26; Acts 2:23; 4:28; 1 Pet. 1:20; Rev. 13:8), and
as Logos existed from eternity as well (John 1:1, 3; 8:58; Rom. 8:3; 2 Cor. 8:9;
Gal. 4:4; Phil. 2:6; etc.). As a result of all this, Scripture offers us a multifaceted
and glorious picture of the work of redemption. The pact of salvation makes
known to us the relationships and life of the three persons in the Divine Being
as a covenantal life, a life of consummate self-consciousness and freedom.
Here, within the Divine Being, the covenant flourishes to the full. . . . *The
greatest freedom and the most perfect agreement coincide.* . . . It is the triune
God alone, Father, Son, and Spirit, who together conceive, determine, carry
out, and complete the entire work of salvation.[54]

Note, says Bavinck, that the "greatest freedom and the most perfect agreement coincide." There is, in the Godhead, quite apart from creation, a free,
voluntary agreement that he—Father, Son, and Holy Spirit—in the person
of the Son, will condescend to relate to his creation and to save a people for
himself, and all to his own glory. This work began in eternity; it was carried out by the triune God; and it was mediated from the beginning by the
second person of the Trinity, the Son of God. We see him there, as Bavinck
reminds us, all through the Old Testament. We see him take on a human
nature, permanently and for all eternity, "when the time had fully come."
This work of the triune God was voluntary. He freely determined to do it.
In that determination, he freely determined to relate to that which was not
him, and thus to that which was less and of a different order than he is. It is
God's "voluntary" condescension, therefore, initiated in eternity past, that
forms the impetus behind the gospel itself.

C. Condescension

In what we have seen thus far, we can begin to understand why God's free
will, his voluntary choice, automatically includes and entails that he will
condescend. Thus, as we have looked at what it means for God to determine
to covenant with us, we cannot help also including the fact of his condescen-

---

[54]Bavinck, *Reformed Dogmatics*, 3:214–15, my emphases.

sion. There are, however, a couple of important aspects to his condescension that need to be explicitly stated.

First, what does it mean for God to condescend to and to be with his creation? Certainly the notion of "condescend" or "coming down" is a metaphor. God does not literally move from a higher location to a lower one, given that God is always and everywhere present. The metaphor, however, is intuitive enough that most would see immediately what we generally mean when we affirm that God has condescended. We mean that God freely determined to take on attributes, characteristics, and properties that he did not have, and would not have, without creation. In his taking on these characteristics, we understand as well that whatever characteristics or attributes he takes on, they cannot be of the essence of who he is, nor can they be necessary to his essential identity as God. In other words, given that whatever properties he takes on are a result of his free knowledge and will, he did not *have* to take them on; he could have chosen not to create or decree anything. Thus, his condescension means that he is *adding* properties and characteristics, not to his essential being, as the triune God (since that would mean that God was essentially mutable), but surely to himself (more on this later).

From the beginning (Gen. 1:1; John 1:1), we see God bringing into existence that which did not exist previously. Even if we affirm, as we must, that creation was known by God "prior to" his creating it, it did not exist *as creation* until that point of his bringing it into existence.

But just what does this voluntary divine condescension entail? We should note that, as for God's relationship to what he creates, it entails everything that he does, says, and (as we will see) is.[55] The very fact that God brings something into existence to which he himself is in some way related entails automatically an act of condescension.

That is because of who God is essentially. Given that God is supremely perfect and without need or constraint, to begin to relate himself to what is limited, constrained, and not perfect is, in sum, to condescend.[56] For example, the very fact that Scripture tells us that "the Spirit of God was hovering over the face of the waters" (Gen. 1:2) is evidence of God's condescension; he had to "come down" to hover over the waters. God, as infinite Spirit, has no need

---

[55] When I say that God's condescension involves everything that he is, I am not saying that all that he is is exhausted in this act of condescension; that would deny what I have already affirmed with respect to God's essential character.

[56] To say that creation is not perfect is not to say that it was not good, as God himself declared it to be. It is simply to say that it was inherently dependent and thus not in any way necessary, as a perfect being would be.

to constrain himself by hovering over the face of the waters. He is altogether infinite, without constraint. He "hovers" just by his omnipresence. But he does hover, and he condescends to do so.[57]

Or, to use another example, the very fact that Scripture tells us that "God said, 'Let there be light,' and there was light" (Gen. 1:3; cf. John 1:1–3) is evidence of condescension. God did not have to speak at all. He is not in need of language in order to communicate (especially since, in this case, there was no one to whom to communicate except himself) or to create. Neither does he need to speak in order to create. He could create without saying a word. But he spoke, and it was. He condescended to speak, and it was. His Word is evidence of his condescension to us.[58]

Not only so, but just after Adam and Eve sinned, "they heard the sound of the LORD God walking in the garden in the cool of the day" (Gen. 3:8).[59] God condescended to his creation in order to begin and maintain a relationship with that creation, more specifically, with those he had made in his image. Evidence of (something of) the extent of that condescension is found in the next verse as well: "But the LORD God called to the man and said to him, 'Where are you?'" (Gen. 3:9). In condescending to relate to Adam and Eve, he is, like them (not essentially, but covenantally), restricted in his knowledge of where they might be hiding in that garden.

It is for this reason that the Confession summarizes God's condescension in the word *covenant*. The condescension itself includes a contract that God makes with his human creatures, a contract that requires, first, God relating himself to us and, second, an understanding of our relationship to him.[60] In the garden, since there was no sin yet introduced into the cosmos, the contract consisted of Adam's obedience to God's specific commands, especially with respect to the tree. Those commands presuppose God's condescending communication to Adam, and Adam's responsibilities as he relates to his Creator.

---

[57]The point made by asserting the Spirit's hovering is that he is present in a special way with that which he has created.

[58]It is not central to the argument here that God literally, with words, spoke creation into existence (though it seems this is exactly what he did). Even if God did not literally speak creation into existence, the fact of creation itself entails God's condescension. In creating, he also "stooped down" to relate himself to that creation. As we will see, his Word-become-flesh is the supreme evidence of God's condescension.

[59]For an analysis of this "theophany," see James A. Borland, *Christ in the Old Testament* (Chicago: Moody, 1978), 83–86.

[60]Once God relates himself to us, there is no reciprocal decision on our part. We necessarily relate to God. The onus is then placed on us to understand that relationship obediently. Even if we fail so to understand it, however, it is always and everywhere present, into eternity.

When, however, sin did enter into the cosmos, such that the whole creation fell (cf. Rom. 8:18–23), while the goal of God's condescension changed, the fact and mode of it remained the same. He continued in his relationship to us (though admittedly that relationship was characterized by wrath and by grace in a way that it was not before the fall into sin). The goal of that relationship, after the fall, was (in part) the redemption of some who had fallen into sin.

(1) I Have Come Down

The quintessential example of that goal in the Old Testament is found in Exodus 3.[61] This text reveals a number of truths, some which we have already seen, and some which we cannot elaborate here. At least three truths, however, evident in this passage, help us to see more clearly the reality of God's condescension. First, remember how God initially identified himself to Moses: "And he said, 'I am the God of your father, the God of Abraham, the God of Isaac, and the God of Jacob.'"

As we have already seen, the first way in which Yahweh describes himself is as Moses's God, the God of Moses's father, Abraham. This is typical throughout the Old Testament when God wants his people to know that he is their God (see Ex. 6:7, e.g., as well as Jer. 7:23; 11:4; etc.). He identifies himself as the covenant God. Notice, just prior to this passage in Exodus 3, we read, "And God heard their groaning, and God remembered his covenant with Abraham, with Isaac, and with Jacob. God saw the people of Israel—and God knew" (Ex. 2:24–25).

The mention of Abraham, Isaac, and Jacob is meant to remind us of God's relationship to his people, a people of his own choosing (John 15:16), a people for God's own possession (1 Pet. 2:9). Exodus 3 opens with the reminder that God is a covenant God, and that he knows the sufferings of his people in Egypt.

When God appears to Moses in the burning bush, he announces himself as the God of the covenant, more specifically, as Moses's God, and thus as the God of Israel. The passage is, therefore, replete with covenant language. Notice Exodus 3:7, 9:

> Then the LORD said, "I have surely seen the affliction of my people who are in Egypt and have heard their cry because of their taskmasters. I know their sufferings. . . . And now, behold, the cry of the people of Israel has come to me, and I have also seen the oppression with which the Egyptians oppress them.

---

[61]Much of what follows is an edited version of K. Scott Oliphint, "Most Moved Mediator," *Themelios* 30, no. 1 (2004): 39–51.

Some theologians and theologies would have us believe that the finite god of Israel just happened to glance at his people in Egypt and then, because what he happened to notice moved him to act, he determined to do something about it.

What God is actually saying to Moses, however, is an elaboration of his initial announcement to him. He is telling Moses what it means that he is a covenant God. There is an intensity about the language that communicates clearly that God is identifying himself with the suffering of his people. That intensity is communicated, in the first place, when God says that he has "surely seen" the suffering of his people.[62] In the second place, we are told twice (2:25 and 3:7) that God knows the suffering of his people. In the context of God's covenant faithfulness to his people, it would be impossible to understand God's knowing in these passages as something intellectual or strictly mental, as if God learned something at a given point in the history of his people. The knowing here is covenantal knowing.[63]

God comes to Moses, then, and announces two things. First, he announces his covenant status, that he is a covenant God and as such has identified himself with the suffering of his people. Second, Moses has been chosen as God's instrument to deliver the Lord's people from their bondage.

The second thing to note in this text is, we will remember, that as Moses is called to the task of deliverer, he claims to need more information. He may realize the commitment of God to do what he says he will do, but Moses also realizes that if he is to be God's instrument, he will need to know as much as possible about the authority of the One who is sending him. So, he asks for God's name. He wants to know what God is like; he wants to know exactly who is sending him into Egypt. And God answers, "I AM WHO I AM." As we have already discussed, in this text God is declaring his self-existence. Though he initially announces himself as the God who is with his people, and thus in history, when he is asked to give his name, he announces himself as the God who is also above history; he alone is the "I AM."[64]

Once we understand this, once we see the supreme significance of God's announcement of his name in the context of his covenant, the most impor-

---

[62]The intensity of the language is clearer in the original Hebrew. For example, in v. 7, God says, רָאֹה רָאִיתִי ..., an idiom that communicates resolve and intensity on the part of the one "seeing."

[63]It is the kind of knowing, for example, that we see in Gen. 4:1, where Adam "knew" Eve and she conceived. It is a knowing of identity, a knowing of intimacy, a knowing that highlights the union of the ones known to the Knower (see Isa. 63:9ff.).

[64]So, says Owen, "This fire was a type or declaration of the presence of God in the person of the Son. For with respect unto the Father he is called an Angel, the Angel of the covenant; but absolutely in himself, he was Jehovah, the 'God of Abraham.'" Owen, *Works*, 1:401.

tant words to understand in this passage are these four in verse 8: "I have
come down."[65] These four words could easily serve to frame the core of our
understanding of God from Genesis to Revelation. There is no way to understand both who God is and his dealings with his creation without seeing this
principle running throughout Scripture. It is the *yarad* (יָרַד, "descend, go or
come down") principle; it is the Emmanuel ("God with us") principle. It is
the principle of the covenant.

This principle is nothing new in the history of theology. What, then, is the
principle of the covenant? In order for God to relate to us, in order for there
to be a commitment on the part of God to his people and more broadly to
his creation, there had to be a "voluntary condescension" on God's part. In
order for us to have anything to do with God whatsoever, God had first to
"come down," to stoop to our level. So, says Calvin:

> For who is so devoid of intellect as not to understand that God, in so speak-
> ing, lisps with us as nurses are wont to do with little children? Such modes of
> expression, therefore, do not so much express what kind of a being God is, as
> accommodate the knowledge of him to our feebleness. In doing so, he must,
> of course, stoop far below his proper height.[66]

What does God's divine "stoop" look like? It looks like the Lord God
walking in the garden in the cool of the day (Gen. 3:8); it looks like the angel
of the Lord (who is the Lord himself) calling to Abraham (Genesis 22), or to
Moses (Exodus 3), or to Israel (Judges 2). Because of his voluntary condescension, the Lord protects and delivers his people (e.g., Ps. 34:7), and he fights
for them (e.g., Isa. 37:36). All of this "relationality" on the part of Yahweh,
the "I AM," can happen only because he willingly decided to condescend to
our level, to the level of the created.

This old covenant *yarad* principle is unveiled explicitly in the symbol of
the burning bush and its manifestation of God's inner being. Here we have
in miniature an extraordinary illustration of that undying biblical principle
that God's ultimate purpose in Creation, while he maintains his "Godness,"
is to glorify himself as he dwells with his people.

This *yarad* principle is, in one sense, basic to our understanding of all of
Scripture. It is the principle that we must use in order to understand how
God can remain who he is and at the same time interact with his creation.

---

[65]The four words in English are actually just one Hebrew word, וָאֵרֵד, taken from the verb יָרַד.
[66]John Calvin, *Institutes of the Christian Religion*, trans. Ford Lewis Battles, ed. John T. McNeill,
2 vols., The Library of Christian Classics (Philadelphia: Westminster Press, 1960), 1.13.1.

The *yarad* principle of the exodus becomes the Emmanuel principle of the new exodus, the deliverance of the Lord's people from the bondage of sin.

We have already seen how devoid of this basic principle many theologians appear to be. To use another example, after stating that Scripture doesn't speak of God as timeless, William Hasker notes:

> The other main difficulty about divine timelessness is that it is very hard to make clear logical sense of the doctrine. If God is truly timeless, so that temporal determinations of "before" and "after" do not apply to him, then how can God act in time . . . ? How can he know what is occurring on the changing earthly scene? How can he respond when his children turn to him in prayer and obedience? And above all, if God is timeless and incapable of change, how can God be born, grow up, live with and among people, suffer and die, as we believe he did as incarnated in Jesus?[67]

Or consider Nicholas Wolterstorff:

> If God were eternal, he could not be aware, concerning any temporal event, whether it was occurring, nor aware that it will be occurring, nor could he remember that it had occurred, nor could he plan to bring it about. But all of such actions are presupposed by and are essential to, the biblical presentation of God as a redeeming God. Hence God is presented by the biblical writers as fundamentally in time.[68]

Is it possible that the proponents of these views have not seen this *yarad-cum*-Emmanuel principle? There are, as a matter of fact, (inadvertent) flashes of insight in some of the "openness" literature. Pinnock insists, against Robert Strimple's criticism, that open theists are not Socinian, since they are Trinitarian and orthodox in their christology.[69] John Sanders, even more explicitly, claims that his christology actually organizes his thinking about God.

> Christology is the great stumbling stone to the classical view of omnipotence. Our views of divine power, providence and sovereignty must pass through the lens of Jesus if they are to come into focus regarding the nature of God.

[67]William Hasker, "A Philosophical Perspective," in Clark H. Pinnock et al., *The Openness of God: A Biblical Challenge to the Traditional Understanding of God* (Downers Grove, IL: InterVarsity, 1994), 128.
[68]Nicholas Wolterstorff, "God Everlasting," in *God and the Good: Essays in Honor of Henry Stob*, ed. Henry Stob, Clifton Orlebeke, and Lewis B. Smedes (Grand Rapids: Eerdmans, 1975), 200.
[69]Clark H. Pinnock, *Most Moved Mover: A Theology of God's Openness*, Didsbury Lectures, 2000 (Grand Rapids: Baker Academic, 2001), 107n122.

Metaphors such as king and potter must be interpreted in the light of Jesus rather than our normal understanding of kings and potters.[70]

This is exactly right, though the depth of it seems to escape many who maintain God's inherent dependence (given creation). The way in which we are to think about God finds its focus, as I have said, in the *yarad* principle, which principle itself reaches its climactic expression in Emmanuel, God with us, the person of Jesus Christ.

Let us, then, begin to take seriously the fact that our christology organizes our understanding of God's relationality. How, specifically, does the person of Christ help us to understand who God is and how he relates to us?

(2) Emmanuel

We must first acknowledge that Christ is the climactic, quintessential revelation of God. He is the One who is, as Paul reminds us, "the image of the invisible God" (Col. 1:15), and "in him all the fullness of God was pleased to dwell" (Col. 1:19). He is, as the angel announced, *Emmanu-El*, that is, God with us (Matt. 1:21). "He is the radiance of the glory of God and the exact imprint of his nature" (Heb. 1:3).

Though we will not work through a detailed exegesis of these texts, orthodox christology has always understood these passages in a particular way. We can briefly elaborate on that understanding by looking more closely at another passage, Philippians 2:5–8.

We should recognize at the outset that we do not do justice to this passage simply by concentrating on its christology. The point the apostle makes by way of christology pertains to our sanctification; he wants us to model the behavior, the "mind" (φρονεῖτε, *phroneite*), exemplified in Christ, specifically the attitude that culminated in Christ's incarnation. Given our present concerns, however, we will focus our attention on the christology at hand. First, the passage:

> Have this mind among yourselves, which is yours in Christ Jesus, who, though
> he was in the form of God, did not count equality with God a thing to be

---

[70] John Sanders, *The God Who Risks: A Theology of Providence* (Downers Grove, IL: InterVarsity, 1998), 116. Among the open theists, Sanders seems to give the most credence to the notion of anthropomorphic ideas and concepts in Scripture but, because of his Enlightenment assumptions, is never able to frame his discussion in terms of orthodox theology. See, for example, pp. 21ff. For a fine critique of the open theist's views of anthropomorphic language, see Douglas M. Jones, "Metaphor in Exile," in *Bound Only Once: The Failure of Open Theism*, ed. Douglas Wilson (Moscow, ID: Canon, 2001).

grasped, but made himself nothing, taking the form of a servant, being born in the likeness of men. And being found in human form, he humbled himself by becoming obedient to the point of death, even death on a cross. (Phil. 2:5–8)

This has been a controversial passage, not so much because of what it says, as we will see, but because of what it has sometimes been twisted to say. There are two central ideas present in this text that relate to our concerns and that have been the focus of controversy. We will see, however, that these ideas serve to confirm orthodox christology. Those two ideas are "form [μορφῇ, *morphē*] of God," and "made himself nothing" (ἐκένωσεν, *ekenōsen*).[71]

What does Paul mean when he says that Christ was in the "form of God" (μορφῇ θεοῦ)? We should first note that the word translated "form" is used only here in the entirety of Scripture.[72] For that reason, the determination of its meaning finds its locus within its immediate context.[73] We should also note, that the word itself is characterized by a broad range of meanings, making the immediate context all the more important.[74]

Within the context, we find two markers that help us see what Paul is telling us. The first marker is the correspondence that is apparent between Paul's phrase "form of God" and the phrase "equality with God" (ἴσα θεῷ). Whatever one makes of the differences between these two phrases, there can be little question that the two are meant to point to the same reality, and that the one helps us see the meaning of the other. According to Silva, "it would be a grave mistake to ignore Käsemann's point that in the literature of the Hellenistic religions *morphē theou* and *isotheos physis* 'are parallel and even become synonymous.'"[75] Paul's notion of Christ being in the form of God, therefore, is tantamount to the notion of equality. Being in the form of God means being equal to God.

The second marker that helps us see something of Paul's meaning in this passage lies in the parallel phrase "form of a servant" (μορφὴν δούλου, *morphēn doulou*). What Paul has in mind in using this phrase is itself further explained by the "likeness of men" (ὁμοιώματι ἀνθρώπων, *homoiōmati anthrōpōn*).

---

[71]Other phrases and words in this context offer some difficulty exegetically, among which is Paul's speaking of Christ as not considering his own position as "a thing to be grasped" (ἁρπαγμὸν— *harpagmon*). My purpose in focusing on these two, however, is simply to place the *yarad* principle in the forefront of our discussion.

[72]With the possible exception of Mark 16:12.

[73]This is important for all words, but is even more so, exegetically, with hapaxlegomena.

[74]Moisés Silva, *Philippians*, The Wycliffe Exegetical Commentary (Chicago: Moody, 1988), 115. For the notion of semantic extension, see also Silva, *Biblical Words and Their Meaning: An Introduction to Lexical Semantics* (Grand Rapids: Zondervan, 1983), 77.

[75]Silva, *Philippians*, 114.

The word "form" in this passage, therefore, is chosen by Paul in part to communicate two analogous, though not identical, situations.[76] The "form of God" is further explained as Christ being equal to God. But, as we noted above, Paul is not immediately concerned in this passage to give us a Christian-theistic ontology. He is concerned to present the quintessential example of how we, as the Lord's people, are to think and live. The second use of "form," then, refers not so much to the being of Christ himself, but to his status as incarnate. In that case, "form" is used to express the role that Christ assumed when he agreed to be "born in the likeness of men."

The clear and initial implication of this text is that the preincarnate Son of God, as the second person of the Trinity, determined voluntarily to come down in such a way that he would identify himself with humanity. He came by taking on our likeness and by taking the role of a servant of the Lord. According to Fee, therefore, the word "form," with respect to God, can be best understood as "that which truly characterizes a given reality."[77] It points us to the reality of Christ's deity.

What then does Paul mean when he says that this preincarnate Son, who was in the form of God but who took on the form of a servant "made himself nothing"? Here controversy has raged, especially since in some translations the phrase is translated "emptied himself" (e.g., NASB). Paul explains what he means when he notes that this self-negation, whatever it is, had to do with the fact that Christ did not count his equality with God "a thing to be grasped" (ἁρπαγμὸν, *harpagmon*). This word has attached to it some ambiguity that can be clarified only by its context. In other words, whenever ambiguous words are employed, the only proper method of discovery lies in the (less ambiguous) context in which those words appear. The force of what Paul is saying, therefore, should not rest on a supposed resolution to the ambiguity apart from its context here but, if possible, on clearer signs along the way. In this context and because of it, the meaning of the passage becomes clearer.

We are, says Paul, to incubate within ourselves the same mind-set that Christ himself had when he chose to come down to us. More specifically, we are told, "Do nothing from rivalry or conceit, but in humility count others more significant than yourselves" (Phil. 2:3). We are not, then, to hold on to whatever status or position we think we might own, but rather to consider that the position or status of others is more significant.

---

[76] Again, given the semantic extension of the term, it is the perfect term to use in this case.
[77] Gordon D. Fee, *Paul's Letter to the Philippians*, The New International Commentary on the New Testament (Grand Rapids: Eerdmans, 1995), 204.

In this light and because of this context, it becomes clearer to us what Paul is saying about our Savior. In his decision to take on the likeness of humanity, he did not simply look to his own position or status, nor did he count that position or status something that he should, in every way, protect and maintain. Rather he considered the position of those who are lower, who could not reach up to his position, and he determined to stoop down to their level.[78]

We should be clear here. Paul is emphatically not saying that the reason the Son of God became man was something intrinsic in us. Christ did not come because we deserved it or because there was something in us that motivated his coming. Rather, Paul is pointing out to us the depth and breadth of humility as it is expressed in the decision of the Son of God to become man. He is explaining what humility, even humiliation, is. It is the decision to give up what may be rightfully ours for the sake of others. It is to be for someone else rather than for oneself. It is, in a word, to be *selfless* in our attitude.

The ambiguous phrases, then, become clearer. It is not as though Christ emptied himself of something; that is not what Paul actually says. His actual point is that Christ emptied *himself* by becoming something that he was not previously, something that, by definition, required humility and ultimately humiliation (Phil. 2:8). For Christ to make himself nothing, says Paul, was for him to humble himself, and he humbles himself by being born in the likeness of men and by becoming obedient to the point of death. So, as Paul describes it in this passage, the self-emptying is, in point of fact, a self-adding. Hence Turretin:

> Here also belongs the verb *ekenōse*, which is not to be taken simply and absolutely (as if he ceased to be God or was reduced to a nonentity, which is impious even to think concerning the eternal and unchangeable God), but in respect of state and comparatively because he concealed the divine glory under the veil of flesh and as it were laid it aside; *not by putting off what he was, but by assuming what he was not*.[79]

---

[78] I should note here that I am *not* interpreting Paul to say that Christ considered his own essential nature and deity as something not to be maintained; there is a distinct difference between one's nature and one's status.

[79] Turretin, *Institutes*, 2:314. Though it cannot be pursued here, it is instructive to note that Turretin links an understanding of the Trinity to an understanding of the hypostatic union: "For as in the Trinity, the unity of essence does not hinder the persons from being distinct from each other and their properties and operations from being incommunicable, so the union of natures in the person of Christ does not prevent both the natures and their properties from remaining unconfounded and distinct" (2:311). The serious point to be made here is that a confusion or ignorance or, worse, denial of the orthodox notion of christology could imply the same with respect to the Trinity, such that Christianity could be replaced for another religion altogether.

We see this principle displayed for us, albeit in nascent form, in the Old Testament as well. We remember Moses's bold request that the Lord display the fullness of his glory to him (Ex. 33:18). This would be certain death, Yahweh told Moses. So, Yahweh in his mercy did show Moses his glory, but only as veiled; Moses could only glimpse the back of Yahweh as he passed by the cleft of the rock in which Moses was hidden. Was Yahweh less than fully God as he passed by Moses? Certainly not. His proclamation as he passed by, what Luther called the "Sermon on the Name," was meant to remind Moses that the "I AM" was present. Rather he was accommodating himself to Moses in a way that demonstrated both his glory ("The Lord . . . the Lord . . .") and the veiling of the fullness of that glory. Yahweh came down and showed himself to Moses even as he hid himself from him.[80]

The *yarad-cum*-Emmanuel principle in Philippians should therefore be obvious. The triune God made a free decision that the Son of God would come down and add to himself created properties (i.e., a human nature) of humiliation. It was not necessary for him to decide to humble himself; he had every right to continue without adding to himself the humiliating status of humanity. But he determined not to exercise that right. The One who is equal to God, who is in the form of God, who is himself God (John 1:1), did not stop being God (such a thing would be impossible), but rather he took on something that was not a part of him previously. He took on human nature (John 1:14).

To reiterate, Christ does not become the opposite of himself by taking on human nature. It is not as though he gives up deity in order to become man. This pattern is nowhere given in Scripture; it is in fact an impossibility. Rather, just as the "I AM" remains Yahweh when coming down to be the God of Abraham, Isaac, and Jacob, so the second person of the Trinity remains God while coming down to be the God-man. This is the covenant. And, as the Westminster Standards remind us, Christ is the "substance" of the covenant (WCF 7.6, WLC 35; cf. Col. 2:8ff.).

---

[80]In a fascinating comparison between John 1:14 ("And the Word became flesh and dwelt among us, and we have seen his glory, glory as of the only Son from the Father, full of grace and truth") and Ex. 33–34, Ronning notes: "We can appreciate that 1:14 alludes to the OT pattern of God dwelling among his people and manifesting his glory, which entails the conclusion that 'the Word' must be a divine title or allude to the name of God. . . . The OT background of John 1:14–18 points especially to the revelation of God to Moses in Exod 33–34, where the corresponding Targum passages make abundant use of the concept of the divine Word in order to convey the idea that Moses saw the glory of the divine Word, but did not see the face of God." John L. Ronning, *The Jewish Targums and John's Logos Theology*, 68–69.

The christology I have been delineating here, as I have said, is nothing new. Any cursory glance at the church's position on the hypostatic union will bring out the same points. Moreover, the position of the Chalcedonian Creed is ample witness that the thinking of so many who would make God essentially dependent is fatally deficient. That Creed reminds us that the incarnation has never been seen as God's abandoning any of his attributes. As a matter of fact, it is in the incarnation that we begin to see how God can relate to his creation without becoming less than God. The Creed affirms that the Son of God, as God, is to be "acknowledged in two natures, inconfusedly [ἀσυγχύτως], unchangeably [ἀτρέπτως], indivisibly [ἀδιαιρέτως], inseparably [ἀχωρίστως]." The Creed goes on to affirm concerning this hypostatic union of the two natures, "The distinction of natures [is] by no means taken away by the union, but rather the property of each nature [is] preserved, and concurring in one Person and one Subsistence, not parted or divided into two persons, but one and the same Son, and only begotten, God the Word, the Lord Jesus Christ."[81] Many who hold to God's essential dependence seem not to have seen the profound implications of this. They seem mired in a kind of theological Eutychianism, in which there is no way that God can take on another nature unless he abandons (at least part of) his own.[82]

If we take the Chalcedonian Creed seriously (and the church, both Catholic and Protestant, has done so since the Creed was written), then the theological priorities of our thinking in this matter become clearer to us. First, we should be clear that there are two crucial concepts in the Creed, and thus in our thinking about God and his relationship to us, that define the parameters of how we are to understand God's accommodation to us. Those two concepts are person and nature.

It should be said at this point that the notions of person and nature, with respect to God, while highly complex (especially as they relate to the Trinity) will be in the background of all that we discuss in this book. In wanting to affirm all that God is essentially, we are for the most part affirming those characteristics and attributes that accrue to God's nature (not, of course, to the neglect of his person). However, in highlighting God's will, for example,

---

[81] I should not leave the impression here that the Chalcedonian Creed was all that was said, or needed, for the church with respect to the incarnation. More statements were needed and given through ecumenical councils. Specifically, there was a need to further clarify that Jesus Christ is *one* person (by way of anathemas in the Second Council of Constantinople, AD 533) and whether there were two wills or just one in Christ (clarified in Constantinople in AD 680). These matters need not detain us here, but it is important to remember that the church further clarified these issues after Chalcedon.

[82] More on the Chalcedonian Creed and its implications in the next chapter.

we are also highlighting aspects of God's personal characteristics. This in no way implies that there is a division between God's nature and person; his will is identical to his essential character. The distinction, however, may be helpful in that there are activities relative to God's personal character (e.g., God's deciding *x*) that do not accrue to aspects of his nature per se. That is, when God decides to do something, it is not his aseity or his immutability that decides, though those attributes remain what they are; it is the personal God who decides. This distinction could help avert theological disaster.

For open theists, for example, person and nature are virtually identical. To the extent that God takes on the nature of created reality, he must be subject to (different aspects of) creation. In orthodox theology historically, however, priority has always been given to person over nature. The reason for this is that what belongs to person is independent and individuated in a way that what belongs to nature is not. God's accommodation presupposes that he *was*, and was (triune) *person*, before coming down to the created level. It is for this reason, it seems to me, that theology has historically attempted to delineate who God is apart from his accommodation, in order thereafter to explain God's accommodation itself. God, as we have seen in the Old Testament, or Christ, as we see more clearly in the New, is a person with distinct character-istics and attributes, prior to his accommodation to and with his creation.[83]

While there are careful distinctions here that must be maintained with respect to God (e.g., that God's essence is identical with God himself), there is absolutely no question that what orthodox christology has always taught is that God came down in the second person of the Trinity, who was and remains fully God, and he took on created attributes and properties without thereby in any way changing his essential deity. To think, as some do, that because God interacts with creation he must necessarily change or in some way limit his essential deity, is in effect to fail to see God's condescension, climactically in the incarnation, for what it is. While we cannot comprehend just what it means for one person fully to possess two distinct natures, we must affirm it in order for the gospel, in its fullest biblical sense from Genesis to Revelation, to be what it is.[84]

---

[83] As Turretin notes, a person or hypostasis is an "intellectual suppositum," having its own incommunicable existence. A person participates in a nature, which itself (on the created level at any rate) is communicable. For the best summary of this terminology, albeit in a Trinitarian context, see Richard A. Muller, *Post-Reformation Reformed Dogmatics: The Rise and Development of Reformed Orthodoxy, ca. 1520 to ca. 1725*, vol. 4, *The Triunity of God*, 2nd ed. (Grand Rapids: Baker, 2003), 167–95.

[84] It strikes me that one of the root problems with open theism is that its proponents are, in the end, more rationalistic than the very "Hellenists" they seek to oppose. To maintain that in

A brief word of warning (which I will develop later) is in order to some who want to set forth and defend the orthodox view of God and his relation to the world. Among defenders of the orthodox view, there seems to me to be some confusion over the concept *anthropomorphic*. It is thought that, for example, when Scripture speaks of God changing his mind, we are to read that anthropomorphically, but that when Scripture says that God is not a man that he should change his mind, we are to read that literally.

It could perhaps be more helpful if we were to see that all of God's revelation to us is anthropomorphic.[85] Or, to use the more classic terminology, all of God's revelation to us is ectypal. It comes to us from he who is the Archetype and thus, by its very nature, is ectypal.[86] It is, then, essentially accommodated revelation; it is revelation accommodated to our mode of being and our mode of understanding.

That all of God's revelation is ectypal, however, does not mean that every truth given to us in Scripture automatically and immediately refers to God as accommodated. To paraphrase Kant, though all of our knowledge begins with God's accommodation, not all our knowledge necessarily refers to accommodation. Our knowledge of God presupposes his accommodating himself to us, but the very knowledge that he gives us can and does refer at times to that which is nonaccommodated, that is, to God apart from, "outside," or "before" creation.

It may be best, therefore, at least in these discussions, to drop the locutions of *literal* and *anthropomorphic* when referring to God and our knowledge of him, as if some of what we know of God has a direct reference point, and other things that we know are simply metaphorical. When Scripture says that God changes his mind, or that he is moved, or angered by our behavior, we should see that as literal.[87] It refers us to God and to his dealings with us. It is

order to relate to creation God must essentially change is to deny the unfathomable mystery that just is "God with us."

[85]Hence, Bavinck notes, "Inasmuch as the revelation of God in nature and in Scripture is specifically addressed to humanity, it is a human language in which God speaks to us of himself. For that reason the words he employs are human words; for the same reason he manifests himself in human forms. *From this it follows that Scripture does not just contain a few scattered anthropomorphisms but is anthropomorphic through and through*" (Herman Bavinck, *Reformed Dogmatics*, vol. 2, *God and Creation*, ed. John Bolt, trans. John Vriend [Grand Rapids: Baker Academic, 2004], 99, my emphasis). It should be noted here that when we speak of all of revelation as anthropomorphic, or accommodated, we are referencing the *mode* of God's activity to us, not necessarily the truth revealed.

[86]For the best recent discussion of this idea, see Willem J. van Asselt, "The Fundamental Meaning of Theology: Archetypal and Ectypal Theology."

[87]Or, as John Frame notes (after affirming God's transcendence, and in also affirming his immanence), "God is not merely *like* an agent in time; he really is *in* time, changing as others

as literal or as real as God being the God of Abraham, Isaac, and Jacob. But we should also see that the God who really changes his mind is the accommodated God, the *yarad-cum*-Emmanuel God who, while remaining the "I AM," nevertheless stoops to our level to interact, person-to-person, with us. His change of mind does not effect his essential character, any more than Christ dying on the cross precluded him from being fully God. He remains fully and completely God, a God who is not like man that he should change his mind, and he remains fully and completely the God who, in covenant with us, changes his mind to accomplish his sovereign purposes.

Within the context of our previous discussion of the *Eimi/eikon*, we should note here that what we see in Exodus 3 (and elsewhere in Scripture) is the "I AM," the *Eimi*, taking on an *eikon*, an image, in order to show his limited creatures who he is and what he is like.[88]

What else should we expect, when we realize the implications of what it means that God took on human nature for the sake of his people in order, as God, to accomplish their salvation?

God comes in Christ, one person in two natures, in order that he might be the most-moved Mediator, who alone, as God and man, can accomplish what is needed for us and for our salvation. This subject will occupy us in coming chapters.

(3) Adopting or Adapting?

One more aspect of God's accommodation needs to be mentioned here.[89] In order to clarify what kind of accommodation I have in mind, it may help to distinguish between accommodation as *adoption* and accommodation as *adaptation*. Here we can stick fairly closely to the etymology of the two

---

change. And we should not say that his atemporal, changeless existence is more real than his changing existence in time, as the term *anthropomorphic* might suggest. Both are real." John M. Frame, *The Doctrine of God* (Phillipsburg, NJ: P&R, 2002), 566.

[88] The *eikon* (image) that God takes on in Exodus 3 is not, strictly speaking, the sign of the burning bush, but is rather the nature of the angel of the Lord himself who, as it turns out, just is the Lord.

[89] Worth noting here is Letham's comment on the notion of condescension in the seventeenth century: "In Protestant scholasticism, long entrenched by the time of Westminster, *condescensio* was used for God's accommodation of himself to human ways of knowing in order to reveal himself. This was closely related to *gratia dei* (the grace of God), the goodness and undeserved favor of God toward man, and to *gratia communis* (common grace), his nonsaving, universal grace by which, in his goodness, he lavishes favor on all creation in the blessings of physical sustenance and moral influence for the good. These are the clearest senses of the terms for the Assembly, for they saw grace as fully compatible with law, not offsetting or limiting it, as in the late medieval notions of congruent and condign grace." Letham, *Westminster Assembly*, 225–26.

words. To *adopt* means to opt for, or to choose, something that then becomes a part of who one is. To *adapt* means to modify something so that it might fit within a particular context or environment.

These definitions are somewhat wooden, certainly not exhaustive, and not designed to be rigid distinctions. It should be seen, however, that any adaptation presupposes some kind of adoption, given that one cannot fit within a particular context without adopting new properties. On the other hand, it is possible for one to adopt new properties without, at the same time, adapting to a particular context or environment. To use a fairly obvious example, a husband and wife may choose to adopt a child without in any way attempting to adapt to a particular context or environment.

On the other hand, much of the discussion of God's accommodation has in view a certain adopt-in-order-to-adapt argument, which itself is focused primarily on language and literary customs dominant when God's revelation was being written. The entire discussion of linguistic and contextual accommodation with respect to revelation is massive and is not the focus of my present argument. However, as an adopt-in-order-to-adapt model of accommodation, we can at least briefly note an example or two.

In "Jean-Alphonse Turrettini on Biblical Accommodation: Calvinist or Socinian?," Martin Klauber and Glenn Sunshine argue that the son of François moved definitively in the direction of Socinianism in his view of God's accommodation. This move was not influenced directly *by* Socinianism, but rather was a result of its inherent rationalism.[90] Because Turrettini wanted to define God's accommodation in such a way as to allow for a less-than-accurate communication from God to man (given that God was *adapting* current customs and contexts in his accommodation), various biblical passages, he argued, were not to be understood as providing historical truth.

> Turrettini's use of accommodation allows him to argue that neither scientific nor historical accuracy is important in light of the clear spiritual lessons that

---

[90]A point made by Klauber and Sunshine, which cannot be developed here, is the close relationship between Turrettini's near-Socinian view of God's accommodation and his rationalistic approach to apologetics: "For Turrettini, accommodation was closely related to the use of rational proofs to support biblical authority. . . . He directs his arguments almost exclusively toward the non-believer or the deist, who would require more objective proof for the truth of Scripture and of the Christian faith. The proofs are so incontestable for Turrettini that any reasonable individual should be convinced of the divine origin of Scripture. His insistence on such proofs follows the Socinian approach quite closely. Remonstrant theologians such as Philippe van Limborch also typically employed similar defenses of the Christian faith." M. I. Klauber, and Glenn S. Sunshine, "Jean-Alphonse Turrettini on Biblical Accommodation: Calvinist Or Socinian?," *Calvin Theological Journal* 25 (1990): 14–15.

one can gain from Scripture, especially from its more primitive forms. For example, he does not defend a literal reading of the biblical account of the creation or the fall but lists a series of religious lessons that these stories teach. He has serious problems with the biblical account of the creation and the fall of man and does not attempt to defend their historicity.[91]

This adopt-in-order-to-adapt view of accommodation can only lead, if followed consistently, to a view of Scripture that is contrary to Scripture's self-witness and acceptable only in the context of a liberal, or unbelieving, theology. It takes a view of God's accommodation that requires that he adapt even the errors and falsehoods of a current context in order to fit into that context. Once accommodation is taken to that extreme, there is little room left for an orthodox view of Scripture and its inspiration.[92] This extreme view of accommodation, at least in part, marks a definitive shift from an orthodox view of God's revelation to a rationalistic one. In comparing the traditional Calvinistic view of accommodation to its rationalistic permutation, Muller notes:

> This traditional view of accommodation stands in contrast with the notion of a necessary accommodation of truth itself to the conventions of language or to particular cultural contexts, an alternative understanding of accommodation that, in rationalist hands, pointed toward the replacement of a Scriptural norm in theology with rationalist philosophy. The rise of this rationalist understanding of accommodation, moreover, marks the transition of philosophy and biblical interpretation from the traditionary modes of Christian philosophy and allied patterns of pre-critical exegesis, still dominant in Protestant circles for the greater part of the seventeenth century and the high orthodox era, to the modes of philosophy and interpretation characteristic of the "transitional" or latitudinarian theologies of the end of the seventeenth and the beginning of the eighteenth centuries, and to the critical and rationalist modes of interpretation dominant in the eighteenth century.[93]

---

[91]Ibid., 20.

[92]This view is gaining ascendancy again in evangelical circles. Note, for example, Bruce Waltke's concise critique of the view of Pete Enns as espoused in the latter's *Inspiration and Incarnation*. Enns, according to Waltke, maintains that "some diversity in the Bible implies contradictions" and also maintains "that the New Testament writers used stories invented during the Second Temple period as a basis for theology; and that they employed the highly arbitrary pesher method of interpretation, which was used in IQpHab. According to this method of interpretation, the people who believe they are living in the eschaton impose their convictions on reluctant Old Testament texts" (Bruce K. Waltke and Charles Yu, *An Old Testament Theology: An Exegetical, Canonical, and Thematic Approach* [Grand Rapids: Zondervan, 2007], 34n18). This notion of the New Testament writers accommodating erroneous ideas in order to interpret the Old Testament is tantamount to Turrettini's notion of accommodation and is replete with the rationalism of the Enlightenment, leading ultimately to a secular, unbelieving view of biblical revelation.

[93]Richard A. Muller, *Post-Reformation Reformed Dogmatics: The Rise and Development of*

But God's condescension is not like the rationalist mode of Turrettini and others. Certainly, there is an adapting that must take place as God "lisps" (Calvin's word) to us in his revelation. But that adapting is inextricably linked to the *adopting* of certain properties, attributes, and characteristics, as God "stoops" to the level of his creation. Or, to put the order aright, whatever God *adopts* with respect to his accommodation determines what he will *adapt* in that accommodation. If God's accommodation includes adapting to erroneous views, contexts or ideas, then he must necessarily adopt those views, contexts, or ideas as his own. Thus, adapting erroneous views has the repugnant implication of God adopting a lie in order adequately to communicate to his creatures. This, of course, cannot be the case.

If we think of God's accommodation in terms of its quintessential example in the incarnation, we can begin to see that, although God does take on human properties, stooping to our level in order to reveal himself to us and to redeem a people, those human properties and attributes in no way oppose his essential character. They are, of course, of a totally different order than his essential character, so in that way they seem to be antinomic. But—and this is all-important—there is no evil or sin included in God's accommodation in Christ. So, while there certainly are limitations imposed when such human properties are adopted (and thus adapted to our weakness), those limitations are not of such a nature as to involve God in the opposition of his goodness. They do not include sin (and thus error) of any sort.

Given this biblical view of God's accommodation, we should recognize that all that we are, know, and do, *even with respect to God*, is itself *eikonic*; it is essentially *image*. That is, who God is and what God knows are inherently *archetypal*. It is original with God and belongs only to him. Only God can know who he is *as he is*, and know that exhaustively. Only God can be identical with himself. Nothing else can be in any way identical to or with God. If it were, it would be God.

This brings us back to where we began in this chapter. God's accommodation, therefore, makes it necessary for us to recognize that God alone is *Eimi*; everything else (and man in a unique way) is *eikon*. As Turretin says, "In man, objects are the exemplar, and our knowledge is the image; *but in God the divine knowledge is the exemplar, and objects are the image*, or the likeness of the exemplar given expression."[94] God's creating activity included the fact

---

Reformed Orthodoxy, ca. 1520 to ca. 1725, vol. 2, *Holy Scripture*, 2nd ed. (Grand Rapids: Baker, 2003), 305.

[94] John W. Beardslee III, ed., *Reformed Dogmatics: J. Wollebius, G. Voetius, F. Turretin*, A Library of Protestant Thought (New York: Oxford University Press, 1965), 339, my emphasis.

that what was in his mind was brought into being as something *external* to him. And that which is external to God's mind must necessarily be *ectypal*; it must be from the Archetype, but not identical to it. Much more could and should be said with regard to accommodation, but the point to be made here is that it may be useful for us to see God's creative activity as a kind of divine translation.[95] Granted, God's translation is *sui generis*, it nevertheless has some of the typical characteristics of a translation. We can note a few.

As I have said, we should recognize that, when God created, that which was created resided first in the triune God's mind (Heb. 11:3; Rev. 4:11). What God made, therefore, came from the original, his own thoughts. He did not create those very thoughts, but what he thought was spoken into existence, and from that speaking, what he thought was created. That creation, however, was a translation of God's thoughts. It could not be identical with his thoughts, in part because those thoughts partake of his eternal character in a way that creation could not. Rather, it was taking the original as it resided in his mind and "carrying it across" as, and into, creation itself. Creation, then, is God's translation of what was in his mind from eternity.[96]

It is a translation (from God's thought to creation) not simply of things and essences, but of being as well. This is an important point, in part because it separates our understanding from (at least some of) the discussion of meta-physics in the medieval period. According to W. Norris Clarke, the medievals objected to the notion that, in creating, God would have created more being. If such were the case, then God's infinity would not reach to his being, since "more being" would be at the point of creation. "As the medievals put it, God + creatures = *plura entia, sed non plus entis*."[97]

The problem with this medieval metaphysical notion, however, is that the starting point of the discussions, which (as for Aristotle) was being *qua* being, is one that requires a univocal conception and use of the word *being*. A univo-cal conception of being does not allow a fundamental (ontological) difference

---

[95]Cornelius Van Til, because of his insistence on the ontological distinction between the Creator and the creature, pressed this kind of ingenious and illustrative language. He often referred to creation as God's interpretation. By that he meant, I take it, that what God spoke into existence was that which was always in his mind, and what was produced by that speaking was his interpretation of the same.

[96]Turretin notes that all things created were first ideas preexistent in God's mind, which therefore were "nothing else than the very divine essence itself." He goes on to argue that "in man, the things themselves are the exemplar and our knowledge is the image; but in God the divine knowledge is the exemplar and the things themselves the image or its expressed likeness" (Turretin, *Institutes*, 1:312). For a contrary view, see James F. Ross, "God, Creator of Kinds and Possibilities."

[97]That is, more beings, but not more being. W. Norris Clarke, "Charles Hartshorne's Philosophy of God: A Thomistic Critique," in *Charles Hartshorne's Concept of God: Philosophical and Theological Responses*, ed. Santiago Sia (Dordrecht: Kluwer Academic, 1990).

between God and his creation. Norris thinks the medieval principle of participation answers the problem in that it provides for more "sharers in being" without affirming any kind of "qualitative intensity of the perfection of being itself."[98]

But this confuses the issue. We should be able to affirm both that God's being is infinite and that, by virtue of creation, there is more being. We can affirm that, however, only if we begin our discussion not with a univocal notion of being, but with the *Eimi/eikon* distinction of being. Beginning with that distinction, we can affirm that God's existence is infinite, independent, immutable, and so on. His being is *Eimi*. At the same time, we can affirm that God's creative activity results in being that is fundamentally and essentially *eikon*ic; it is dependent, finite, mutable, and such. Does this mean there is *more* being? In one sense it does, just as it means there are more people, more things, more relationships. The more, however, is the more of a different kind; it is the more of a class that is in no way identical to, and certainly not equal to, God's existence, person, intra-Trinitarian relationships, and so forth. Nothing, therefore, not even being, is added to God in any essential way (though, as we will see, something is added to God in a covenantal way).[99]

This provides for both continuity and discontinuity in the relationship of our knowledge to God's knowledge, as well as the overall relationship of the *Eimi/eikon*. There is continuity in that God's translation can be counted on to be wholly accurate, true to the original, referring to the same thing, and meaningful. That which God thought from eternity, "comes across" at a point in time—"in the beginning"—such that it becomes something that it was not prior to "the beginning." What it becomes is not identical with the original; that would be impossible. The thoughts of God could not be, by definition, created. But it becomes a proper and true translation or interpretation of that which has always been, that which God has eternally thought.

But there is discontinuity as well. No matter how accurate the translation, the original does not, and could not, become the translated. So it is with

[98]Ibid., 108.
[99]Thomas, at points, falls prey to a univocal notion of being and thus denies that anything contingent or accidental can pertain to God: "For being cannot participate in anything that is not of its essence, although that which is can participate in something. The reason is that nothing is more formal or more simple than being, which thus participates in nothing. But the divine substance is being itself, and therefore has nothing that is not of its substance. Hence, no accident can reside in it" (Thomas Aquinas, *Summa contra Gentiles*, trans. Charles J. O'Neil, 4 vols. [Notre Dame: Notre Dame University Press, 1957], 1:121–22). I would agree with Thomas that no accident can reside in God, but would also argue that, given creation as another kind of being, God can "have" properties that obtain in creation without in any way changing who he essentially is. As we will see, our supreme example of such is the person of Christ.

God's translation, God's creation. No matter how accurately it represents God's thoughts (and it does represent them accurately), the fact of the matter is that it re-presents those thoughts; it re-presents them as created, which, in their original form, they were not. There is nothing in creation that can ever be identified with those thoughts, since God's thoughts necessarily function in a different context (an infinite, eternal, holy, incomprehensible context), a context that has different constituent "parts," a different "syntax."

There is an impermeable (for us), ontological boundary, therefore, between God and creation. It is a boundary that is impossible to transgress. It would be just as impossible for God essentially to become a created being as it would for creation to become in any way identical to God. The boundary, then, is creation.[100]

So how are we to know God and to think any thoughts at all after him? If the boundary is as radical as all that, what does that mean for our knowledge of God and of his character (not to mention creation itself)?

As God creates, he establishes the boundary between creation and himself, and (this is the point so often missed) he crosses that boundary. (Just what this means for our understanding of God we'll look at later.) He establishes that boundary by creating something that essentially is not, and could not be, what he essentially is. He crosses that boundary by communicating into creation. He communicates into creation in his word, in his works, and supremely in himself.[101] This communication is God's revelation both to and in his creation.

Creation, then, is inextricably linked with God's revelation. It is revelation in that God "speaks" through that which he has made. God's attributes have been revealed and seen through the things that were made "since the creation of the world" (Rom 1:20). Not only so, but since the creation of the world, God has spoken. In speaking, he has revealed something of who he is, as well as his will for his creation.

Given the dual metaphysical construct of *Eimi/eikon*, the "I AM"/image, therefore, we should begin to see that, just as the very being of creation was given by and is dependent upon God the Creator, so is our knowledge of God and of creation dependent upon him. This dependence requires not just an acknowledgment so that we can tip our theological hat to God and then go our merry way in pursuit of the truth (which is what much of theistic philosophy appears to do); but it invites us to see the knowledge situation generally as dependent, first of all, on what God has said and done.

---

[100]This is, in part, what is behind the philosophy of the South African philosopher Hendrik Stoker in his *Die Wysbegeerte van die skeppingsidee*.

[101]In himself, that is, as the Word of God becomes flesh (John 1:14). More on that below.

Herman Bavinck sums up the nature of *eikonic*[102] being and knowledge in the following five ways:

1. All our knowledge of God is from and through God, grounded in his reve-lation, that is, in objective reason.
2. In order to convey the knowledge of him to his creatures, God has to come down to the level of his creatures and accommodate himself to their powers of comprehension.
3. The possibility of this condescension cannot be denied since it is given with creation, that is, with the existence of finite being.
4. Our knowledge of God is always only analogical [*eikonic*] in character, that is, shaped by analogy to what can be discerned of God in his creatures, having as its object not God himself in his knowable essence, but God in his revelation, his relation to us, in the things that pertain to his nature, in his habitual disposition to his creatures. Accordingly, this knowledge is only a finite image, a faint likeness and creaturely impression of the perfect knowledge that God has of himself.
5. Finally, our knowledge of God is nevertheless true, pure, and trustworthy because it has for its foundation God's self-consciousness, its archetype, and his self-revelation in the cosmos.[103]

God's accommodation, his condescension, therefore, from a biblical per-spective, includes God adopting certain aspects of creation in order to adapt to our weaknesses. It does *not* include God adapting the errors and misrep-resentations of a given culture or context in order simply to communicate on our level. God's condescension is a sinless and errorless condescension. He does not, because he *cannot*, adopt that which is untrue so that we might understand him. In order to understand him, we must know the truth, not that which is contrary to truth.

We will see in the next chapter what it means for God to condescend and adopt creaturely properties. We will begin to see what it means for God to come down to our level. In all of this, however, we must firmly and decisively reject any notion of accommodation that requires that God participate in erroneous habits, customs, or contexts in order that we might know him. It is *the truth*, as it is in Christ, that we must know. And the way to that truth *is* the Truth himself.

---

[102]Bavinck, of course, does not use the word *eikonic*; he uses the notion of analogical or ectypal. However, because the concept of analogy can be confusing, given its abundant use in philosophical theology, it seems best to coin a term that will carry less historical baggage.
[103]Bavinck, *Reformed Dogmatics*, 2:110.

CHAPTER 3

Before Abraham Was . . .

> There He lies, in mighty weakness,
> David's Lord and David's Son;
> Creature and Creator meeting,
> Heaven and earth conjoined in one.
>
> HORATIUS BONAR

A. Introduction

We have seen that the tension that exists between God's essential character and his dealings with creation has its focus, ultimately, in God's character. The tension, in other words, revolves around the scriptural teaching on God's aseity, on the one hand, and, on the other, God's real interaction with creation, especially man, all to the glory of his own name.

In the conclusion to the previous chapter, I begin to address this tension from the perspective of the person of Christ in the incarnation. I noted there that Scripture confirms *both* that the Son of God, in the incarnation, remains fully God and that he takes on the form of a servant. The incarnation, therefore, is a *mode* of assumption (in that the Son assumes a human nature) by the second person of the Trinity.

All that I have said thus far concerning God's activity in and toward creation applies climactically to the appearance of the Son of God in human nature some two thousand years ago. That event was the result, as we have seen, of a free decision of the triune God—a decision to condescend. The condescension of which we (and Westminster Confession 7.1) speak is *not*, we should note again, something centrally *spatial*. God is present everywhere, so we should not think of the condescension that is the incarnation as the Son of God entering into a spatial context in which he was otherwise absent.[1] Rather, as we saw from our look at Philippians 2, the condescension of the incarnation *is* an assumption of new properties (namely, a human nature) by the Son of God, who all the while maintained (as is necessarily the case) his full, independent deity as God.[2]

What follows in this chapter may at first glance look to be an aside, a tangent, parenthetical to the subject at hand. However, it should be stated here at the beginning of this chapter that the material that follows is central, crucial, and fundamentally interpretive of everything I have thus far said and everything I will go on to say in later chapters. The subject of this chapter, therefore, is meant to set forth and clarify the entire atmosphere in which discussions of God and his relationship to creation can thrive and grow. What I hope to proffer in what follows is a *revelational* grid through which we can know and understand God. We must take seriously the quintessential revelation of God in Christ, without which no one can know or understand God truly, and through which one can begin to see the depth and majesty of his relationship to creation.

B. Christological Constraints[3]

In order better to understand how we might construe God's aseity relative to creation, we need first to think specifically about the person of the Son in the

---

[1] It is important to note that the incarnation was not centrally spatial, in that God's condescension in any form or mode presupposes his essential deity and thus, in this case, his omnipresence. In a curious assessment of the incarnation, Paul Helm notes: "In the Incarnation there is uniquely powerful and loving and gracious focusing of the divine nature upon human nature, *rather than a transfer of the Son of God to a spatio-temporal location.* This focusing makes it possible for us to say that the Son is so present with human nature that there is a union of natures in Jesus Christ. . . . The character of this divine presence sanctions the language of person with respect to the result" (Paul Helm, *John Calvin's Ideas* [Oxford: Oxford University Press, 2004], 64, my emphasis). Whatever else Helm might mean by this "focusing," it should be stated that the incarnation has never been thought to be a "transfer" of the Son of God to a spatio-temporal location. Condescension, as we have seen, means taking on covenantal properties, not occupying a space otherwise vacant of God's presence.

[2] Assuming a human nature, of course, will have spatial implications, in that the Son of God will be spatially contained according to his human nature, once assumed. But it is not the case that he will occupy a "place" in which he was otherwise absent.

[3] Parts of sections B–D are adapted from material found in K. Scott Oliphint, *Reasons for Faith: Philosophy in the Service of Theology* (Phillipsburg, NJ: P&R, 2006); Oliphint, "Something

incarnation and then move to a more general discussion of the Son's activity in redemptive history. Specifically, we need to remind ourselves of some of the basic principles of orthodox theology regarding the *person* of the Son, in distinction from his *work*.

What follows will be somewhat technical in places. If this were a book on christology, we would have the opportunity to develop and further define the importance of the categories and discussions below. However, given our particular focus, we will need to get to the meat of the matter quickly in order to apply these categories to our discussion of theology proper. We should state as well that, with all of the good and proper attempts to think biblically about the incarnation and the person of Christ, none of these discussions and categories is intended in any way to dissolve the fundamentally mysterious character of what God has done in his Son. This in no way should encourage us simply to dismiss the technical theological tenets, but neither should such tenets tempt us to think that we may undermine or mute the clear biblical mystery that is the incarnation. To mute that mystery would be to mute the glory of God (cf. Rom. 11:33–36). It is important, however, to be as biblically and theologically precise as we can be, *just because* in that precision the mystery and glory of God stand out in bold relief.

We shall begin our thinking about the incarnation with the Westminster Confession of Faith. What happened at the incarnation? The second person of the Trinity became man. Did he become man by giving up his deity, or a part of his deity? The Confession (8.2) puts it well:

> The Son of God, the second person in the Trinity, being very and eternal God, of one substance and equal with the Father, did, when the fulness of time was come, take upon Him man's nature, with all the essential properties and common infirmities thereof, yet without sin; being conceived by the power of the Holy Ghost, in the womb of the Virgin Mary, of her substance. So that two whole, perfect, and distinct natures, the Godhead and the manhood, were inseparably joined together in one person, without conversion, composition, or confusion. Which person is very God, and very man, yet one Christ, the only Mediator between God and man.

The reason I have called this section "Christological Constraints" is that, whatever we have to say about the characteristics of God relative to himself and to creation must, at the very least, not contradict or in any way undermine

Much Too Plain to Say," in *Resurrection and Eschatology*, ed. Lane G. Tipton and Jeffrey C. Waddington (Phillipsburg, NJ: P&R, 2008).

that quintessential revelation of God in Christ. Or, to put it the other way around, God's revelation of himself in Christ should provide the controls and constraints that we need to keep in mind in order biblically to articulate the attributes and characteristics of God himself as he relates himself to us throughout history.

One word of warning here: we should not succumb to the temptation to think that just because we are trying to be careful in our articulation of the person of the Son of God, the matters we are discussing have no practical import and we are attempting to exhaust what is altogether incomprehensible. We should keep in the forefront of our minds that the driving force behind a proper articulation of the incarnation and of Christ was the hope that the church would know and understand him better, and in knowing and understanding him better, be better able to serve and worship him—both in life and in thought.

It is important to understand that the church has wrestled with these questions, not as abstract questions of theology, but in order that we might speak biblically and properly about God, and about his revelation to us. These were, first of all, discussions and questions of obedience, and not of speculation.

One other important note concerning our attempt to articulate the reality of God in the flesh is found in a reminder from Turretin.

> In the Christian religion there are two questions above all others which are difficult. The first concerns the unity of the three persons in the one essence in the Trinity; the other concerns the union of the two natures in the one person in the incarnation. Now while they mutually differ . . . , still the one greatly assists in the understanding of the other. For as in the Trinity, the unity of essence does not hinder the persons from being distinct from each other and their properties and operations from being incommunicable, so the union of natures in the person of Christ does not prevent both the natures and their properties from remaining unconfounded and distinct.[4]

Scriptural Support

We need not repeat here what we saw in our last chapter with respect to the incarnation. Other passages could be considered, of course, but the teaching of Scripture from Philippians 2:5–7 gives us an ample picture of the incarnation, at least for our initial purposes here. Another point or two, however, may be useful.

---

[4]Francis Turretin, *Institutes of Elenctic Theology*, trans. George Musgrave Giger, ed. James T. Dennison Jr., 3 vols. (Phillipsburg, NJ: P&R, 1992–1997), 3:311.

In his penetrating discussion of the apostle Paul's theology, Herman Ridderbos, with his proper concern for the redemptive-historical impetus of Paul's thought, is also concerned to point out that Paul's christology necessarily includes affirmations of Christ's preexistence as the Son of God.

> However much Paul's Christology finds its point of departure in Christ's death and resurrection and to whatever degree he draws the lines from thence on the one to the incarnation and on the other to the future of the Lord, all this does not alter the fact that *the whole of his preaching of the historical and future revelation of Christ is supported by the confession of Christ as the Son of God, in the supra- and prehistorical sense of the word.*[5]

In other words, any biblical notion of the redemptive-historical must have as its foundation the affirmation of the ontological Son, that is, the Son of God *as God* and not, first of all, as Mediator. In thinking, then, of Christ "in the supra- and prehistorical sense of the word," we're thinking now of Christ as preexistent, that is, as the Son of God. This preexistence is both primary and necessary if there is to be any true and biblical understanding of what the incarnation is.[6]

Geerhardus Vos, another champion of the centrality of the redemptive-historical aspects of Scripture, says much the same thing as Ridderbos. Vos notes that Jesus's sonship traces back to his eternal deity. Vos adds:

> The Messiahship is in Jesus' life the secondary thing, not merely in the order of being, but also in the order of importance. When seen in the perspective sketched above, the Messiahship will have to be classed with the things that are relative, not with the order of absolutes. This relativeness it shares with all other historical things, as compared with the inner life of the Deity.[7]

Perhaps this point need not be made. However, given a certain skepticism concerning the preexistence of Christ presently, we need to be clear here in our rejection of such skepticism.[8] The general point that we need to get clear

---

[5]Herman N. Ridderbos, *Paul: An Outline of His Theology*, trans. John Richard DeWitt (Grand Rapids: Eerdmans, 1975), 68, my emphasis.
[6]This is the orthodox view of the incarnation and is in direct contradiction to Karl Barth's strange construction of christology. See Bruce McCormack, "Christ and the Decree: An Unsettled Question for the Reformed Churches Today," in *Reformed Theology in Contemporary Perspective*, ed. Lynn Quigley (Edinburgh: Rutherford House, 2006).
[7]Geerhardus Vos, *The Self-Disclosure of Jesus: The Modern Debate About the Messianic Consciousness* (New York: Doran, 1926; repr., Phillipsburg, NJ: P&R, 2002), 102.
[8]Note, for example, the helpful analysis in Simon J. Gathercole, *The Preexistent Son: Recovering the Christologies of Matthew, Mark, and Luke* (Grand Rapids: Eerdmans, 2006).

in our minds is that *ontology defines and determines history*.[9] More specifically, with respect to christology, the existence of the Son of God *as God* is
primary and interpretive of his existence *as Christ*, that is, as God who has
assumed a human nature. In that sense, there is a priority to ontology, more
specifically, to the ontological Trinity, in that he becomes the determining
factor and the primary factor in all our discussions.

Notice, in this context, Colossians 1:15. There Paul notes that Christ is "the
image of the invisible God."[10] When this passage reveals Christ as image, it is
not speaking of a copy; rather, as Scripture elsewhere affirms, it is speaking of
Christ as the visible manifestation of the being of God himself.[11] For Christ
to be the image of God is to manifest who he is as God. In other words, Paul
is saying here what Hebrews 1:3 says when it speaks of "the Son" as "the
radiance of [God's] glory and the imprint of his nature."[12] This "imprint"
(χαρακτήρ, *charaktēr*) refers to an exact replica of something; it was used of
a seal made on wax. In this case, the author to the Hebrews is telling us that
Christ is the exact imprint of God's very being.

Again, as Ridderbos puts it, when Paul speaks of Christ as "the image of
the invisible God" (εἰκὼν τοῦ θεοῦ τοῦ ἀοράτου—Col. 1:15; cf. 2 Cor. 4:4) or
as "in the form of God" (ἐν μορφῇ θεοῦ—Phil. 2:6), he is describing Christ
"not, as is the case when he calls him the last Adam (1 Cor. 15:45ff.), as the
second man, but . . . as the Pre-existent One in his divine glory."[13] So, "it
can even be maintained that by the name Image of God in the passages in
question Paul intended to elucidate precisely 'the eternal relationship of the
Father to the Son.'"[14]

The One who came down in the incarnation, therefore, is the One who is
and always has been God. He is the One who is begotten of the Father. He is

---

[9]This is just another way of saying that the triune God creates and controls "whatsoever comes
to pass," and thus all that is created finds its meaning, ultimately, in him alone. This is one
of the many affirmations that, for example, process theology, with its concern to do justice
to God's relationship to the world, would not and cannot affirm. Process theology's "dipolar
theism," with its view of actuality as relatedness, reduces God so that his essential attributes are
only "abstract." See John B. Cobb Jr. and David Ray Griffin, *Process Theology* (Philadelphia:
Westminster Press, 1976).

[10]. . . ὅς ἐστιν εἰκὼν τοῦ θεοῦ τοῦ ἀοράτου . . .

[11]Paul also notes that Christ is the "firstborn of all creation." We cannot pursue it here, but
firstborn of creation, when taken in the context of v. 16 and the rest of Scripture, refers to
Christ as the fountain and source of creation, not as created. For a helpful discussion of this
phrase, see Ridderbos, *Paul*, 53ff.

[12]. . . ὃς ὢν ἀπαύγασμα τῆς δόξης καὶ χαρακτὴρ τῆς ὑποστάσεως αὐτοῦ . . .

[13]Ridderbos, *Paul*, 71.

[14]Ibid.

the second person of the Trinity who himself partakes of all of the essential properties of God, given that he is himself fully God.

There is much more that could be pursued with respect to Scripture's teaching on the person of Christ. What I have offered here and in the previous chapter only skims the surface. I will expand on this biblical foundation below. From here, however, we can move on, assuming that the basic biblical contours of christology that the church has affirmed throughout its history are firmly in place. Given our brief look at Philippians 2 and Colossians 1, we move to the historic formulation of the person of Christ and then to some of the more salient implications of that formulation for our study in theology proper.

C. The Creed and Controversies

The controversies leading up to the Council of Chalcedon were primarily two. We need only mention them briefly.

In the first place, a man by the name of Nestorius, in his confirmed opposition to Arianism (which taught, among other things, that Christ was a created being and not eternal), began to teach and preach against the notion of *Theotokos*, that is, that Mary could be called the "Mother of God." In his zeal to safeguard the deity of Christ, Nestorius began to teach that there could be no hypostatic union in the incarnation; instead of the assumption of a human nature by the second person of the Trinity, it was *a man* that was assumed. This lead to the notion that Christ must be two persons, or that there was a double personality in the person of Christ. Thus, according to Nestorians, Mary was the mother of the man Jesus, but not of the person of the deity.

In response to this, and in order to affirm Mary as *Theotokos*, some church fathers, following perhaps a man by the name of Eutyches, began to teach that the Son of God, in taking on human flesh, was of one nature. Thus, instead of a two-nature christology, Eutychianism taught a one-nature christology, in which the divine nature completely absorbed the human nature at the incarnation.

The Chalcedonian Creed (AD 451) was written in part to affirm what the church had thus far believed regarding the incarnation,[15] but also to denounce these other views as heretical. As we noted in the last chapter, the Creed

---

[15]"The dogma of Chalcedon is ancient tradition in a formula corresponding to the needs of the hour. So we cannot say that the Chalcedonian Definition marks a great turning point in the christological belief of the early church." Alos Grillmeier, SJ, *Christ in Christian Tradition*, vol. 1, *From the Apostolic Age to Chalcedon (451)*, trans. J. S. Bowden (New York: Sheed and Ward, 1965), 487.

affirms that the Son of God, as God, is to be "acknowledged in two natures inconfusedly [ἀσυγχύτως], unchangeably [ἀτρέπτως], indivisibly [ἀδιαιρέτως], inseparably [ἀχωρίστως]." Notice that the first two negatives—ἀσυγχύτως and ἀτρέπτως—are directed against Eutychianism. The Creed affirms that the two natures of Christ are not changed by virtue of the union, nor are they in any way confused. The second two negatives—ἀδιαιρέτως and ἀχωρίστως—are directed against Nestorianism. The two natures are neither divided nor separated, so that Christ is not two persons, nor is he two distinct personalities. It goes on to affirm, concerning this hypostatic union, that with regard to these two natures,

> The distinction of natures [is] by no means taken away by the union, but rather the property of each nature [is] preserved, and concurring in one Person and one Subsistence, not parted or divided into two persons, but one and the same Son, and only begotten, God the Word, the Lord Jesus Christ.

It is important to note that, while preserving the full integrity of each of the two natures, the Creed also affirms that both natures are unified in the one person.[16] That person is designated as "God the Word"—thus highlighting his identity as God, the Logos, the second person of the Trinity—and as "the Lord Jesus Christ"—thus highlighting his identity as the incarnate Mediator. Neither of these natures is diminished, we should note, but, and this is all-important, *neither are they thereby on a par with each other.* The divine is presupposed by the human, in that the divine is essential to the person, without which he would not *be*, and therefore would not be (the Son of) God. And the human is contingent; it has its origin in the free decision of God (in the *pactum salutis*). There was nothing in God, or the Son of God, that made his incarnation absolutely necessary.

This personal unity affirmed at Chalcedon is indeed mysterious, and the human mind will never be able to exhaust its character. The four negatives in the Creed are meant only to ensure that our thinking about this one person is biblical. Thus, the two natures in the one person are neither confused nor changeable. That is, they do not merge into each other in such a way as to lose their distinctive characteristics or properties, and neither does either nature change into something it is not. This does not mean, of course, as we will see below, that each of the two natures is always visibly active in the same way; the

---

[16]Note Grillmeier: "The Alexandrians were shouting μία φύσις [one nature], the Antiochenes δύο φύσεις [two natures]. Chalcedon made its choice and said: Christ is one and the same Son, Lord, Only-begotten, but ἐν δύο φύσειν [in two natures]! Christ is one in 'two natures'" (ibid., 485).

fact that they are not confused does not mean that they are equally displayed. The fact that they are not changeable does not mean that, for example, the human nature of Christ does not grow or exist in time. The unchangeability refers to the *natures* themselves. The divine nature does not change (since, as we saw previously, it *cannot* change), and the human nature does not change into something other than fully human (yet without sin).

Likewise, given that the two natures exist in the one person, they cannot be divided in such a way as to exist as a dual personality in the one person of Jesus Christ. Jesus was not schizophrenic as a result of the incarnation.[17] This qualification serves to emphasize that it is the *person*, who himself is one, that delimits and defines the natures, and not vice versa. So also, neither of the two natures can be separated such that, *in Christ*, the divine could exist without the human; nor could the human exist without the divine. Again, as we will see below, this does not mean that the existence of the divine is dependent on the human. It means that, *once united in the person of Jesus Christ*, the incarnate Son of God, the one will exist inseparably with the other in the same person.

D. The Whole Christ

Before we move to a discussion of distinctions and disagreements with respect to the person of Christ and the hypostatic union, it is crucial to understand where orthodox Christianity has, in the main, been in agreement.

When speaking of a hypostatic union, we are not thinking strictly of a union of two natures—one divine, the other human—which would then constitute a third thing, the person. (This will have important implications when we move again to thinking of God's own characteristics.) Rather, to think properly about the hypostatic union, we must grasp two crucial points.

1. The first, as I have indicated above, is that the hypostatic union affirms a *unio personalis*. This all orthodox theology affirms. If, negatively, it is not strictly that two natures united into one person, positively it means that the Son of God, the second person of the Trinity, took on a human nature and remained one person. Two subpoints are important to remember in this regard.

---

[17]This seems to be the implication, for example, in N. T. Wright's assessment of Christ's self-consciousness: "My case, has been, and remains, that Jesus believed himself called to do and be things which, in the traditions to which he fell heir, only Israel's God, YHWH, was to do and be. I think he held this belief both with passionate and firm conviction, and with the knowledge that he could be making a terrible, lunatic mistake." N. T. Wright, "Jesus' Self-Understanding," in *The Incarnation*, ed. Stephen T. Davis, Daniel Kendall, SJ, and Gerald O'Collins, SJ (Oxford: Oxford University Press, 2002), 59.

a. Negatively, if in this union a completely new person had come to be, then that person would either be within or without the triune God. If he were without, then he could not be God; if within, then the Trinity would be a Quadrinity. In either case, the result is counter to orthodoxy and Scripture.

b. Because the person to whom the human nature unites is the same, and because he is the second person of the Trinity, the priority and presupposition of the incarnation is the ontological, specifically the ontological Trinity. There could be no human nature to which to unite without the ontological Son of God, the second person of the Trinity. To put the matter more generally, the temporal presupposes (and in no ultimate way opposes) the ontological.

2. The second point to be grasped, and related to the first, is that in the history of christology, the human nature of Christ is denoted both as *anhypostatic* and *enhypostatic*. *Anhypostatic* means that the human nature was impersonal or non–self-subsistent. In other words, apart from its union with the person of the Son of God, it was nothing; it did not have its own existence apart from the person. It exists (subsists) only in the person of the Son of God. This idea goes back at least to John of Damascus and was an important advance in a biblical exposition of the hypostatic union.

By *enhypostatic* is meant the positive of *anhypostatic*. Literally, it means "in-person." That which is *enhypostatic* has its subsistence in a person. This idea makes clear the notion that the person is not constituted by a combination of two natures. Rather, it affirms that the person is divine and, as divine, he takes on the nature of humanity.[18]

(1) Mixed Natures?

The basic notion of *unio personalis* (one united person) was and is noncontroversial in the history of the church. Orthodox theology has always affirmed this basic union.[19] From this fundamental agreement, however, matters become

---

[18]Note Bavinck: "But Reformed theology stressed that it was the person of the Son who became flesh—not the substance [the underlying reality] but the subsistence [the particular being] of the Son assumed our nature," and, "The Reformed prefer to say that the person of the Son, rather than the divine nature, as Lutherans said, had become human" (Herman Bavinck, *Reformed Dogmatics*, vol. 3, *Sin and Salvation in Christ*, ed. John Bolt, trans. John Vriend [Grand Rapids: Baker Academic, 2006], 259, 275). All of this will become important when we think again of the attributes of God, so keep these distinctions in mind.

[19]"Belief in the unity in Christ is expressed in accordance with tradition. . . . This is done first in quite simple periphrastic expressions: 'we confess that our Lord Jesus Christ is one and the same Son.' This εἷς καὶ ὁ αὐτός occurs twice in this double formula and four times as a simple αὐτός. It reaches far back in to the early patristic period, say to Ignatius of Antioch (Ad Eph. 7.2), whose christological framework is built in such a way as to predicate the divine and the human of one and the same subject. The Nicene concern is again taken up, just as it had been

a bit more complex. Once the personal union is affirmed, the next obvious question that we are confronted with is just how we should think about the relationship of the divine person to his assumed human nature. Even if the heresies of Nestorianism and Eutychianism are avoided, questions still loom about the relationship of the divine nature in the person of the Son of God to the human nature that he has taken on.

One of the primary questions is, Is there any sense in which we can speak about a *communication of properties* (*communicatio idiomatum*) in the person of Christ while affirming all that the Chalcedonian formulation says? The answers to this question have divided theological traditions, more or less, since the early church.

Debate over the *communicatio idiomatum* reached its zenith during the Reformation, as we will see. Since that time, it has been identified more with Lutheran than with Reformed theology.[20]

In order to think properly about this, we need to draw another distinction or two. First, discussions of the *communicatio* have distinguished between its characterization either *in concreto* or *in abstracto*. To put it simply, the *communicatio* is *in concreto* when the properties are referred to the person, and it is *in abstracto* when the properties are referred to the nature. In other words, crucial to this entire discussion—particularly in a Reformed understanding of the incarnation—person is concrete, and nature is abstract.

The discussions of the *communicatio* during the time of the Reformation centered on the Lutheran notion (ultimately, it seems, rejected by Luther himself) that Christ was physically present in the Lord's Supper. Rejecting transubstantiation, Lutherans argued for a real presence of Christ in the Supper that is grounded in the omnipresence of the person of Christ, including both natures. That is, Christ is really with the elements and is not by those elements changing into another substance (i.e., consubstantial). So, "the whole Christ" is omnipresent.

---

interpreted in Ephesus: that it is one and the same Logos who dwells with the Fathers and 'who for us men and for our salvation came down from heaven, and was incarnate and was made man.'" Grillmeier, *Christ in Christian Tradition*, 1:483–84.

[20]In order to get straight what we mean here, we need to see that, especially since the Reformation, there are three different types of *communicatio*. *Communicatio apotelesmaticum*—here ἀποτὲλεσμα refers to a conclusion or completion of work. We will not need to dwell on this since it is not centrally germane to our context here. This aspect refers to the operations or the work of Christ as Mediator, as the God-man—his propitiatory death, for example. *Communicatio maiestatecum*—the *maiestas Dei* refers to the majesty of God in his essence and is usually coupled with *gloria*. My discussion here reflects the discussion in Richard A. Muller, *Dictionary of Latin and Greek Theological Terms: Drawn Principally from Protestant Scholastic Theology* (Grand Rapids: Baker, 1985), 72f.

In Lutheran theology, therefore, since the human nature of Christ is *enhy-postatic*—i.e., since it cannot subsist without the person of the Son of God, who is divine—the human nature of Christ participates in the divine attributes. It participates in the *maiestas et gloria Dei* (the essence and glory of God).

To be clear, both Lutherans and the Reformed agree that the properties of either nature can be communicated to the person. What the Lutherans wanted to further maintain, however, is that (at least some of) the properties of the divine nature (omnipresence, omniscience, etc.) are communicated to the human nature. The Reformed (along with the rest of Christendom, for the most part) have denied this.

To think of the *communicatio* in the way Lutheranism does is to think of it *in abstracto*. The communication is thought to take place with respect to the natures involved, and not directly with respect to the person. But historically the *communicatio* has been affirmed when thought of *in concreto*, that is, not in reference to the natures (in the abstract), but in reference to the person. As Grillmeier notes:

> We can trace quite clearly in the Chalcedonian Definition the wish of the Fathers to take the Nicene framework as their starting point: . . . In the view of Chalcedon, Christ is not just a *homo deifer* or a human subject, *habens dei-tatem*, but the God-Logos, *habens humanitatem*, or rather, *habens et deitatem et humanitatem*. The person of Christ does not first come into being from the concurrence of Godhead and manhood or of the two natures, but is already present in the person of the pre-existent Logos. Thus the Chalcedonian picture of Christ, too, is drawn in the light of the Logos.[21]

Turretin, as well, notes:

> The communication of attributes . . . is an effect of the union by which the properties of both natures became common to the person. Hence the phraseology (or the manner of speaking) concerning Christ arises, by which the properties of either nature are predicated of the person of Christ, in whatever manner it is denominated.[22] This is done either directly, when what belongs to the divine nature is predicated of the person denominated from the divine nature, and what belongs to the human nature of the person denominated from the human

---

[21]Grillmeier, *Christ in Christian Tradition*, 1:490.
[22]Note that a proper use or understanding of the *communicatio*, at least from a Reformed perspective, requires that the properties of the natures are referred to the *person*. Thus, again, the person is central in discussions of this sort. This emphasis is one that the Reformed maintained over against the Lutherans and is central to any understanding of the properties of each and either nature.

nature (as when the Word is said to have been in the beginning with God and God [Jn. 1:1]; when the Son of man, it is said, must be delivered to death and crucified [Lk. 9:22]. Or it is done indirectly, as when what belongs to the deity is predicated of the man Christ and to the humanity of Christ as God (as when suffering is ascribed to God [Acts 20:28] and ubiquity [which is proper to deity] is ascribed to the Son of man [Jn. 3:13]).[23]

So what of the *communicatio idiomatum*? Here perhaps Calvin's affirmation of it can help us.

It is equally senseless to despise the "communication of properties," a term long ago invented to some purpose by the holy fathers. Surely, when the Lord of glory is said to be crucified [1 Cor. 2:8], Paul does not mean that he suffered anything in his divinity, but he says this because the same Christ, who was cast down and despised, and suffered in the flesh, was God and Lord of glory. In this way he was also Son of man in heaven [John 3:13], for the very same Christ, who, according to the flesh, dwelt as Son of man on earth, was God in heaven.[24]

So, if we affirm the *communicatio idiomatum*, we can do so just so long as what we are affirming is that the properties of either nature are rightly referred to the person, who is himself the Son of God, the Lord Jesus Christ. I will want to say a bit more on this below. Before I do, however, one more aspect of this Lutheran controversy needs to be underlined.

(2) Outside of Christ

The *extra calvinisticum* (I'll call it the *extra*, for short) or the "Calvinistic 'outside'" is another label that surfaced in the context of Lutheran theology.[25] Lutherans gave this label to what they saw as the error of a Reformed christology. Even though this notion of the *extra calvinisticum* arose out of the controversy over the Lord's Supper with the Lutherans, the concept itself is not restricted to Calvin. Some have argued, rightly it seems, that it should

---

[23]Turretin, *Institutes*, 2:322.

[24]John Calvin, *Institutes of the Christian Religion*, trans. Ford Lewis Battles, ed. John T. McNeill, 2 vols., The Library of Christian Classics (Philadelphia: Westminster Press, 1960), 4.17.30.

[25]One historical note that may be obvious but should be noted here: The discussions and debates over the sacrament of the Lord's Supper that were so central to much of the Reformation were concerned, in the main, with a proper doctrine of Christ. The sacrament per se was not the matter in dispute. What made the debates so intense was that everyone recognized that there was a direct connection between how we think about the sacrament and how we think about the person of Christ. These debates, therefore, were crucial for a biblical christology.

be better labeled the *extra catholicum*, in that it represents the majority view of the church in history.

The *extra* that is affirmed by the Reformed and opposed by the Lutherans is that the incarnation in no way constrained the divinity of the Son of God. His divinity was not "tied" to his incarnation in an exhaustive way; it surpassed it and thus was "outside" the person as incarnate. So, the supposed error, according to Lutheranism, is this: the person of the Son of God is not contained within the person of Christ as the God-man, but rather the former transcends, in his deity, the latter. There is, then, an "outside" (*extra*) aspect to the Son of God *as incarnate*. One reason for this assertion of the *extra* was the affirmation of the standard formula *Finitum non capax infiniti*—the finite cannot contain the infinite. But this view of the *extra* goes back to the early church. The church father Athanasius, in his work on the incarnation, notes:

> *The Word was not hedged in by His body, nor did His presence in the body prevent His being present elsewhere as well.* When He moved His body He did not cease also to direct the universe by His Mind and might. No. The marvellous truth is, that being the Word, so far from being Himself contained by anything, He actually contained all things Himself. In creation He is present everywhere, yet is distinct in being from it; ordering, directing, giving life to all, containing all, yet is He Himself the Uncontained, existing solely in His Father. . . . Existing in a human body, to which He Himself gives life, He is still Source of life to all the universe, present in every part of it, yet outside the whole; and He is revealed both through the works of His body and through His activity in the world. . . . His body was for Him not a limitation, but an instrument, so that He was both in it and in all things, and outside all things, resting in the Father alone. At one and the same time—this is the wonder—as Man He was living a human life, and as Word He was sustaining the life of the universe, and as Son He was in constant union with the Father. Not even His birth from a virgin, therefore, changed Him in any way, nor was He defiled by being in the body.[26]

So, as the Son of God takes to himself a human nature, he is not contained within the human nature that he assumes—"the Word was not hedged in by his body."

Not only so, but as Calvin notes, to think as the Lutherans do—that the human nature absorbed and partook of the divine attributes—would be to create a kind of "third thing." One quotation from Calvin summarizes the position well.

---

[26]Athanasius, *The Incarnation of the Word, Being the Treatise of St. Athanasius (De incarnatione verbi dei)*, trans. Sister Penelope, CSMV (London: Geoffrey Bles, Centenary, 1944), 45–46.

But some are carried away with such contentiousness as to say that because of the natures joined in Christ, wherever Christ's divinity is, there also is his flesh [this is the Lutheran notion of ubiquity], which cannot be separated from it. As if that union had compounded from two natures some sort of intermediate being which was neither God nor man! So, indeed, did Eutyches teach, and Servetus after him. But from Scripture we plainly infer that the one person of Christ so consists of two natures that each nevertheless retains unimpaired its own distinctive character. And they will be ashamed to deny that Eutyches was rightly condemned. It is a wonder they do not heed the cause of his condemnation; removing the distinction between the natures and urging the unity of the person, he made man out of God and God out of man. What sort of madness, then, is it to mingle heaven with earth rather than give up trying to drag Christ's body from the heavenly sanctuary?

They bring forward these passages for their side: "No one has ascended into heaven but he who descended from heaven, the Son of man, who is in heaven"; and again: "The Son, who is in the bosom of the Father, he has made him known." It is, equally senseless to despise the "communication of properties," a term long ago invented to some purpose by the holy fathers. Surely, when the Lord of glory is said to be crucified, Paul does not mean that he suffered anything in his divinity, but he says this because the same Christ, who was cast down and despised, and suffered in the flesh, was God and Lord of glory. In this way he was also Son of man in heaven, for the very same Christ, who, according to the flesh, dwelt as Son of man on earth, was God in heaven. In this manner, he is said to have descended to that place according to his divinity, not because divinity left heaven to hide itself in the prison house of the body, but because even though it filled all things, still in Christ's very humanity it dwelt bodily, that is, by nature, and in a certain ineffable way. There is a commonplace distinction of the schools to which I am not ashamed to refer: although the whole Christ is everywhere, still the whole of that which is in him is not everywhere. And would that the Schoolmen themselves had honestly weighed the force of this statement. For thus would the absurd fiction of Christ's carnal presence have been obviated.[27]

The crucial point to remember here is that Calvin and the majority of theologians in church history want to emphasize and safeguard (what I have called) the *Eimi/eikon* distinction. Paul Helm says this about the *extra*:

According to the Chalcedonian view of the Incarnation . . . , whatever is essential to the divine nature cannot be yielded up in the Incarnation. That is, if there are properties that are essential to God being God . . . then in becoming

---

[27]Calvin, *Institutes*, 4.17.30.

incarnate God cannot cease to be omnipotent or omniscient. . . . By insisting
on the extra, Calvin is arguing that the Son of God is God, and therefore has
God's essence. In other words, the Son has all of God's essential properties.
. . . Therefore, if the Incarnation is truly the Incarnation of the Son of God,
then it must preserve the divinity of the Son of God unaltered or unimpaired.[28]

Of course, the Lutherans would not want to deny the deity of Christ.
However, what they do deny is that this deity accrues to Christ in that he is
the Son and not in that he is man. According to the Lutherans, the "deifying"
of Christ accrues both to his divine *and* human natures.

This compromises the *Eimi/eikon* distinction not only at the level of the
Creator, but at the level of the creature as well. For Calvin and the rest, at
issue was not simply correct theology, but also the biblical picture of the
gospel. For example, if the human nature of Christ took on (at least some
of) the properties of God, how could Christ become like us in *every way*,
yet without sin? How could he be like us *in every way* if his human nature
participates in divine properties?

This point of the reality of a true and genuine *human* nature is, according
to Bavinck, one of the things that the *extra*, in a Reformed context, highlights.

> Reformed theologians . . . had fundamentally overcome the Greek Roman and
> Lutheran commingling of the divine and human, also in Christology. While
> rigorously maintaining the unity of the person, they applied the rule "the finite
> is not capable of [containing] the infinite" also to the human nature of Christ
> and maintained this rule not only in the state of humiliation but even in that of
> Christ's exaltation. *In that way Reformed theology secured space for a purely
> human development of Christ, for a successive communication of gifts, and
> for a real distinction between humiliation and exaltation.*[29]

The point of Christ's full humanity, which he has freely taken on by way
of his condescension, can often either be muted or exaggerated. There can
be, on the one hand, in the interest of Christ's perfection, an interest also in
minimizing or expunging texts of Scripture that speak to his emotions and
the process of his growth.[30] On the other hand, there can be a tendency to
dismiss or, worse, deny his deity in favor of a "true" humanity.

---

[28]Helm, *John Calvin's Ideas*, 61–62.
[29]Bavinck, *Reformed Dogmatics*, 3:258–59, my emphasis. We should note here as well that
Thomas Aquinas, at least to some extent, affirms the humanity of Christ as that which truly
develops. See, for example, *Summa theologica* 3.9.4.
[30]"The church fathers gradually came to believe that Christ was not deficient in knowledge. The

One response to these extremes that is virtually unparalleled for its exegetical weight and biblical balance is found in B. B. Warfield, "The Emotional Life
of Our Lord."[31] Without repeating or attempting to elaborate on Warfield's
arguments, we can recognize in the general thrust of his article that the reality of Christ's passions, as given in numerous texts in the New Testament,
speaks not to any sinfulness in him, but to his full and vibrant humanity.
For example:

> The sight of Mary and her companions wailing at the tomb of Lazarus, agi-
> tated his soul and caused him tears (Jno. xi. 35); the stubborn unbelief of
> Jerusalem drew from him loud wailing (Lk. xix. 41). He sighed at the sight
> of human suffering (Mk. vii. 34) and "sighed deeply" over men's hardened
> unbelief (viii. 12); man's inhumanity to man smote his heart with pain (iii. 5).
> . . . Not only do we read that he wept (Jno. xi. 35) and wailed (Lk. xix. 41),
> sighed (Mk. vii. 34) and groaned (Mk. viii. 12); but we read also of his angry
> glare (Mk. iii. 5), his annoyed speech (Mk. x. 14), his chiding words (e.g. Mk.
> iii. 12), the outbreaking ebullition of his rage (e.g. Jno. xi. 33, 38); of the agita-
> tion of his bearing when under strong feeling (Jno. xi. 35), the open exultation
> of his joy (Lk. x. 21), the unrest of his movements in the face of anticipated
> evils (Mt. xxvii. 37), the loud cry which was wrung from him in his moment
> of desolation (Mt. xxvii. 46).[32]

Bavinck's point above, that "Reformed theology secured space for a purely
human development of Christ," is amply demonstrated in Warfield's article.[33]

One further perspective on the *extra* before we move on: Although it is
impossible in a short space to do justice to the complexity of Barth's theology,
it may be helpful to offer a couple of summary points relative to his concerns
for an orthodox christology in order to provide one more context in which, at
least by contrast, we should think of the *extra* in relation to the incarnation.

As he does with most historic Christianity, Karl Barth has a problem with
the historic Christian notion of the *extra*. His problem relates directly to his

---

Reformed taught that Christ's infused and acquired knowledge was not immediately complete
but gradually increased." Bavinck, *Reformed Dogmatics*, 3:312.
[31]Benjamin Breckinridge Warfield, "The Emotional Life of Our Lord," in *The Person and Work
of Christ*, ed. Samuel G. Craig (Philadelphia: Presbyterian and Reformed, 1950).
[32]Ibid., 127.
[33]We will discuss this below, but it may be useful to mention here that there is no fundamental
disagreement in this ascription of the emotional life of Christ and the truth of God's impassibility.
When, for example, the Westminster Confession of Faith affirms that God is "without body,
parts or passions," it is obviously referring to God as he is in himself, rather than God as
condescended, since, *as condescended*, God *does* have a body (and parts, and passions), in that
the second person of the Trinity assumes one, into eternity.

unusual ontology. Barth's ontology has been labeled "actualistic." Included in that label is an opposition to any "essentialistic" ontology, as well as the notion that God's freedom, which itself is ultimate, is the determining condition for his being. In other words, it is God's choices, all of which are and must be free, that determine exactly who God is. The problem that Barth seems to have with the *extra*, given his ontology, is that a notion of essence lurks in the background. That notion of essence carries with it at least two theological problems, as Barth sees it.

First, how can one relate the essence of God, in this case of God in Christ, to the Christ of history? On Barth's view, if there is a Logos without flesh (*asarkos*) outside of the Logos in the flesh (*ensarkos*), then this Logos *asarkos* is an indeterminate state of being that is above and prior to the determination to enter time. And if indeterminate, then there is or can be (who can really know?) a radical discontinuity between the Logos *asarkos* and the Logos *ensarkos*.

The second problem for Barth is related to the first. If there is a Logos *asarkos* that transcends and even predates the Logos *ensarkos*, then, in the words of Bruce McCormack:

> The decision to assume flesh in time could only result in something being added to that already completed identity; an addition which has no effect upon what he is essentially. Being the Redeemer, in this view, tells us nothing about who or what the Logos is in and for himself. It is merely a role he plays, something he does; but what he does in time has no significance for his eternal being.[34]

Barth's "solution" to this problem is what McCormack calls a "covenant ontology." This is identical to what he elsewhere calls an "actualistic ontology." It means that the act of God incarnating himself—which is relationality, not in the abstract but in the concrete—is of the essence of God himself.

So, says Barth:

> We have consistently followed the rule, which we regard as basic, that statements about the divine modes of being antecedently in themselves cannot be different in content from those that are to be made about their reality in revelation. . . . The reality of God in His revelation cannot be bracketed by an "only," as though somewhere behind His revelation there stood another reality of God;

---

[34]Bruce McCormack, "Grace and Being: The Role of Gracious Election in Karl Barth's Theological Ontology," in *The Cambridge Companion to Karl Barth*, ed. John Webster (Cambridge: Cambridge University Press, 2000), 97.

the reality of God which encounters us in His revelation is His reality in all the depths of eternity.[35]

The important point to note here is that Barth denies the *extra* because, at least in part, he can think of no way in which God can determine to relate himself to his creation except in that this is who God is essentially. To posit some essence of God that then determines to relate to creation is to place an impenetrable barrier between this essence and who God is as revealed.

It should be said here, though it cannot be developed, that either Barth's notion of God at this point requires that God's freedom is who he essentially is, so that his freedom is his essence, or it makes God as dependent on creation as creation is on him. If Barthians would reply by saying that the only reason God is essentially "for us" is his free decision, then that free decision stands behind and above—it transcends—who God is "essentially" and thus it becomes an "essence" in and of itself. Thus, either Barth's actualism is essentialism in disguise, with the unhappy consequence of a capricious god, or it is another version of a god whose "godness" is defined by who we are, rather than the other way around.

The importance of the *extra* is that it attempts to lay out as clearly as possible what the mystery of the incarnation entails. It seeks to affirm something that is most important to affirm with respect to the incarnation in that the Son of God did not (indeed, as we have seen, he *could not*) give up any essential aspect of his deity in order to assume a human nature.

(3) Be Careful What You Say

One final clarification with respect to the person of Christ is needed before we move on. Though this discussion remains somewhat technical, the goal to which it points is important for our purposes, especially as we come later to consider certain biblical passages that appear to contradict each other regarding God's character.

The notion of reduplication, or what is sometimes called the "reduplicative strategy," goes back at least as far as Aristotle and is employed typically to deal with statements sometimes called *qua* (or "as") statements of the form "x as A is N."

This strategy was employed by Aquinas, and by the Reformed as well, to speak truthfully and without bare contradiction about the person of Jesus

---

[35] Quoted in ibid., 100.

Christ. So, in answer to the question of whether this is true, "Christ as Man is a creature," Aquinas says:

> I answer that, When we say "Christ as Man" this word "man" may be added in the reduplication, either by reason of the *suppositum* or by reason of the nature. If it be added by reason of the *suppositum*, since the *suppositum* of the human nature in Christ is eternal and uncreated, this will be false: "Christ as Man is a creature." But if it be added by reason of the human nature, it is true, since by reason of the human nature or in the human nature, it belongs to Him to be a creature, as was said.[36]

So, says Thomas, it is legitimate to speak of "Christ as man" so long as we recognize that the "as man" has its referent, not in the "suppositum," which is the divinity of Christ, but in the human nature.

As we might expect, problems have been raised concerning this strategy. Thomas Morris thinks that such a strategy cannot avoid absurdity because it cannot avoid contradiction:

> Consider any conjunctive reduplicative proposition of the form 'x as A is N and x as B is not N.' If the subjects of both conjuncts are the same and the substituends of N are univocal across the conjunction, then as long as (1) the reduplication predicates being A of x and predicates being B of x, and (2) being N is entailed by being A, and not being N is entailed by being B, then the reduplicative form of predication accomplishes nothing except for muddying the waters, since in the end the contradiction stands of x being characterized as both N and not N.

In other words, argues Morris, suppose one affirms both that "Christ as God is infinite, and, Christ as man is not infinite." Given that the subject of both conjuncts (Christ) is the same, which it is, and that "infinite" is used in the same way in both conjuncts, which it is, and as long as the reduplication predicates "being God" of Christ and "being man" of Christ, which it does, and "being infinite" is entailed by being God, and not being infinite is entailed by being man, which each is, then, says Morris, the contradiction stands, since Christ is characterized as being infinite and not infinite.

There is much that can be said here in response. One response from Eleonore Stump, though not without its own problems, is that something can be predicated of a whole if it is true of some constituent part of that whole, even if it is not true of other parts of the whole. Stump puts it this way:

---

[36]Thomas Aquinas, *Summa theologica*, trans. Fathers of the English Dominican Province, 3.16.10.

So a whole can borrow properties from its constituents. . . . Consequently, there is no reason for denying that Christ can have properties borrowed from either his human nature or his divine nature, even if the natures are not integral parts of Christ and the properties are contradictories. Because each of the incompatible properties is had in its own right by a different constituent of the whole and because they attach to the whole only derivatively, in consequence of the fact that the whole has these constituents, there is no incoherence in attributing both otherwise incompatible properties to the whole.[37]

In some ways, this brings us back to our discussion of the *communicatio idiomatum*. Stump maintains that, given that there are two natures in the one Christ, what can be predicated of each nature in its own right can be predicated as well of the person. One more quotation from Turretin may clarify:

From "the whole Christ to the whole of Christ" or "from the person of Christ to the natures" the argument [of ubiquity] does not hold good. Nor can what is attributed to the person be at once predicated of the natures because the person indeed claims for itself the properties of both natures, but one nature does not claim for itself the properties of the other, which belong to the person. Otherwise the natures would be confounded.[38]

We can speak of Christ in ways that appear incompatible, given that, as a unique individual, he is a combination of two distinct and fundamentally different natures.

Recall that in our discussions of the *communicatio*, I affirmed a Reformed notion of this, provided it is understood that the *communicatio* has to do with ascribing properties of either nature to the person of Christ. In that sense, what we have in the Reformed *communicatio* is a reduplicative strategy, but it is one that has its focus, not in the real communication of properties between natures, but in the real communication of any of the properties to the one person, who is the Mediator, the Logos, Jesus Christ. This is because, as we saw above, the *communicatio* has reference to the *person* (*in concreto*) and not to the *natures* (*in abstracto*). Thus, the Reformed notion of the *communicatio* has been rightly called a verbal predication (*praedicatio verbalis*) of properties from both natures to the person.

Thus, as we discussed above, it is legitimate to ascribe real emotions and passions to God (focused in the Son). Not only so, but we can fully affirm

---

[37]Eleonore Stump, "Aquinas' Metaphysics of the Incarnation," in *The Incarnation*, ed. Stephen T. Davis, Daniel Kendall, SJ, and Gerald O'Collins, SJ (Oxford: Oxford University Press, 2002), 217.
[38]Turretin, *Institutes*, 2:328.

that Jesus *really did* grow in wisdom and in favor with God (Luke 2:52).
To repeat, he *grew* in these qualities, and it is legitimate (because Scripture
speaks this way) to say this about *the person*. We need not explain away the
reality of this growth, as if it were beneath Christ. It is, to be sure, *beneath
God*, until and unless he freely decides to condescend to us and to take on
properties that are not essential to him but are of an entirely different nature
than who he is essentially. Once he has decided to condescend and has done
so, however, he really and fully takes on those properties, not metaphorically or figuratively. Thus we could say that in God alone are the *Eimi* and
the *eikon* brought together into a real and perfect unity, in the one person
of the Son of God.

One more qualification with respect to the union of the *Eimi/eikon* in
Christ is pertinent here, given certain objections that have surfaced in church
history. I will be arguing below that there are essential properties relative to
God (i.e., the Son of God) and other contingent (accidental?) properties that
God takes on. Would that imply that the uniting of a human nature to the
Logos was an accidental union? Aquinas, and Owen following him, say no.

In his elaboration of the hypostatic union of the two natures in the person of Christ, John Owen notes that this union was a "substantial" union,
"because it was of two substances or essences in the same person, *in opposition unto all accidental union*, as 'the fullness of the Godhead dwelt in
him bodily.'"[39] The notion of an "accidental union," which Owen rejects,
may seem to be exactly what we are affirming when we speak of the Son of
God taking on contingent (i.e., covenantal) properties—that is, taking on
a human nature as a result of his free decision. Surely, if those properties
are contingent (freely chosen and not a result of any necessity in him), then
they are not essential to who he is (viz., the Son of God) and thus could be
construed to be accidental.

Thomas Aquinas is even more specific. He objects to the idea of an accidental union of a human nature with the Son of God. The relevant question
in Thomas is whether human nature was united to the Word in the manner
of an accident. Thomas answers:

> Whenever a predication is accidental, substance is not the predicate (*non praedi-
> cat aliquid*), but quantity, quality or some other modifier of the subject. If, then,
> human nature came to Christ in the manner of an accident, when we say that

---

[39] John Owen, *The Works of John Owen*, ed. W. H. Gould, Ages Digital Library CD ed., 16
vols. (Edinburgh: Banner of Truth, 1977), 1:293, my emphasis.

he is a man, we would not be predicating substance of him (*non praedicaretur aliquid*), but quantity, quality or some other accident.

In light of the objections of Aquinas and Owen (and others), it is crucial that we make some fine distinctions.

First, we should note that the way in which we are using the notion of *contingent* or *covenantal* (and its possible synonym *accident*) is with respect to things that are not absolutely necessary. In other words, we are confining our use of those concepts in distinction from our notion of essence, which itself has to do with what something is necessarily. So, that which is contingent or accidental, in this context, is something that is not absolutely essential or necessary (i.e., it is possible for it to be otherwise).

Second, and important for a proper understanding of Thomas and Owen, it was the metaphysics of Thomas (and of Owen as well in this case) that disallowed any notion of accidental union in Christ.[40] For Thomas, there were only three modes of union available, given the structure of his metaphysics, and none of them were sufficient to describe the mode of union of the incarnation.

The third mode of union, which is the one most relevant to our discussion, is the union of an accident with a *supposit* (hypostasis). Thomas rejects this option because, for him, *a nature could not be an accident*. A nature is, rather, in the case of a human being, a *substantial* form of a particular material thing. Because it was a human nature that Christ assumed and not simply a combination of properties (such as, having brown hair, being *x* inches tall, etc.), there can be no union of accidents with a person (*supposit*). The properties conferred on Christ by virtue of this union were all those properties that are essential to a human nature.

The objection to any kind of accidental union, therefore, takes its place, not in the context of what is ultimately necessary and what is merely possible, but rather in the context of a substance metaphysic, in which concepts such as human nature were thought to entail a substantial form.[41] In that sense,

---

[40]Most of what follows is taken from the discussion of Thomas's view of the incarnation in Stump, "Aquinas' Metaphysics of the Incarnation."

[41]Stump says, "He does *not* characterize an accident as any property a thing has in some but not all of the possible worlds in which it exists, so that every feature a thing fails to have in all the worlds in which it exists has to count as an accident" (Eleonore Stump, *Aquinas* [New York: Routledge, 2003], 112). In other words, we are thinking of contingency in the context of what God freely chooses to do, such that possibilities are actualized by virtue of his free choice, whereas Thomas would think of accidental or contingent properties in the context of *substances*. Speaking of substances, it should be said here, for the sake of clarity, that contrary to some Thomas holds not that a person is *substantially* a soul with a body, but that a person is *substantially* body and soul. For a contrary view to that of Thomas, see J. P. Moreland and Scott Rae, *Body and Soul:*

our notion of contingent is not accidental, in that it does not presuppose a substance metaphysic. Rather, it has to do with what God does necessarily, on the one hand, and what he does freely, on the other.

The christology we have been delineating here is nothing new. Any cursory glance at the church's position on the hypostatic union will bring out these same basic points. To put this matter another way, and to repeat: We know that our foundation for knowledge is in God's revelation to us. But, particularly when it comes to a knowledge of God, one of the things we must do is look to the quintessential revelation of God in Jesus Christ. In him we have the perfect union of God and creation in the uniting of the two natures in one person. So, if we want to know how God can relate to his creation, we should look to the example of that relationship in the person of Christ. In him we have the picture of God's covenant with his people. Because Christ is the union of two natures, he brings together, in a way that only God could accomplish, the union of both "I will be your God" and "you will be my people." In Christ, we have both "our God" and "his people."

E. In the Beginning?

All that we have discussed thus far will go a long way in helping us to think biblically—*revelationally*—about God and his relationship to creation. Specifically, it should help us to see how God can condescend without giving up who he is essentially, all the while relating—*really and truly*, not just metaphorically or figuratively—to his creation and to his human creatures.

One more aspect to this discussion, as it bears on the second person of the Trinity, should be broached here. In order to begin to see the exhaustive and universal activity of the second person of the Trinity, we should first note his universal presence, as condescended, and then highlight that his universal presence also finds its focus in his appearance to and with the Lord's people in covenant history. One of the most profound and concise passages in which to see the universal and revealing activity of the second person of the Trinity—the Logos—is found in the prologue to John's Gospel.

(1) The Word Was

The importance of this section for what follows should be kept in mind. What I hope to accomplish in our brief study of John's prologue is in one sense quite

---

Human Nature and the Crisis in Ethics (Downers Grove, IL: InterVarsity, 2000). For a helpful analysis of this view, see Christina Van Dyke, "Not Properly a Person: The Rational Soul and 'Thomistic Substance Dualism,'" *Faith and Philosophy* 26, no. 2 (2009): 186–204.

simple. I hope to show (at least some of) the biblical basis for the fact that the second person of the Trinity has always been the Mediator between God and man. Thus, any revelation of God to man comes by way of that Mediator. I also hope to strengthen the notion that, while the incarnation is *sui generis*, that does not mean it has no precedents at all in covenant history. The Christ who comes as incarnate is the same person who came "in the beginning" and who has always come as God to man.

In his careful and incisive article on the prologue in the Gospel of John, Geerhardus Vos concludes:

> The unique feature of the Prologue consists in this, that it views the *cosmical function of the preexistent Christ as a revealing function and places it in direct continuity with His revealing work in the sphere of redemption.* Not that the Messiah has a share in the creation of the world or in providence, but that *in mediating both He acts as the revealing Logos of God . . . . It not only vindicates for nature the character of a revealing medium through which God speaks,* but also links together creation and redemption as both mediated by the same Logos.[42]

In order to apply the truth of this prologue to our particular concerns of a revelational hermeneutic with respect to God's relationship to creation, we need to note some of the more salient points of Vos's exegesis of this central and magnificent passage.[43]

The first and more obvious point of John's prologue is that the Logos himself preexisted the creation.[44] This can be seen in part from the opening verses.[45] The Logos *was* (ἦν) in the beginning. That is, when creation began,

---

[42]Geerhardus Vos, "The Range of the Logos Title in the Prologue to the Fourth Gospel," in *Redemptive History and Biblical Interpretation: The Shorter Writings of Geerhardus Vos,* ed. Richard B. Gaffin Jr. (Phillipsburg, NJ: Presbyterian and Reformed, 1980), 90, my emphasis. This article originally appeared as Geerhardus Vos, "The Range of the Logos-Title in the Prologue to the Fourth Gospel," *Princeton Theological Review* 11 (1913): 365–419. The reader is encouraged to refer to this entire article for analyses and questions that, owing to our more specific focus, must be excluded in what follows.

[43]The material that follows will be summaries and extrapolations from Vos's article, and such statements will mark the page number in Vos's article in parentheses. Again, the reader should consult that article for the more careful exegetical work that grounds the material presented here.

[44]For a fascinating and helpful analysis of the relationship of the concept of Logos to the Old Testament, see John L. Ronning, *The Jewish Targums and John's Logos Theology* (Peabody, MS: Hendrickson, 2009). Ronning argues that the Logos concept is not something taken over from Greek philosophy, in the first place, but was taken by Greek philosophy from earlier Jewish theology.

[45]Ἐν ἀρχῇ ἦν ὁ λόγος, καὶ ὁ λόγος ἦν πρὸς τὸν θεόν, καὶ θεὸς ἦν ὁ λόγος. οὗτος ἦν ἐν ἀρχῇ πρὸς τὸν θεόν (John 1:1–2).

the Logos already existed. As most commentators will recognize, this opening is calculated to refer us back to the beginning of Scripture, Genesis 1. So,
John continues, not only was the Logos in the beginning, but this Logos is
both distinct from God (πρὸς τὸν θεόν) and identical to God (θεὸς ἦν ὁ λόγος).
This much is noncontroversial among orthodox Christians and scholars, and
it forms the background for everything else John will say in this prologue.[46]
The specific verses that will be our concern here are John 1:1–5, 9–11:

> In the beginning was the Word, and the Word was with God, and the Word was
> God. He was in the beginning with God. All things were made through him,
> and without him was not any thing made that was made. In him was life, and
> the life was the light of men. The light shines in the darkness, and the dark-
> ness has not overcome it. . . . The true light, which enlightens everyone, was
> coming into the world. He was in the world, and the world was made through
> him, yet the world did not know him. He came to his own, and his own people
> did not receive him.

In verse 3, Scripture affirms that through the Logos everything was made
that has been made.[47] As God, he himself is the Creator of all that is.[48] After
verse 3, however, interpretations of the prologue divide between understanding
John as referring primarily to the activity of Christ (the Logos incarnate) in
redemption, and reading John as referring to the activity of the Logos in creation generally. Vos notes that he is inclined to stick with the "older exegesis,"
which views John 1:1–5, 9–11 primarily from the standpoint of the Logos's
activity in creation, or in creation *as well as* redemption.[49]

After John affirms the Logos to "be" before the foundation of the world,
and to be the One through whom all creation came to be, he goes on, in verse
4, to tell us that life itself was in the Logos and that this life was the light of
men. The life here referred to is not the life that comes by way of redemp-

[46]For a helpful summary of the "History of Religions Approach" to the Logos, as well as the
notion of the Logos and "Wisdom" literature, see Herman Ridderbos, *The Gospel of John: A
Theological Commentary*, trans. John Vriend (Grand Rapids: Eerdmans, 1997), 27–36.
[47]There is some question whether ὃ γέγονεν, at the end of v. 3 actually belongs to v. 4. This
need not detain us here. Most commentators agree that it belongs with v. 3. See Andreas J.
Köstenberger, *John*, Baker Exegetical Commentary on the New Testament (Grand Rapids:
Baker Academic, 2004), 29–30.
[48]According to Ridderbos, there is no strong reason to suggest that δι' αὐτοῦ must be seen as
designating the Logos as the medium of creation (see Ridderbos, *Gospel of John*, 36–37). What
v. 3 does note clearly is that the Logos created *everything* (πάντα).
[49]Vos, "Logos Title," 90.

tion, though that will be a central point in this Gospel.[50] Rather, in the logic of John's argument, the life that is in the Logos is the life that is given to all of creation. That John speaks of this life just after affirming the Logos to be the Creator indicates that the life itself is the life of creation.[51] According to Vos (65), then, the Logos is not first of all revealer as presented here, but the omnipotent life giver, the One who gives life *to all* (πάντα—v. 3).

The question now is whether the "light" of which John speaks in this verse is the light of redemption or of creation. The reference to light seems to apply to man in God's image, that is, to every person. John has yet to introduce the specific activity of redemption as found in Christ. His immediate concern continues to be the cosmic activity of the Logos. So, verses 3 and 4 tell us that the Logos created everything and, moreover, gave life to everything that is alive. More specifically, having given life to all things that live, he also gave life to man, and to everyone he also gave light. The life that he gave to man *is* light, in distinction to the life that he gave to all else. Man's life is the life of light, given by the Logos. According to Vos (75):

> By far the simplest exegesis, and that which best avoids all difficulties, is to make the imperfect tense [of verse 4] refer to the point of time fixed by verse 3 and let it describe something that was true at and since that point in time. On this view the connection between verse 3 and verse 4 is so close and self-explanatory, that no particle or adverb of more precise definition is required.

In other words, says Vos, the Logos is the Logos in creation (v. 3) as well as in the activity of maintaining and sustaining the creation; he is the Logos in creation *and* in providence (v. 4). Life and light came from him and continue in him.[52]

---

[50]The prologue in this Gospel, while it has unmistakable connections to the rest of the Gospel, is itself unique. John is setting the stage for what is to come. In so doing, he will use words, concepts, and ideas, some of which are themselves meant to be seen in the context of the prologue and not primarily in the context of the rest of the Gospel. So, in v. 4, while "life" and "light" play a major role in John's discussion of Christ and the good news of the gospel, John will use these terms in the prologue in a way that sets the stage for their later use, but is not identical to those terms used after the prologue. In other words, there is a reason that the prologue is its own context within the larger context of the whole Gospel.

[51]Note, for example, "In John ζωὴ is generally eternal or spiritual life, but here it is more comprehensive. In the Logos was life, and it is of this life all things have partaken and by it they exist." W. Robertson Nicoll, ed., *The Expositor's Greek New Testament*, vol. 1 (Grand Rapids: Eerdmans, 1970), 685.

[52]Vos rightly notes that, had redemption rather than creation been in view here, priority would have been given to the notion of light. It is the light of the gospel that brings new life, not the reverse. If redemption were in view, John would have said, "In him was light, and the light was the life of men." But John states the opposite, following on his affirmation that the Logos

The question arises, Why is there a transition from the imperfect tense in verse 4 to the present tense in verse 5? That is, John tells us that life and light *were* in the Logos from the point of creation onward, but then, in verse 5, he moves to the present tense: "the light shines in the darkness." Why the change in tense?

Most commentators today seem to think that the present tense in verse 5 is a clear indication of a reference "to the light that came when Christ entered the world and that now shines."[53] This interpretation takes the subsequent verses, which refer to John the Baptist and his announcement of the incarnate Christ as the light, as indicating the light that shines in verse 5. That is, the author moves to the present tense in verse 5 as he transitions from creation generally to the announcement, in verses 6–8, of the coming of Christ (τὸ φῶς—v. 8) by the Baptist.

Vos, however, mounts a considerable argument that the reference here is to the Logos's activity in creation and nature, not simply in redemption. Vos offers two possibilities for the interpretation of the present tense in verse 5 (77). Perhaps the present tense refers to the present "illuminating function of the Logos" (φαίνει) in distinction from his light-giving activity at creation in the past (ἦν). If this were what John meant, however, we would expect the insertion of some temporal adverb or particle (in that he would be moving from creation and providence to Jesus's earthly life), rather than a leap from verse 4 (past) to verse 5 (present) without any grammatical indication. But no such indicator is given. The second option, which Vos prefers, is worth quoting here:

> The second interpretation of the present φαίνει—the one that in our view deserves the preference—makes the Evangelist advance from the general proposition that the world when created was as such dependent on the Logos as its source of life and light, to the specific reflection, or after-reflection, that this holds true even now under the reign of darkness in the world. The light that functioned at the beginning functions also in a world which is positively darkened through sin. The only difference is that under these circumstances there is a conflict between it and the world. (77)

---

created all things. In this case, the Logos mediates both life and light, in that order. "Here the Logos-revelation is actually mediated through the subjective life which man in dependence on the Logos possesses. The life here naturally produces the light. The meaning here is . . . that the life which man receives carries in itself and of itself kindles in him, the light of the knowledge of God" (76).

[53]Ridderbos, *Gospel of John*, 39; see also Köstenberger, *John*, 31.

The point John wants us to see in verse 5 is not, therefore, that the Logos has come as incarnate to overcome sin, at least not specifically (though that will certainly be a theme set out in the rest of this Gospel), but that the Logos, who himself created all things and gave life and light to man, continues, even with the entrance of sin in the world, to give this light to all men. The progression in John's thinking here, therefore, is not so much historical but "logical, from the general to the specific" (77). That is, the apostle moves from the general statement of the Logos and his relation to creation generally, to the more specific situation of the world affected and infected by sin. Or, to put it in terms of the background to this prologue, John moves from Genesis 1 to Genesis 3. The "and" (καὶ) at the beginning of verse 5 is sufficient to link these thoughts together in this way. Vos goes on to say that, with respect to verses 4 and 5, "there is no place for the incarnate Christ" (79). It seems likely, therefore, from the structure of John's prologue thus far, that he is thinking about the activity of the Logos *at* creation and *in* creation, generally, and more specifically, *in* creation even as it has been affected by sin.[54]

The next reference within our particular purview concerns the activity of the Logos in verse 9. Specifically, we hope to ascertain what John means in verse 9 by the relative clause "which enlightens everyone." The immediate surrounding verses help us. We have already seen that the Baptist came to bear witness about the light, who is the Logos. The apostle makes clear that this One who is the light is the One who preexists John the Baptist. The prologue, then, is making a connection, beginning in verse 6, to both the preexistence of the Logos (cf. vv. 15, 30) and the announcement of this Logos who is coming. As we have seen, according to Vos, the prologue moves, rather seamlessly it seems, between the historic announcement and reality of the incarnation and the truth of the eternal, ontic identity of the One who comes in the flesh. This movement in the prologue is a natural transition from the

---

[54]When we come to vv. 6–8, however, there can be no question that we have entered the time period of the incarnation. The apostle turns our attention to John the Baptist and his announcement of the coming of the Christ. Not only so, but he links this historical moment to the fact that this Logos who is coming is himself the light. Given our particular focus, we need not enter that discussion here, but a point or two is worth mentioning. According to Vos, introducing the Baptist brings to the fore the question of the relationship between the ontic and the historic. Vos thinks that the "cosmical light" is represented, at least in part, in vv. 7–9 (80). This can be seen in that, in vv. 15 and 30, the Baptist compares himself and his ministry to the preexistence of the Logos (note the presence of ὅτι πρῶτός μου ἦν in both verses). Though in v. 6 John speaks as a historian, in v. 8 he resumes the tone of the theologian. This alternating between the present historical situation and the preexistent metaphysical affirmation of the Logos marks both the uniqueness of the prologue and its connection to what is to follow in the rest of the book.

identity of the Logos as the Son of God, and therefore as God, to his identity
in the flesh as the Christ.

In verse 9, John reiterates the point already made, that this Logos is the
"true light" (Ἦν τὸ φῶς τὸ ἀληθινόν),[55] but he also notes that this Logos who
is the true light "was coming into the world" (ἐρχόμενον εἰς τὸν κόσμον). In
this latter phrase, the question again is whether John is referring to a general
activity of the Logos, as One who was coming into the world generally, or
to the Logos coming as incarnate, as Christ. The latter seems to be the more
obvious meaning. Given that the Baptist has come to announce the incarnate
coming of the Logos, it seems natural to assume that "was coming into the
world" means that the Logos was in the process of coming as incarnate at the
time of the Baptist's ministry (cf. John 11:27). But how shall we then understand the relative clause "which enlightens everyone"? Is the enlightening of
everyone by the Logos meant to be connected with the incarnate coming of
the Logos, or does it refer to a more general "enlightening"? Köstenberger,
following Raymond Brown, chooses the former.

> As the "true light," Jesus is here presented as the source of (spiritual) light.
> That light enlightens every person. . . . The present verse does not suggest uni-
> versalism—the ultimate salvation of every person—for John does not speak
> of *internal* illumination in the sense of general revelation . . . , but of *external*
> illumination in the sense of objective revelation requiring a response.[56]

So also, Ridderbos:

> Because of [Jesus's] uniqueness, it is also true of this light that it "enlightens
> every person" (cf. vs. 4b). This statement describes the light in its fullness and
> universality. It does not say that every individual is in fact enlightened by the
> light (cf. vss. 5, 10f.) but that by its coming into the world the light is for every
> human being that by which alone he or she can live (cf. 8:12).[57]

Both of these commentators recognize the universality necessitated in the
relative clause. There can be no question that John affirms that "everyone"
(πάντα ἄνθρωπον) is enlightened by the true light. What is problematic in both
of these interpretations, however, is that the full force of the verb "enlightens"

---

[55]There is a question as to whether τὸ φῶς is the subject and ἦν . . . ἐρχόμενον the predicate or
the subject is supplied from the previous verses. Without rehearsing the details, I have chosen
the latter, which is given in the ESV translation. For more on these two options, see Vos, 80–82.
[56]Köstenberger, *John*, 35–36.
[57]Ridderbos, *Gospel of John*, 43.

(φωτίζει) seems to be muted or undermined. John does not say that the light *could* enlighten everyone, or that it *may* enlighten everyone, or even that it *will* enlighten everyone; rather, he clearly affirms here that the light *enlightens* everyone. The use of this verb, according to Vos, "clearly passes beyond the sphere of objective potentiality into that of subjective effectuation" (82).

Not only so, but setting aside for the moment verses 6–8 as a "Johannine intermezzo,"[58] verse 9 seems to be closely connected, terminologically and conceptually, to verses 4 and 5. The life, which was in the Logos and was the light of men (τὸ φῶς τῶν ἀνθρώπων), and which itself shines (φαίνει) in the darkness, is the selfsame *true* light (τὸ φῶς τὸ ἀληθινόν) who enlightens everyone (ὃ φωτίζει πάντα ἄνθρωπον). In other words, if the light *is* the light of men, even in the midst of the darkness of a sin-stained world, there can be little question, given John's use of the verb φωτίζω, that the true light actually *enlightens* everyone.

The flow of thought in verse 9, therefore, seems to be that this Logos of whom John has spoken so majestically, and who is the One who is life and light for every person, is himself, at the time of the Baptist's ministry, coming into the world. That is, the Logos is about to embark on a more specific, redemptive ministry in a way that has heretofore not been seen in the world. His "coming" is going to be a coming quite distinct from his universal presence and ministry, in that it will be a new and different "coming" into the world. We see, then, a connection, in verse 9, between the redemptive and the general, or cosmical, aspects of the activity of the Logos. "In other words, the purpose of the relative clause may well be to identify the redemptive light with the cosmical light." Furthermore, says Vos:

> If it be objected that such a specific reference to the φωτίζειν to natural revelation would have to be indicated in some way in order to be understood, we answer, that it is sufficiently indicated by the object πάντα ἄνθρωπον. A light of which it is said that it enlightens every man, is thereby clearly enough characterized as the general light which is common to the world as such. (82)

The most natural and obvious understanding of the relative clause, therefore, is that this true light *actually*, in terms of his *subjective* (not merely objective and potential) activity, enlightens everyone, even as the life that is in the Logos *is* the light of every person (vv. 4–5). Thus, there is a universal, *revelational*

---

[58]Ibid., 42.

activity attributed to the Logos prior to and apart from his appearance in the flesh.

The question that remains, for our purposes, concerning the general activity of the Logos, as John describes that activity in the prologue to his Gospel, is how specifically to understand his activity in verses 10 and 11 (since these verses, as we will see, are linked closely to v. 9). Two questions that need clarification in these verses are, what does John mean by "the world" (ὁ κόσμος) in verse 10 and, related to that, what does John mean when he says that the Logos came to "his own" (τὰ ἴδια, οἱ ἴδιοι) in verse 11? Is the apostle, in these two verses, referring to the Logos as incarnate, such that his activity in the world and among his own relates to his incarnation, or is John referring us to a more general, cosmic activity of the Logos (or both)?

John uses the word "world" seventy-eight times in his Gospel, far and away more than any other Gospel. Depending on context, it can mean the physical creation (e.g., 17:5), the mass of sinful humanity (e.g., 8:23; 15:18–19), or, as is often the case, the universe as it now resides under the curse of sin (e.g., 9:5; 12:48). Given the uniqueness of the prologue, in that the apostle sets out to affirm the cosmic activity of the Logos and to relate that activity to his now-new redemptive work as incarnate, we need to see how "world" is used in this section. Of the four uses in the prologue (vv. 9–10), we have already seen that, in verse 9, the apostle is affirming the incarnate coming of the Logos into the world at the time of the Baptist's ministry (which time, given John 11:27, would include the entirety of his earthly ministry as incarnate). As verse 9 tells us, the Logos, who is the universal light, is coming in a unique way (and, as stated in vv. 6–8, a uniquely *redemptive* way).

The point thus far, therefore, which should not be underestimated for its theological import, is that this Logos has been active and present since the time of creation, sustaining *and revealing* himself, but is now focusing his sustaining and revealing efforts in such a way that "his own" might be redeemed. *Without in any way undermining the uniqueness and once-for-all character of the incarnation, we should not think that, prior to his incarnation, the Logos has been inactive or absent from his creation, only to appear for the first time in these last days.* To be clear, he does appear only in these last days *as incarnate* (i.e., as taking on a human nature), but his incarnation is summarily his last, climactic act *in the world*, which itself prepares the way for the new, recreating activity of his Spirit *in the world* in these last days (cf. John 7:32–39).

Given this use of "world" in verse 9, how should we understand the three uses (of the four in the prologue) of "world" in verse 10? In order to see what the apostle is affirming here, we must also take account of what he says in verse 11, specifically the correlation between "the world" that did not know him (οὐκ ἔγνω), and his own (τὰ ἴδια, οἱ ἴδιοι) who did not receive him (οὐ παρέλαβον). There is obviously a parallel here between that which did not know him and those who did not receive him. But is John referring to the same entity in both cases? Is he simply saying the same thing in two different ways?

What is clear in these two verses is that John moves from the more general "the world" to the more specific "his own." The first question, then, is whether "the world" to which the Logos came as incarnate is what John refers to in verse 10, or is he referring again to the more general, cosmic, activity of the Logos in the world as his creation? Because verse 9 seems obviously to refer to the incarnate coming of the Logos, it could easily be inferred that the same subject—the incarnate Logos—is the subject of discussion in verse 10.

There are a couple of clues, however, that indicate that John is again bringing together the cosmic activity of the Logos with his redemptive work. First, John notes in verse 10 that the Logos *was* (ἦν) in the world. This verb points us back to the discussion of the Logos in verses 1–5. But why would John affirm in verse 9 that the Logos was coming into the world (ἐρχόμενον εἰς τὸν κόσμον), and then move backward, as it were, to affirm that he *was* in the world? It seems John wants us to understand that this world into which the Logos "was coming" in a uniquely redemptive way is the same world in which he already *was*, the same world, as John says in the next clause, that "was made through him." In other words, the clause that points us back to the creation of the world through the Logos interprets for us what John means and why he says that the Logos *was* in the world. He is telling us that this world to which the Logos is coming as incarnate is the world that he created, *in which he has always been present to reveal himself.*[59]

Not only so, but the more general indictment of the world in verse 10 itself points to the presence of the Logos in the world generally, in the context of a world of darkness, which darkness, John has already reminded us, has not apprehended (κατέλαβεν)[60] the Logos. When John tells us, therefore, that

---

[59]Note Bavinck's remarks: "It was the Son himself who immediately after the fall, as Logos and as Angel of the covenant, made the world of Gentiles and Jews ready for his coming. He was in the process of coming from the beginning of time and in the end came for good, by his incarnation making his home in man." Bavinck, *Reformed Dogmatics*, 3:280.

[60]Though we have not engaged the discussion over whether κατέλαβεν is best translated by "overcome" or by "apprehend," I take the verb in v. 5, κατέλαβεν, to be best translated as "apprehend," given that either translation is, by itself, legitimate. While "overcome" seems to be the standard translation (and is the translation preferred in the ESV), nevertheless, given what I have said concerning v. 10, and given its close correlation with v. 5, κατέλαβεν seems best understood as "apprehend." This is the translation also preferred by Vos: "Of the two

this world, as created by the Logos and in which the Logos *was*, did not know (οὐκ ἔγνω) the Logos, he is now reiterating more specifically how the world in darkness has responded to this pervasive and universal, enlightening presence of the Logos himself. That the world did not apprehend the Logos, even though his presence exhaustively permeates his creation and enlightens everyone, means at least in part that the world he created, because of the entrance of sin (darkness), in some sense did not know him.[61]

One final interpretive element remains: what does John mean in verse 11 when he becomes more specific with respect to the truths affirmed in verse 10? Not only was the Logos not known by the world, which was his own creation (v. 10), but now in verse 11 we see that his own, to which the Logos came, did not receive him. What, then, does John mean when he speaks of the Logos coming to "his own"?

According to Vos, the usage of ἴδιος (*idios*) settles nothing as to the import of verse 11 (86). Vos sees a close connection between the words ἴδια (*idia*) and ἴδιοι (*idioi*) in verse 11, and the clause "and the world was made through him" (καὶ ὁ κόσμος δι' αὐτοῦ ἐγένετο) in verse 10. "It is certainly most natural to assume that this latter clause prepares the way for and explains the characterization of those to whom the Logos came as His [own] ἴδιοι" (87).

To what, then, do the two terms translated "own" (ἴδια and ἴδιοι) refer? Do they refer to Israel, thus to the incarnate Christ? Or do they refer to the revelation of the Logos to the world he had made? Vos thinks the latter, and here his reasoning is subtle, as he believes is John's. Four points are adduced.

1. There is a close connection between the two terms (ἴδια and ἴδιοι) in verse 11 and the clause "and the world was made through him" in verse 10. We can assume that the clause in verse 10 prepares the way for and explains the characterization of those to whom the Logos came as his own (ἴδιοι) (87).

---

interpretations of κατέλαβεν that which takes it as "apprehended" in the noetic sense deserves the preference. Most of the Greek commentators take it in the other sense of "laying hold upon" for the purpose of getting in one's power. But this latter signification, which the verb undoubtedly has, falls quite short of the proposed rendering "overcame it not." . . . It is plain that the rendering "the darkness has not overtaken it," or even "the darkness has not laid hold upon it," introduces a weakening element into the context. The prelude to the tragic note of verses 10 and 11, which has been justly recognized in verse 5c, also speaks against this interpretation, while it is admirably expressed by the other." (77–78n27).
[61] According to Vos: "The issue between knowing and not-knowing naturally reminds us of the religion of nature and man's universal failure to apprehend the light supplied by the Logos" (87). The world, that is, everyone, knows the Logos, but everyone refuses to apprehend him. Or, to use Pauline terminology, everyone both knows (Rom. 1:20–21) and does not know (1 Thess. 4:5; 2 Thess. 1:8) God.

They were his own because he had made them. On the other view, which sees Israel as "his own," the terms emerge unprepared for and unexplained.

2. The pointed parallelism between "he was" (ἦν—v. 10) and "he came" (ἦλθεν—v. 11), on the one hand, and "did not know" (οὐκ ἔγνω—v. 10) and "did not receive" (οὐ παρέλαβον—v. 11), on the other hand, can best be seen as a parallelism between the Logos-relation to the natural world and the Logos-relation to the world of redemption. "Our point is that the delicately shaded contrast [between ἦν and ἦλθεν as indicating the lasting cosmical relationship and the redemptive approach as a unique historical event, respectively] perceptible in the use of these two words by the Evangelist is obliterated by the other exegesis [i.e., the exegesis that sees ἴδια and ἴδιοι as Israel]" (87). The same applies to οὐκ ἔγνω and οὐ παρέλαβον.

> The issue between knowing and not knowing naturally reminds us of the religion of nature and man's universal failure to apprehend the light supplied by the Logos. On the other hand, the issue between receiving and not receiving points to a definite, historical act on the part of the Logos [not the incarnate Christ] *whereby he aggressively made his appearance among those who were his own.* (87, my emphasis)

3. In the presence of the highly generalized contrast between nature and redemption that furnishes the keynote to the prologue, the appearance of Israel here would be more or less anomalous (88).

4. Finally:

> The view which understands verse 10 of the presence of the incarnate Logos in the world and verse 11 of His coming to Israel encounters a difficulty when the last clauses of both verses are to be explained as marking two successive and distinctive steps in the ill-reception of the Logos. . . . How or where did the world reject the incarnate Christ, apart from His not being received by Israel? The clearly perceptible climax in the tragic note as between verse 10c and verse 11c requires that the two clauses shall not be related to the same thing. . . . Two distinct failures to appreciate the Logos, by two distinct subjects and two distinct relations are spoken of. (88)

So, given verses 10–11, we have a "twofold addition to the evidence for a cosmical Logos-function already discovered" (89). The Logos was by nature in the world made through him, and the cosmos is the Logos's own; it is his. The production of the world through the Logos is not simply a past fact. "It is a fact resulting in a continuous relationship, for only as such could it offer a reason why the world could and should, under normal conditions, have so known and received the Logos as is implied in both verse 10c and verse 11c" (89).[62] The world would know the Logos, not by creation in and of itself, but "only if the origin of the world through the Logos established *a perpetual relation of immanence* in the world and proprietorship of the world" (89, my emphasis).

But it may be that there is a way to think of the progression of verses 10 and 11 as having a logical, historical, and theological impetus. Perhaps we could think of the progression this way: the Logos, who made the world and whose the world is, not only made the world, but actually was in the world that he made, revealing himself and coming to his own. Given the darkness of sin, however, the world did not acknowledge him for who he is. Not only so, but though he came to a world that is his (τὰ ἴδια), even his own people (οἱ ἴδιοι) did not receive him.

Enough has been said to make at least the following assertions: (1) The Logos, who himself as the second person of the Trinity, always was with God and always was God, created all that is and *has been making himself known since the time of creation*. (2) Given the entrance of sin, the light of men, which is to say the knowledge of the Logos that has been given to all men, has been received by men, though never, since the entrance of sin, apprehended by them apart from a gracious act of God. Thus, God is both known (because the Logos who made man also enlightens him with such knowledge) and not known (because the power of sin is such that man will not apprehend the Logos as he reveals himself). The light that characterizes who man is—which is actual knowledge of God by and through the Logos—has never, since sin entered the world, been acknowledged by men who remain in their sins. (3) Even as the Logos has made himself known to all men, he has as well come to his own, and they too have rejected him. Thus, as the apostle will set forth in the rest of this Gospel, the Logos has come to be the light to those who continue to live in darkness. The "life and light" has come to be "light and life" to those who have not apprehended but have rejected him. As John will go on to say (v. 12), those who do receive him, who believe in his name, have the right to become children of God, since they themselves are born of God.

Thus, what we have in the prologue to John's Gospel is an affirmation, not only of the universal *creative* activity of the second person of the Trinity, but—important for our particular concerns—of the universal *revealing* activity of the Logos since the time of creation. John's point seems to be that the

---

[62]Note, as Vos points out, the adversative καὶ before both clauses in vv. 10c and 11c.

world into which the Logos came as incarnate is the world in which the Logos has always been revealing himself, to the world and to his own people. The coming of the Logos in the flesh was not, therefore, some kind of revelational *surprise*, unprepared for or unheard of, especially by the Lord's own people. As Jesus himself said, any faithful understanding of Moses would have rendered his appearance in the flesh as something awaited and now fulfilled, not as something completely out of the blue (see John 5:46).

(2) The Angel of the Covenant

According to Herman Bavinck:

> The whole revelation of God is concentrated in the Logos, who became "flesh" and is, as it were, *one single act of self-humanization*, the incarnation of God. If God were to speak to us in a divine language, not a creature would understand him. But what spells out his grace is the fact that *from the moment of creation God stoops down to his creatures*, speaking and appearing to them in human fashion.[63]

Bavinck is here affirming what we have seen the prologue to John's Gospel affirming as well.[64] The Logos—the second person of the Trinity—is described here as acting to reveal God in "one single act of self-humanization." That is to say, the incarnation is the pinnacle and climax of a *process* of God's revealing himself since the time of creation. This is what we have learned from John's prologue. However, and this point again cannot be overemphasized, the incarnation is *sui generis* in God's activity of self-revelation. There is nothing identical to it and nothing so complete and completely suited for God's redemptive and revelatory purposes. But, even as *sui generis*, the incarnation of the Son of God is not without its precedents and prior signals in redemptive history. This is Bavinck's point above. God began the process of revealing himself via the Logos "from the moment of creation." That process

---

[63]Herman Bavinck, *Reformed Dogmatics*, vol. 2, *God and Creation*, ed. John Bolt, trans. John Vriend (Grand Rapids: Baker Academic, 2004), 100, my emphases.

[64]Elsewhere Bavinck notes: "The world itself rests on revelation; revelation is the presupposition, the foundation, the secret of all that exists in all its forms. . . . In every moment of time beats the pulse of eternity; every point in space is filled with the omnipresence of God; the finite is supported by the infinite, all becoming is rooted in being. Together with all created things, that special revelation which comes to us in the Person of Christ is built on these presuppositions. The foundations of creation and redemption are the same. The Logos who became flesh is the same by whom all things were made. The first-born from the dead is also the first-born of every creature. The Son, whom the Father made heir of all things, is the same by whom he also made the worlds." Herman Bavinck, *The Philosophy of Revelation* (Grand Rapids: Baker, 1979), 27–28.

culminates in "the Son," who is "the radiance of the glory of God and the exact imprint of his nature" (Heb. 1:2–3). As we have seen, this language in Hebrews implies a strict identity of the Son with God himself.

This identity is perhaps nowhere more explicitly stated by the Savior himself than in John 8: "So the Jews said to him, 'You are not yet fifty years old, and have you seen Abraham?' Jesus said to them, 'Truly, truly, I say to you, *before Abraham was, I am.*' So they picked up stones to throw at him, but Jesus hid himself and went out of the temple" (vv. 57–59).

There can be little doubt that Jesus uses *ego eimi* (ἐγὼ εἰμί) in this passage to identify himself clearly as the One who appeared to Moses on the mountain (in Exodus 3) and who gave himself the name of Yahweh.[65] According to Raymond Brown, "no clearer implication of divinity is found in the Gospel tradition."[66] The implication of Jesus's words becomes all the more clear when we see that the Jews, upon hearing these words, picked up stones to throw at him. It was obvious to them that he had blasphemed by making himself out to be Yahweh himself. Calvin recognizes this identity of the Son of God in Exodus 3.

> Therefore, although at that time, properly speaking, he was not yet the messenger of his Father, still his predestinated appointment to the office even then had this effect, *that he manifested himself to the patriarchs, and was known in this character. Nor, indeed, had the saints ever any communication with God except through the promised Mediator.* It is not then to be wondered at, if the Eternal Word of God, of one Godhead and essence with the Father, assumed the name of "the Angel" on the ground of his future mission.[67]

Even more strongly, in his comments on Acts 7:30, Calvin says:

---

[65]Note, for example, "For Poole, as for a majority of the seventeenth-century orthodox exegetes, the determinative text is Exodus 3:2–6, and the others are read in terms of their relationship to it. At verse 2, Poole comments that 'the Angel of the Lord' is clearly 'not a created angel but the angle of the covenant, Christ Jesus, who then and ever was God, and was to be man, and to be sent in the world in our flesh.'" Then, in a footnote to this, Muller notes, "And note Ainsworth, Annotations upon Exodus, Ex. 3:2 in loc., citing rabbinic exegesis to the effect that the Angle of the Lord is the Redeemer.'" Richard A. Muller, *Post-Reformation Reformed Dogmatics: The Rise and Development of Reformed Orthodoxy, ca. 1520 to ca. 1725*, vol. 4, *The Triunity of God*, 2nd ed. (Grand Rapids: Baker, 2003), 315.

[66]Raymond E. Brown, *The Gospel According to John I–XII*, Anchor Bible Series (Garden City, NY: Doubleday, 1966), 194.

[67]Commentary on Exodus 3 in John Calvin, *The Comprehensive John Calvin Collection*, CD ed., The Ages Digital Library System, 2002.

Therefore, let us, first of all, set down this for a surety, *that there was never since the beginning any communication between God and men, save only by Christ*; for we have nothing to do with God, unless the Mediator be present to purchase his favor for us. Therefore, this place doth plentifully prove the divinity of Christ, and teacheth that he is of the same essence with the Father. Furthermore, he is called an angel, not only because he had the angels always to bear him company, and to be, as it were, his apparitors [aids]: but because that deliverance of the people did shadow the redemption of us all, for whose sake Christ was to be sent of his Father, that he might take upon him the shape of a servant together with our flesh. It is certain, indeed, *that God did never appear unto men as he is, but under some shape agreeable to their capacity*; notwithstanding, there is another reason why Christ is called by this name, because he being appointed by the eternal counsel of God to be unto men the minister of salvation, doth appear unto Moses to this end.[68]

So, according to Calvin, the saints throughout covenant history never had any communication with God except through the second person of the Trinity, who condescended to reveal himself.[69] Bavinck states the same: "It was the Son himself who immediately after the fall, as Logos and as Angel of the covenant, made the world of Gentiles and Jews ready for his coming. *He was in the process of coming from the beginning of time and in the end came for good, by his incarnation making his home in man.*"[70]

We should recognize that there is a strong and persistent tradition in orthodox theology that sees the condescension of God in the Old Testament as appearances of the second person of the Trinity. As Calvin argues:

The orthodox doctors of the church have rightly and prudently interpreted that chief angel to be God's Word, who already at that time, as a sort of foretaste, began to fulfill the office of Mediator. For even though he was not yet clothed with flesh, he came down, so to speak, as an intermediary, in order to approach believers more intimately. *Therefore this closer intercourse gave him the name of angel. Meanwhile, what was his he retained*, that as God he might be of ineffable glory.[71]

---

[68]Commentary on Acts 7:30 in ibid.
[69]In his commentary on Genesis 48:16 (ibid.), Calvin also notes, "He had not yet indeed been sent by the Father, to approach more nearly to us by taking our flesh, but because he was always the bond of connection between God and man, and because God formally manifested himself in no other way than through him, he is properly called the Angel."
[70]Bavinck, *Reformed Dogmatics*, 2:280, my emphasis.
[71]Calvin, *Institutes*, 1.13.10, my emphasis.

To cite one example of the "orthodox doctors" whom Calvin has in mind, Ambrose, commenting on John 8:56ff., says:

> Otherwise, if our adversaries will understand this passage as referred to the Father, then the rest of the record does not agree with it. For the Father did not appear to Abraham, nor did Abraham wash the feet of God the Father, but the feet of Him in Whom is the image of the man that shall be. Moreover, the Son of God saith, "Abraham saw My day, and rejoiced." It is He, therefore, Who sware by Himself, [and] Whom Abraham saw.[72]

Not only so, but Ambrose also argues that it was the Logos who appeared to Moses on the mountain.

> This is the God of Abraham, the God of Isaac, the God of Jacob, Who appeared to Moses in the bush, concerning Whom Moses saith, "He Who is hath sent me." It was not the Father Who spake to Moses in the bush or in the desert, but the Son. It was of this Moses that Stephen said, "This is He Who was in the church, in the wilderness, with the Angel." This, then, is He Who gave the Law, Who spake with Moses, saying, "I am the God of Abraham, the God of Isaac, the God of Jacob." This, then, is the God of the patriarchs, this is the God of the prophets.[73]

We will need to say more in the coming chapter concerning this revelation of God, but we cannot avoid the obvious implication of our study thus far. The implication is this: if in fact the revelation of God in covenant history is accomplished via the Logos, the second person of the Trinity, then the quintessential revelation of God in Christ becomes our guide as we attempt to understand and interpret God's interaction with, and relation to, creation. More specifically, could it be that the way in which Christ interacts with the world to which he comes in the flesh forms the proper, biblical ground upon which we understand his interaction with the world from the beginning and into eternity?

What begins to emerge from our study in christology, in other words, is that, given the full deity of the second person of the Trinity, and given his status as the One through whom everything was made, and given his triune commission to be the One who reveals God, it seems our understanding of "God revealed" should find its focus in God's condescension by way of the

---

[72]Ambrose, "Exposition of the Christian Faith," bk. 2, chap. 8, in Philip Schaff, *The Nicene and Post-Nicene Fathers*, Series 2, vol. 10 (Oak Harbor, WA: Logos Research Systems, 1997).
[73]Ibid.

Logos, culminating in the "Logos-in-the-flesh," God with us, Emmanuel, the Lord Jesus Christ. We shall look at this in more detail in the next chapter. First, one more note of clarification is in order.

F. One for All and All for One

It might be argued, given our investigation of the revelation of God as it finds its focus in the second person of the Trinity, that it is *only* the second person of the Trinity who is revealed to us. This would be a natural, perhaps even logical, consequence of the conclusions we have thus far reached. If the revelation of God is by way of the Son, then surely it is the Son of God who is revealed.

It should not be thought, however, that, because the Son of God is revealed, *only* the Son of God is revealed in that revelation. This, it would seem, was Philip's mistake.

> Philip said to him, "Lord, show us the Father, and it is enough for us." Jesus said to him, "Have I been with you so long, and you still do not know me, Philip? Whoever has seen me has seen the Father. How can you say, 'Show us the Father'? Do you not believe that I am in the Father and the Father is in me?" (John 14:8–10)

Philip failed to understand that the revelation of the Son was itself a revelation of the Father.

Given the essential unity of the Godhead, when one person of the Godhead is revealed, *God himself* is revealed, even in his triunity. Historically, distinctions have been made between the *actions* of the three persons of the Trinity and the *works* of the triune God.[74] We can think of God's *actions* as being distinguished among the three persons—the Father sends the Son, for example—whereas, the *works* of God allow no such division. Thus, John Owen, in his work on the Holy Spirit, affirms:

> It is a saying generally admitted, that *Opera Trinitatis ad extra sunt indivisa* [The external works of the Trinity are indivisible]. There is no such division in the external operations of God that any one of them should be the act of one person, without the concurrence of the others; and the reason of it is, because

---

[74]We need not discuss further Trinitarian distinctions such as God's actions and works *ad intra* as distinguished from his actions and works *ad extra*. Our focus here will be on God's activity *ad extra*.

the nature of God, which is the principle of all divine operations, is one and the same, undivided in them all.[75]

This affirmation of the unity of God's works does not at all mean that all three persons actually *did* the exact same external works. It does not mean, for example, that Father, Son, and Holy Spirit all assumed a human nature. The affirmation that the external works of the Trinity are indivisible means, rather, that it is *God*, and not simply one person of the Godhead, who acts in redemption.

> This trinitarian argument leads to a distinction between incarnation as the common work (*opus commune*) of all persons in the Trinity which terminates in the person of the Son and the assumption of human nature, which, in a restrictive sense, is the personal work of the Son alone. *Inchoatively*, the incarnation is a common work of the divine persons but *terminatively* it is the work of the Son. In this latter sense, incarnation is the *opus proprium* [proper work] of the Son, a personal rather than an essential work, not a common but an economical or dispensative work (*opus oeconomicum*). Similarly, if the one divine substance is incarnate, it is nevertheless true that it is not the divine nature *simpliciter* that is incarnate but the *natura divina determinata in Filio, id est, hypostasis seu persona Filii* ["the particular divine nature in the Son, that is, the hypostasis or person of the Son"].[76]

Given that each of the three persons is fully and completely God, any revelation of one of the persons is, *ipso facto*, a revelation of God himself, rather than a revelation only of the person. That revelation of God has its focus in one person, but is not thereby truncated or simply "confined" to the person.[77]

---

[75]Owen, *Works*, 3:202.

[76]Richard A. Muller, *Christ and the Decree: Christology and Predestination in Reformed Theology from Calvin to Perkins* (Durham, NC: Labyrinth, 1986), 137. The point here is not that the divine nature of the Son is in any way different from that of the Father or the Spirit; quite the opposite. The point is that the one God is revealed as the one God, but is revealed in and through the person of the Son, rather than of the Father or the Spirit.

[77]Some arguments have been offered in the history of theology to the effect that if it is the Son who is incarnate and not the Father, the Son must be of a different essence than the Father. This logic may hold true for things created, in that such things can be different instantiations of a universal "essence," but no such thing is possible with the triune God. So, says, Muller: "The argument . . . does not apply to the infinite, simple, and individual essence of the Godhead: for here is a single essence or substance that cannot be separated or divided, but in which there are distinct incommunicable properties, three in number that identify distinct, but not essentially separate hypostases. Identity of essence in no way implies the removal of variations or distinctions. Thus, the one divine essence is incarnate, but only in one of its hypostases or persons." Muller, *Post-Reformation Reformed Dogmatics*, 4:211.

This basic theological principle with respect to the Trinity has its impetus in what could easily be the brightest of the golden threads running through all of Scripture—the name of God as Yahweh. As we have seen, this name is used over five thousand times in the Old Testament. As such, it is meant to define and determine everything else that is said and is meant to be a reminder of who God is as "I AM." What is most striking about this name in the New Testament (though it may be so familiar to us that its majesty is muted) is that it is attributed to Jesus Christ.

In this context we should mention the advance made by Calvin and others with respect to the full and unequivocal deity of Jesus Christ, the Son of God.[78] Calvin was concerned that the phrase "God of God [θεός ἐκ θεοῦ], Light of Light, very God of very God" as articulated in the Nicene Creed could too easily imply that the Son's *deity* is from his Father. While there can be no question that the Son's *sonship* is derived from his Father—that is, that his personal properties are dependent on the personal properties of the Father—it is illegitimate to move from that to a notion that the Son's deity was anything less than *a se*. His deity, like that of the other persons of the Trinity, was from himself, and not from the Father.[79] So, says Calvin:

> And they [opponents of this doctrine] will not benefit at all by another evasion, that Christ was God in his Father. For even though we admit that in respect to order and degree the beginning of divinity is in the Father, yet we say that it is a detestable invention that essence is proper to the Father alone, as if he were the deifier of the Son. For in this way either essence would be manifold or they call Christ "God" in title and imagination only. If they grant that the Son is God, but second to the Father, then in him will be begotten and formed the essence that is in the Father unbegotten and unformed.[80]

It is not the case, then, according to Calvin, that the Son has his deity from the Father. With respect to the Son's deity, he is *a se* or *autotheos* (αὐτόθεος). Of course, as Calvin notes of a certain order in the Godhead (which is not a hierarchy of being), the Father is first, but not as to deity. Father, Son, and Spirit are all three *autotheos*. In this same context, Calvin counters antagonists: "But they are obviously deceived in this connection, for they dream of individuals, each having its own separate part of the essence. Yet

---

[78]For a fuller exposition of what follows, see, "Calvin's Doctrine of the Trinity," in Benjamin Breckinridge Warfield, *Calvin and Augustine* (Philadelphia: Presbyterian and Reformed, 1974).
[79]This was, according to Warfield, in contrast to Valentine Gentilis, who was insisting that only the Father's deity could be *a se*, only the Father was αὐτόθεος.
[80]Calvin, *Institutes*, 1.13.24.

we teach from the Scriptures that God is one in essence, and hence that the essence both of the Son and of the Spirit is unbegotten."[81] So, for Calvin, the one essence of God is not distinguished among the three persons. Charles Hodge quotes him:

> "If the distinction between the Father and the Word be attentively considered, we shall say that the one is from the other. If, however, the essential quality of the Word be considered, in so far as He is one God with the Father, whatever can be said concerning God may also be applied to Him the Second Person in the glorious Trinity. Now, what is the meaning of the name Jehovah? What did that answer imply that was spoken to Moses? I AM THAT I AM. Paul makes Christ the author of this saying." This argument is conclusive.[82]

It is necessary for us, as we think through the implications of christology for theology proper, to adopt Calvin's (and the subsequent Reformed) emphasis on the absolute aseity of the Son (and the Spirit). Without that affirmation, the assertion of the Savior that he is "I AM" cannot be maintained and sustained for what it is. Jesus is the "I AM," the *a se* God. He is Yahweh.

As a matter of fact, the most primitive confession of the church in the New Testament is that "Jesus is Lord" (cf. 1 Cor. 12:3). To make that confession is not simply to say that he is the One who rules heaven and earth, though it is certainly saying that. To say that Jesus is Lord is also to say that the One who names himself in Exodus 3:14, who is revealed throughout the Old Testament, who is himself self-complete, has a revelatory focus in the One who has assumed a human nature. That is, by the time we get to the revelation of Jesus Christ in the New Testament, it becomes clear that this Yahweh, of whom the entire covenant history speaks, is the same One who is the Son of God now come in the flesh.

This is the focus of Paul's christological argument in Philippians 2:5–11. As we have already seen, Paul gives us, in the beginning of this passage, a magnificent description of what it means for the Son of God to have taken on the "form of a servant." The humiliation of this gracious act finds its *telos* in the glorious exaltation of verses 9–11: "Therefore God has highly exalted him and bestowed on him the name that is above every name, so that at the name of Jesus every knee should bow, in heaven and on earth and under the earth, and every tongue confess that Jesus Christ is Lord, to the glory of

---

[81]Ibid., 1.13.25.
[82]*Calvin's Letters* (Philadelphia: Presbyterian Board), 1:55–56, quoted in Charles Hodge, *Systematic Theology*, 3 vols. (London: James Clarke, 1960), 1:467.

God the Father." The point that Paul is making here is *not* that the name of Jesus *simpliciter* will be the cause of the bowing of every knee on that day. As Calvin says, "But worse than ridiculous is the conduct of the Sorbonnic sophists, who infer from the passage before us that we ought to bow the knee whenever the name of Jesus is pronounced, as though it were a magic word which had all virtue included in the sound of it."[83] In other words, the name of Jesus itself holds no intrinsic power or worth. Rather, the impetus behind Paul's point is that this Jesus is himself Yahweh, and he has now accomplished his redemptive work.[84]

For this reason, just to cite one more example, Peter can quote from Isaiah 8:13, which is a clear reference to Yahweh, and apply it to Jesus Christ. Note the two passages.

> Do not fear what they fear, nor be in dread. But the LORD of hosts, him you shall honor as holy. (Isa. 8:12–13)

> Have no fear of them, nor be troubled, but in your hearts honor Christ the Lord as holy. (1 Pet. 3:14–15)

Peter, under the inspiration of the Holy Spirit, interprets Isaiah 8:13 for the church by claiming its referent to be "Christ the Lord," the One who was announced to the shepherds on the day of his birth: "For unto you is born this day in the city of David a Savior, who is Christ the Lord" (Luke 2:11).

References of this sort could easily be multiplied (compare Isa. 40:3 with Mark 1:3; Ps. 107:28 with Mark 4:35–41; Deut. 31:8 with Heb. 13:5; Isa. 8:13–14 with Rom. 9:33; Isa. 45:20–25 with Rom. 14:11). The radical nature of this ascription of this most holy name of God to Jesus Christ not only shows us the *status* of Christ, but also displays before us the seamless way in which God has revealed himself throughout covenant history. The One who condescends in the Old Testament is the same One who condescends,

---

[83]Comment on Phil. 2:11 in Calvin, *Comprehensive John Calvin Collection.*

[84]It is necessary to remember some distinctions that cannot be developed here. There is no question that much of the New Testament ascribes lordship to Christ in light of his accomplished redemptive acts. This is undoubtedly Paul's meaning in Phil. 2:11 (see also, e.g., Acts 2:36). The lordship of Christ is a declaration of his completed work. However, neither should we lose sight of the fact, seen clearly in John 8:58, that this redemptive lordship presupposes the full deity of the Son as Yahweh. So, any declaration of *lordship* with respect to Christ and his work can have its meaning only in the context of his identity as the "I AM." To put it another way, any contingency, such as Christ's rule over creation, must presuppose his essential deity as the *a se* Lord—Yahweh.

definitively and uniquely, in the person of Jesus Christ, in order finally and climactically (this side of the second coming) to reveal himself to us.

G. Conclusion

We have covered a good bit of theological territory in this chapter. It may be helpful to summarize the central points, in that those points will be the foundation on which our next chapter will be built.

I have affirmed that it was and is the second person of the Trinity *through whom* creation was made and *through whom all* mediation between God and man has since taken place. As we move from "the beginning" forward to the time of the incarnation, we have seen that, in taking on a human nature, the Son of God in no way denied or gave up his deity.[85] Rather, the same person, in taking on a human nature, remained *one person* who himself possessed two natures without any confusion, division, change, or separation (Chalcedonian Creed). The two natures were not confused by the assuming of a human nature, neither were they divided in the one person. They were not changed, in that neither the divine nature (which is essential to the Logos) nor the human nature (freely assumed) became anything other than what each nature is. Neither were the natures separated such that two persons were required.

It is legitimate, therefore, in that Scripture itself does this, to ascribe the properties of either nature to the one person. Further clarifications and qualifications are, of course, legitimate as well. The Lord himself says that he does not know the time of his own coming (Matt. 24:36; Mark 13:32), but that the Father does. Given what we have discussed about the *extra*, we must affirm that this agnosticism has its focus in the human nature assumed, and not in the divine nature, in that the latter is necessarily omniscient. This does not make the statement any less "literal"; it only shows that what we have in the person of Christ is a *mysterious* unity, a unity in which there can be real ignorance together with exhaustive knowledge.

And here we must remind ourselves of our previous discussion of antinomy. In the one person of Christ, there is an apparent antinomy in that the rules and boundaries intrinsic to humanity—e.g., limited knowledge—seem to be in direct conflict with the necessary aseity of the Son. This antinomy

---

[85]"Even the incarnation does not indicate a change in God, inasmuch as the Logos was incarnate by 'conversion' into flesh—rather the flesh was assumed by the person or hypostasis of the Word, as God eternally willed." Richard A. Muller, *Post-Reformation Reformed Dogmatics: The Rise and Development of Reformed Orthodoxy, ca. 1520 to ca. 1725*, vol. 3, *The Divine Essence and Attributes*, 2nd ed. (Grand Rapids: Baker Academic, 2003), 317.

is resolved in the Godhead alone. We dare not minimize it for the sake of attempting a more thorough understanding of how the mind of One who is both essentially divine and contingently, covenantally human could work. This antinomy surely results in paradoxical statements—statements such as "The Lord of glory was crucified" (1 Cor. 2:8)—but that is as it should be, given the wondrous mystery that is the incarnation.

In anticipation of coming discussions, we also noted that the revelation of God has, from the beginning, come to us by way of the Logos, the second person of the Trinity, the Son of God. He was the One who appeared to Moses and the prophets, and it was through him that God, who had condescended to them, was revealed. In this revelation, however, it was not the unique properties or character of the specific *person* of the Godhead that was revealed, but it was *God himself* whom the Logos revealed. The Logos was not acting simply as the second person of the Trinity; he was acting as the one God. Thus, the Son of God condescending *is* the condescension of God.

Alert readers will likely be able to see where we are going from here. I could hint at our coming discussions by way of some questions that relate directly to the subject matter of this chapter, questions that also are relevant to the entirety of our subject, "God with us." Some of those questions would be:

1. Can we see the various ascriptions of God throughout Scripture as analogous to those of Christ?
2. Is there an *extra* aspect to the entirety of God-as-revealed throughout Scripture?
3. May we employ the reduplicative strategy, together with the Reformed notion of the *communicatio idiomatum*, in order better to understand why Scripture seems to attribute different and seemingly contradictory properties to God?
4. Could it be that the four Chalcedonian categories—without confusion, change, division, or separation—can also be applied to God as condescended throughout covenant history?

I will broach these questions in the next chapter and argue for an affirmative answer to each. In doing so, we will not be straying from the traditional Reformed understanding of who God is. I will, however, attempt to add something to that understanding that may shed more light on other concerns about God's character discussed in the history of theology proper.

CHAPTER 4

(The Son of) God with Us

All praise to Thee, eternal God,
Who, clothed in garb of flesh and blood,
Dost take a manger for Thy throne,
While worlds on worlds are Thine alone.
Hallelujah!

MARTIN LUTHER

It remains for us in this chapter to begin to tie together all that we have previously discussed regarding the Son of God in relation to theology proper. Specifically, given our affirmation of God's aseity and all that aseity entails, how can our understanding of christology help us to articulate a biblical understanding of God's relationship to creation?

Given what we have thus far said about biblical christology, the primary "hermeneutic" for understanding the relationship of God to the world is to look to Christ himself, so that we understand God's relationship to the world, first, by understanding the biblical teaching on the person of Christ.

Before we move on to apply what we have discussed thus far to God in his condescension, a couple of points need to be remembered. First, no orthodox theology denies that before anything was created, there was God. This should be obvious. Given the distinction I have already articulated between the *Eimi* and the *eikon*, and given that those two categories exhaust all that is, before there was anything created—anything that was *eikon*—there was only God, the *Eimi*.

Since that is true, it follows that God was *a se*. That is, he exists, and existed, in and of himself. Since there *was* nothing else before creation, it would be impossible for God to be dependent in any way prior to creation. This much should be easily affirmed. Prior to his creating activity, God existed as a complete and perfect Being. He lacked nothing, and there was nothing on which he depended in order to be who he essentially is, the triune God.

Second, when we look at God's condescension throughout Scripture, certain things are beyond controversy. First, there can be no question that God appears to his people from the beginning. These appearances of God entail that he is making himself known by way of properties and qualities that would otherwise not belong to him.[1]

To refer again to one example: it seems clear that, whatever else is going on in Exodus 3 with respect to God and his appearance to Moses, the Lord appears to Moses "in a flame of fire out of the midst of the bush." The One who appears, as we have seen, is first called "the angel of the LORD" and subsequently simply "the LORD." The fire in the bush is *not* the appearance of Yahweh; rather, it is the context in which Yahweh's messenger, his angel, appears. This angel of Yahweh who speaks from the midst of the bush is called "God" by Christ himself (Mark 12:26).

Or as we see later on, in Exodus 33 Yahweh descends in a cloud and stands with Moses. He passes by Moses so that Moses can see only his back, and he declares his name and his character to Moses again. This One who passes by Moses is Yahweh himself, and he has taken on certain created properties in order that Moses might meet with him, see him, and worship him there.

So, given these two aspects of God's activity—his character *as God* and his character *as God in relation to creation*—we can begin to see in Scripture just how God both remains who he is and interacts with his creation as he sovereignly guides, directs, and controls it. As we have just seen in the previ-

---

[1] To be clear here, I am *not* saying that once God created, he determined to be essentially what he was not prior to creation. That God determined himself to be essentially different seems to be the point that Neil MacDonald wants to stress, following Karl Barth. MacDonald's view of condescension is by way of God's *self*-determination, such that God does indeed essentially change. This view, again consistent with Barth and thus not orthodox, sees God's freedom as ultimate and, we should note, quite arbitrary. See Neil B. MacDonald, *Metaphysics and the God of Israel: Systematic Theology of the Old and New Testaments* (Grand Rapids: Baker Academic, 2007).

ous chapter, the supreme example of this interaction is found in the second person of the Trinity.

A. Christology Guides Theology Proper

Because the person of Christ is the quintessential example of God's remaining who he is essentially, even in his interaction with creation, we would do well to think carefully about how our understanding of Christ's person helps us to see what is taking place throughout covenant history as God relates to his human creatures.

Briefly put, explanations of God's interaction with creation have tended in one of two directions. Either God gives up aspects of his essential character and is, thereby, essentially constrained by his creation, or those passages in Scripture that indicate constraint or limitation in God as he interacts with creation are metaphorical or somehow "improper."[2]

Neither of these tendencies allows the proper, gospel emphasis of Scripture to shine. The first option detracts from the glory of God in that man, and not God, becomes the sovereign in his own affairs. Because God is thought to have given up something of his "Godness," it is man, not God, who determines by virtue of his own choice just what happens. Man is thought to be self-determining; God, therefore, cannot be sovereign. Neither can he be omniscient, nor omnipotent. Exactly which essential attributes are thought to be forsaken by God depends on how radically free man is thought to be. Whatever the case, God has to give up something of who he is essentially in order for man to be free.

The second option seems akin to theological docetism, in which Scripture's ascription of God's interaction with creation is relegated to an *appearance* of such interaction, rather than something that really takes place. In attempting to avoid both of these tendencies, we will take what we have learned thus far and apply it to our understanding of God throughout covenant history.

B. Both/And

We may begin with a quotation from a book promoting Arminian theology.

---

[2]E.g., "There is a sense in which (certainly according to the orthodox doctrine of Scripture and its interpretation) Scripture itself 'confirms' the conclusion that affections are only improperly or figuratively predicated of God—'when it says in one place that which really does not belong to God which it ascribes to him in another.'" Richard A. Muller, *Post-Reformation Reformed Dogmatics: The Rise and Development of Reformed Orthodoxy, ca. 1520 to ca. 1725*, vol. 3, *The Divine Essence and Attributes*, 2nd ed. (Grand Rapids: Baker Academic, 2003), 558.

A great deal hangs on whether God is portrayed as an all-determining Power who gets glory even from the damnation of sinners or as a compassionate Lover who enters into the struggles of his significantly free creatures. The writers of this book contend that it makes the difference between having good news or having bad news to offer people whether we start with God's goodness or with his power. Does God love the people next door or has God perhaps excluded them from salvation? Do our choices make any difference or have they been preprogramed from the beginning? Did God devise all the evil in the world or is there something limiting his sovereignty?[3]

A slight paraphrase will help us discern the false dichotomy expressed here. We need only rephrase a few words, but with the central figure being Christ rather than "God."

A great deal hangs on whether Christ is portrayed as an all-determining Power who derives glory even from the condemnation of sinners or as a compassionate Lover who enters into the struggles of his creatures. . . . Does Christ love the people next door or has Christ perhaps excluded them from salvation? Do our choices make any difference or have they been planned from the beginning? Does Christ control all the evil in the world or is there something limiting his sovereignty?

When we rephrase things this way, some of the tensions produced by the questions and statements take on a different tone. Given what we have seen about the incarnation, it should be no intellectual stretch to affirm that Christ is, in fact, "an all-determining Power" as well as a "compassionate Lover." Not only so, but we need not pose a dichotomy that Christ himself does not see. For example, note how Jesus describes himself and his ministry.

I thank you, Father, Lord of heaven and earth, that you have hidden these things from the wise and understanding and revealed them to little children; yes, Father, for such was your gracious will. All things have been handed over to me by my Father, and no one knows the Son except the Father, and no one knows the Father except the Son and anyone to whom the Son chooses to reveal him. (Matt. 11:25–27)

Clearly, Jesus is praising his Father for the sovereignty he exercises in salvation. As Calvin says of this passage, "That some arrive at faith, while

---

[3]Clark H. Pinnock, in *The Grace of God, the Will of Man*, ed. Pinnock (Grand Rapids: Academie, 1989), ix–x.

others remain hardened and obstinate, is accomplished by his free election; for, drawing some, and passing by others, he alone makes a distinction among men, whose condition by nature is alike."[4] Jesus is thanking God, his heavenly Father, for the fact of his sovereign character. This does not, however, cause Jesus to be casual or in any way apathetic about the necessity of a general call to repentance and faith. Immediately after he gives thanks to his Father for his sovereign electing purposes, Jesus says to the crowd: "Come to me, all who labor and are heavy laden, and I will give you rest. Take my yoke upon you, and learn from me, for I am gentle and lowly in heart, and you will find rest for your souls. For my yoke is easy, and my burden is light" (Matt. 11:28–30).

We shall return to this in the next chapter, but for now we should note that there is no incoherence in the Savior's mind between God's electing purposes, on the one hand, and the responsibility of all to come to Christ, on the other. These two truths are united in the one great plan of the triune God for the salvation of his people, and the regeneration of all things.

In order to articulate the synthesis between the christology we noted in the previous chapter and the issues of tension that abound in theology proper, we need to ask, Can we apply, with certain qualifiers, all that we have discussed concerning christology to theology proper—that is, to our understanding of God himself as he relates to creation?

(1) Theology Proper and Proper Communication

More specifically, we could ask, Is there a (preincarnate) *communicatio idiomatum* with respect to God as condescended? That is, are properties of both deity and humanity ascribed to God prior to the incarnation? Compare the following two examples:

> And the LORD relented from the disaster that he had spoken of bringing on his people. (Ex. 32:14)

> For I the LORD do not change. (Mal. 3:6)

Remember that the *communicatio*, as we have discussed it, requires not that the properties of one constituent part be communicated to the other (as in Lutheran theology), but that properties of either be properly ascribed

---

[4]Commentary on Matthew 11:25ff. in John Calvin, *The Comprehensive John Calvin Collection*, CD ed., The Ages Digital Library System, 2002.

to the (one) person. Though we need to make clear that we are *not* dealing in the Old Testament with a permanent assumption of a human nature (as we have in the incarnation), whatever kind of "assumption" this is, we can affirm that in his condescension Yahweh relented, while in his essential deity Yahweh does not change. Not only so, but whatever relenting Yahweh does, it is always done within the context of his sovereign plan (thus, again, the contingent presupposes the necessary).

In other words, even as Scripture attributes both divine and human attributes and properties to the Son of God as incarnate, so also does it attribute essential and covenantal properties to God as condescended. Thus, Yahweh remains the "I AM"; there is no possible world in which he is essentially dependent on something external to himself. Whenever, therefore, Scripture notes that Yahweh does not change, not only does such immutability accrue to his plan for his people (which is the immediate concern in Mal. 3:6 above), but the immutability of his plan has its roots in God's own immutability *as God*. His plan, then, is an expression of his immutable character. This is, in part, the point that the author to the Hebrews is making.

> So when God desired to show more convincingly to the heirs of the promise the unchangeable character of his purpose, he guaranteed it with an oath, so that by two unchangeable things, in which it is impossible for God to lie, we who have fled for refuge might have strong encouragement to hold fast to the hope set before us. (Heb. 6:17–18)

The "two unchangeable things" to which the author refers are the oath that God swore (cf. Heb. 7:20ff.) and the fact that it is contrary to God's character to lie.[5] That is, the God who *cannot* lie swore an oath. In this context we can see the inextricable link between God's character and what he purposes to do.

But the immutable character of God does not translate into a kind of static, removed, and uninvolved abstraction, as some have wanted to claim.[6] Rather, the God who is immutable and whose plan and purpose for creation and his people will not fail nevertheless can and does relent.

This relenting in no way changes who God is essentially; neither does it require us to think that God was taken by surprise at a certain turn of events, or that something unexpected threatened to thwart his plan or, in itself, caused

---

[5] Or perhaps the two unchangeable things are his promise and his oath. If so, both are grounded in the impossibility of God to lie, and thus in his immutable character. God *cannot* lie because of who he essentially is as God.

[6] See Gregory A. Boyd, *God of the Possible: A Biblical Introduction to the Open View of God* (Grand Rapids: Baker, 2000), 17.

him to change course. Instead, we should take seriously the fact that God has covenanted with us and that in that relationship he interacts with us, really and truly, and thus certain covenant activities of his will change and adjust according to the attitudes and actions of his people, all within his all-comprehensive plan.

Perhaps it will help to think of this situation more globally. We should not pass over lightly the fact that, in Scripture, from the entrance of sin and into eternity, the Lord is fighting against and contending with sin and evil. Remember, just to use one example, what the Lord says to Joshua?

> When Joshua was by Jericho, he lifted up his eyes and looked, and behold, a man was standing before him with his drawn sword in his hand. And Joshua went to him and said to him, "Are you for us, or for our adversaries?" And he said, "No; but I am the commander of the army of the LORD. Now I have come." And Joshua fell on his face to the earth and worshiped and said to him, "What does my lord say to his servant?" And the commander of the LORD's army said to Joshua, "Take off your sandals from your feet, for the place where you are standing is holy." And Joshua did so.
>
> Now Jericho was shut up inside and outside because of the people of Israel. None went out, and none came in. And the LORD said to Joshua, "See, I have given Jericho into your hand, with its king and mighty men of valor." (Josh. 5:13–6:2)

The parallels between some of the language of this passage and the language that we have seen in Exodus 3 are unmistakable. The clear indication is that Joshua is confronted here with the "Divine Warrior."[7] That is, he is in the presence of Yahweh himself (thus, like Moses, he is commanded to remove his sandals, given the holiness of the ground). Now we must ask the obvious question in this context, Why does this Divine Warrior even fight the fight? In so doing, by virtue of his covenant with his people he determines to take on properties such as wrath, patience, and vengeance. All of these properties presuppose his *covenantal* dependence. None of them, however, demand that his essential character be in any way denied, negated, or undermined, any more than the Son of God's assumption of a human nature required a (*per impossibile*) setting aside of his essential deity.

Examples could easily be multiplied. In fact, the entirety of history, and into eternity, to be understood properly, presupposes God's covenantal prop-

---

[7]For more on this, see Tremper Longman III and Daniel G. Reid, *God Is a Warrior* (Grand Rapids: Zondervan, 1995).

erties, in that he, from the beginning, works with his creation and his human creatures in order to accomplish his sovereign purposes. In his condescension, he never denies his essential character, but neither is his essential character that which alone is predominant in his interactions with creation.[8]

In a more general sense, the fact that God interacts at all with creation presupposes his covenantal character. Once he determines to relate to us, that relation entails that he take on properties that he otherwise would not have had. He limits himself while remaining the infinite God.[9] The fact that he is Creator means that he is now related to something *ad extra* to which he was not related before.

This relationship of God to creation has been expressed in ways that seem to undermine its reality. For example, Aquinas, in answering the question "whether names which imply relation to creatures are predicated of God temporally," explains:

> Since therefore God is outside the whole order of creation, and all creatures are ordered to Him, and not conversely, it is manifest that creatures are really related to God Himself; whereas in God there is no real relation to creatures, but a relation only in idea, inasmuch as creatures are referred to Him. Thus there is nothing to prevent these names which import relation to the creature from being predicated of God temporally, *not by reason of any change in Him, but by reason of the change of the creature*; as a column is on the right of an animal, without change in itself, but by change in the animal.[10]

Ascriptions of God, therefore, according to Thomas, which imply a relationship to creation, are predicated of God, but are to be understood as denoting a change in the creation, not in God. The notion of God as Creator, to use Aquinas's example here, is properly thought to be a temporal and not an eternal notion, in that the relationship entailed by such a notion is predicated "really" of the creation itself, and only "ideally" of God. In other words, when we say, "God is the Creator," it is the "idea" of God as Creator that is predicated of him, whereas it is the "reality" of creation's relationship to

---

[8]I will elaborate on this more below. What I mean by this, generally speaking, is that God's interaction with creation necessarily hides, rather than reveals, his infinity, aseity, eternity, etc. The implications of such attributes are given in various ways, but are not given directly via his covenantal dealings.

[9]Exactly *what* limitations there are in God's covenantal character can be defined *only* by Scripture. Thus, the Arminian notion that God limits his sovereign control cannot be sustained, because Scripture indicates no such thing.

[10]Thomas Aquinas, *Summa theologica*, trans. Fathers of the English Dominican Province, 1.13.7, my emphasis.

God that is thus predicated. The "real relation" is in the created thing, or the creation, and not in God.

Stephen Charnock picks up this same theme in his discussion of God's immutability. Though he wants to affirm some kind of eternal sense in which God is Creator, he nevertheless also affirms Aquinas's point.

> Nor is there any new relation acquired by God by the creation of the world. . . . As a tree is now on our right hand, and by our turning about it is on our left hand, sometimes before us, sometimes behind us, according to our motion near it or about it, and the turning of the body; there is no change in the tree, which remains firm and fixed in the earth, but the change is wholly in the posture of the body, whereby the tree may be said to be before us or behind us, or on the right hand or on the left hand. God gained no new relation of Lord or Creator by the creation; for though he had created nothing to rule over, yet he had the power to create and rule, though he did not create and rule: as a man may be called a skilful [sic] writer, though he does not write, because he is able to do it when he pleases. . . . So the name Creator and Lord belongs to God from eternity, because he could create and rule though he did not create and rule. But, howsoever, if there were any such change of relation, that God may be called Creator and Lord after the creation and not before, it is not a change in essence, nor in knowledge, nor in will.[11]

We can appreciate and affirm the thrust of what Aquinas and Charnock (with others) set forth here. They are concerned to guard that God is essentially immutable. They also want to ascertain just how we can predicate something relational of God all the while affirming his immutability. For both men, the reality of the relation is in the creature, not in God. As Charnock notes, God's creative activity brings about no essential change in God. That much is certainly true.

In citing the *Commonplaces* of Peter Vermigli, Muller notes that "when God is said to 'repent' this signifies no change—no imperfection or inconsistency—in God, but instead a change in us."[12] Furthermore, according to Vermigli, "when it is said, that God waxed angry, it is not so to be understood as though God were troubled with affects; for that belongeth unto men: but according to the common and received exposition of these places, we understand it, that God behaved himself like unto men that be angry." And, "these words show, that God is not variable in these kind of promises and threaten-

---

[11]Stephen Charnock, *The Existence and Attributes of God*, 2 vols. (Grand Rapids: Baker, 1979), 1:339.
[12]Muller, *Post-Reformation Reformed Dogmatics*, 3:556.

ings; for he speaketh not absolutely and simply, but upon condition. But the fulfilling, or making void of the conditions, is looked for in us: wherefore the change must not be attributed unto him, but unto us."[13]

This is the tack taken by Charnock as well.

> God is not changed, when of loving to any creatures he becomes angry with them, or of angry he becomes appeased. The change in these cases is in the creatures; according to the alteration in the creature, it stands in a various relation to God: an innocent creature is the object of his kindness, an offending creature is the object of his anger; there is a change in the dispensations of God, as there is a change in the creature making himself capable of such dispensations. God always acts according to the immutable nature of his holiness, and can no more change in his affections to good and evil, than he can in his essence.[14]

There is in these discussions, however, not only a good and proper attempt to affirm God's essential immutability, but also an understanding of God's activity that fails to ring true to what Scripture itself affirms of God. Our discussion thus far should help us to see how this way of thinking can pose problems, and the problems posed go much deeper than mere language. They greatly influence how we think about the reality of God's redemptive purposes for his people. Put simply, they bear on the actual truth of the matter and thus impinge on how we read Scripture and how we think of God in relation to us and his creation.

When Scripture speaks of the anger of the Lord,[15] are we supposed to think not that the Lord is angry, but that *we* are? What does it mean to say that the change is in us when Scripture speaks of Yahweh as angry? Or are we simply to read those passages as referring to God's *activity* toward us, but not to his *disposition* toward us? No honest reading of Scripture can lend itself to such an idea. Surely such passages are not teaching that we, rather than the Lord, are angry, or that the Lord acts in a way that we call angry even though he himself continues to exist solely in "happy repose."

Or, as Charnock puts it, are we to think that, in this case, "an offending creature is the object of his anger," but that being the "object of his anger" denotes a change *in us* such that it does not change God in any way? Charnock

---

[13]Ibid.

[14]Charnock, *Existence and Attributes of God*, 1:345.

[15]As it does in Ex. 4:14; Num. 11:10, 33; 12:9; 25:3–4; 32:14; Deut. 6:15; 7:4; 11:17; 29:20, 27; Josh. 7:1; 23:16; Judg. 2:14, 20; 3:8; 10:7; 2 Sam. 6:7; 24:1; 2 Kings 13:3; 24:20; 1 Chron. 13:10; Ps. 106:40; Isa. 5:25; Jer. 4:8; 12:13; 23:20; 25:37; 30:24; 51:45; 52:3; Lam. 2:22; Zeph. 2:2–3.

uses the example of the sun: "Is the sun changed when it hardens one thing and softens another, according to the disposition of the several subjects? Or when the sun makes a flower more fragrant, and a dead carcass more noisome?"[16]

There can be no question that the relation one has to God will significantly alter one's own disposition and destiny. That much is certainly true. But is it adequate simply to think that when Scripture speaks of God being gracious, on the one hand, and wrathful, on the other, the *same* disposition in God causes these differences *in us*? Is God's anger toward one person an identical disposition as his grace and covenant love toward another? There seems to be no reason to think so, and it seems clear that Scripture does not speak in these terms; such ideas violate basic linguistic sensibilities.

Rather, when Scripture says that the Lord's anger was kindled, *it really was kindled*. Because God is personal, we should expect that he will react in different ways to things that please and displease him. These ascriptions of God in Scripture are *not* meant simply to tell us more about ourselves, but rather are meant to show us more of who God is, especially as he interacts with his human creatures. They are meant to show us who God is in light of his gracious condescension, generally, and of the gospel, more specifically, as given progressively throughout covenant history.

Does this mean that God is mutable and that he has given up his immutability? No more so than when we affirm that when Christ was angry (see, e.g., Mark 3:5; 10:14),[17] he gave up his deity, or that his anger could be "real" only if his immutability were denied. On the contrary, as we have seen, we can truthfully predicate both aspects and properties of Christ; the *communicatio* means that both aspects of Christ's character can (and must) be affirmed. So also with God. He both is immutable *and* in his condescension takes on covenantal properties in order really and truly to relate himself to us.

The penchant to shift the focus of Scripture's ascription of God's affections from himself to us in order to guard his essential deity, while admirable and understandable, does not do justice to the reality of God's real and gracious condescension since the beginning of creation.[18] It fails to recognize that

---

[16]Charnock, *Existence and Attributes of God*, 1:345.

[17]For an illuminating and helpful exposition of Jesus's anger, see Benjamin Breckinridge Warfield, "The Emotional Life of Our Lord," in *The Person and Work of Christ*, ed. Samuel G. Craig (Philadelphia: Presbyterian and Reformed, 1950), 107ff.

[18]In a section discussing the Reformed orthodox notions of the love and grace of God, Muller argues that, historically, God's condescension, even before the fall, was seen to be an act of his grace. "Divine grace, as indicated both in the doctrine of the divine attributes and in the developing Reformed covenant theology of the seventeenth century, is not merely the outward favor of God toward the elect, evident only in the post-lapsarian dispensation of salvation; rather is it one of the perfections of the divine nature. It is a characteristic of God's relations

what God has done in Christ through his condescension he has been doing from the dawn of time. The condescension of the Son of God in becoming Jesus Christ points us back to his condescension elsewhere in Scripture. To undermine or in any way minimize that condescension is, to that extent, to miss the glory of the goodness and grace of God as he sovereignly acts to accomplish all of his purposes.

(2) Theology Proper: Above and Beyond

What about the *extra calvinisticum*? Is there any application of that biblical truth to theology proper? Remember Helm's point: "According to the Chalcedonian view of the Incarnation . . . , whatever is essential to the divine nature cannot be yielded up in the Incarnation. That is, if there are properties that are essential to God being God . . . then in becoming incarnate God cannot cease to be omnipotent or omniscient." The crucial point to be noted here has implications across the entire theological spectrum, especially in the context of the Arminian/Calvinistic debate. Did God give up his sovereignty at the point of creation? Did he cease to control his creation in certain areas? The general implication of the *extra* is that God remains completely and essentially God, even while he interacts covenantally with his creation.

So, again, we think of Exodus 3: even though the "angel of the LORD," who was himself "the LORD," came down (v. 8) as the God of Abraham, Isaac, Jacob, and Moses, he did not thereby give up his independence. He remained, as he reminded Moses, "I AM WHO I AM." His coming down did not necessitate a lack of deity or alter his essential nature. What is true of the incarnation is true also of other "incarnations" of God in Scripture.

Let us take one example from Scripture that might seem, at first glance, to undermine God's essential character, and attempt to understand it from the perspective of the *extra* as applied to God's condescension.

In that magnificent passage in Genesis 22, Abraham is put to the test. God commands him to take Isaac for a sacrifice. As Abraham shows himself obedient, the Lord intervenes: "But the angel of the Lord called to him from heaven and said, 'Abraham, Abraham!' And he said, 'Here am I.' He said, 'Do not lay your hand on the boy or do anything to him, for now I know that you fear

---

to the finite order apart from sin, in the act of divine condescension to relate to finite creatures" (Muller, *Post-Reformation Reformed Dogmatics*, 3:570). Muller continues, "There is, both in the orthodox Reformed doctrine of God and in the orthodox Reformed covenant theology of the seventeenth century, a consistent identification of grace as fundamental to all of God's relationships with the world and especially with human beings, to the point of the consistent assertion that the covenant of nature or works is itself gracious" (ibid., 3:570n512).

God, seeing you have not withheld your son, your only son, from me'" (Gen. 22:11–12). What could God mean here when he says, "Now I know that you fear God"? Surely, because God knows all things and nothing is darkness to him, he knew not only that Abraham would fear God, but also what Abraham would do in every possible situation, including this one.[19] And, he knew what he had decreed, which included every aspect and moment of this event.

Turretin comments on this passage:

> Thus he tried Abraham (not in order that he might know his faith and obedience by this experiment, which he was previously ignorant of, since even before he professed that he knew his piety [Gen. 18:19], but in order to make known to the world and the church his remarkable faith). If it is said that God then knew that he feared him ("Now I know that thou fearest God, seeing thou hast not withheld thine only son from me," Gen. 22:12), this is not to be understood absolutely of the knowledge which God obtained, but transitively of the knowledge which he gave to others (as similar words are often used in the Scriptures).[20]

What Turretin seems to say here is that when God says, "Now I know," what he actually means is "Now others will know," or, "Now I can give knowledge of this event to others." Turretin indicates that this "now I know" phrase is to be understood "transitively" and not "absolutely." That is, Turretin is making a grammatical argument here about the verb "know." He argues that when God says, "Now I know," there is a direct object implied, so that it is not understood "absolutely." If "know" were understood absolutely, there would be no direct object implied, in which case the "know" would refer to God himself.

Turretin's commentary, however, misconstrues the actual grammar of the statement.[21] Calvin's comment on this verse is closer to the mark.

> The exposition of Augustine, "I have caused thee to know," is forced. But how can any thing become known to God, to whom all things have always been present? Truly, by condescending to the manner of men, God here says that what he has proved by experiment, is now made known to himself. And he speaks thus with us, not according to his own infinite wisdom, but according

---

[19] Just to be clear, God's knowledge of all possibilities *does not*, as in Molinism, entail libertarian freedom. God knows all possibilities because of who *he* is, not because of who we are.

[20] Francis Turretin, *Institutes of Elenctic Theology*, trans. George Musgrave Giger, ed. James T. Dennison Jr., 3 vols. (Phillipsburg, NJ: P&R, 1992–1997), 1:212.

[21] The verb used, יָדַעְתִּי, is first person, singular, qal perfect of יָדַע.

to our infirmity. Moses, however, simply means that Abraham, by this very act, testified how reverently he feared God.[22]

Calvin is correct that Augustine's construal of this passage is forced; so also, I would say, is Turretin's. In whatever ways a phrase like this is used, what it does *not* communicate is that the "knowing" is (exclusively) located somewhere other than in the subject who utters the statement. So, a passage like this should not be read as, "Now, I have caused you to know," or, "Now, others will know," for the simple reason that it is not what the statement says. These things may certainly be true, but their truth is not what is communicated in the statement "Now I know."

As Calvin says, we should understand the statement in this way: "Truly, by condescending to the manner of men, God here says that what he has proved by experiment, is now made known to himself." Does this mean that God, *as God*—as essentially who he is, as the *Eimi*—did not know what Abraham would do? It cannot mean that, which is why we have the kinds of explanations given by Augustine and Turretin. They are trying to make sense of the statement, given the clear emphasis in Scripture that God is *a se*. God not only knew what Abraham would do in this situation by virtue of his exhaustive decree, but knew it by virtue of his exhaustive self-knowledge.

So why does God say of himself, "Now I know . . ."? He says this, in part, *not* because he wants us to map this expression of his knowledge onto his essential character. Rather, we have to take seriously God's condescension. Once God condescends, we should recognize that, in taking to himself covenantal properties, he takes to himself as well the *kind* of knowledge (and will, to be discussed later) that accrues to those properties. Or, to put it another way, one of the covenantal properties that he takes to himself is the development of knowledge that is conducive to his interaction with his creation generally, and specifically with his people.

This is, of course, the case with the Son of God who came in the flesh: "But concerning that day and hour no one knows, not even the angels of heaven, nor the Son, but the Father only" (Matt. 24:36; cf. Mark 13:32). Having taken a human nature, he took as well properties that accrue to that nature. Calvin's commentary helps us understand what Christ is saying here.

But many persons, thinking that this was unworthy of Christ, have endeavored to mitigate the harshness of this opinion by a contrivance of their own; and

---

[22]Calvin's commentary on Gen. 22:12 in Calvin, *Comprehensive John Calvin Collection*.

perhaps they were driven to employ a subterfuge by the malice of the Arians, who attempted to prove from it that Christ is not the true and only God. So then, according to those men, Christ did not know the last day, because he did not choose to reveal it to men. But since it is manifest that the same kind of ignorance is ascribed to Christ as is ascribed to the angels, we must endeavor to find some other meaning which is more suitable.[23]

Suppose we take Calvin's explanation here and place it into the more general context of God's condescension in which, as we noted above, God's knowledge is somehow restricted. We could now propose to transfer the comments of Calvin (about Christ) to comments on Genesis 22 this way:

> But many persons, thinking that this was unworthy of God, have endeavored to mitigate the harshness of this opinion by a contrivance of their own; and perhaps they were driven to employ a subterfuge by the malice of the Arminians, who attempted to prove from it that God is not the true and *a se* God. But since it is manifest that the same kind of ignorance is ascribed to God as is ascribed to creatures, we must endeavor to find some other meaning which is more suitable.

The "some other meaning which is more suitable" is the meaning that sees God's free and gracious condescension as exhibited from the beginning of creation and as itself proleptically pointing us to that climactic condescension that is the incarnation. So the lack of knowledge that God has, as given to us in Genesis 22:12, is a covenantal lack; it is a lack in which God's relationship to his people includes his real and literal interaction with us. It is a lack, which itself presupposes his essential deity and eternal decree, in which the Lord is *patient* toward us (2 Pet. 3:9). That patience surely includes his "waiting to see" how we might react in the face of trials and sufferings. And since contingency is real in God's creation, it is not until we act/react that God, as condescended to that contingency, sees/knows what we will do (even though he always knows it, as who he is essentially).

It is useful, again, to note Calvin's comments on the ignorance of Christ as we think about this more generally in terms of God's covenantal properties.

> As to the first objection, that nothing is unknown to God, the answer is easy. For we know that in Christ the two natures were united into one person in such a manner that each retained its own properties; and more especially the Divine nature was in a state of repose, and did not at all exert itself, whenever it was

---

[23]Calvin, "Commentary on the Harmony of the Gospels," vol. 3, in Calvin, *Comprehensive John Calvin Collection.*

necessary that the human nature should act separately, according to what was peculiar to itself, in discharging the office of Mediator.[24]

Calvin anticipates objections to Christ's admission of ignorance. We can paraphrase Calvin again here in anticipating possible objections to God's covenantal lack of knowledge.

> For we know that in God's condescension two kinds of properties accrue to him in such a manner that each retained its own properties; and more especially the Divine nature was in a state of repose, and did not at all exert itself, whenever it was necessary that the covenantal character of God should act separately, according to what was peculiar to itself, in discharging the office of Mediator.[25]

"Discharging the office of Mediator," therefore, which covers the entire span of redemptive history (of which more below), involves some aspects of God's character that refer us more specifically to his covenantal character, and others that refer us more to his divine, essential character. Even so, the mediatorial work itself was done according to both aspects of his person. He was not simply Mediator in his assumption of covenantal characteristics. But it was and is just *because* in that assumption he remains who he is essentially that he is Mediator according to his condescension, that is, as *God* but God *with us*. Both aspects of his character are, from the beginning, included in his mediation.

This is a good place to note another Reformed distinctive concerning the person of the Son that further bolsters our discussion of God's interaction with creation. In the context of a sixteenth-century dispute over the precise nature of the mediation of the Son of God, Reformed theology argued that "Christ was a mediator in both natures," and "that he had also fulfilled the office of mediator already in the days of the Old Testament."[26] The importance of this debate is deep and wide, extending from the Romanist insistence on mediation according to Christ's human nature only, and the implications of such a view, to the insistence of mediation according to Christ's divine

---

[24]Ibid.

[25]By using the phrase "act separately" here Calvin is not Nestorian; he is simply making distinctions that must be made theologically; i.e., since there are two natures in Christ, we may properly ascribe certain activities of his to one nature, and not to the other, even though such ascriptions in no way undermine the unity of his person.

[26]Herman Bavinck, *Reformed Dogmatics*, vol. 3, *Sin and Salvation in Christ*, ed. John Bolt, trans. John Vriend (Grand Rapids: Baker Academic, 2006), 364. See also Turretin, *Institutes*, 2:379ff.; John Calvin, *Institutes of the Christian Religion*, trans. Ford Lewis Battles, ed. John T. McNeill, 2 vols., The Library of Christian Classics (Philadelphia: Westminster Press, 1960), 2.14.3, 6.

nature only, in which, for example, the righteousness of Christ accrues to us only by way of his divinity.[27] We shall happily leave those debates aside here in order not to diverge from our more particular focus.

Given what we have discussed in the previous chapter about the Logos, it should not surprise us that the particular work and office of mediation is given to the Son from the point of creation (condescension) and into eternity.[28] The implications for our discussion are, at least, that the second person of the Trinity is himself the Mediator between God and man even when there is no human nature assumed. More generally, we could say that the pattern of Christ at the time of the incarnation—a pattern often described as humiliation and exaltation (e.g., Phil. 2:4–8)—had its beginning at the point of condescension. In other words, condescension itself is humiliation; it is God coming down (e.g., Ex. 3:8).[29] Speaking of the mediation of Christ, Turretin notes:

> He ought to be Mediator according to that nature in which he could work as Mediator even from the beginning of the world, since he ought to be the same yesterday, today and forever. Now he could not work according to the human, but only according to the divine nature, according to which (as he already existed) he could govern his church and enrich it with all gifts necessary to salvation.[30]

The importance of this discussion can be seen if we recognize that in condescending, God the Son, from the beginning of creation, remained who he essentially is, all the while taking to himself those properties and characteristics sufficient to accomplish his sovereign plan. In so doing, it was *not* simply the assumed covenantal properties, culminating as they do in the assumption of a human nature at the incarnation, that were the conduit through which he would be Mediator. Rather, the fact that *God* (the Son) took on these properties constituted him as the Mediator of all creation and as the salvific Mediator of his people. That which applies to Christ, therefore, with respect

---

[27]This latter view was held by Osiander and is discussed by both Bavinck and Turretin in the references above.

[28]I should state the obvious here, i.e., that mediation itself implies condescension, in that, apart from anything existing *ad extra* with respect to God, there is nothing that necessitates mediation.

[29]There are obvious differences between the general humiliation that is condescension and the more specific humiliation of the incarnation. Just to use one example, when the Lord appeared to Moses in the bush, he fell on his face and was commanded to approach in a reverent and worshipful way. This is not the case with God incarnate until after his work is completed (cf. Rev. 1:10ff.). The differences, however, point both to a continuity and to a discontinuity between God's general condescension in history and the climactic condescension in the incarnation.

[30]Turretin, *Institutes*, 2:381.

to his mediatorial office and work, applies proleptically to the Son of God, the Logos, throughout covenant history. So, says Turretin.

> Again the actions of Christ can be viewed in a threefold order as Christ can be regarded under a threefold relation (*schesei*)—either as God, or as man, or as God-man (*theanthrōpos*). Some are merely divine, which he effects only as God (such as creation and conservation). Others are merely human (such as eating, walking and sleeping). Others are mixed, which are called theandric (*theandrikai*) (such as redemption, to accomplish which both his divine and human natures concurred). Therefore the question is—To which class of these acts does mediation belong? To the merely human (as the papists hold) or to the theandric (*theandrikas*) (which we assert)?[31]

The mediation of God (the Son) is, to use Turretin's word, theandric; it includes, necessarily, both the divine and the human. In the same way, therefore, and proleptically, the mediation of God (the Son) prior to the incarnation is theandric as well. The point is not that it includes the permanent assumption of a human nature, as is the case in the incarnation, but that it includes the fact of God's taking to himself created, covenantal, *human* properties, all the while maintaining, as he must, his essential divinity.

Thus, the *extra calvinisticum* is applicable across the entire spectrum of God's mediatorial work in redemptive history, culminating in the climax of that mediation as expressed and fulfilled in the person and work of God incarnate.

(3) Theology Proper: The Two and One

What about the reduplicative strategy? As we have seen, the reduplicative strategy in a Reformed context could be viewed as a subset of the *communicatio* in that it affirms that opposing propositions can be legitimately applied to the same person, given that that person contains constituent parts that pertain to the whole, in this case, to the person himself. So, to repeat, we may properly speak of God as not knowing and knowing at the same time, of his being limited in space and infinitely omnipresent, of his lacking the power to do something and being omnipotent at the same time.

One further point, mentioned earlier, needs reemphasis here: that the essential takes precedence over the contingent. Just as the two natures in Christ are not on a par with each other, so also the essential and contingent are not two equal aspects of the one God.

---
[31]Ibid., 2:380.

Turretin says this about the incarnation:

> As the body and soul form one person, so the divinity and humanity; and as the
> soul operates through the body (as the organ substantially united to itself) so
> also the divinity through the humanity. . . . But the divinity is properly neither
> a part nor an incomplete nature. Finally, from the soul and the body a certain
> third nature arises; but not from the divinity and humanity.

What, therefore, does it mean that Christ's divinity operates through his
humanity? In part, it means that Christ's divinity is manifested through the
human nature that he assumed (Col. 1:15; Heb. 1:1–3). What this means
for our more general purposes is that when Scripture speaks of God as not
knowing, that is simply a manifestation of his covenant character, and that
manifestation is operative and sustained only by virtue of his essential character. So, there is no way in which the contingent can undermine or finally
subvert the essential. Using incarnational language here, we could say that all
of God's covenantal or contingent properties, which are really and literally
his, are nevertheless *anhypostatic* and *enhypostatic*. As *anhypostatic* they
are non–self-subsistent. Any properties that he freely determines to assume
are what they are only as they are assumed by the personal God, the Logos,
on the basis of his essential character. So also, as *enhypostatic*, they necessarily exist and subsist because of who he is as the Logos and because of his
essential character.[32]

So, we are back again to the ontological Trinity, revealed as it is through
the Logos, as the foundation and ground of everything else. If we in any way
minimize the essential character of the ontological Trinity, as Arminianism
and like theologies do, then (at least some) properties that are freely assumed
by God will of necessity have an independent status; they will be what they
are quite apart from who God is essentially.

This means, as I have said, that the essential or ontological forms the
backdrop for and interprets the covenantal or contingent or historical, *and
not vice versa*. There is an asymmetrical relation between the essential and
the contingent, just as there is between the divine and the human in Christ.
The divine is primary and the human is secondary in how we understand
this relationship. So also, the contingent is secondary, not primary. While it

---

[32] The properties that the Son of God assumes prior to the incarnation are neither, technically,
anhypostatic nor *enhypostatic*, in that, for either to be the case, he would be assuming a *nature*
and not simply properties of that nature. The point I am making here is simply that it is the
person who assumes these properties and not a *nature* of that person.

remains the mode in which God deals with his creation from beginning to end, it is not the primary or foundational mode either of God's own existence or of his character as he relates to us.

Two general methodologies are called into question when we begin to think that God, by virtue of his relation to creation, cannot be who he essentially is.

The first basic problem in all of these discussions about God and virtually all of his essential characteristics is that those thinking about such things typically begin in the wrong place. They begin with some notion of creation or an aspect of creation—e.g., time—and then try to extrapolate from that notion to God's character. And in that extrapolation, there is no proper attention given to the fact of God's condescension; invariably, the relationship of God to creation is determined somehow to limit God's essential character *because of* that relationship.

But this is just another attempt at a method of natural theology that excludes the necessity and authority of revelation. Such discussions must begin with revelation—and in this case with the supreme manifestation of God's revelation in Christ—in order to understand how God can remain God and at the same time relate to the world. What is desperately needed, in other words, is a revelational (including a supremely christological) hermeneutic.

The second methodological problem has to do with our standard notions of compatibility, and this has implications not only across the philosophical spectrum, but most especially across the theological spectrum.

A couple of reminders will help us elaborate on this problem with respect to the reduplicative strategy. What if we begin to define our notion of compatibility by way of the reality of the incarnation? Remember that Eleonore Stump argues for rational predication based on the notion that the whole can borrow properties from its constituents, even when the constituents appear to be incompatible.[33] We will remember as well that Thomas Morris remains unconvinced that this strategy in any way diminishes the dilemma.[34]

---

[33]Recall, "So a whole can borrow properties from its constituents. . . . Consequently, there is no reason for denying that Christ can have properties borrowed from either his human nature or his divine nature, even if the natures are not integral parts of Christ and the properties are contradictories. Because each of the incompatible properties is had in its own right by a different constituent of the whole and because they attach to the whole only derivatively, in consequence of the fact that the whole has these constituents, there is no incoherence in attributing both otherwise incompatible properties to the whole." Eleonore Stump, "Aquinas' Metaphysics of the Incarnation," in *The Incarnation*, ed. Stephen T. Davis, Daniel Kendall, SJ, and Gerald O'Collins, SJ (Oxford: Oxford University Press, 2002), 217.

[34]Recall also, "Consider any conjunctive reduplicative proposition of the form 'x as A is N and x as B is not N.' If the subjects of both conjuncts are the same and the substituends of N are univocal across the conjunction, then as long as (1) the reduplication predicates being A

To put Morris's argument in a form that relates to our particular concern, we could rephrase it this way:

> Suppose one affirms both that "God as God is immutable, and, God as condescended is not immutable."[35] Given that the subject of both conjuncts is the same, which it is, and that "immutable" is used in the same way in both conjuncts, which it is, and as long as the reduplication predicates "as God" of God and "as condescended" of God, which it does, and "immutable" is entailed by being God, and "not immutable" is entailed by God condescending, which each is, then the contradiction stands since God is characterized as being immutable and not immutable.

It seems that both Stump and Morris have a legitimate point.

Stump is saying that two things that have otherwise incompatible and contradictory properties can coexist in the context of something else, which she calls the whole. As Stump points out, there are other things, complex in their essential make-up, to which we can coherently attribute otherwise incompatible properties. When we say, therefore, that Christ is infinite, we speak truly because what we say refers, not to Christ's human nature, but to his divine nature. In terms of our discussion, when we say that God is immutable, we speak truly because we refer to his essential character.

There are, however, as Stump admits, properties that Christ has "in their own right" and other properties that are borrowed from one or the other of his natures. While discerning which properties are which is not the immediate concern of the reduplicative strategy, delineating these properties may be beyond the capacity of such a strategy. There are two primary reasons for this. First, Stump notes that

> in the case of Christ, who is a composite of one person and two natures, the property of being unlimited in power is a property had by the whole only in virtue of the fact that one constituent of the whole has this property. Furthermore, if

---

of x and predicates being B of x, and (2) being N is entailed by being A, and not being N is entailed by being B, then the reduplicative form of predication accomplishes nothing except for muddying the waters, since in the end the contradiction stands of x being characterized as both N and not N." Thomas V. Morris, *The Logic of God Incarnate* (Ithaca, NY: Cornell University Press, 1986), 48–49.

[35] We need not enter a discussion of the eternal decree here. I will look at that more closely in chapter 5. Suffice it to say at this point that God's decree itself implies God's condescension, in that he has something "in mind" that is *ad extra*, and that he initiated a decree with respect to it. The point to be made here is that even the eternal decree had a "beginning" in that it includes God's free decision and is not something necessary to him, as is his eternity.

all the constituents of Christ other than the divine nature were removed, what remained would still be omnipotent.[36]

But there may be problems with this kind of assessment.

Given our previous discussion of God's essential character, we have already seen that there is nothing in him that is in any way essentially contingent or otherwise not necessary. This is true, as we have noted, of the triune God. Thus, it is true of Father, Son, and Holy Spirit, individually and collectively, as one God. The Father's "Godness" is his essentially, as is the Son's, as is the Spirit's.

Thus, orthodox theology has always held that, in Christ, there was not a union of two persons, but rather a union of the person of the Son of God with human nature. This union did not produce another person, but it produced a change, in that the Son of God became something that he was not, all the while remaining who he essentially is. He became the God-man, Jesus Christ.

What we have in the incarnation is, therefore, not a union of the divine and human natures *simpliciter*. Rather, we have a union of the divine nature, which just *is* the person of the Son of God, with a human nature that, apart from that union, did not subsist.[37]

With regard to the *Eimi/eikon* relationship generally, therefore, two truths, difficult precisely to state, obtain. The first is that the Son of God is the person who took on a contingent property (human nature) and thus became something that he was not previously (while remaining who he is essentially). The second is that Jesus Christ, who is (numerically) the same person as the Son of God, is composed essentially of two natures. That is, though it might have been possible that Jesus Christ not exist (which was not possible of the Son of God), given that he does exist, he exists necessarily as one person with a divine and a human nature.

With respect to Stump's assertion above, therefore, that "if all the constituents of Christ other than the divine nature were removed, what remained would still be omnipotent," we need also to understand that what would remain would not be an omnipotent Jesus Christ. This is because, if all the constituents of Christ other than the divine nature were removed, then the

---

[36]Stump, "Aquinas' Metaphysics of the Incarnation," 215.
[37]"By this, the human nature (which was destitute of proper personality and was without subsistence [*anypostatos*] because otherwise it would have been a person) was assumed into the person of the Logos (*Logou*), and either conjoined with or adjoined to him in unity of person, so that now it is substantial with the Logos (*enypostatos Logō*)." Turretin, *Institutes*, 2:311.

human nature would be removed from him, in which case he would not be Jesus Christ, since to be Jesus Christ he must be both divine and human.

Herein lies a problem. When Stump argues for the reduplicative strategy as a means of coherent articulation with respect to Christ, she argues that there is no incoherence in attributing otherwise incompatible properties to the whole, given that the attribution refers to a constituent part of that whole. As Stump notes, "On Aquinas' view, there is a distinction between a property a whole has in its own right and a property it has in virtue of having a constituent that has that property in its own right . . . , a whole can borrow a property from one of its constituents."[38] Given this, argues Stump, we have "a helpful way to analyse *qua* locutions of the form x *qua* A is N."[39] The "helpful way" is that we can attribute something of the whole that is a property of a constituent part of that whole. The whole to which she refers here is the person of Christ.[40] And the person of Christ is composed of two natures, one of which, the human, would not subsist except as assumed by the person himself, and the other of which is identical with the person, since it refers to his essential character. The divine nature of Christ, therefore, is not in any coherent sense a "part" of Christ. Rather, it just *is* the person who takes on the human nature. But the person of Christ is the same person as the Son of God. So what we actually have in the person of Christ is the same person, who has taken to himself contingent properties (or a contingent property if the unity of human nature is in view), becoming thereby something different while remaining the same essential person.[41]

When speaking of "the whole," therefore, with respect to Christ, we are speaking of a "whole" that is contingent (given that it necessarily includes a human nature). What we have in Christ, therefore, is a person whose essence is identical with him, who is essentially who he is, and who in history takes on new properties, assuming to himself a human nature, all the while remaining the same person. All we need do here is change our specific reference, namely, "Christ," to the more general reference of covenant history, "God with us,"

---

[38]Stump, "Aquinas' Metaphysics of the Incarnation," 212.

[39]Ibid.

[40]Turretin makes a distinction between the masculine and neuter use of the term *whole*, such that the former refers to the person and the latter to the natures. The former refers to "the whole Christ," while the latter refers to "the whole of Christ." It seems, however, that what is referenced is, on the one hand, an essential property of Christ and, on the other, that which is contingent in him. See Turretin, *Institutes*, 2:321.

[41]Obviously, I am using both *essentially* and *essential* here in different ways. The Son of God becomes something essentially different in that, once he takes on a human nature in this world, he cannot be who he is without that nature. It is (hypothetically) necessary that he be both human and divine. Yet he remains who he essentially is because he is essentially and necessarily divine.

and the discussion is the same. The "whole" to which we refer is God who has condescended—the same person who is essentially God, but now having taken on contingent properties.

The rejoinder to Morris, given this construal of the hypostatic union, could be somewhat different than Stump's. It may be that what we are actually predicating in reduplication (with respect to "God with us" generally and Christ more specifically) is not in fact contradictory.

We will remember Morris's charge of contradiction, even given the reduplicative strategy. The conditions laid down by Morris seem to obtain: When we say, "God as essentially God is immutable," and, "God as condescended is not immutable," the subject of both conjuncts must be the same. Also, it must be that the reduplication predicates "as essentially God" of God and "as condescended" of God. And "being immutable" is entailed by being God, and "not being immutable" is entailed by being condescended. So far, so good.

But one other condition must obtain, according to Morris, for there to be contradiction, namely, that the "substituends of N are univocal across the conjunction." But are they? Is it the case that when we say, "God as essentially God is immutable," and "God as condescended is not immutable," we are using the term "immutable" univocally? Perhaps not.

If we take the notion of immutable to be, as we have seen, an essential property of God's and thus also identical to him, then when we say, "God as essentially God is immutable," we are not in the first place predicating something of the whole in virtue of one of its constituent parts. Rather, we are predicating something of the whole (God) that he has in his own right (since the whole is the person and the person is the Logos). Thus, immutability is not constitutive of the person, but just is the person (given simplicity). What we are also saying is that it is not possible for the Logos to be essentially mutable; immutability is of the essence of who the person of the Logos is (since he is the same person as the Son of God).

This, however, does not hold true for "God as condescended is not immutable." Here "not immutable" is a contingent property of God's, something not of the essence of the person.[42] It seems, therefore, that the term "immutable" cannot be used univocally, since in the one case its reference is essential to (and identical to) its predicate (the Son of) God, and in the other case its refer-

---

[42]It is, of course, of the essence of the person of Christ, but it is not of the essence of the (same) person of the Son of God. Thus, it is essential that the Logos be infinite, but as essentially infinite he is only contingently not infinite. It is surely the case that if he determined to be infinite only, then he would not be Christ, but the Son of God. This is only to affirm that he would be the same essentially with different (or no) contingent properties.

ence is to something contingent and dependent on creation, that is, covenant properties. And, as Aquinas argues, whenever the same term is used both to refer to God and to refer to something created, it cannot be used univocally. We must affirm, then, that the word itself is used analogically.

Thus, to respond to Morris and agree with Stump (using our more general *Eimi/eikon* locution): while there is no contradiction per se between the propositions "God as essentially God [*Eimi*] is immutable" and "God as condescended [*eikon*] is not immutable," so that the propositions can be somewhat understood, we nevertheless encounter quickly our own intellectual limits when we ponder the fact that the person who took on covenant properties, and eventually a human nature, is the same eternally as the Son of God, though from the time of creation he is different (though not essentially), and this difference obtains into eternity. To put it in our own terms, then, the *Eimi/eikon* properties, being themselves ontologically or essentially incompatible, can be made compatible by God as they are brought together in one person. That is, orthodox theology (and specifically orthodox christology) has always admitted that things and properties that seem to us to be fundamentally incompatible, even contradictory at times, can indeed be brought together into a coherent whole, whether in a person or something else.

Morris, however, has a point as well. That two contradictory properties can reside in one person does not thereby remove the contradiction. To put it another way, just because the two *are* one does not automatically mean that we can articulate that "oneness" in an intellectually satisfying way. Thus, because it is the one person who has these conflicting properties, it makes it difficult for us to describe his character without quickly reaching our intellectual boundaries.

(4) Theology Proper: Back to the Word

If Christ be Jehovah, and if the name Jehovah implies self-existence, then Christ is self-existent. In other words, self-existence and necessary existence, as well as omnipotence and all other divine attributes, belong to the divine essence common to all the persons of the Trinity, and therefore it is the Triune God who is self-existent, and not one person in distinction from the other persons. That is, self-existence is not to be predicated of the divine essence only, nor of the Father only, but of the Trinity, or of the Godhead as subsisting in three persons. And, therefore, as Calvin says, when the word God is used indefinitely it means the Triune God, and not the Father in distinction from the Son and Spirit.[43]

---

[43]Charles Hodge, *Systematic Theology*, 3 vols. (London: James Clarke, 1960), 1:467.

Here Hodge recognizes what I have wanted to argue all along. Yahweh is, in fact, the second person of the Trinity, who became incarnate. As such, he is self-existent, as are the Father and the Spirit. Because God is self-existent, each person of the Godhead is.

Once we recognize that the person who is the subject of this combination of conflicting properties is the person of the Logos, the Word, the Son of God, it becomes easier for us to articulate the reality of these properties.[44]

The history of the church's affirmations regarding the second person of the Trinity, with its focus in the Chalcedonian Creed, gives us substantial and significant theological precedent in which we can accept and affirm that there is a mysterious harmony in these attributes and know how we might more helpfully categorize them.

Recall the language of the Creed. The Son of God, once he assumes a human nature, is to be "acknowledged in two natures, inconfusedly [ἀσυγχύτως], unchangeably [ἀτρέπτως], indivisibly [ἀδιαιρέτως], inseparably [ἀχωρίστως]." While we must be careful not to muddle the technical terms used here, it seems useful to think of the characteristics and properties of "God with us"—i.e., God as condescended—in the same way. So, for example, the word "natures" (φύσεσιν) should probably be reserved for the respective characteristics, as a whole, that were united in the incarnation. In other words, the taking of covenant properties by the Logos throughout covenant history must be distinguished from that singular moment "when the fullness of time had come" and God sent forth his Son to be born (Gal. 4:4f.).

Having said that, we should not hesitate to affirm that, in taking on covenantal properties while remaining who he is essentially, the Son of God partakes of two different and sometimes seemingly incommensurable kinds of properties, each kind of which should be acknowledged inconfusedly, unchangeably, indivisibly, and inseparably. That is, the impassibility/passibility of the Logos (prior to his incarnation) requires that we neither confuse the two (as if the properties of the one, i.e., the *Eimi*, accrue to the other, i.e., the *eikon*), change the one into the other (so that they are unified via some kind of property merger), divide them (as if they do not reside in the one person), or separate them (as if they are not actually unified).

---

[44]The argument I have been presenting throughout does not stand or fall on the fact that it is, throughout covenant history, the second person of the Trinity who is the subject of our discussion. Given what I have said thus far, however, it seems clear that it *is*, and *that* it is allows us more easily to contextualize the difficult matter of conflicting properties, since the church has affirmed these truths of the Son of God from its earliest creeds.

We will remember that the first two negatives—ἀσυγχύτως and ἀτρέπτως—are directed primarily against Eutychianism. Those negatives affirm that the two natures of Christ are not changed by virtue of the union, nor are they in any way confused. In what we have argued, we want to avoid a *theological* Eutychianism as well, in which, for example, God the Son's taking on the property of passibility means that his impassibility changes. The second two negatives—ἀδιαιρέτως and ἀχωρίστως—are directed primarily against Nestorianism. The two natures of Christ are neither divided nor separated, so that Christ is not two persons, nor is he two distinct personalities. This problem is not as acute in theology proper. What might be more to the point, as we have said, is that we must avoid a theological docetism, in which it is argued that the real properties of passibility, anger, patience, and so forth are simply what "seem" to be, rather than what really are.

In a discussion of Luke 24:27 ("And beginning with Moses and all the Prophets, he interpreted to them in all the Scriptures the things concerning himself"), John Owen explains various ways in which Christ was represented in the Old Testament.

> It was so represented and made known under the Old Testament, in his personal appearances on various occasions unto several eminent persons, leaders of the church in their generations. This he did as a *praeludium* to his incarnation. He was as yet God only; but appeared in the assumed shape of a man, to signify what he would be. He did not create a human nature, and unite it unto himself for such a season. . . . So he appeared to Abraham, to Jacob, to Moses, to Joshua, and others; as I have at large elsewhere proved and confirmed. And hereon, also, because he was the divine person who dwelt in and dwelt with the church, under the Old Testament, from first to last, in so doing *he constantly assumes unto himself human affections*, to intimate that a season would come when he would immediately act in that nature.[45]

Once we understand that it is the Son of God, prior to his incarnation, who is interacting with his creation all along, we need not in any way be reticent to affirm those covenantal properties that Scripture seems so easily and seamlessly to ascribe to him. In such assignments, it is preparing us for that climactic representation of the Logos in Jesus Christ.[46]

---

[45]John Owen, *The Works of John Owen*, ed. W. H. Gould, Ages Digital Library CD ed., 16 vols. (Edinburgh: Banner of Truth, 1977), 1:50, my emphasis.
[46]And if Scripture is preparing for the incarnation throughout covenant history, there is no way in which the coming of Christ could have been a surprise.

So why the reticence? Why the reluctance to affirm both aspects of God's character throughout covenant history? There are no doubt a host of answers to this question. But surely one of the primary answers brings us back to our discussion of antinomy and paradox. Once the *Eimi*, as the independent and *a se* God, takes to himself—that is, to his person—anything that is dependent and created, there is bound to be a perceived conflict of laws operating.

As I alluded to in the last chapter, in her excellent discussion of the metaphysics of the incarnation, Eleonore Stump asks just what kind of union it could be, according to Aquinas, that unites the divine person of the Son of God with a human nature. Her conclusion is that Thomas had no category of union available to him to explain how the incarnation could take place.

> So what does configure the whole into one thing? Aquinas himself concedes that he has no answer to this question. If the mode of union for Christ *were* any of the modes of union his metaphysics recognizes, then, he says, it would be the mode of union between a substantial form and the matter it configures. But since this mode of union is also ruled out as a mode of uniting the human nature of Christ to the person of Christ, the best that can be said is that whatever exactly the mode of union is for Christ, it is analogous to the mode of union of substantial form and matter into one supposit. Strictly speaking, Aquinas is compelled to conclude, *the mode of union for Christ is unique*. It is not the same as any other union found among created things, and therefore it cannot be analyzed in terms used to understand any other sort of union. In fact, Aquinas thinks, we have to grant that this mode of union is in a certain respect incomprehensible. He says, "to explain this union perfectly is not possible for human beings."[47]

Granted, as I have been at pains to affirm, the union effected in the incarnation is *sui generis*; there is no other union like it.[48] However, as I have also been at pains to affirm, the assumption of covenantal properties by the Son of God, from the beginning of creation onward, is itself a proleptic pointer to that one unique event. We therefore must recognize that to the extent that such properties are assumed, a certain union is effected as well, a union that brings together the *Eimi* and the *eikon*, a union of both created and essential properties. As in the incarnation, so also in every manner of God's assumption

---

[47]Eleonore Stump, *Aquinas* (New York: Routledge, 2003), 424–25, my emphasis.
[48]Not only is the union *sui generis*, but the incarnation as a means and mode of revelation is altogether unique as well (cf. Heb. 1:1ff.). As unique, however, it does have its own "types and shadows" in redemptive history. See, for example, Thomas Taylor, *Christ Revealed: Or, the Old Testament Explained. A Treatise of the Types and Shadows of Our Saviour Contained Throughout the Whole Scripture: All Opened and Made Usefull for the Benefit of God's Church* (1635; repr., Delmar, NY: Scholar's Facsimiles and Reprints, 1979).

of covenantal, human properties, we simply cannot comprehend the mode of union at all. What God has done since the beginning of time is to unify two disparate "laws," that is, the "laws" that define his essential character[49] and the "laws" that inhere in creation and created properties.

This "antinomic" situation will inevitably result in paradox. Given that there are opposing laws at work, laws that inhere in two different "kinds" of reality—God's and creation's—which themselves are unified by way of the one person of (the Son of) God, any proper attempt at explaining that union will result in paradox. This is as it should be, and it highlights for us the glorious mystery that just is God with us.

In an essay on the problem of evil and the so-called "puppet objection" (a problem to which we will turn in the next chapter), Paul Helm notes:

> I shall invoke Augustine's strategy and underline the sui generis character of the divine-human relation. (Recall his reference to "a way unspeakably strange and wonderful" in the quotation from his Enchiridion given earlier.) While this move is philosophically unsatisfactory, since philosophers like to have answers to their questions, it is nevertheless highly appropriate. For, after all, the divine-human relation is sui generis. What could be more extraordinary than the relation between the transcendent Creator and Lord of all and his creation, including his human creatures? If God is sui generis, then any relation between anything else and God looks likely to be sui generis as well.[50]

Isn't this Paul's point in Romans 11:33–36? Having discussed the problems of the salvation of ethnic Israel, the Gentiles, election, and reprobation, doesn't the apostle himself, under the inspiration of God the Holy Spirit, catch and record a sense of this magnificent mystery? Surely if the ways of God are beyond our comprehension, then the fact that he unites himself to his creation is among the chief of those ways.

C. Slow to Anger

So, there can be little question, it seems, as one reads of the varying appearances of Yahweh throughout covenant history that, in order to appear at all, Yahweh takes on created properties and characteristics. He condescends to present himself, and in doing so he takes characteristics and attributes that belong to creation.

---

[49]Strictly speaking, the only "laws" that define and delimit God's essential character just are that character. There is nothing outside of God or beside him that determines who he is essentially.
[50]Paul Helm, "Evil, Love and Silence" (unpublished manuscript, 2010).

It may be useful, in this regard, to elaborate on some of the standard terminology that is used to describe this activity on God's part.

In his comment on Genesis 6:6, Calvin notes:

> The repentance which is here ascribed to God does not properly belong to him,
> but has reference to our understanding of him. For since we cannot comprehend
> him as he is, it is necessary that, for our sakes he should, in a certain sense,
> transform himself. That repentance cannot take place in God, easily appears
> from this single consideration, that nothing happens which is by him unexpected
> or unforeseen. The same reasoning, and remark, applies to what follows, that
> God was affected with grief. Certainly God is not sorrowful or sad; but remains
> forever like himself in his celestial and happy repose: yet, because it could not
> otherwise be known how great is God's hatred and detestation of sin, therefore
> the Spirit accommodates himself to our capacity.[51]

Calvin's explanation of this and like passages is consistent with later Reformed
explanations.

> As for the understanding of divine affections generally, we have seen little discern-
> ible movement or development from the Reformation into the era of orthodoxy.
> The basic understanding of what divine affections are, namely, *ad extra* relations,
> not indicative of a change in God, together with the exclusion of "passions,"
> belongs in common to the Reformers and the orthodox. . . . In sum, the Reformed
> interpretation of the divine affections was in the interest, not of a metaphysical
> structure, but of a consistent view of the way God relates to the human race.[52]

The "consistent view" of which Muller speaks seems to include at least the
following ideas: Whenever Scripture attributes affections to God,[53] it is incumbent
on the reader to make sense of such attributions against the clear backdrop of
God's aseity—an aseity, we should remember, that is necessary to his character.
That is, as I have said, it cannot be denied that, prior to creation, there was only
God, and that *as God* he was altogether complete and independent. The hermeneutic applied to passages that speak of God's *dependence* must, therefore,
be governed and controlled by his essential *independence*,[54] and not vice versa.

---

[51]Calvin, *Comprehensive John Calvin Collection.*
[52]Muller, *Post-Reformation Reformed Dogmatics*, 3:588.
[53]With the exception of love (and possibly goodness), which will not detain us here.
[54]To the extent that Arminian and "open" theologies deal with this question, they too must
acknowledge God's independence prior to creation. They do this, in the main, by arguing that
such independence is in no way essential to God, but is given up (at least partially) at the point
of creation. So, just to use one example, William Lane Craig notes: "Thus, even if it is not the

Not only so, but the "consistent view" of the Reformed has been that those passages which speak of God's affections do so "metaphorically," or "improperly" or "anthropopathically." In concluding his comments on the passage above, for example, Calvin says this:

> Moreover, this paternal goodness and tenderness ought, in no slight degree, to subdue in us the love of sin; since God, in order more effectually to pierce our hearts, *clothes himself with our affections*. This figure, which represents God as transferring to himself what is peculiar to human nature, is called ἀνθρωποπάθεια [*anthropopatheia*].[55]

Given our discussion up to now, it is instructive to note how, at least in some cases, the notion of *anthropopatheia* has been understood. In a description of the term, Bullinger notes:

> The Ascribing of Human Attributes, etc., to God. Greek, ἀνθρωποπάθεια, from ἄνθρωπος (anthropos), man, and πάθος (pathos), affections and feelings, etc. (from πάσχειν, paschein, to suffer). This figure is used of the ascription of human passions, actions, or attributes to God. The Hebrews had a name for this figure, and called it דֶּרֶךְ בְּנֵי אָדָם (Derech Benai Adam), the way of the sons of man. The Greeks had another name for it: SYNCATABASIS (Syn'-cat-ab'-a-sis), from σύν (syn), together with, κατά (kata), down, and βαίνειν (bainein), to go: a going down together with: i.e., God, by using this figure, condescends to the ignorance and infirmity of man. Hence, the Latin name for it was CONDESCENSIO, condescension.[56]

The intersection of the notion of *anthropopatheia* and condescension in this explanation should be highlighted. As Bullinger notes, the Greek way of articulating just how to understand God's affective identification with us is denoted by the term *syncatabasis*, a term that means "going down together" (denominated in Latin, as Bullinger notes, as *condescensio*). This is simply

---

case that God is temporal prior to His creation of the world, He nonetheless undergoes an extrinsic change at the moment of creation which draws Him into time in virtue of His real relation to the world. So even if God is timeless without creation, His free decision to create a temporal world also constitutes a free decision on His part to exist temporally" (William Lane Craig, *Time and Eternity: Exploring God's Relationship to Time* [Wheaton, IL: Crossway, 2001], 87). So far, so good. Given Craig's Arminianism, however, libertarian freedom trumps God's sovereignty. Thus, God determined to give up his sovereignty at the point of creation. See William Lane Craig, "Middle Knowledge: A Calvinist-Arminian Rapprochement?," in Pinnock, *The Grace of God, the Will of Man*.

[55]Calvin, *Comprehensive John Calvin Collection*.

[56]Ethelbert William Bullinger, *Figures of Speech Used in the Bible* (New York: Yound, 1898), 287.

another way of defining what I have dubbed "covenant condescension." The term *anthropopatheia*, therefore, assumes that God has come down, and that he has come down *covenantally*, in order to relate to us in a way that would be suitable to who we are.

John Owen, in his able defense of Reformed Christianity against Socinianism, addresses the question, answered by the Socinians in the affirmative, "Are there not, according to the perpetual tenor of the Scriptures, affections and passions in God, as anger, fury, zeal, wrath, love, hatred, mercy, grace, jealousy, repentance, grief, joy, fear?"[57] In response, Owen gives four reasons why such affections and passions cannot be properly affirmed of God. It may help to clarify and enhance our discussion if we interact with Owen's responses.[58] It should be understood, however, that I want to interact with Owen only in the context of complete agreement with his objections to Socinianism. Owen makes clear that he is concerned to refute the particular ways in which the Socinians ascribe affections and passions to God. In response to the views of John Biddle, the father of English Socianism, Owen says,

> The main of Mr Biddle's design, in his questions about the nature of God, being to deprive the Deity of its distinct persons, its omnipresence, prescience, and therein all other infinite perfections, he endeavors to make him some recompense for all that loss by ascribing to him in the foregoing query a human visible shape, and in this, human, turbulent affections and passions.[59]

Because of Socinianism's aversion to an orthodox theology proper, we must first heartily and without reservation agree with the thrust of Owen's arguments.

Owen's first reason to answer negatively to his question (above) is this:

> 1. Affections, considered in themselves, have always *an incomplete, imperfect act of the will* or volition joined with them.[60]

Here Owen is considering an affection as that which "lies between the firm purpose of the soul and the execution of that purpose."[61] In other words, affec-

[57]Owen, *Works*, 12:147.
[58]Other Reformed theologians could be pursued here; we focus on Owen as one of the most able and helpful representatives of the Reformed answer to these question. For a useful summary of other responses, see Muller, *Post-Reformation Reformed Dogmatics*, 3:551ff.
[59]Owen, *Works*, 12:147.
[60]Ibid., 12:149.
[61]Ibid.

tions, in this context, arise because of a lack of execution of what one wills to do. Owen's biblical counter to this idea references Isaiah 14:24; Ephesians 1:11; Romans 11:33–36; and Isaiah 40:14, 18. In these passages, it is clear that God executes what he determines to do. Socinianism would deny the clear teaching of God's unconditional sovereignty, which these passages supply.

In discussions of God's will, however, the Reformed have, at times, made a distinction between the decretive will of God and the preceptive will. When discussing the decretive will of God, we are referencing the ideas set forth in the passages Owen uses above. We are affirming that God controls "whatsoever comes to pass," and he "works all things by the counsel of his own will."

With respect to the preceptive will of God, on the other hand, we are not thinking of something that God decrees or purposes to carry out, but rather of something that is in conformity to his character, thus to his revealed desires. So, while it may be the desire of God that none perish, that desire is not referencing God's own determinative decree, but rather his character as condescended to us. Obviously, conformity to God's character is to be preferred, and is to be preferred *in excelsis* in God. So, the references to the preceptive will of God are references to God's preference that his human creatures conform to his character, which preference, we must say, is significantly different from his decree.

The distinction itself could be somewhat misleading. It seems to indicate two aspects of the identical thing. But what God "wants," so to speak, is a different thing, from a scriptural standpoint, from what he determines. In determining, he makes a free decision that certain things will necessarily be certain ways. In wanting certain things to be certain ways, he does not necessarily determine them, but he desires them. To put the want and the determination together is, in fact, difficult for us. If God takes no delight in the death of the wicked, why doesn't he just save them all and thereby be maximally delighted? If it really is God's desire that none should perish, why not let none perish and fulfill that desire?

Or, to use another example, when God commands Israel to repent (e.g., Ezek. 14:6), it would be impossible to think that the repentance of Israel is not his will and desire. Moreover, when Christ calls the crowd to come to him (Matt. 11:28ff.), that call expresses his will; he is not calling them insincerely or artificially expressing his intent. God (and Christ) *really does want* what he requires or offers in such circumstances.

Does this mean that God's affections, tied as they are to his will and volition, are such that the execution of that will is not fulfilled? It seems that it does, but not according to his *Eimi* character; only according to his *eikon* character. As we have seen, that which is an implication of his independent character—his unconditional decree, in this case—always and everywhere has priority over any contingent aspect of God's activity and character. This is where Owen's refutation of Socinianism is exactly right. So, in whatever way God's preceptive will is unfulfilled, that in no way denies, frustrates, or otherwise undermines what he has unconditionally and eternally purposed to do.

Owen's second objection to a Socinian understanding of God's affections is this:

> 2. They have their *dependence on that wherewith he in whom they are is affected*; that is, they owe their rise and continuance to something without him in whom they are.[62]

Here, Owen's concern again is that we not affirm the Socinian notion of an ultimately dependent God.

> Is he in dependence upon any thing without him? Is it not a most eminent contradiction to speak of God in dependence on any other thing? Must not that thing either be God or be reduced to some other without and besides him, who is God, as the causes of all our affections are? "God is in one mind, and who can turn him? what his soul desireth, that he doeth," Job 23:13.[63]

In affirming Owen's general point, however, we may also recognize that God has condescended in such a way that his disposition toward his human creatures is indeed dependent on them, though not, of course, in any ultimate way; God remains the "I AM." But, as condescended, God has determined that he would react to what takes place in creation and, specifically, in and with man. What else could Scripture mean—what else could *Yahweh* mean—when he says that he is "slow to anger" (cf. Ex. 34:6; Num. 14:18; Neh. 9:17; Pss. 86:15; 103:8; 145:8)? Surely Scripture is not telling us to believe that, in his patience and slowness to anger, the Lord bears no such relationship to us. To affirm such a thing would be tantamount to affirming that Scripture enjoins us to believe what is not the case in reality. If we are simply to believe that God is slow to anger, even though he is not, then we are encouraged by Scripture to believe a proposition to be true when it is false. This kind of language in Scripture cannot be relegated to mere metaphor. The Lord's disposition toward us in cases like this necessarily depends on our responses to him in this world.

---

[62]Ibid.
[63]Ibid.

When the Bible says that the Lord is slow to anger, there are two covenantal characteristics highlighted: he is slow, that is, patient with us. Thus, there is a real relationship to time in which God takes on temporality; and his anger, though tied to this patience, is nevertheless real. We should not simply *believe* he is angry or could become angry; *he really is angry*.

This in no way asserts an absolute dependence in God, any more than the suffering of Christ was absolutely dependent on the choices and actions of those who crucified him (Acts 2:22–23). It does, however, affirm a *real and proper* dependence of God on that which takes place in creation, all of which, of course, takes place according to his decree and in the context of his voluntary condescension. Even though decreed, these events still necessitate the activities decreed. Not only so, but God does react to these events, and they determine his disposition toward us, though not in any ultimate or essential way. His reactions are never surprises, and nothing comes to him or happens that is not first decreed by him. Whatever the "kind" of dependence that God's condescension entails, it is not a dependence that inheres in him essentially. As a matter of fact, it may be more accurate to say that, though these characteristics accrue to him, really and truly, they are never in fact *in him* at all. Only his essential characteristics are identical to him and thus in him, which leads to Owen's next point.

Third, says Owen:

> 3. Affections are necessarily *accompanied with change and mutability*; yea, he who is affected properly is really changed; yea, there is no more unworthy change or alteration than that which is accompanied with passion, as is the change that is wrought by the affections ascribed to God.[64]

The reason why Owen affirms that affections necessarily entail change and mutability is that affections have been typically defined in terms of God's relationships *ad extra*. In other words, affections in this sense are not something internal to God's own essential character and being, but they had their genesis in that which was created and thus external to God.

> This understanding of the divine affections as movements or attractions in some sense defined by their external object is a significant element of the Reformed orthodox system, both in terms of the implications of the concept for the orthodox theology as a whole and in view of the frequently heard claim that the older theology was so caught up in an Aristotelian conceptuality of God

---

[64]Ibid.

as Unmoved Mover that it paid scant attention to the biblical language of God in relation to his world.[65]

In the context of Owen's true and proper arguments against Socinianism, there can be no compromise in God's essential aseity. Thus, any notion of affections that, as in Socinianism, seeks to deny or undermine that aseity cannot be sustained as biblical or orthodox.

However, as I have been anxious to aver, given God's condescension *to* and *with* his creation, there need be no reason to deny God's aseity by affirming the reality of his affections. In his condescension, the *a se* God remains independent, all the while taking on covenantal properties. As Muller also notes:

> In the words of the Leiden *Synopsis*, the divine affections "are nothing other than the ardent (*ardens*) will of God toward us," known in terms of its power and its effects in creatures—known, therefore, by diverse objects, varied effects, and different ways of operating *ad extra*. Such affections are *"truly and properly"* predicated of God when care is taken to avoid the attribution of any imperfection to the Godhead.[66]

There is a way, then, "truly and properly" to predicate affections of God, so long as such attributions and predications never serve to deny his essential character.

Part of Owen's concern in this discussion, it seems, is that nothing external to God affect him "internally." That is, Owen seems amenable to the notion that outward actions/effects might elicit certain *actions* from God, but he wants to guard against any notion that such outward actions by us would initiate any change of God's inward affections.

> We say, then, anger is not properly ascribed to God, but metaphorically, denoting partly his vindictive justice, whence all punishments flow, partly the effects of it in the punishments themselves, either threatened or inflicted, in their terror and bitterness, upon the account of what is analogous therein to our proceeding under the power of that passion; and so is to be taken in all the places mentioned by Mr B.[67]

Note that anger is not properly ascribed to God, but vindictive justice and punishments are. Thus, Owen's concern here is not that something external

---

[65]Muller, *Post-Reformation Reformed Dogmatics*, 3:560.
[66]Ibid., my emphasis.
[67]Owen, *Works*, 12:151.

to God influences his *actions*, but rather that something external to God influences his *attitude* or *affections*.

The reason for this is likely twofold: (1) If what happens in creation affects God internally (and affections are typically thought to be internal), then he cannot be considered "perfect." That is, he is incomplete in some way in that the attitude that he takes to something external to himself depends on what happens in creation. (2) Related to this, any internal affection that is produced or caused by what is external to God would automatically reduce God's life to something at least in part determined by what we do.

God's *actions*, on the other hand, are simply God's display of his character relative to the character of his creatures. Vindictive justice, therefore, is God's display of his holiness relative to the sin that seeks to oppose him. Thus, God can remain, it seems, in his "celestial and happy repose" even as he works to punish sin.

This way of thinking, however, seems *not* to put the cart before the horse, but to posit a cart *without* a horse. To think that God's vindictive justice has no corollary in his affections is to think that God's retributive acts are motivated, if at all, by the selfsame "happy repose" that is his blessedness. Not only so, but it is to think either that the effect—vindictive justice—is without a compatible cause in God or that it is its own cause. This, too, seems unnecessarily to twist the plain meaning of Scripture.

Fourth, says Owen,

> 4. Many of the affections here ascribed to God *do eminently denote impotence*; which, indeed, on this account, both by Socinians and Arminians, is directly ascribed to the Almighty.[68]

This of course follows from everything Owen has thus far said, and it only makes explicit what is implicit in his other three points. With this point, again, I am in full agreement regarding Socinians and Arminians. Their view of affections does, in certain cases, denote impotence, in that God is simply not able to involve himself in certain aspects of man's activities. Things happen, therefore, and happen *to God*, according to these theologies, that God is unable to avoid. As Owen goes on to say, "They make him affectionately and with commotion of will to desire many things in their own nature not impossible, which yet he cannot accomplish or bring about (of which I have elsewhere

---

[68]Ibid., 12:150.

spoken)."[69] There is, therefore, a certain essential impotence attributed to God that extends to his affections.[70] This understanding of God's character is not consistent with Reformed orthodox theology.

We should also see, however, that, once God determines to condescend to his creation, that determination itself includes limiting characteristics and properties that God assumes. Because God determines to do this, all limiting characteristics and properties are *self*-limiting, first of all. There is nothing outside of God that initially limits him; nor is there anything that ever limits his essential character.

But, just to use one example, when God determines to defend himself as the Divine Warrior, he thereby determines to limit his own activity in such a way as to conform to various constraints and contexts in creation. He does not *have* to do this; he freely chooses to do it, and there is nothing in God that makes this determination necessary, as we have already seen. But he does do it, and in "fighting the good fight" alongside his people, as the commander of the Lord's army (Josh. 5:14; cf. Joel 2:11; Rev. 19:13–14), he assumes created properties and determines not to fight according to the application of his all-powerful character.

As we have seen above, the concept of God taking on human characteristics—specifically, in this case, human emotions, often designated as "anthropopathic" characteristics—is denoted by the Hebrews as the "way of the sons of man," and by the Greeks as a "coming down." In other words, what we have been discussing all along as God's covenantal condescension, what others have called anthropopathisms, just *is* his assumption of human characteristics.

This is important for a number of reasons, not the least of which is that it better articulates a response to what is often seen to be mere metaphor. For example, Greg Boyd writes, "The language about God 'changing his mind,' 'regretting,' and so on should be taken no less literally than language about

---

[69]Ibid. The "elsewhere spoken" to which Owen alludes includes, at least, his "A Display of Arminianism," in which he notes: "They deny the irresistibility and uncontrollable power of God's will, affirming that oftentimes he seriously willeth and intendeth what he cannot accomplish, and so is deceived of his aim; nay, whereas he desireth, and really intendeth, to save every man, it is wholly in their own power whether he shall save any one or no; otherwise their idol free-will should have but a poor deity, if God could, how and when he would, cross and resist him in his dominion" (ibid., 10:29–30).

[70]To be clear, orthodox theology has always held, because Scripture teaches, that there are certain things that God cannot do; he cannot lie, for example. The difference, however, in a Reformed understanding of omnipotence and an Arminian one is that, in the latter, the other reason God cannot do certain things is because he is essentially constrained by the libertarian will of his creatures. In Reformed theology, God's only constraint on his essential character is that character itself.

God 'thinking,' 'loving,' or 'acting justly.'"[71] While there may be some justifica-
tion to Boyd's thinking that some have wanted illegitimately to minimize these
biblical ascriptions of God, any understanding of God's condescension that
we have thus far developed certainly affirms the "literal" character of these
properties in God. That is to say, God really does take on these properties.
Though they are contingent and not essential to who he is, he nevertheless
assumes them to himself as he interacts with his human creatures.

Relenting and Repenting

We should acknowledge that, as difficult as it may be at times to ascribe affections and passions to God, there are indeed degrees of difficulty. It seems no
huge stretch to think of God as loving and gracious, or perhaps, given his
holiness, as angry and wrathful.

When it comes to passages that indicate that the Lord relents or repents,[72]
however, it becomes more difficult to find consistency, given God's comprehensive decree. How could the Lord both decree "whatsoever comes to pass"
and then relent from a particular direction or change his mind from what he
might have previously announced? According to Muller, "Given that the attribution of repentance to human beings indicates both a detestation of what
has been done and an alteration of the path taken by future acts, repentance
cannot be applied to God in a literal sense."[73] When the matter is stated that
way, we can see why there has been a reluctance in Reformed theology to
ascribe repentance or relenting to God.

It should be obvious by this point in our discussion, however, that there
is a literal way in which we can apply the notion of relenting to God, that is,
by virtue of his taking on covenantal properties. The Lord relents in that, as
he interacts with us covenantally, his interaction allows for (because he has
decreed it) the reality and responsibility of our choices, and of contingency
generally. Thus, he may determine (covenantally) to respond to his people or
his creation in a particular way, but may "change his mind"[74] with respect to
his initial response.

---

[71]Boyd, *God of the Possible*, 170n2.
[72]The Hebrew (root) word often used, נחם, is translated as "repent" (e.g., KJV), "relent" (e.g.,
ESV), and "changed his mind" (e.g., NASB). See Ex. 32:14; 2 Sam. 24:16; 1 Chron. 21:15; Jer. 15:6;
26:13; 26:19; Ezek. 24:14; Joel 2:13, 14; Amos 7:3, 6; Jonah 4:2; Zech. 8:14.
[73]Muller, *Post-Reformation Reformed Dogmatics*, 3:558.
[74]For God to "change his mind" in this context would entail that, included in his covenantal
properties, is a covenantal "mind" such that he condescends to us, even with respect to his
knowledge and the actions that proceed from it. This, again, would be analogous to a "two minds"
theory of the incarnation, as argued, for example, by Aquinas (e.g., *Summa theologica* 3.5.4).

Or perhaps it is best to think of it this way: even as the Lord really and truly interacts with his people in such a way that he fights the battle necessary to defend his own glory, in fighting that battle he necessarily acts according to, and in response to, the various choices and opportunities with which his people are confronted.

We shall discuss the reality and legitimacy of our choices, given God's comprehensive decree, in the next chapter. We can begin to see, however, that the same God who effected the eternal decree nevertheless sees our choices as, in some way, affecting what he will do "next."[75]

D. Conclusion

In what we have thus far seen, it appears there is a biblical and Christocentric way to begin to organize and understand why Scripture attributes properties to God throughout covenant history that are difficult to reconcile with his obvious and essential character as *a se*.

As we noted earlier in this chapter, when Scripture tells us, on the one hand, that "the LORD relented from the disaster that he had spoken of bringing on his people" (Ex. 32:14) and, on the other hand, that "I the LORD do not change" (Mal. 3:6), we can now understand why both aspects of the Lord's character are true of him. His pronouncement that he does not change relates directly to his salvific promises to his people. Not only so, but his immutable promises are grounded in his immutable character. So, we rightly understand that the Lord is telling us something of his essential character when he reminds us of his immutability.

When the Lord tells us in his Word that he relented from the disaster that he had threatened, we need not explain this in such a way as to diminish the clear, covenant implications of his actions. In condescending to interact with his people, the Lord really did relent from what he would otherwise have done. This is in no way an improper or metaphorical way of speaking. It is, in fact, a way of speaking that takes seriously the condescension of the Lord from the beginning, including the *gospel* condescension, that is part and parcel of the Lord's interaction with his people from Genesis 3 into eternity.

In other words, what we have contained in these verses is a "reduplicative strategy," a *communicatio idiomatum*, in which the properties of both aspects

---

[75]We should remember, as well, that Christ saw no conflict between the eternal decree (which he himself, as God, had made) and the reality of an appeal that God change his mind (cf. Matt. 26:39; Mark 14:36).

of God's character are properly attributed to his person, and that person is the Son of God, the Word, the Lord Jesus Christ.

But the conclusion to which we have come is much more sweeping than simply lining up various seemingly contradictory verses. Because the condescension of the Lord takes place from the beginning, we should understand *all* of God's dealings with creation as necessarily entailing that God has assumed properties not essential to him. In other words (again in reference to the Westminster Confession 7.1), when we think of God's voluntary condescension as expressed by way of *covenant*, we will take seriously that *all* of God's dealings with creation are covenantal dealings. This will also help us see the richness and depth of the statement that "Christ is the substance of the covenant" (WCF 7.6, WLC 35; cf. Col. 2:8ff.). He is, in that, from the beginning, he condescended to relate himself to us in such a way as to take on characteristics that were and are not essential to him in any way. What the history of God's dealings with us points toward is covenant condescension, inconceivable fully to comprehend, but nevertheless central to a basic understanding of God and his relationship to creation. Thus, in every aspect of his relationship to creation it was necessary for him (only because he freely chose) to take on characteristics that were otherwise not his and that are in no way essential to who he is.

Does this mean that God is not simple? Do we deny the simplicity of God by arguing that God condescends to take on properties that were not his and that are not essential to him? This would be the case only if the same were true of him in the incarnation. If the fact of the incarnation undermines or otherwise denies the doctrine of God's simplicity, then so also for his general covenantal condescension. But, as we have seen, particularly in our discussion of the *extra calvinisticum*, just because the Son of God takes on a human nature does not in any way deny his essential deity. All of the attributes of deity that are his prior to the incarnation remain his even as incarnate. So also, just because God condescends to take on covenantal properties does not in any way mean that he becomes less than who he is essentially. The *extra calvinisticum* applies as much to the Son of God in covenant history generally as it does to him in the reality of the incarnation.

It might be helpful here to note again Turretin's explanation of the incarnation as a "self-emptying" and to apply that now to God's covenantal condescension more generally.

> Here also belongs the verb *ekenōse*, which is not to be taken simply and absolutely (as if he ceased to be God or was reduced to a nonentity, which is impious even to think concerning the eternal and unchangeable God), but in respect

of state and comparatively because he concealed the divine glory under the veil of flesh and as it were laid it aside; not by putting off what he was, but by assuming what he was not.[76]

In all of God's dealings with creation, even as he takes to himself created properties, there is a kind of self-emptying, "in respect of state and comparatively because he conceals the divine glory." And he does this, throughout history and into eternity, "not by putting off what he was, but by assuming what he was not." There is, therefore, no change in God's essential character in any of his dealings with creation; there is, though, a graciously free and willing humiliation that, when understood properly, should serve only to humble and amaze the hearts of any who have seen this voluntary condescension for what it truly is.

There is, therefore, a divinely instituted and initiated compatibility between God's own essential character and the character of his creation. Once the Lord determines to condescend, this compatibility, as we have seen, is not such that the properties, which themselves are brought together in one person, can be in any way confused, changed, divided, or separated. However, because they are brought together in one person, they are thereby rendered compatible.

But the compatibility that *is* God condescended does not consist of the same degree of difficulty in our attempts to understand it. The fact of the Lord's immutability, as that applies to his covenant faithfulness to us, is easy enough to see. It is just because the Lord is immutable that his decree will not change. But the fact of the Lord's comprehensive decree in the light of his relenting and repenting is much more difficult for us to put together.

In the next, and final, chapter, I will attempt to apply what we have thus far understood to the more difficult areas of compatibility that confront us in Scripture. In so doing, I hope to address how we should think of such difficulties in light of the fact that as the Lord takes to himself covenantal properties, we cannot thereby confuse, change, divide, or separate his essential properties from those which he has freely chosen to take. This may help us to see why it is only in a Reformed context that a fully robust understanding of God is possible.

---

[76]Turretin, *Institutes*, 2:314. Though it cannot be pursued here, it is instructive to note, as earlier, that Turretin links an understanding of the Trinity to an understanding of the hypostatic union: "For as in the Trinity, the unity of essence does not hinder the persons from being distinct from each other and their properties and operations from being incommunicable, so the union of natures in the person of Christ does not prevent both the natures and their properties from remaining unconfounded and distinct" (2:311). The serious point to be made here is that a confusion or ignorance or, worse, denial of the orthodox notion of christology could imply the same with respect to the Trinity, such that Christianity would then be replaced for another religion altogether.

CHAPTER 5

Things Secret and Revealed

> God moves in a mysterious way
> His wonders to perform;
> He plants his footsteps in the sea,
> And rides upon the storm.
>
> Deep in unfathomable mines
> Of never-failing skill
> He treasures up his bright designs,
> And works his sovereign will.
>
> Blind unbelief is sure to err,
> And scan his work in vain.
> God is his own interpreter,
> And he will make it plain.
>
> WILLIAM COWPER

In this last chapter, I hope to set out, at least in a preliminary way, how we might construe God's *activity*, given the distinction I have been developing of God's essential/covenantal (*Eimi/eikon*) properties.

Before we move into a discussion of God's activity, however, it is important to note that there is no one-to-one correspondence between the essential/covenantal distinction and classical delineations of God's attributes. There *is*, it seems, an identity or near identity between (what we have called) God's essential properties and God's incommunicable attributes, for example. Since both categories (essential and incommunicable) have their focus in God's aseity, it is natural that they would more or less coincide. Not only so, but since both categories highlight God's character quite apart from anything else *ad extra*, we should expect that there will be significant overlap and identity between the two.

There is not, however, such coincidence between the (so-called) communicable attributes of God and (what I have called) his covenantal properties. This is no criticism of the standard classifications of attributes. What those classifications attempt to set forth, while not opposed to our specific concerns in this book, have more to do with God's character *as God* than with his freely chosen relationship and activity in and with the universe that he has made. Again, however, even these two classifications will have some overlap. God's character as a just God, for example, will certainly have much to do with the way in which he relates himself to his creation.

The concern in our previous chapters, however, is broader than a classification of God's attributes will allow. The fact that God changes his mind covenantally is no warrant for ascribing the attribute of uncertainty or of essential ignorance to God. As I have said, such change is a property that God takes on just because he has covenanted to create and redeem a people and to condescend in order to effect his sovereign purposes. This, it seems, is one of the reasons that the best interpreters of Scripture have given precedence to passages that declare God's character, and then have interpreted passages that seem to conflict with that character in light of that declaration, and not vice versa. So, it is right and proper for the church—hermeneutically, biblically, theologically—to interpret Exodus 32:14 in light of Malachi 3:6. God's proclamation that his character is such that he does not change (Mal. 3:6) must take precedence over Yahweh's plain statement that he relents (Ex. 32:14).[1] Just *how* this precedence is applied and articulated has been one of our primary points of discussion all along. But there is no question that the precedence must be there and must fashion and shape anything else we say concerning God and his activity.[2]

---

[1] I recognize that there are more complex issues here. My concern at this point is for the principle that Scripture interprets Scripture, given the closed canon.

[2] To reiterate what we have previously said, another way of articulating this precedence is that ontology determines and guides history, not vice versa. Thus, the character of God *as God*

With that in mind, I hope to apply the distinction of God's essential and covenantal (*Eimi/eikon*) properties to the way(s) in which his activity for, in, and through his creation has been addressed. As in previous chapters, the intent here is to see whether God's decision to condescend and the implications of that decision help us better to understand God's relationship to and with his creation, and with his people. Before we proceed, one more reminder is in order.

A. In Praise of Paradox

I mentioned in the introduction that we must get used to the idea that antinomy and paradox will inevitably surround discussions such as this one. But the appeal to antinomy, paradox, and mystery is oftentimes troubling to those sympathetic to a less-than-Reformed understanding of God's character and decree. In an attempted refutation of Calvinism and the "problem" of divine sovereignty, Jack Cottrell complains:

> Calvinistic discussions of this problem are laced with words like *paradox*, *antinomy*, *contradiction*, and *mystery*. As Klooster says, "Divine sovereignty and human responsibility are paradoxical and beyond human comprehension." Despite this rather agnostic attitude, Calvinists have spent much time and energy trying to explain the unexplainable.[3]

It may be that some Calvinists have given the impression that, in our discussions of the mysteries of the faith, we are attempting to exhaust what is inexhaustible. But surely Cottrell would not fault Calvinists any more than he would Arminians for attempting to bring together, as much as possible, what God's revelation teaches concerning these mysteries. It is certainly not the case that the relationship of God to the world is absolutely inexplicable; rather, in whatever ways it is explicable, it will always remain for us incomprehensible as well.

This is yet another reason why it seems best to begin our discussions with the doctrine of Christ, specifically the person of Christ. Both Reformed and Arminian have agreed historically that when the Son of God became man, he did not give up his deity, his "Godness," in order to take on a human nature.

---

determines and guides whatever else he is and does relative to his creation. As always, our movement with respect to a proper knowledge of God is from the top down, not from the bottom up.

[3] Jack W. Cottrell, "The Nature of Divine Sovereignty," in *The Grace of God, the Will of Man*, ed. Clark H. Pinnock (Grand Rapids: Academie, 1989), 98.

Arminians, like the Reformed, have historically been Chalcedonian in their affirmation of the incarnation.

Yet the Chalcedonian affirmations have always been seen to be *paradoxical*, even *antinomic*.[4] The Chalcedonian Creed is one example of the church's attempt—and an accepted and acceptable attempt, at that—to "explain the unexplainable." Not only so, but given that the incarnation itself is *the* "explanation" and application of God's relationship to creation, we should expect that every other instantiation, indication, and explanation of such a relation would itself be paradoxical and antinomic and, in the end, incomprehensible.

The "explanations" therefore given by the Reformed of the relationship of God to creation, including his actions and reactions, will themselves be shrouded in mystery. Nevertheless, explanations are given both in biblical revelation and in theology. If we *begin* with christology, rather than with some abstract concept of antinomy, paradox, or mystery, we can start to see that *all* explanations of God's relationship to creation can be understood properly only within the context of God's relationship to creation as expressed in the incarnation. This, it seems to me, expands and enhances the Christ-centered approach to God's revelation in such a way that the glory of God in his condescension, typified centrally in the gospel, is seen for what it is.

In all of this we must keep in mind, however, that there is no antinomy or contradiction in God. He is completely and exhaustively coherent in all that he says, does, and is. Thus, the admission of antinomy and paradox in Christianity points us to the complexity of God's simplicity, the unfathomable depth that is God's complete and incomprehensible perfection, for which, among other things, we worship him (Rom. 11:33ff.).

B. Continuities (and Discontinuities) of Condescension

The relationship of God's attributes and character to the attitudes, activities, and actions that come about by way of his condescension is perhaps not as straightforward as we might expect at first glance. We cannot assume, for example, that all of God's covenantal properties are implied by his essential character.

There are, of course, properties that he takes on by virtue of creation that are inextricably tied to, in that they are consistent with, his essential character. God's holiness, defined as his unique transcendence, is directly implied by his aseity and "Godness." His justice, in that he always does what is right,

---

[4]We should remember here that antinomy and paradox are always modes of creaturely expression; in God there is complete coherence and harmony such that no antinomies or paradoxes exist.

is an implication of his goodness (which just *is* his essential character). His exhaustive knowledge of himself implies his exhaustive knowledge of creation as well; that is, he could not be omniscient with respect to himself and also be *essentially* ignorant of any aspect of creation. These and other characteristics of God are relatively uncontroversial.[5]

As we have already seen, however, the truths about God that have been most perplexing are those that imply a decided discontinuity between God's essential character and properties that undermine, or seem to negate or deny, that character. God's covenantal lack of knowledge, to use an example we have already noted, is inconsistent with his essential exhaustive knowledge. Because of that inconsistency or discontinuity, one of the primary options taken historically has been to explain such a lack in terms that are no part of the biblical text itself.

Recall, to use an example I have already mentioned (in chapter 4), Turretin's explanation of the Lord's words in Genesis 22:12 (". . . for now I know that you fear God, seeing you have not withheld your son, your only son, from me"): "This is not to be understood absolutely of the knowledge which God obtained, but transitively of the knowledge which he gave to others (as similar words are often used in the Scriptures)."[6] Turretin's explanation is understandable, especially given the attacks that he was addressing from the Socinians and others. But critics of Turretin can be excused for charging that such explanations do not do justice to the text itself. As a matter of fact, to understand the text covenantally (whereby God takes on properties that establish and maintain his condescending commitment to us) is to see again the glory of God in the gospel. He interacts with Abraham, and that interaction is real, it is significant, and its outcome is verified in the context of that relationship.

God could have truthfully said to Abraham, "I have known from eternity both what you would do, in every detail, and that I would provide a substitute for you. I put you to this test so that your faith would be strengthened and so that *you* would know, by way of experience, just how deeply committed to me you are." This, and many other similar statements, God could have genuinely said to Abraham.

The point of the passage, however, is not that God knows the end from the beginning in any and every situation or in Abraham's life, *true as that is*. The point of the passage is that God's covenant with his people, and with

---

[5]"Relatively" uncontroversial because, as we have seen, once creation becomes a part of the equation, some want to maintain that God's essential attributes change according to *its* character.
[6]Francis Turretin, *Institutes of Elenctic Theology*, trans. George Musgrave Giger, ed. James T. Dennison Jr., 3 vols. (Phillipsburg, NJ: P&R, 1992–1997), 1:212.

Abraham as the father of his people, is one that really and truly, not simply metaphorically, involves God in the process. It is a commitment in which he has come down, covenantally "hiding" those essential properties that remain his, in order to bind himself to us and to our lives in such a way that his interaction with us involves a real, ongoing, empathetic relationship. He really does identify with us, and he moves with us in history, "learning" and listening, in order to maintain and manage the covenant relationship that he has sovereignly and unilaterally established, the details of which he has eternally and immutably decreed.

This, of course, is what Christ did. He came to earth and was tempted in all points just like us (Heb. 4:15), yet in this temptation he did not say, "I will not sin because I am God, so these temptations are of no significance; they are futile." From one perspective, that is true enough. Instead, however, "although he was a Son, he learned obedience through what he suffered" (Heb. 5:8). This learning surely included a knowledge component, as Jesus "increased in wisdom and in stature, and in favor with God and man" (Luke 2:52). This "increase" is no fantasy; it is the foundation for the very gospel of God. It in no way negates or denies his full deity. Though it might seem to undermine his essential character, it is just that essential character, which itself remains and obtains throughout his existence, that highlights for us and emphasizes to us the glory of his sacrificial humiliation in condescension. As is the case with Christ climactically, so it is also with (the Son of) God in covenant history.

So, God takes on covenant characteristics that are consistent with his essential character. But he also takes on covenant characteristics that seem to us to be inconsistent with that character. As with Christ, however, these inconsistencies are not such that we must explain them away or twist the texts to make them say the opposite of what they say. They appear as inconsistencies precisely because of God's condescension, and that condescension has the gospel as its central focus and Christ as its substance. So, the explanation of those inconsistencies is to be found in God's free act of mercy and grace, his stooping down to be "one of us" as he providentially works out his meticulously sovereign plan in history. This way of understanding these tensions has its focus in what God has freely done, and what he has sacrificed, in order to relate himself to us and to conquer the sin that has taken his creation captive.

C. Problems and Possibilities

As we have seen, God's covenant condescension is an act of his free will that effects a change. It does *not* effect a change *in* God, that is, essentially, any more than the incarnation effected a change *in* the Son of God. God remains *a se*, altogether immutable, infinite, and eternal. But there is a change with respect to God, in that, by virtue of his own free decision, he takes on properties and characteristics that he otherwise would not have had. In other words, as I have said, the metaphor of "condescension" just *is* the taking on of covenant properties; it is not a literal "coming down," since God is exhaustively located everywhere. And as we have seen, that act of God's free will is inextricably linked with his free knowledge.

As is always the case when we consider who God is, numerous deep and complex questions remain concerning God's character and his *activity* of condescension.[7] How, we might ask, does the eternal God *begin* to do something he was not doing "previously"? To put it another way, how can the eternal God "take on" anything that he did not eternally have? Would not such an "assumption" or "taking on" require some kind of distinguishing "moment" (temporal or otherwise) in God's eternal activity?

Perhaps even more perplexing, how could God, who is himself necessary and simple, determine anything at all that was not itself both necessary and identical with him? If God's will just *is* his nature (in that there are no "parts" that compose God), in what way could his will be free, thus relativized (to something), without his nature itself being so relativized?

Let me first state explicitly what is implicit in all discussions of this sort. What I am seeking to expound is a matter of "good and necessary consequence" of biblical truth about God. Since God is *a se*, since his knowledge is in no way dependent on creation, and since creation itself is a free act of God, the goal is to articulate properly—i.e., biblically—from a limited perspective, *how* it might be that God acts, knows, and wills with respect to creation. In seeking to respond to these questions, then, I will not be able to produce anything close to a full explanation. I do hope, however, to set the contours of the discussion so that the direction of a fuller response might be clearer.

I must also make clear before we begin our foray into these discussions that I will endeavor to avoid a speculative or abstract theology. Any theology

---

[7] Worth noting at this point, and relative to our entire discussion below, is the relationship of God's will to his character: "The Reformed orthodox . . . insist on understanding the doctrine of God's will as an integral part of the larger doctrine of the attributes—indeed, as a connecting link in the chain or circle of attributes that, together in their unity, provide us with an understanding of what God is and of the way that God relates to the world" (Richard A. Muller, *Post-Reformation Reformed Dogmatics: The Rise and Development of Reformed Orthodoxy, ca. 1520 to ca. 1725*, vol. 3, *The Divine Essence and Attributes*, 2nd ed. [Grand Rapids: Baker Academic, 2003], 433). Thus, our discussion of God's will is meant to be a "connecting link" between God's character and what he chooses to do relative to that character.

that "hangs in the air," as it were, without being grounded in the truth of Scripture (or in the good and necessary consequences of that truth) is not worth the ink used to write it. Thus, we cannot hope to know in any precise detail what God's will in itself is.[8]

There are, however, certain aspects of God's will that must be affirmed in the context of an orthodox understanding of his attributes. To put the matter summarily and in two central points: (1) God's will in no way compromises his simplicity. However we think of God's will, as in everything else that we have discussed, it both is essential to him as a personal God and is in no way a "part" of him, such that it was added to him or is essentially distinct from his character *as God*. (2) God's will is free, in that he is able to and *does* make choices and commits himself to actions that were in no way necessary. These two points must be kept in mind throughout our discussion. Give up either one, and orthodoxy is compromised. If we give up 1, we deny God's aseity, making him dependent on something external to himself. If we give up 2, then creation becomes necessary, and, again, his essential aseity is compromised. Whatever else we have to say about God's will and the relationship of that will to his character, these two points cannot be subverted or denied.

So, there is a complex and ultimately incomprehensible web of ideas that comes together when we begin to think of God's activity, especially as we attempt to delineate that activity by way of God's covenantal condescension. In order to think about God's activity, especially in relation to his power, his will, his decree, and his providence in and over creation, we need again to enter the labyrinth of distinctions surrounding his knowledge, will, and power.

Recall from chapter 2 the close relationship that obtains between God's knowledge and his will. God's necessary knowledge, as we saw, is identical with who he is. He did not acquire it, nor is it in some way added to who he is as God. For this reason, and in line with God's character, this necessary knowledge that God has is sometimes called his simple knowledge; like God, it is not composed of parts. Moreover, God's knowledge is not something added to his being. Given God's essential simplicity, his knowledge *is* his being, in that he does not first exist and then know.[9] He does not need to acquire

---

[8]"Far from being an excessively 'speculative' doctrine in the modern sense of the term, the orthodox discussion of the divine will was deeply rooted in the redemptive and historical elements of Christian theology and indicative of the a posteriori character of much Reformed theology in the era of Protestant scholasticism: for the distinctions made by the orthodox concerning the divine willing were not a matter of rational speculation but rather a result of the examination of biblical texts and traditional discussions of the *voluntas Dei*" (ibid.).

[9]This identity of knowledge and being, however, is not without distinctions; it is not, therefore, a blank identity. More on this below.

knowledge in any way. Even his free knowledge is not an acquired knowledge. Included in his existence is his exhaustive knowledge.

Whatever is not necessary but is known and willed to be contingent (i.e., it is/was possible for it to be or not to be), as an object of God's knowledge, is related to God's free knowledge and will. This knowledge, too, he did not acquire.[10] Traditionally, it is in this category that we begin to see more explicitly the relationship between God's knowledge and God's will. As a matter of fact, as we have seen, oftentimes the *modes* of God's free knowledge and of his will were thought to be coterminous.

Necessarily linked with this discussion is one more set of characteristics that God has and that needs to be introduced here. Typically discussed in conjunction with God's knowledge and will is God's power. The reason for this, as we noted in chapter 2, is that God's self-knowledge, *along with all possibilities*, was included in God's simple, necessary, or natural knowledge. One of the primary reasons that all possibilities have been included in the natural knowledge of God is that, in exhaustively knowing himself, he exhaustively knows as well his own power. Therefore, God knows all that is possible, based on that power.

Thomas's explanation of this notion may be helpful. In *Summa theologica* 1.14.5, Thomas asks, "Does God know things other than himself?" After a series of objections and denials, he responds:

> God must know things other than himself. For he evidently understands himself perfectly; otherwise his existing would not be perfect, since his existing is his understanding. But if something is known perfectly, *its power must be known perfectly. Now the power of a thing cannot be known perfectly unless the objects to which the power extends are known.* Hence, since God's power extends to other things by being the first efficient cause which produces all beings, . . . God must know things other than himself. This will be still more evident if we add that the very being of God, the first efficient cause, is his act of knowing. So, whatever effects pre-exist in God as in the first cause must be in his understanding; and everything there must be in the condition of intelligibility.[11]

---

[10]I should note again that I am making distinctions here in order to preserve the biblical notions of God as *a se* as well as the contingency of creation. Though these distinctions are proper and theologically necessary, we must remember that God never acquires any of his knowledge, with respect to his essential character. Both necessary and free knowledge are included in his exhaustive knowledge, which is identical with his being God.

[11]Brian Leftow and Brian Davies, *Aquinas: Summa Theologiae, Questions on God*, Cambridge Texts in the History of Philosophy (Cambridge: Cambridge University Press, 2006), 175–76, my emphasis.

Here we see, initially, Thomas's emphasis, again, on God's simplicity. God must understand things other than himself because, if he did not, he could not be a perfect Being, given that his existence and understanding are identical. For God, to lack in understanding is to lack in being, which is impossible. So, God must understand himself and understand things other than himself *through himself.*

Thomas then goes on to connect God's knowledge of other things with his power. Given that there is no lack of knowledge in God as God, that is, he understands himself completely and exhaustively, it follows that he exhaustively understands his own power. For Thomas, an exhaustive understanding of God's power would necessarily include an exhaustive understanding of those things to which that power extends. So, in understanding himself perfectly (i.e., exhaustively), God naturally and necessarily knows all possible things beyond himself. This link between God's knowledge and power is explained thus by Turretin:

> Although the knowledge of God is one and simple intrinsically no less than his essence, yet it can be considered in different ways extrinsically as to the objects. But it is commonly distinguished by theologians into the knowledge of simple intelligence (or natural and indefinite) and the knowledge of vision (or free and definite). The former is the knowledge of things merely possible and is therefore called indefinite because nothing on either hand is determined concerning them by God. . . . Hence they mutually differ: (1) in object because the natural knowledge is occupied with possible things, but the free about future things; (2) in foundation because *the natural is founded on the omnipotence of God*, but the free depends upon his will and decree by which things pass from a state of possibility to a state of futurition; (3) in order because the natural precedes the decree, but the free follows it because it beholds things future.[12]

The power of God, therefore, grounds and founds the natural knowledge of God, according to Turretin. What he likely means is that God's knowledge of things possible must be included in his natural knowledge, given that such knowledge includes exhaustive knowledge of his power, and included in that power is what God could possibly do. Charles Hodge follows Turretin here.

> This distinction between the possible and actual, is the foundation of the distinction between the knowledge of simple intelligence and the knowledge of vision. The former is founded on God's power, and the latter upon his will. This

---

[12]Turretin, *Institutes*, 1:212–13, my emphasis.

only means that, in virtue of his omniscient intelligence, He knows whatever infinite power can effect; and that from the consciousness of his own purposes, He knows what He has determined to effect or to permit to occur. . . .

It seems to be an inconsistency in those orthodox theologians who deny the distinction in God between knowledge and power, to admit, as they all do, the distinction between the actual and possible. For if God creates by thinking or knowing, if in Him, as they say, *intelligere et facere idem est*, then all He knows must be, and must be as soon as He knows or thinks it, i.e., from eternity. If, however, we retain the Scriptural idea of God as a spirit, who can do more than He does; if we ascribe to Him what we know to be a perfection in ourselves, namely, that our power exceeds our acts, that a faculty and the exercise of that faculty are not identical, then we can understand how God can know the possible as well as the actual. God is not limited to the universe, which of necessity is finite. God has not exhausted Himself in determining to cause the present order of things to be.[13]

There is, then, an inextricable link between God's simple knowledge, his power, and his will. For now, we will focus on this link and deal with God's "knowledge of vision," or free will, further below.

First, just what is this divine power? Simply put, it is that which God can do. But, of course, things are never that simple. Doesn't God's omnipotence require us to affirm that God can do all things? That is how it is often understood (hence the prefix "omni-"). Scripture does say that all things are possible with God (see Matt. 10:26; Mark 10:27; 14:36). However, Scripture surely indicates that there are certain things that God cannot do (e.g., Heb. 6:18). How might we make sense of this?

We first must recognize that any inability that obtains in God does so only by virtue of his own character. The fact that it is impossible for God to lie is a specific example of the more general truth that God cannot change his essential character. He cannot do so, not because *we* say so, but because for God to deny himself would mean that he ceases to be God, which is impossible. Second, we note that other impossibilities—for example, that Judas of Iscariot be redeemed—are impossible only by virtue of what God has *determined* will be the case (John 17:12). Though conditioned on God's determination and not therefore absolutely impossible, they nevertheless are also impossible by virtue of God's (covenant) character. Once God has determined something, that thing will necessarily obtain.

---

[13]Charles Hodge, *Systematic Theology*, 3 vols. (London: James Clarke, 1960), 1:398.

Thus, the power of God has historically been circumscribed, in part, according to what is *possible*. Embedded in God's *knowledge* of his own power—a power that he knows exhaustively—is a knowledge of all that is possible. So, says Muller:

> A further distinction can be made concerning possible things according to the theological distinction between the divine *potentia absoluta* or absolute power, and the divine *potentia ordinata*, or ordained power. Under the *potentia absoluta* anything is possible that does not involve a contradiction; God's absolute power comprehends the broadest category of possibility. But under the *potentia ordinata* only those things are possible that do not conflict with the divinely established order of nature.[14]

In discussing the *potentia* of God, including as it does all possibility, we need a further clarification.

> There is a highly significant point in the language that associates the natural or necessary divine knowledge of all possibility with the *potentia Dei* and the free or visionary knowledge of all actuality with the *decretum Dei*. The latter issue is simple: nothing can exist unless God in some manner wills its existence (whether directly or through the agency of secondary causes). The former issue demands clarification, inasmuch as the usual translation of *potentia* as "power" misses the sense of the term as "potency": the point is that possibilities or possible existents are *in potentia*—in potency or potential—and the potential *for* their existence is the divine potency or power. Thus, God knows both his power and his will: in his power is the potential for the existence of all that is possible; in his will is the foundation of the existence of all that is actual. This also means that, inasmuch as the potential for the existence of all that is possible is the divine *potentia*, the entire category of the possible is necessarily limited by the *potentia Dei*: there is no genuine possibility beyond the bounds of the divine nature.[15]

The clarification and point, then, is this: because the existence of anything possible is in God's *potentia*, included in his simple knowledge is exhaustive knowledge of his power and thus of things possible. So, according to Edward Leigh:

> The object of divine power is all things simply and in their own nature possible, which neither contradict the nature of God, nor the essence of the creatures; those which are contrary to these are absolutely impossible; such things God

---

[14]Richard A. Muller, *Dictionary of Latin and Greek Theological Terms: Drawn Principally from Protestant Scholastic Theology* (Grand Rapids: Baker, 1985), 230–31.
[15]Muller, *Post-Reformation Reformed Dogmatics*, 3:413.

cannot do, because he cannot will them; nor can he will and do contrary things, as good and evil; or contradictory, as to be, and not to be, that a true thing be false, that any thing while it is should not be; God cannot sin, lie, deny, change or destroy himself, suffer; he cannot not beget his Son from eternity: for all these things do *ex diametro* oppose the Divine, Immutable, Simple, most perfect and true essence. God cannot create another God, nor cause a man to be unreasonable, nor a body to be infinite and everywhere, for these things contradict the essential definitions of a creature, of a man and of a body; not to be able to do these things is not impotency but power, for to be able to do opposite things is a sign of infirmity, being not able to remain altogether in one and the same state.[16]

So, God's knowledge is exhaustive; it comprehends everything, including everything he is able to do. What he actually *does*, however, with respect to anything contingent, is denominated both as God's free will and as his *free knowledge*, since such knowledge is inextricably tied to a free act of God's will. This does not mean, we should note, that God cannot know some things until and unless he freely wills them. God knows everything, period, and his essential knowledge of all things is not progressive or discursive in any way. Why not, then, simply categorize God's knowledge as *natural* or *necessary* and then make distinctions with respect to what he *wills*? Why tie God's knowledge to his act of will in this way?

When addressing questions such as these we must keep in mind that we are treading on holy ground; we are at the edge of a glorious abyss the bottom of which we will never reach. Not only, then, must great care be taken, as much as lies within us, but we should also recognize that there will have to be a certain tentativeness to everything we seek to affirm. There are sound theological reasons to affirm much of what we say here. But even as we affirm these truths, we at the same time must admit that we peer into unapproachable light. Our vision of such things, and our ability to grasp and hold them, will always be surrounded by profound creaturely limits.[17] In making these

---

[16]Quoted in ibid., 3:534–35.

[17]So, says Pictet: "Concerning the manner (*modus*) in which God knows all things, we must speak cautiously and not attribute anything unbecoming or unworthy to the ultimate majesty. Maimonides observes, that *to wish to know the mode of the divine knowledge, is the same as wishing to be God*. Now we must not at all imagine that God knows things in the same manner as men, who understand one thing in one way, and another thing in another way, and the same thing sometimes obscurely and at other times more clearly, and who, from things known proceed to things unknown. The divine knowledge is of such a mode, as not to admit of any discursive imperfection, or investigative labor, or recollective obscurity, or difficulty of application. God comprehends all things by one single act, observes them as by a single consideration, and sees them distinctly, certainly, and therefore perfectly," quoted in ibid., 3:413.

distinctions, however, the biblical emphasis of God's essential (and, as I will argue below, covenantal) character is set forth.[18]

One of the main reasons to link God's free knowledge and will in this way is to recognize that there is nothing *ad extra* that essentially constrains God or God's knowledge. Suppose we argued that God's knowledge of all things *ad extra* is not free, but *necessary, simpliciter.* That is, suppose we affirm simply that God's knowledge is *only* necessary and that it includes a knowledge of creation. Would this not entail that God's knowledge is essentially *dependent* on that which is (at least potentially) *ad extra*, that is, creation? The distinction, then, rightly affirms both that God's knowledge is exhaustive and comprehensive, and that his "mode" of knowing must be distinguished. This distinction, then, has its locus in the *objects* known and willed. If such objects are themselves necessary, then they are included in God's natural knowledge and necessary will; if they are contingent, then they are a part of his free knowledge and will.

Despite this fundamental distinction, the notion of possibility relative to God's knowledge and will is itself not always clearly distinguished. Note, for example:

> The knowledge that God must have is a necessary knowledge but it is also natural, inasmuch as God has it by nature rather than by imposition from without—the knowledge that God freely has is a knowledge that coincides with his will for the being or existence of all things *ad extra.* Accordingly, the necessary or natural knowledge of God is the knowledge that God has concerning himself and all possibilities *ad extra* or beyond himself. This knowledge of all possibility is typically associated by the orthodox with the *potentia* or *omnipotentia Dei*, given that the divine potency is the potency for the being of all things. The free or voluntary knowledge is a knowledge of all those possibilities that God freely wills to actualize—namely, his creation, whether past, present, or future.[19]

On a first read, it may sound as though there is a conflict in the way in which God's knowledge is described relative to all possibilities. His free knowledge, says Muller, is "a knowledge that coincides with his will for the being or existence of all things *ad extra.*" This seems to say that all things *ad extra* belong to the category of God's free knowledge (and will). The corollary to this would be that only those things *ad intra* would belong to God's necessary (or natural, or simple) knowledge. But as Muller goes on to note, the neces-

---

[18]Thus, Hodge overstates when, in discussing these distinctions with respect to God's knowledge, he says, "This distinction is not of much importance," Hodge, *Systematic Theology*, 1:397.
[19]Muller, *Post-Reformation Reformed Dogmatics*, 3:406.

sary knowledge of God includes, of course, God himself, but also knowledge of "all possibilities *ad extra* or beyond himself."

It would appear, then, that God's free knowledge encompasses *all things* that are outside of God, and also that his necessary knowledge includes *all possibilities* that are outside of God. How can both of these be true? They can be true if we affirm that possibilities are not "things" in the sense of that which actually exists, but include what God is able to do, some of which he does not do.

In what sense, though, are possibilities not "things"? One way that this has been understood historically is by arguing that possibilities are exemplars in the mind of God, from which he determines which ones will be actual. According to Thomas:

> As ideas, according to Plato, are principles of the knowledge of things and of their generation, an idea has this twofold office, as it exists in the mind of God. So far as the idea is the principle of the making of things, it may be called an *exemplar*, and belongs to practical knowledge. But so far as it is a principle of knowledge, it is properly called a *type*, and may belong to speculative knowledge also. As an exemplar, therefore, it has respect to everything made by God in any period of time; whereas as a principle of knowledge it has respect to all things known by God, even though they never come to be in time; and to all things that He knows according to their proper type, in so far as they are known by Him in a speculative manner.[20]

And further:

> The exemplar is the same as the idea. But ideas, according to Augustine (QQ. LXXXIII., *qu.* 46), are *the master forms, which are contained in the divine intelligence*. Therefore the exemplars of things are not outside God.
> . . . And therefore we must say that in the divine wisdom are the types of all things, which types we have called ideas—*i.e.*, exemplar forms existing in the divine mind (Q. XV., A. 1). And these ideas, though multiplied by their relations to things, in reality are not apart from the divine essence, according as the likeness to that essence can be shared diversely by different things.[21]

But what exactly can we say about these exemplars, and how might they relate to both possibility and actuality?

---

[20]Thomas Aquinas, *Summa theologica*, trans. Fathers of the English Dominican Province, 1.15.3.
[21]Ibid., 1.44.3. For a penetrating analysis of Aquinas on divine ideas, see Gregory T. Doolan, *Aquinas on the Divine Ideas as Exemplar Causes* (Washington, DC: Catholic University of America Press, 2008).

From Actual to Possible?

This notion of God knowing exemplars has a long history in theology. It is another way of articulating the fact that God must know exhaustively *as God*, and that what he knows relates, not simply and only to himself, but to everything else that is or could be as well.[22]

There are, however, a couple of points that may be worth considering with respect to this notion of exemplars, divine ideas, and the related problem of possibilities.[23] James Ross questions the traditional understanding of exemplars.

> Plato's idea that perfect exemplars are logically prior (and prior in being) to imperfect participations was adapted by St. Augustine to make the exemplars dependent in being upon God's nature, not will, preserving the necessity and logical priority of the exemplars without allowing them to be independent of God.[24]

Ross's contention is a modification of the exemplarism of (some) traditional theology. Rather than postulating exemplars in the mind of God according to his natural or simple knowledge, Ross argues that for exemplarism to have any content at all, it must be predicated on God's *will*. His argument seems to include the following.[25]

The exemplarism of Aquinas, according to Ross, does not include an infinite number of possibilities that God knows. Rather, it is an affirmation that,

---

[22]There is a long and complex discussion dealing with the relationship of exemplars to ideas, and then of exemplars to created things. We cannot enter that discussion here. For a sample of the issues involved, see James F. Ross, "Aquinas's Exemplarism; Aquinas's Voluntarism," *American Catholic Philosophical Quarterly* 64 (1990): 171–98; Armand A. Maurer, "James Ross on the Divine Ideas: A Reply," *American Catholic Philosophical Quarterly* 65 (1991): 213–20; and James F. Ross, "Response to Maurer and Dewan," *American Catholic Philosophical Quarterly* 65 (1991): 235–43.

[23]It seems that "good and necessary consequence" can move in either direction with respect to possibility. The strength of the view that attributes all possibility, including possibility *ad extra*, to God's natural knowledge is that it thereby affirms God's essential power as extending across the spectrum of all that could be. The strength of the view described below is that it seeks to ground the possible in the actual, and thus consistently attributes *all* that is *ad extra* to the free will/free knowledge of God. In either case, there remain depths that cannot be plumbed, which is, of course, to be expected.

[24]James F. Ross, "God, Creator of Kinds and Possibilities: Requiescant Universalia Ante Res," in *Rationality, Religious Belief, and Moral Commitment*, ed. Robert Audi and William J. Wainwright (Ithaca, NY: Cornell University Press, 1986), 320.

[25]Readers less interested in the fine points of philosophical theology may want to skip this section. I am attempting in what follows to summarize aspects of Ross's argument, some of which is not completely clear; any errors in summary, however, are entirely my own.

as God is the divine *Verbum*, his knowledge is the pattern for anything and everything else; that much is basic to all theology. Further, says Ross:

> For the exemplarist's purposes, it would not do for God to have an exemplar for one or only some individuals in a way that is conditional upon his having made some actual thing. . . . He must be able to have a complete idea for any and all individuals, irrespective of whether there is an actual finite being at all.[26]

The problem with having a complete idea regardless of what is actual, according to Ross, is that every possibility itself must have a context and content. In a word, it must be *indexed* to something.[27] That context and content need not be actual; it can be possible. But for it to be possible, *it must have its genesis in the actual.* "If, however, God can have exemplars of all individuals with all *indexed* de re necessities[28] without an actual finite being, then what do the indexes indicate? This is what refutes, inter alia, Leibniz's 'complete concept' hypothesis. *Indexicality requires actuality.*"[29] Furthermore, says Ross, "the only way a divine exemplar could include *every* indexed de re necessity of its object is to be the exemplar of an actual thing."[30]

That is, as Ross indicates, God's knowledge of exemplars, in order to be complete—including all necessities that attach to such exemplars—must be *based on* what is actual. Only then can such exemplars be exhaustively indexed; that is, only then can exemplars have both content and context. "Therefore, there is not a domain of exemplar ideas *of individuals.* Indexing without a root in actual being is like pointing without a context."[31]

We can now begin to see how the notion of the "possible" as it is sometimes discussed might be too bare a concept for a cogent discussion of God's knowledge. At least, it may be the case that bare possibility is, in fact, *nothing at all* and therefore is neither known nor considered by God's natural knowledge. The realm of that which is contingent (which would include all possibility), according to Ross, should not be understood as having its locus in the power

---

[26]Ross, "God, Creator of Kinds and Possibilities," 328.
[27]At the risk of oversimplification, "to be indexed" includes, at least, that something be a possible state of affairs with content and context. In other words, my being born in the seventeenth century is a possible state of affairs because it is indexed to *me* (content) and to a *past (actual) state of affairs* (context). Included in Ross's concern is the notion of the truth value of a proposition as well, which will not detain us here.
[28]"De re necessities" are modal claims, in this case about, say, a particular individual *as such* rather than about the truth of a given proposition.
[29]Ross, "God, Creator of Kinds and Possibilities," 328, my emphasis.
[30]Ibid., 329.
[31]Ibid.

of God to make the possible actual. Rather, we should see God's power as "the power to *cause being* ex nihilo. There is no need, then, to think that 'the realm of the contingent' determinately decomposes into actual and possible individuals and common natures or into exemplar ideas for them."[32]

What, then, of exemplars? Exemplars are those ideas, perhaps infinite, in the mind of God that have their foundation in what is actual. This entails, of course, that there is a vast array of things that God could have done but did not do. But it also entails that possibility has its source, not in the *natural knowledge* of God, as has sometimes been understood, but in the *free will* of God to *cause* whatever is, and *not to cause* other things that might have been.

This, we can see, also shifts the focus of discussion of God's *potentia*. That power, as it has reference to God himself, is certainly included in his natural and necessary knowledge. But once that power has reference to possibilities *ad extra*, it has its content, context, and focus in the free determination of the way things are, and thus in his free knowledge and will. So, says Ross, the domain of God's power, instead of "adding actuality" to a possible world, rather,

> is realized with its exercise. What is possible *ad extra* is a result of what God does. God's power has no exemplar objects, only a perimeter (that is, finite being) plus a limit (that of internal consistency, compatibility with the divine being). God creates the kinds, the natures of things, along with the things. And he settles what-might-have-been insofar as it is a consequence of what exists; for example, you might have been wealthier. Thus, there is no *mere* possibility with content (for example, "there might have been Martisils, silicon-based percipients, native to Mars"); there are only descriptions, actual and potential, that might, for all we know so far, have been satisfied. They do not, however, "pick out" any definite content that, if actual, would satisfy them. All content *ad extra* is caused by God. In sum, God creates the possibility, impossibility, and counter-factuality that has content (real situations) involving being other than God.[33]

If Ross is right, then all possibility concerning things that are outside of God must depend on a free act of his will, since it depends on God's free decision to create. In that sense, God *determines* the possible, and from the vast array of possibles picks out the actual.[34]

---

[32]Ibid., 318.

[33]Ibid., 318–19.

[34]This notion might also go against Stump's understanding of Thomas. In Eleonore Stump and Norman Kretzmann, "God's Knowledge and Its Causal Efficacy," in *The Rationality of Belief and the Plurality of Faith*, ed. Thomas D. Senor (Ithaca, NY: Cornell University Press,

The view for which Ross argues, generally, comports with a traditional discomfort, at least for some, with the idea that possibility is included, *simpliciter*, in God's natural knowledge. It may be for this reason that some have wanted to qualify the notion of possibility with respect to God's knowledge and will. According to Muller:

> Alsted indicates that God, first in order, knows himself. Second, God knows all possibilities—*whether those arising immediately out of his will*, or those arising out of his movement, conservation, concurrence, or permissive willing of creatures, or those arising out of the acts of creatures themselves.[35]

Note that this "second" order of possibilities *arises out of God's will or movement*. Thus, possibility would have its locus in the will of God and, following our discussion, in the free will of God. Note also how Van Til demarcates the relationship of possibility to God's knowledge.

> God's knowledge of himself may further be spoken of as *necessary* knowledge. He himself exists as a necessary being. His knowledge of himself is therefore necessary in the sense that it is knowledge of himself as a necessarily existing being. And it is because God has this full and extensive knowledge of himself necessarily, and therefore exhaustively, that he also has a comprehensive knowledge of all possibility beside himself. That possibility itself depends upon God's plan with respect to it. God is free to create what he pleases. *This knowledge that God has of all possibility beyond himself may therefore be called the free knowledge of God*. It is in this way that we may keep a rigid and clear distinction between God's knowledge and his power.[36]

The knowledge that God has of possibility beyond himself is coincident with the *free knowledge* of God, says Van Til. Thus, it is inextricably tied to the free *will* of God. This seems to be, in sum, what Ross is arguing, though in a different context. That which is necessary with respect to God—be it his knowledge or his will—must have as its object anything necessary; that which is free with respect to God—be it his knowledge or his will—must have as *its* object anything that is contingent, which is anything other than God himself.

1995), 99n22, Stump says that God's creating possibilities is not something Aquinas would accept, "since he does not suppose that modality is created by God." It is a different thing to be *determined* and to be *created*, but both require causality in order *to be*.

[35] Muller, *Post-Reformation Reformed Dogmatics*, 3:414, my emphasis.

[36] Cornelius Van Til, *An Introduction to Systematic Theology*, 2nd ed., ed. William Edgar (Phillipsburg, NJ: P&R, 2007), 373.

Thus, the free knowledge/will of God is what grounds and founds what is possible, and what is possible must have the actual as its context and content. The second thing that we must be aware of relative to the distinction between the possible and the actual relates to our discussion above and is summarized by Bavinck: "The *existence* of things, accordingly, depends on God's will, but their *essence* depends on his mind."[37] So, according to Bavinck, *essences* relate to the knowledge that God has of possibilities, while the actualization of (some of) those essences requires an act of God's will to bring about their *existence*.

Given this formulation, just what is the relationship of the essences of things to their existence? According to this construal, their existence depends on God's will—presumably his free will. But what about their essences? They depend on God's mind, if Bavinck is correct. But what is the relationship of those essences to the essences that compose a part of each existing thing? Here things can become confused. Presumably, Bavinck would hold that the relationship of anything finite to the infinite Creator is analogical.[38] So, in this construal, the essences of things that are not a part of creation are included in God's natural or simple knowledge.

However, would this not require that God's knowledge of essences be itself *necessary* in the same way that knowledge of himself is? As we have seen, there is a longstanding tradition that affirms this, given that comprehensive knowledge of God's nature, which he has necessarily, includes comprehensive knowledge of his own power, which itself includes knowledge of all that he can do. Thus, comprehensive knowledge of God's nature *must* include, some would say, knowledge of all essences, even though such essences may or may not be created (i.e., they may be possible or actual).

Without detailing the knotty topic of the relationship of divine ideas to divine exemplars, and of divine exemplars to created essences, at least the following is worth consideration: that which is *ad extra* ought not be considered in any way identical to God's essential nature. Even if God's power includes his ability to think and create all that is *ad extra* (which, of course, it does), nothing that is *ad extra* is absolutely necessary. To ascribe absolute necessity

---

[37]Herman Bavinck, *Reformed Dogmatics*, vol. 2, *God and Creation*, ed. John Bolt, trans. John Vriend (Grand Rapids: Baker Academic, 2004), 238.

[38]Cf. ibid., 2:97–110. Note, however, "Suárez . . . departed from the Thomistic assumption that the divine essence contains the exemplars of finite being, which derives from God and has its being by participation—rather Suárez held that created essences have their own internal coherence and that God creates, in the strictest sense, not essences but existences" (Muller, *Post-Reformation Reformed Dogmatics*, 3:108). It is not clear whether Bavinck is following the Suárezian metaphysical approach here, but his statement seems conducive to it.

to anything that has its referent outside of God is to attribute God's status as a necessary Being to that thing.

Both the essences and the existence of created things, therefore, as well as of all things possible, have their genesis in the free will of God. This seems to be consistent with Ross's concern, above, that the will of God must *determine* both the possible and the actual, since all that is possible presupposes the actual. Doolan seems to make a similar point with respect to Aquinas's notion of exemplars.

> The principle of essence and *esse* [being] in any finite being are thus mutually dependent upon each other, and ultimately they are so because the two modes of *divine exemplarism* are mutually dependent upon each other. As the exemplar causes of created essence, the divine ideas are the causes of a principle of potency that requires a principle of act; as the exemplar cause of the act of being, the divine nature is the cause of an act that requires a principle of limitation.
>
> Neither mode of exemplarism, therefore, can be exercised without the other, and *both are dependent upon the mediation of the divine will*, for an exemplar is effective only because an agent determines the end of that which is exemplified.[39]

Thus, it may be better to recognize, contra Bavinck at this point, that both the *essence* and the *existence* of all things *ad extra* are themselves dependent on God's free will. If that is true, then it would also be true that all things *ad extra* are what they are according to God's covenantal properties and attributes. That is, the Lord freely decides or determines that such things *are* (the actual) or *could be* (the possible) and, in that determination, freely determines as well to relate himself to such things.[40] Therefore, God's relationship to *all things* that are *not* himself is at every point a condescended, covenantal relationship; his relationship to himself, as well as all that such a relationship entails, is such that it is essential to who he is as the one God—Father, Son, and Holy Spirit.

Perhaps another aspect of (some of) the differences between that which is simple and necessary in God, on the one hand, and that which depends on

---

[39]Doolan, *Aquinas on the Divine Ideas as Exemplar Causes*, 243, my emphasis. The point here is not that Thomas (according to Doolan) would agree with my analysis above *in toto*; it is rather that any notion of *ad extra* essence (as well as existence) requires an act of God's free will.

[40]This may comport with a point Brian Leftow considers (more of which, below): "We might see Thomas' God as facing initially a set of alternatives some of which have no modal status at all, and determining their modal status in a single act of will: He renders possible the possible, and contingently impossible the contingently impossible. He (we can suppose) faces no constraints at all in doing so; He has alternatives of distributing modal status differently, though in the nature of the case these aren't initially possible (or impossible) alternatives." Brian Leftow, "Aquinas, Divine Simplicity and Divine Freedom," in *Metaphysics and God: Essays in Honor of Eleonore Stump*, ed. Kevin Timpe (New York: Routledge, 2009), 28.

a free (condescended, covenantal) act of his will, on the other hand, is seen when we consider God's archetypal and ectypal knowledge.[41] Archetypal knowledge is God's knowledge per se. Ectypal knowledge is "knowledge from" the archetypal knowledge of God.

The distinction between archetypal and ectypal knowledge in God is not, first of all, simply a twofold distinction; there is a threefold aspect to this distinction in order to account for theology that is communicable to us.[42] This threefold aspect includes, first, God's archetypal knowledge, known only in and by himself; second, ectypal theology, which resides in the mind of God; and third, ectypal theology, which, based on ectypal theology in God's mind, he communicates to us. According to van Asselt:

> Junius elaborates his remarks on the causes of ectypical theology by making a distinction between (1) the internal concept of ectypal theology in the mind of God and (2) the external form in which God communicates this concept to human beings. The internal concept in the mind of God is his divine will and grace; the external form is the body of knowledge that God decided to reveal to mankind. Junius compares God's internal concept of ectypal knowledge with a source (*fons*), the external form with a lake (*lacus*) derived from the source.
>
> Furthermore, the concept of ectypal knowledge existing in the mind of God must be distinguished from archetypal theology. Junius calls the former *theologia simpliciter dicta* (theology, simply speaking) which differs from archetypal theology in that the latter is incommunicable, while the former is communicable. When communication of ectypal knowledge takes place then *theologia simpliciter dicta* becomes *theologia secundum quid*, i.e., *relational theology* [my emphasis], for it depends upon God's accommodation of himself to a form which finite beings are capable of grasping. Junius calls it a second order theology, ectypal theology *simpliciter dicta* being a first order theology.[43]

Ectypal theology *simpliciter dicta*, to use Junius's terminology, would be coterminous with God's free will (given that it is a part of God's free knowledge). It thus would be that which God knows and which is also contingent. In other words, it includes all that God knows and that is other than his own

---

[41]Keeping in mind the close relationship that obtains between God's knowledge and his will.
[42]As discussed here, this should not be confused with the three *kinds* of ectypal theology. See Willem J. van Asselt, "The Fundamental Meaning of Theology: Archetypal and Ectypal Theology in Seventeenth-Century Reformed Thought," *Westminster Theological Journal* 64, no. 2 (2002): 330ff.
[43]Ibid., 329.

essential character (i.e., things *ad extra* that God knows) and itself forms the foundation of all that he communicates to us. So, there is a "knowledge from (i.e., ec-typal), version 1," which resides in the mind of God alone, and a "knowledge from (i.e., ec-typal), version 2," which comes from 1 and, like 1, has its ultimate source in God's archetypal (per se) knowledge.

The result of our discussion thus far in this section is to highlight the advantage that obtains when we locate both the possible and the actual, with respect to all things *ad extra*, in the free will and knowledge of God; that is, such things presuppose God's covenantal condescension. We must remember, however, that ascribing freedom to God's knowledge and will in no way implies or entails that he acquired these properties as aspects of his essential character. God is simple and thus is "without body, parts or passions" in his essential character. He does, however, take on properties—real relational properties—that do in fact change the way in which he acts and relates *ad extra*. He does this by way of covenantal condescension, which comes by a free act of his will. In taking on these properties, he considers the possible in light of the actual, and he determines to bring into existence some (but not all) of that which is possible. As we will see below, in acting in this way, his condescension stems from eternity and moves into the temporal realm at the point of creation.

D. On the Necessity of Freedom

There is a recent, fascinating analysis of the relationship of God's character to his freedom in Brian Leftow, "Aquinas, Divine Simplicity and Divine Freedom."[44] In evaluating a Thomistic understanding of the relationship of God's simplicity to his freedom, Leftow concludes that there is no obvious way to understand God's freedom, given the notion of divine simplicity; in the end, the simplest Thomistic option to bring these two realities together seems to him to "solve the problem by magic," though some other way to solve it, he thinks, may be feasible.[45]

More important than Leftow's conclusion, however, is his analysis of the problem itself. A close look at his concerns, call them Leftow's Lucubrations, may help clarify how our essential/covenantal (or *Eimi/eikon*) distinction might apply to God's knowledge and will.

---

[44]Leftow sees the problem not so much that God *has* his actual volition, given DDS, as that he *is* that volition. "Substituting a co-referential term for 'God' in 'God = God' shouldn't yield a claim differing in modality. But 'the actual divine volition' and 'God' are co-referential, given DDS." Leftow, "Aquinas, Divine Simplicity and Divine Freedom," 28.
[45]Ibid., 36.

Leftow begins with Thomas's notion of divine simplicity such that

1. God's volition = His essence[46]

In this article, 1 becomes the problematic proposition.[47] It is problematic in that it equates and identifies anything that God wills with his essence. Since his essence is necessary, in that there is no possible world in which it cannot *be*, or be *what* it is, his will must also be necessary.

This is nothing new. Any notion of God's simplicity affirms that, since God is not composed of parts, his will cannot be something different from, or initially apart from, his essential character. If it were, he would depend on something different from or outside of his essential character—something *not* him—in order to be who he is. So, his will must be identical to his character (or essence).

So given that God's essential character is itself necessary—i.e., there is no possibility that it could not *be*, and not be *what (who) it is*—this would entail that God's will is always and only necessary as well. Says Leftow:

> So if God has his essence necessarily, it seems to follow that for Thomas he has His actual volition necessarily. But then it seems that He necessarily wills what He does: that it is not possible that He do otherwise. This is not a problem for Thomas alone. The doctrine of divine simplicity (DDS) is a core commitment of classical theism.[48]

To reiterate (from chapter 1), the doctrine of divine simplicity, what Leftow denominates as DDS, holds that everything that God is essentially, every attribute and property that belongs essentially to him, must be identical with him. Without detailing the arguments for this, we could summarize it this way: Suppose God's infinity were not identical to him. What would be the status of such an attribute? The only option would seem to be that God's essence is in part made up of something that is "not God," in that infinity is *different* from who he is as God. Even without attempting to posit the status of infinity, supposing it to be different from God, we can see that in such a case God would be dependent on something different from himself in order

---

[46]My numbering, not Leftow's.
[47]For another and in some ways similar analysis of Thomas's view of simplicity, see Christopher Hughes, *On a Complex Theory of a Simple God: An Investigation in Aquinas' Philosophical Theology*, Cornell Studies in the Philosophy of Religion (Ithaca, NY: Cornell University Press, 1989).
[48]Leftow, "Aquinas, Divine Simplicity and Divine Freedom," 21.

to be who he is essentially. In that case, God could not be the "I AM" (*Eimi*); he could not be *a se*. He would be, in some ways, similar to us, an essentially dependent being, since he would be dependent on the property of infinity in order to be who he essentially is. So, whatever God is essentially must be identical to him such that he is in no way dependent on anything outside himself or essentially different from him in order to be who he essentially is.

So what happens when we combine the notion of God's simplicity, and all that it entails, with God's will? We have to recognize, first of all, as Leftow's Lucubrations make clear, that God's will cannot be something independent of his essential character; like all of God's essential attributes and properties, it is identical to him and thus participates in all of his essential attributes. Specifically, to reiterate, since God is a necessary Being—i.e., it is impossible that God not exist—his will must be necessary as well.

So, it seems that whatever God does and whatever he wills, he does and wills necessarily. If he does something that is *not* necessary, then the nature or mode of that action cannot be identical with him since he himself is necessary; it must be something that is apart from, perhaps even contrary to, his essential character. That which is not necessary is contingent, and for God to act contingently with respect to something means that there must be some condition (or several) imposed, a condition that brings about that which is not necessary. That which is contingent, then, is conditional and relative; and whatever the conditional or relative element is must be something in which God himself in some way participates. Even if the conditional element is God's own free choice to do *x*, there is still something other than an absolute necessity attached to *x* such that God participates in what is not absolutely necessary.

But Thomas knows that this cannot be the case for God. So, according to Leftow, Thomas affirms that God has one act of will; he *must* affirm this in order to maintain DDS. All that God wills, he wills necessarily. That too is entailed in DDS. But Leftow goes on to note that, even if God has one act of will, distinctions are made by Thomas and his followers as to the *kinds* of necessity entailed. God wills his own nature necessarily; there is no possible world in which he could will otherwise with respect to his own essential character. But he wills creation necessarily only in the sense that, *once determined*, it *becomes* necessary. Thus, attached to all things contingent is a *conditional* necessity of the will of God. This conditional necessity, however, is only necessary once it is determined. Prior to its determination, it need not be at all. But the notion of something able either to be or not to be begins to sound eerily like another way of articulating contingency.

So Leftow has problems with conditional necessity. The first problem seems to revolve around Leftow's notion of God's eternity.

> If *P* is only conditionally necessary, ~*P* could have been true: ~*P* was possible, though it is no longer [that is, it is no longer possible once *P* is determined]. From God's timeless standpoint, when "was" it possible that He not create? If God timelessly limits the possible to worlds in which He creates, "when" were non-creation worlds possible? At God's timeless standpoint, God has already—timelessly—eliminated non-creative worlds from possibility. It is not possible that He do other than create; the best Thomas can do, it seems is claim that non-creation worlds are only contingently impossible, and are so due to God's choice. More worrying, the same applies to worlds in which God creates any other than what were actually the initial creatures. On Thomas' account, it was never possible that God do other than create what He initially did; it merely could have been possible.[49]

Here we run up against the kind of complaint we have seen before. Once eternity is thought to be in some significant ways a flat or static mode of existence, then it seems incoherent to posit points of difference or distinction in such a context. So, for Leftow, because God freely chose, in eternity, to create a particular world, "it was never possible that God do other than create what He initially did." It was never possible, presumably, because God's choice to create what he did was an eternal choice, having neither a "before" nor an "after." Worlds that God would not create were never possible, given that such worlds were eternally eliminated from consideration. And to be eternally eliminated from consideration means the same thing (thinks Leftow) as never being considered in the first place.

But here it seems better to understand eternity, not as a static mode of God's existence (and certainly not as a static "context" in which God exists), but rather as a word describing God's non-successive duration (hereafter, NSD). God's existence, therefore, is *durative*, in that it is continuous, but it is *non-successively* durative in that, as God continues always to exist, that existence does not consist of parts, temporal or otherwise.

This kind of language[50] is an important advance over some notions of eternity, in that so much of the discussion has pitted eternity against time. Time, however, is *successively durative* so that there are elements of temporal existence that are not strictly in opposition to, or otherwise incommensurate

---

[49]Ibid., 28.
[50]For a discussion of this language, see Muller, *Post-Reformation Reformed Dogmatics*, 3:354ff.

with, eternal existence. The key element in each kind of existence, eternal and temporal, is *duration*, and though we have to make clear that a non-successive duration cannot, in and of itself, intersect with a successive duration, there is nevertheless duration in each case. Because each is durative, we can expect that there will be real, significant *action* embedded in that duration.[51]

Consider, for example, the fact that Christ, in praying to his Father, notes that the Father loved him before the foundation of the world (John 17:24). This, of course, is an eternal, NSD love. But we would misunderstand this love of the Father for the Son if we thought it to be a flat or static condition containing no contours or distinctions. Clearly Christ is referring to the fact that there was, in eternity, a meaningful and vital relationship between him and the Father. That relationship surely had elements embedded in it that were evidence of a supreme, familial love between two persons. There were, in other words, distinctions and differences in their relationship that marked it out as a vital, loving, "family" relationship between Father and Son. There is, therefore, an NSD *dynamic* that takes place within the Godhead. These distinctions, elements and differences, however, do not and cannot serve to constitute "parts" in God, any more than distinctions and differences between Father, Son, and Spirit serve to undermine his essential simplicity. Rather, what we must train our minds to grasp is that, in God, there are these distinctions, but they in no way compromise his essential simplicity.

So, just as the Father, Son, and Spirit are distinct, yet each is fully the one God,[52] so also are there distinctions and differences in God's NSD that themselves are also the one God. What is true for the three persons of the Trinity, in other words, is true as well for the multiplicity of aspects, properties, and attributes of God's essential character. None of them can be flattened out so that their distinctiveness is lost; neither can they be thought of as so distinct that they constitute a change in God, or a "part" of God's essential nature that is added to his character.[53]

---

[51] In the words of Bavinck, "The world itself rests on revelation; revelation is the presupposition, the foundation, the secret of all that exists in all its forms. . . . In every moment of time beats the pulse of eternity." Herman Bavinck, *The Philosophy of Revelation* (Grand Rapids: Baker, 1979), 27.

[52] So, for example, as we have seen, the Gospel of John opens with both aspects in view. In the beginning was the Word, who was both *with God* (πρὸς τὸν θεόν), signaling a distinction and difference, and who *was God* (καὶ θεὸς ἦν ὁ λόγος), signaling his identity with God.

[53] Arguing from the greater to the lesser, since orthodox theology has consistently maintained that the one, simple God is distinctly (i.e., differently) Father, Son, and Holy Spirit, it is no theological stretch to maintain as well that the real distinctions present in God's character and attributes are, themselves, the one and simple God as well.

So also with respect to God's will. There was an NSD point at which God determined to create the universe he created. He did make an NSD choice, and it was an NSD choice he did not *have* to make. That choice brought about a distinction and difference with respect to God's own NSD activity, though at no point did such a distinction and difference constitute a change in God, nor did it add "parts" to his essential character.

Rather, as I have been arguing throughout, the NSD free choice of God to decree and create was itself an NSD free choice of covenantal condescension. God descended, as it were, even while remaining NSD eternal, in order to commit himself to a particular plan, including the creation of the universe. At the NSD point when God had not yet determined what he would do, it was indeed possible that he do something else, perhaps infinitely other things. Just because the choice is itself NSD eternal does not exclude an NSD point at which there was no such choice; to think that way would be to think of an eternity that disallowed any distinction or difference. But there are eternal, NSD distinctions and differences (again, as evidenced in the distinct and different persons of the Trinity), and God's choice to do one thing and not another is but one of those. So, Leftow's Lucubration, that God's freedom does not comport with an eternal God, is not a significant one. Particularly when what is being discussed is the will of God, we should affirm that God can and does choose things that are in no way necessary for him to choose. Once chosen, they have their own necessity, but that necessity is indeed conditional; it presupposes God's own NSD free choice.

Precisely *how* God's free and contingent choices comport both with his essential necessity and with divine simplicity is beyond our ability completely to grasp. But this is nothing new and should not thereby be rejected or deemed suspicious. It is also beyond our ability to grasp exactly how the Son of God, for example, can himself be identical to God yet also be distinct and different as one person of the Godhead. He is identical to God, yet identical with distinctions that must be maintained; the personal attributes cannot be ignored or minimized in order to make sense of essential simplicity. So also with God's free choices. God choosing freely is a property that God has essentially, thus it must be identical to/with him. But it is also a property with distinctions that cannot be flattened out for the sake of a more conducive notion of simplicity. The identity and the difference are both essential, both affirmed; the one and the many are equally ultimate in God.

Leftow's second concern with respect to the relationship of God's freedom to his essential character as simple revolves around the notion of extrinsic modalities. Here Leftow wants to challenge Eleonore Stump's explanation. According to Stump:

> Because some but not all . . . objects of (God's) act of will might have (differed, there is) a logical distinction between the conditionally and the absolutely necessitated objects of that single act of will . . . (If) with regard to some but not all of its objects, God's will . . . might have been different . . . this . . . shows us . . . a difference in the ways in which the single act of divine will is related to the divine nature, on the one hand, and to created things, on the other (stemming) from logical differences among (its) diverse objects . . . that one thing is related in different ways to different things does not entail that it has distinct intrinsic properties, only distinct *Cambridge* properties.[54]

It is at this point that we can begin to focus the tension that obtains with respect to God's essential character and his freedom. A part of Leftow's response to Stump merges nicely with our concerns and discussion thus far.

Leftow doubts that Stump's deference to extrinsic modalities is a legitimate move for Thomistic metaphysics. He argues (in part) that Thomas's metaphysics disallows the notion that God's being free is in some way extrinsic to him. Leftow lists four problems with the notion of extrinsic modality in God.

Leftow's first problem has to do with the relation of the divine nature to the divine will. He rightly notes that God's will does not produce his nature.[55] "If identity is a relation at all, it is an intrinsic relation."[56] Given that identity, there seems to Leftow to be no way coherently to allow for an extrinsic modality with respect to God's will. "So, *pace* Stump, any property God's will has solely in virtue of its relation to the divine nature is intrinsic."[57]

This latter point, however, need not constrain our understanding of God, according to traditional orthodox theology. As we have already seen, the fact that God's will has the properties *both* of necessity *and* of freedom (as does his knowledge) affirms that God's simplicity is replete with distinctions and differences, all the while remaining one and simple. So, there is indeed the property of freedom that God's will has. That property entails that God does some things that he does not have to do. In doing those things (e.g., decree-

---

[54]Leftow, "Aquinas, Divine Simplicity and Divine Freedom," 29–30. Though we will not delve into the controversy over Cambridge properties, sufficient for this discussion is the notion that a Cambridge property is an extrinsic property that requires no change in the one having such a property.

[55]Contra Karl Barth, for example.

[56]Leftow, "Aquinas, Divine Simplicity and Divine Freedom," 32.

[57]Ibid.

ing and creating), he condescends to relate himself to something *ad extra*. In
that relationship, he takes on additional properties, which, though they are
real and require actions and reactions on God's part, never change or affect
his essential character.

Perhaps it would help to recognize that God's will is best delineated as
a *personal* rather than an *essential* property of his.[58] To be personal rather
than essential in no way separates the properties; they are all included in his
simplicity. But it does seem more conducive to our discussion to realize that
God's necessary and free will are (is!) a property he has by virtue of his being
a personal God. That is, it is a person who chooses, not a nature or essence.
In this way, too, we begin to see how crucial it is (as in christology, discussed
previously) to view the will of God *in concreto* rather than *in abstracto*.

Thus, while the necessity of God's existence is an essential property of his,
that necessity, as an essential property, is not in conflict with, even though
it is distinguished from, the necessity (and freedom) of his will. Thus, God,
who is himself necessary, necessarily wills his own character (even as his
character determines that will, and not vice versa). Included in his will is the
determinative delight in himself. But he also freely wills other things *ad extra*.
Once those things are willed, he takes on properties that relate him to them
in certain ways and with certain constraints. To deny that the triune God
has the freedom to determine such things is to opt for a notion of necessity
that is opposed to his personal character (in that he would then have no real
choice) and that would only serve to limit him in such a way that he would
not be who he in fact is.

We will comment on Leftow's second problem below. His third and fourth
problems are related. Both problems, according to Leftow, leave one in the
awkward position of affirming extrinsic modality with respect to God's activity *because of* those things that are related to him *ad extra*. In other words,
"the contingency of God's effects renders it (extrinsically) contingent that
God's will has some of its content"; and, with respect to his fourth problem,

> if [God's] "willing creatures to exist" is an extrinsic description, the existence
> of creatures will help explain the event's falling under it, rather than *vice versa*.

---

[58]To be clear, distinctions have been made with respect to God's will in terms of the *voluntas
essentialis* and the *voluntas personalis*. The former highlights that God necessarily *has* a will;
it is essential to his character. The latter highlights the character of that will relative to the
persons of the Trinity. For more on this, see Muller, *Post-Reformation Reformed Dogmatics*,
3:453. My emphasis here is closer to the latter distinction, but is meant also to highlight that
God's will has its locus in himself as *personal*, in that, included in the notion of personal is
the ability to choose.

This is unintuitive: surely there are creatures because God wills there to be, rather than its being the case that God wills there to be because there are creatures.[59]

Both of these concerns argue that the existence of things *ad extra*—e.g., creatures created by God—is the *reason* or *cause* of the supposed extrinsic modality with respect to God's will. On Leftow's account, once there is contingency ascribed to something that God has (or *is*), then a "part" or "constituent" has been added to God's will such that simplicity can no longer be affirmed. "What other," asks Leftow, "than a difference in part, accident or property *could* account for an intrinsic description's applying contingently?"[60]

With respect to both of these concerns, we must again reiterate how best to understand God's simplicity. It is *not* the case that God's simplicity obviates any difference or distinction; the Father is simple, the Son is simple, and the Holy Spirit is simple. Each of the three persons is distinct in his own right, all the while being identical and equal to the one God. There is distinction, there is difference, *and* there is identity.[61]

Leftow's second problem with the notion of extrinsic modality relative to God's will highlights aspects of the discussion above concerning the relationship of God's power and will. Quoting the bulk of Leftow's concern will help clarify the matter:

> Thomas holds views which imply that if there "are" possible worlds, prior to all Creation, they exist "in God's power," in the strong sense that what makes talk of them true is really God's power. God's power is intrinsic to Him. If all possible worlds exist in God's power and God's power is intrinsic to Him, then if God is contingently F, the worlds which make it the case that God's being F is contingent are intrinsic to God.[62]

The central problem here, according to Leftow, is that whatever is contingent with respect to God being, say, Creator, must on Thomas's account be *intrinsic* rather than extrinsic, since such contingencies are located in God's

---

[59]Leftow, "Aquinas, Divine Simplicity and Divine Freedom," 32, 33.
[60]Ibid., 33.
[61]It should be made clear here that I am not attempting to defend or otherwise substantiate the *Thomistic* understanding of simplicity. While so much of what Thomas affirmed with respect to theology proper is foundational to orthodox theology generally, it may well be that his methodological separation between understanding that God is *one*, on the one hand, and that he is *triune*, on the other, served to undermine his right and proper affirmation of God's simplicity. The point that I am making is that an understanding of simplicity necessarily has God's triunity in its immediate purview. To affirm simplicity by reason alone, only later to bring in a notion of the Trinity by way of revelation, is to rend asunder what God has joined together.
[62]Leftow, "Aquinas, Divine Simplicity and Divine Freedom," 32.

power. This is just another way of stating what we were discussing above, in chapter 4, section B (1).

But what if our supposition, as argued above, is correct: that everything *ad extra* has its source first of all in a free determination of God? This would *not*, we should note, move the freedom of God's will from being intrinsic ("in God's power") to being extrinsic, since God's will is an intrinsic property of his.[63] It would not, therefore, alleviate Leftow's Lucubrations.

What it *would* do, however, is provide for a distinction (which, as we have noted, does not destroy or undermine the doctrine of simplicity) in which God's necessary will is such because the object of that will is necessary, and his free will is what it is because of *its* object.[64] It would allow for the fact that God makes a decision that he did not have to make; there was no necessity for him to decide as he did relative to that which is contingent. It would also allow us to posit a free decision by God to condescend and relate himself to what is *ad extra*, which involves taking on properties that were not his otherwise, all the while remaining the "I AM." That is, the *Eimi* chooses to take on *eikon* properties, properties that require an *ad extra* relationship.

This is another argument for the position broached above: that *both* the possible *and* the actual, with respect to all things *ad extra*, have their genesis in the free will of God, first of all. If that is true, then, to put it in theological terms, there was a point in eternity in which there was nothing but the triune God. Then, owing to God's free, NSD decision, he determined that he would relate himself to that which is other than himself—both the possible and the actual (this would include his eternal decree, about which I'll say more below). Then, he freely determined to bring about what he had determined would be actual, which itself was a subset of all that is/was possible. This is covenant condescension, and God takes on new properties in executing it; the *Eimi*, who himself is and always remains *a se*, takes on the *eikon*, in that he determines to relate himself to something(s) *ad extra*.

But this in no way sacrifices, undermines or negates who he is as the simple One-in-Three. He remains who he is, but he decides to be something else as well; he decides to be the God of the covenant. It was, to be sure, a monumental

---

[63]That is, as noted above, it is essential to who he is as a personal God.

[64]A point made by Muller is important to highlight here: "Necessity and freedom are neither contraries nor contradictories: the contrary of necessity is impossibility; the contrary of freedom is coercion" (Muller, *Post-Reformation Reformed Dogmatics*, 3:434n360). As a matter of fact, one of the most consistent implications of all discussions of necessity and freedom, whether relative to God's own character, or to man, is that the former is presupposed by the latter. Where there is necessity, there will also and always be freedom that is grounded in, rather than contrary to, that necessity.

decision. It changed the *mode* of God's existence for eternity; he began to exist according to relationships *ad extra*, which had not been the case before. But it in no way changed his essential character. Is this not the wonder of the gospel, from Genesis to Revelation?[65]

As we noted, Leftow's Lucubrations reach no real conclusion; he attempts to articulate a dual notion of "God willing" in terms of necessity and "God willing in the accompanied manner" (i.e., accompanied by the will to create), but that introduces a different "manner" in God, which disallows DDS.

Our discussion thus far, however, seems to be a better way of understanding the tensions that Leftow's Lucubrations highlight. The matter will remain fundamentally incomprehensible to us; this is what we should expect. But to see God in covenant history making decisions, acting, and reacting, all the while remaining the great *Eimi* of history, should move us a long way toward understanding the reality of his free decisions with respect to all things *ad extra*. And the central focus of that freedom is in his eternal decree.

(1) The Free Decree

It remains for us, finally, to merge our concerns above with a discussion of the decree(s) and providence of God. The way in which Turretin approaches the topic of God's decrees and predestination provides a nice foray into our proposed merger. Turretin firsts asks whether the decrees are in God and, if so, how.

> Concerning these decrees the question is How are they in God—essentially or only inherently . . . and accidentally? The former the orthodox maintain; the latter is maintained by Socinus and Vorstius who, to overthrow the simplicity of God and to prove that there is a real composition in him, maintain that they are accidents properly so called. Against these, we thus argue.[66]

Turretin goes on to argue that decrees cannot be accidental in God because (1) that would undermine his simplicity, (2) he could not then be perfect, since something (i.e., the decrees) would be added to him, and (3) he could not be immutable, since adding decrees to him would constitute a change in him.

---

[65]That is, to focus the point, is it not a wonder that the Son of God, in taking on a human nature, changed his mode of existence for eternity, all the while remaining the one true God? From the time of the incarnation and into the eternity of the new heavens and the new earth, he will always be God incarnate, even while he remains who he eternally is. Is it any wonder that we have no sufficient intellectual tools to comprehend this?

[66]Turretin, *Institutes*, 1:311.

Since, therefore, these three cannot be the case with God, Turretin affirms that the decrees are in God essentially, but with a relation that is outside of God (perhaps something akin to the "extrinsic modality" notion we saw above).[67]

Turretin then posits that, with respect to the relationship of the necessity and the freedom of the decree, "three things come to be carefully distinguished in the decree":

> (1) the essence of God willing and decreeing after the manner of a principle;
> (2) its tendency outside himself, without however any internal addition or change because it indicates nothing but an external respect and habitude towards the creature, after the manner of a relation; (3) the object itself or the things decreed, which have a reason of the end. In the first mode, the decree is necessary, but in the latter free.[68]

That is, given that Turretin has located the decree in the essence of God himself, there has to be some sense in which it is necessary. That sense, he wants to say, is with respect to God willing and decreeing "after the manner of a principle." What he seems to be saying here is that the *genesis* or *source* (*principium*) of the willing and decreeing is in God himself. About that, there should be no debate.

But does the fact that God is the *source* of the decree require that it be "in him" so that it partakes of his necessity? It wouldn't seem so, particularly when we remember that God is the *source* and *principle* of *all things*, including all things created, though there is no absolute necessity attached to creation.

For Turretin, however, this notion of God willing and decreeing "after the manner of a principle" is linked with his understanding of the decree as an exemplar cause.[69] It is an exemplar cause "because the decree of God is (as it were) the idea of all things out of himself, after which as the archetype . . . they, as the ectypes . . . , are expressed in time."[70] In other words, as he puts it, "the decrees are rightly said to be identified with the essence, conceived after the manner of a vital act determining itself to the production of this or that thing out of itself."[71]

There seem to be problems, however, with an identification of the decrees with God's essence. Unlike the tensions between necessity and freedom discussed above, in this case the decrees of God must necessarily be identical to

---

[67]Ibid., 1:312.
[68]Ibid., 1:313.
[69]He also argues that the decrees are an efficient cause, but that need not detain us here.
[70]Turretin, *Institutes*, 1:312.
[71]Ibid.

him, at least in their status as exemplars. Perhaps Turretin is thinking of the decrees here in the same way as he might think of creation: that they each begin as ideas in the mind of God—ideas that, once willed by God, become (causal) exemplars.

It is difficult to see how such a proposal as Turretin's avoids the necessity of God's decrees per se. The act of God's decree, as he says, is an immanent and intrinsic act *in God*, even though the act itself has its terminus in something outside God.[72] There seems to be no way, on this construal, to make the actual willing of God's decree free, since it is identical with his simple essence.[73] Turretin thinks he can avoid such a conclusion by stating the following:

> The liberty of the divine decree does not hinder it from being God himself because it is free only terminatively and on the part of the thing, but not subjectively and on the part of God. It is free in the exercised act inasmuch as it resides in the liberty of God to decree this or that thing. It is not free in the signified act because to decree anything depends upon the internal constitution of God by which he understands and wills.[74]

Turretin says here that the divine decree is free "only terminatively," but then also that it is free in the "exercised act inasmuch as it resides in the liberty of God."

The language here seems confused. How might we understand the notions that the divine decree is free *"only terminatively,"* and therefore not subjectively, and then that it is free also in the exercised act in that it *"resides in the liberty of God"*? How can that which is *only terminative* and *not subjective* at the same time *reside in* the freedom of God? It may be that Turretin at this particular point was (rightly) so concerned with the heresy of Socinianism that he wanted to affirm what was obvious in orthodox theology—i.e., God's simplicity—while wanting to safeguard some kind of notion of God's freedom. To do that, he needed to countenance a certain necessity with respect to the decree, so that it might be consistent with God's simple essence, while asserting some notion of the freedom of God's will in the decree. The statements as they stand, however, cannot easily be read to make sense.

---

[72]Ibid., 1:311.

[73]To be clear, Turretin does affirm the freedom of the decree, and to interpret his position as demanding only necessity is to miss his insistence on that freedom. Our concern has more to do with just *how* his particular statements go together. It is worth noting that Muller insists that any interpretation of Turretin and his Reformed contemporaries that ascribes a necessity to God's decree per se, misses the point. See Muller, *Post-Reformation Reformed Dogmatics*, 3:433f.

[74]Turretin, *Institutes*, 1:313.

It should be clear by now that there is another, third, way to construe this scenario that would neither acquiesce to Socinianism, which is Turretin's right and proper concern, nor require that God's decrees be essential to him or in some way necessary (or, to use Turretin's phrase, "in him"). It seems impossible to impose any kind of necessity on God's decree from a biblical perspective, except insofar as *once the determination has been made*, it *becomes* necessary. It is, therefore, only conditionally necessary, in that it presupposes God's free decision.

Perhaps this is what Turretin wants to say. He surely believes God's will to be both necessary and free.[75] As with Aquinas, he affirms that God wills himself necessarily and he wills creation freely. As we have seen, Turretin believes that God's free will with respect to creation also has its own subjective necessity, in that (Turretin agrees with Aquinas), for God to remain simple, the act of the will to create must itself partake of God's own essential necessity.

However, perhaps we could read Turretin as affirming that the characteristics of God's will, as both necessary and free, are characteristics themselves of the essence of who God is *as God*. In other words, God could not be in every way constrained by his own will, such that he could *not*, in any case, choose to do something that is directed toward that which is essentially "other" than himself (e.g., decree and create). That choice that God necessarily has is a free choice. So, the necessity that attaches to God's free will is that he has that freedom essentially; both freedom *and* necessity are necessarily a characteristic of his will.

The choice *itself*, however, can be seen as an act of God, in which he determines to consider that which is contingent, and determines to bring about (some of) that contingency. This choice, however, can in no way be thought of as necessary. Neither can the contingency of the event be attached only to the contingent objects themselves; otherwise God would have necessarily (and not freely) determined that which is contingent. Thus, the *locus* of the choice of God to decree and to create ought to be seen in his covenantal condescension. The choice of God to decree and create presupposes a free choice to assume covenantal properties.

To put it another way, once God determines to relate himself to that which is *ad extra*—whether in his eternal decree or in creation itself—he thus necessarily freely determines to relate himself, by way of a commitment, to that which is *not* himself. This can be nothing other than divine condescension; it is the taking on of properties and attributes that he would otherwise not

---

[75]Ibid., 1:218f.

have had, and the properties and attributes themselves are less than, because in no way identical to, who God is essentially. And just one of those properties is that he freely acts to be in covenant with what is external to himself. In other words, while God's freedom is an essential characteristic of his will, the free *act*, in that it is an event (even if in eternity), is an act of condescension.

To repeat what we discussed in chapter 2: with respect to God's decree, the *pactum salutis* is a free act of God in which he determines to covenant with himself *and with that which he will create*. This covenant of redemption between Father, Son, and Holy Spirit, as I have said, is at the heart, and forms the foundation, of God's entire covenantal relationship with creation. So, to repeat what Vos says:

> The covenant of redemption is nothing other than proof for the fact that even the work of redemption, though it springs from God's sovereign will, finds its execution in free deeds performed in a covenantal way. . . . Instead of the covenant idea being presented here in a forced way, one must much rather say that only here does it fully come to its own. For it is only in the triune Being that that perfect freedom dominates which the covenant idea appears to demand.[76]

Again, as we noted in chapter 2, the covenant idea "appears to demand" the perfect freedom of the triune Being because, as we have seen, it presupposes God's determination freely to condescend and to act—to create and relate to that creation. Therefore, as Vos says, the covenant idea "comes to its own"; it finds its impetus and source in this eternal counsel of the triune God.

This is yet another reason why it is important to think of God in terms of his essential character and of his covenantal character. To fail to do that is to begin to confuse what is contingent with what is necessary. It is to blend the free and the necessary in such a way that each of the two is obscured, and thus God's own character is, in some important ways, undermined.

In the Beginning Was . . . the Decree?

Another illustration of similar and related points may help us to see how God's character can be undermined in discussions of his decree. In an essay that seeks to defend Karl Barth's understanding of the relationship of Jesus Christ to the decree of God (as that decree includes both predestination and

---

[76]Geerhardus Vos, "The Doctrine of the Covenant in Reformed Theology," in *Redemptive History and Biblical Interpretation: The Shorter Writings of Geerhardus Vos*, ed. Richard B. Gaffin Jr. (Phillipsburg, NJ: Presbyterian and Reformed, 1980), 245–46.

reprobation),[77] Bruce McCormack provides a vivid illustration, by way of contrast, of just how crucial it is to maintain orthodox distinctions and categories when discussing these matters.[78] We will not need to rehearse the bulk of his essay; much of it is not central to our concerns here.

What is central to our concerns is the way in which McCormack declares Barth's "Christocentrism" to stand as a critique of Calvin's understanding of Christ's relationship to the divine decree. According to what I will call the BarMc Declaration,[79] the central criticism of Calvin's view of the decree and predestination is this:

> Calvin's doctrine of predestination is *not* decisively controlled by Christology. Christ, for Calvin, is the divinely appointed *means* for the execution in history of the decree of election. Predestination . . . as the decree in which the ends of all human beings is determined, stands above and prior to the decision to effect election through the provision of a Mediator. For Barth, that was a move which could only have disastrous consequences. If Christ is only the means to an end which was itself established without reference to that which would occur in and through him, then that can only mean that the being of the divine Subject which determines himself for predestination is a being which is not controlled and determined by that which occurred in Christ. Indeed, God's activity in the covenant of grace is, in the strictest sense imaginable, *accidental* to what he truly is. What was in the beginning with God, as John's Gospel puts it, was the decree, not Jesus Christ.[80]

The point that the BarMc Declaration wants to make, generally, is that Calvin's view of predestination was *not* Christocentric, whereas Barth's was. Calvin was unable to place Christ at the center of his understanding of predestination and the decree because he thought there to be a decision and a God (especially *the Son of God*) who was in back of or prior to the incarnate Christ. For the BarMc Declaration, this could not be the case.

---

[77] Westminster Confession of Faith 3.3: "By the decree of God, for the manifestation of His glory, some men and angels (1 Tim. 5:21, Matt. 25:41) are predestinated unto everlasting life; and others foreordained to everlasting death (Rom. 9:22–23, Eph. 1:5–6, Prov. 16:4).

[78] Bruce McCormack, "Christ and the Decree: An Unsettled Question for the Reformed Churches Today," in *Reformed Theology in Contemporary Perspective*, ed. Lynn Quigley (Edinburgh: Rutherford House, 2006).

[79] Because I believe McCormack to be fairly and accurately representing Barth in this discussion, and in order to avoid the cumbersome "for McCormack and for Barth" kinds of locutions, in the interest of verbal economy I will simply refer to McCormack's discussion of Barth's declarations as the "BarMc Declaration."

[80] McCormack, "Christ and the Decree," 130–31. See also Cornelius Van Til, *Christianity and Barthianism* (Philadelphia: Presbyterian and Reformed, 1962), 61.

This criticism of Barth's brought about no reply, according to McCormack, until Richard Muller responded some forty years later.[81] The sum of Muller's response, according to the BarMc Declaration, is this:

> "As mediator," Muller says, "Christ is subordinate to the decree while as Son of God he is one with the Father and in no way subordinate. The Son *as God* stands behind the decree while the Son *as Mediator* is the executor of the decree." Hence, Christ is both Subject and Object of election for Calvin and Barth's critique falls to the ground—or so Muller thinks.[82]

At this point in the discussion, McCormack's reasoning seems completely opaque. He goes on to argue that any change in the role of the eternal Son would necessitate either an ontological change or a commitment to Nestorianism.

> I will simply observe that one may, with consistency, avoid introducing ontological change in speaking of the adoption of a new role (with the subordination which that entails) *only* by taking the route of Nestorianism. If the presence of the eternal Son in Jesus were as the Nestorians described, then the eternal Son could take on the role of the Mediator without any consequences for his divine being.[83]

What seems odd about the reasoning here is McCormack's penchant to pretermit orthodoxy in his evaluation of the available options in this discussion. Surely the church has recognized that there are orthodox options available such that one need not choose either an ontological change or Nestorianism.

There is no need to rehearse the history of christology here. Even with its differences, however, the consistent thread of orthodox christology includes the fact that the Son of God, without ceasing to be who he is, took on a human nature at the incarnation. In that assumption, there was no change in the Son of God as God, while there certainly was a new relationship established, and thus the taking on of new properties, for eternity. All of this should be clear by this point, since it forms the foundation of all that I have argued thus far.

---

[81] This is a curious statement, at best, in that Cornelius Van Til, decades prior to Muller, did respond precisely to these, and many other, aspects of Barth's theology and, though critical of Barth, generally understood Barth to be saying what McCormack understands him to be saying. See Van Til, *Christianity and Barthianism*; and Van Til, *The New Modernism: An Appraisal of the Theology of Barth and Brunner* (Philadelphia: Presbyterian and Reformed, 1947).

[82] McCormack, "Christ and the Decree," 133.

[83] Ibid.

There is no need, therefore, to posit the options as *either* a Nestorian christology *or* a Barthian christology. The other, obvious, option is an orthodox christology. The problems persist in the BarMc Declaration:

> Muller needs a state of existence in the Son above and prior to his state of existence defined by his role as Mediator in order to be able to counter Barth's claim that Jesus Christ is not, for Calvin, the Subject of election. He needs such a primal state because Jesus Christ, in the economy, is so clearly subordinate to the Father. If he is going to be able to say that Jesus Christ is, nonetheless, the Subject of election, he has to say that the subordination characteristic of the economy was not always true; that the identity of the eternal Son is not determined by what he does in the economy.

We will pause here simply to note that it is not that *Muller* "needs a state of existence above and prior to his state of existence defined by his role as Mediator." It is rather that the history of orthodoxy has affirmed such a thing, and it has done so based on solid and consistent exegesis (e.g., see chapter 3, B and following), along with creedal fidelity based on that exegesis.

To put it another way, it could be that the exogenous theology of the BarMc Declaration causes the conundrum. A theology that begins with orthodoxy, instead of standing outside of it, would not have seen Muller's assessment as anything other than an explanation of orthodox christology via Calvin. McCormack continues:

> But such a solution does not make Jesus Christ the Subject of election at all. Rather, it makes the eternal Son—a Person of the Trinity whose identity is not determined by the decision for the covenant of grace—to the [*sic*] be the Subject of election; a Person whose identity is either undetermined or determined in ways beyond our knowing. In either case, he is, as Subject of election, a contentless placeholder in a system of thought.[84]

As the BarMc Declaration continues, McCormack wants to focus his concern on the way(s) in which we can construe the character of God, given our understanding of Christ. This part of the discussion will help focus our concerns as well. Specifically:

> We come back to Barth's question: what must God be if God can live a human life, suffer and die? How can God experience these things without undergoing some kind of fundamental change on the ontological level; without, in other

---

[84]Ibid., 134.

words, ceasing to be God? What are the ontological conditions in the eternal God which allow for this possibility?[85]

Barth's answer to these questions will stun anyone familiar with orthodox theology/christology, whether Romanist or Protestant. In order to see the extreme and aberrant view of the BarMc Declaration, we need to have before us the bulk of McCormack's response to the questions he poses above.

> Barth's answer to this series of question [*sic*] is, first, that God can be the Subject of the *assumptio carnis* [assumption of the flesh] without undergoing any fundamental ontological change because the *assumptio carnis* is *essential* to him. And, secondly, the *assumptio carnis* is essential to God because God has *willed* that it be so. . . . God is so much the Lord that he is sovereign even over his own being. In a primal decision, God assigned to himself the being he would have for all eternity. That which is truly "essential" to him . . . consists finally in a *decision* whose content is the covenant of grace. Against the essential*ism* of the ancient Church, which made the self-identical element in God to consist in a mode of being which is untouched, unaffected, by all that God does, Barth said: there are no heights and depths in the being of God in which God is not already a God "for us" in Jesus Christ. No wedge may be driven, therefore, between a being of God in and for himself and a being of God "for us." God "is" in himself (in eternity) what he is in the covenant of grace.[86]

Anyone familiar with the history of orthodox Reformed theology will see a host of bright red warning flags in the BarMc Declaration here. Not only so, but readers who have followed the argument thus far in this book will, I trust, readily see the deep and deadly problems that plague Barth's maverick theological construct. A few comments, nevertheless, may help make the problems more explicit.

First, what could the BarMc Declaration mean by asserting that the *assumptio carnis* is essential to who God is? What it clearly *does not* mean, according to the quotation above, is that the assumption of the flesh is *necessary* to who God is. The BarMc Declaration eschews any notion of essential*ism*. So, it would not be fair simply to assert that the declaration envisions no possible world in which the assumption of the flesh does not obtain. Such a view would

---

[85]Ibid., 139.

[86]Ibid. For those interested in Barth's discussion of these points, McCormack substantiates his claims by referring to Barth, *Church Dogmatics*, 4.1.193, 186–210; 2.2.6–7, 77, 64. See also Van Til, *Christianity and Barthianism*, 75f.

make the assumption of the flesh a necessity with respect to God's being. The BarMc Declaration clearly asserts the contrary:

> If, as Barth says, the decree is truly primal and there is no state or mode of existence in God above and prior to it, then surely the decree is not freely made. Must it not, therefore, be a necessity for God? At this point, I would have to confess: I don't think any of us can understand how an eternal decision can be a free one. Every doctrine of predestination will have to raise the flag of mystery at some point; on Barthian soil, this is the point to do so.[87]

So, God's primal decision to assume a human nature is of the essence of who God is, and is a free decision.

Given our discussion in this chapter, we can heartily agree with BarMc that the notion of freedom in God is a difficult one to understand properly and biblically. The problem here is not that there is a recognition of, or deference to, mystery. The problem is that such a deference seems as arbitrary as the theology that drives it. How, we might ask, can it be that what is *essential* to God has its impetus in his *free* decision. That can be only if what is *essential* to God, above and beyond anything else, is his *freedom* (which, of course, Barth would affirm).

One would be hard-pressed, however, to find an argument anywhere in the history of orthodox theology, not to mention orthodox Reformed theology, that asserts such a strange idea. Not only so, but given what we have thus far discussed, one would be hard-pressed to find a biblical assertion—either directly or by good and necessary consequence—that would even hint at such an idea. It is difficult to avoid the suspicion that what the BarMc Declaration *really* eschews is the truth of God as revealed in Holy Scripture.

For example, to continue with the reasoning of BarMc, it is asserted that, since the decree is eternal, there can be no "before" or "after" with respect to it. So also, one cannot ask as to the relationship of this primal decision to the One who decides (God). God assigns to himself his own being, BarMc declares, and to ask how that can be is to confuse time and eternity. There can no more be a Being "before" this act of his will than there can be one "after." There just *is* this Being, who is himself *only* in his act, including his act of the *assumptio*, and that because he is himself eternal.[88]

---

[87] McCormack, "Christ and the Decree," 141. See also Van Til, *Christianity and Barthianism*, 61.
[88] As Van Til notes with respect to this "act," "How then can we speak truly, that is concretely, rather than abstractly about Christ? We can do so only by speaking of him as *Act*. Abstract thinking is thinking of static entities, such as God in himself and man in himself. To think

We have discussed a way out of this BarMc quagmire already, so it need not detain us here. It is important to highlight, however, that even though the BarMc Declaration at this point weaves together a few notions that have their home in orthodox theology—notions such as God's freedom and his eternity, as well as an affirmation of the decree as eternal—the particular Gordian knot that is tied is surely done with *scienter*, and can be nothing other than theologically myopic.

If we affirm the standard biblical and theological notion of God's necessity—an affirmation, as we have seen, that alone can do justice to his character as *Eimi*—then, along with that affirmation, we must also affirm that *anything* that God does relative to what is *ad extra*, including his eternal decree, must flow *from* his necessity (as the triune "I AM"), through his free decision, and thus must be located within the context of his gracious condescension. The BarMc Declaration would agree with the "freedom" aspect of the previous statement; what BarMc leaves out, and what is central, crucial, and foundational to *anything else* that we say about God, is that he must be and remain the "I AM," even as he freely determines to establish and maintain a covenantal relationship in which there is a certain mutual dependence. There must be, in other words, first and foremost, the *Eimi*, who himself determines to be related covenantally to that which is not himself.

One more concern of the BarMc Declaration needs attention. McCormack seems to think that unless the *schwerpunkt* (focal point) of the *assumptio carnis* as essential is accepted, there is no way, for Calvin (and presumably those who follow him, such as adherents to the Westminster Standards) to affirm the full deity of Christ.

> But what Barth is asking here is whether Calvin's doctrine of predestination does not finally render incoherent and ineffectual his affirmation of the deity of Christ. . . . Once the demotion (if I may put it that way) of Christ in the decree has established a distinction between the "eternal Son" and the incarnate Son, what is the relationship between the two? And, even more importantly, how can we know what the relationship is?[89]

It is difficult to make sense of such questions; surely their genesis is not naïveté. McCormack is well aware that such questions have been asked and

---

truly, that is concretely, about God is to think of him as living and therefore as acting for man in Christ." Van Til, *Christianity and Barthianism*, 13–14; see also 44f.

[89] McCormack, "Christ and the Decree," 140. As Van Til notes, "Orthodoxy, says Barth, has such an absolute God, with an absolute plan prior to and independent of Christ. This means that for orthodoxy Christ is not the electing God. Christ is then merely an instrument for accomplishing the work of salvation of men." Van Til, *Christianity and Barthianism*, 106.

answered in the church. These questions must, therefore, stem from a highly contextualized and myopic standpoint.[90] To entertain them as serious questions, one must live, move, and exist only in a Barthian box, without recourse to the real world of orthodox theological discourse. In such a box, the only way to affirm the full deity of Christ is if he is *what* he is and *who* he is from and in eternity. For him to *be* something in eternity that he is/was *not* in time is to create a category (i.e., that of eternal, static "being") with no content.

As we have already seen, however, Scripture is clear that the Christ who came when the time had fully come (Gal. 4:4; Eph. 1:10) is the same One who, prior to that coming, was the Logos of God, who himself is and was fully God (John 1:1). There is indeed mystery with respect to who this One is in all his fullness and deity, quite apart from his revealing himself to us (Matt. 11:27f.; cf. Rom. 8:26–27). That mystery is no miasmic morass, as the BarMc Declaration seems to think. Instead, it is the very glory of God (Rom. 11:33–36). It teaches us that this Logos, who was in the beginning, and who was *asarkos* in the beginning, became *ensarkos*; he took on a human nature in the fullness of time—he condescended to redeem a people (Phil. 2:1–10).

Is there any coherent way that such a construal could render the Logos as less than fully and completely God? If what we have noticed in previous chapters is correct, if the Son of God remained all that he is, even while condescending to us throughout covenant history, and climactically in Christ, is there even a hint of ontological change or ontological subordinationism in such an idea? There is, only if notions of God, Christ, salvation, redemption, condescension, time, eternity, and so forth are reconfigured in such a way as to be fundamentally absent and thus unrecognized in the history of the church. Such is the BarMc Declaration.

There is one more strand in the BarMc Declaration that deserves mention, though it can be dismissed fairly quickly. McCormack thinks that we must read Philippians 2:5ff. as Paul's affirmation that God suffered and died. To read it any other way, he thinks, misses the climactic point in the passage that Jesus is Lord. He is right, of course, that this is Paul's conclusion. For the BarMc Declaration, however,

---

[90]In conjunction with these strange ideas is a similarly strange understanding of God as triune. So, according to Van Til, Barth's view of God as *Act*, and therefore as *Geschichte*, includes for Barth that "the older theology, including protestant orthodoxy, failed to see this basic point. It was not truly christological in its approach. It sought for formal-logical foundations for its doctrine of the trinity back of the revelation of God in Christ. Over against this we must insist that 'God is, who He is, in the act of his revelation.' Thus do we deal with the living God, not with some abstract essence" (ibid., 36–37).

> The important thing to see . . . is that the affirmation of two natures *in one Person* cannot, with any consistency, allow us to attribute that which is accomplished in and through the human nature to the human nature alone—as though the human nature were a subject in its own right. Consistency demands that we ascribe that which is accomplished in and through the human nature to the person of the union—which, as the Chalcedonian formula says, is none other than the Logos, the Second Person of the Trinity.[91]

BarMc's concern is that Calvin and "the overwhelming majority of pre-modern theologians" missed the central truth that the human nature of Christ could not be considered as a subject in its own right.

We can dispense with this rather quickly because we have already dealt with the substance of what the "overwhelming majority" in the church thought in this regard. Recall that, according to Bavinck, "Reformed theology stressed that it was the person of the Son who became flesh—not the substance [the underlying reality] but the subsistence [the particular being] of the Son assumed our nature," and, "The Reformed prefer to say that the person of the Son, rather than the divine nature, as Lutherans said, had become human."[92]

Thus, *the subject*, given a Reformed understanding of the *communicatio idiomatum*, is the *person* of Christ himself. But affirming such a thing does not, thereby, negate any attribution of characteristics, actions, and properties to one of the two natures that is his by virtue of the incarnation. To think that it does would be to negate, for example, that when I make a decision, *both I* make that decision and *my will* decides. To make of myself *and* of my will a subject does no injustice, ontologically or otherwise, to who I am in my activity. Thus, there is no Nestorianism present just because one attributes, for example, Christ's growth in wisdom to his person *as Christ* or to his human nature.

There is no ontological change in God. Such change is impossible, *not* because God isn't free, but rather because God is necessarily who he is; he cannot and will not become ontologically less than he is. It is only *in* that necessity that freedom has its proper place, which brings us to our final consideration.

(2) The Secret Nod of God

> For providence is so connected with the divinity that it cannot be asserted or denied without either asserting or denying God himself. Hence the Scriptures

---

[91]McCormack, "Christ and the Decree," 138–39.
[92]Herman Bavinck, *Reformed Dogmatics*, vol. 3, *Sin and Salvation in Christ*, ed. John Bolt, trans. John Vriend (Grand Rapids: Baker Academic, 2006), 3:259, 275.

everywhere separate God from idols by the argument of providence (Is. 41:22, 23; 42:8, 9; Job 12:7–9). By the heathen, God and providence . . . are used promiscuously. Not only they who deny the existence, but also they who deny the providence of God, are condemned as atheists.[93]

I will not be able to do justice to the biblical teaching of God's providence in this section, nor is it my intention to do so. Clearly, as Turretin notes above, the existence of the Christian God entails that he be in control of all that he has made.[94] That much is certain.

This meticulous and comprehensive control, however, as should be clear by now, brings to mind certain conundrums that need to be mentioned here. The first conundrum has to do with the relationship of God's providence to necessity and contingency. The second conundrum has to do with the relationship of God's providence more specifically to our responsible choices.

We need not rehearse the history of debate on this important topic at this point. All we need affirm, first, for our purposes is the notion of *concursus*,[95] in that God's providence includes *both* his meticulous control over all things *and* the reality, as well as the mode, of the activity necessitated in and by those contingent things that are providentially controlled.

To put the matter in general terms, everything that Scripture affirms about providence, and thus all that we are to say and think about providence, has to do with the relationship of the necessary (God) to the contingent (creation). More specifically, therefore, we need to attempt to articulate just how we might best think of God's eternal and immutable decree in relation to those contingent things that are done and performed in time on the basis of that decree. How, we might ask, can that which is necessary and foundational[96]

---

[93]Turretin, *Institutes*, 1:492.

[94]For concise and clear explanations of the biblical teaching of God's providence, see John Calvin, *Institutes of the Christian Religion*, trans. Ford Lewis Battles, ed. John T. McNeill, 2 vols., The Library of Christian Classics (Philadelphia: Westminster Press, 1960), 1.16–17; Turretin, *Institutes*, 1:489–538.

[95]*Concursus* is "a corollary of the doctrines of God as *primum movens* and of providence as *continuata creatio* that defines the continuing divine support of the operation of all secondary causes (whether free, contingent, or necessary). For any contingent being to act in a free, a contingent, or a necessary manner, the divine will which supports all contingent being must concur in its act" (Muller, *Dictionary of Latin and Greek Theological Terms*, 76). Virtually all orthodox theology affirms some version of concurrence. Debates, for example, between Molinists and certain compatibilists revolve around questions of whether concurrence is relative to the *event* or to the *agent*, and whether or not God's concurrence is intrinsically "neutral" or efficacious. We will not engage those debates here.

[96]I am thinking here of the necessity of God's decree *given his free determination*. Thus, though the decree is conditionally necessary, once determined by God, what is decreed *must* take place.

accrue to any event without that event itself being necessary? Any Christian construal of providence understands the urgency of this question.

There are full and detailed studies available on this question.[97] Those are worth consulting for a much fuller picture than what I will present here. Helping us to focus our discussion of this important matter, however, a recent, concise treatment of the relevant issues is available. I will seek to provide the basic contours of my thinking about providence by highlighting a few aspects of the interactions on that and related matters in Bruce Ware (ed.), *Perspectives on the Doctrine of God: Four Views*.

Specifically, because the chapter "Divine Providence and the Openness of God"[98] is a concise exposition of the tenets of free-will (including "openness") theism relative to God's providence, incorporating those concerns here should also help us see how our discussion thus far addresses the concerns of openness theism (as well as Arminianism),[99] all the while maintaining the truths set forth in a Reformed doctrine of God.

Sanders sees the divide between (what he calls) the "Hatfield" free-will theists and the "McCoy" theological determinists as a sixteen-hundred-year struggle. According to him, "The watershed separating these two families is whether one affirms that God is ever affected by and responds to what we do."[100] This is not quite right, even as Sanders's own questions indicate: "Does God tightly control everything such that what God wants is never thwarted in the least detail? Does God ever take risks? Is God ever influenced by what we do, or does everything work out precisely as God eternally foreordained?"[101] The central problem, therefore, is *not* whether God is affected by or responds to what we do (though that can be *a* problem in this discussion); the central problem lies in what is presupposed by those responses with respect to God's character. Do God's reactions to our decisions, for example, require that those decisions be the first and primary cause of his reactions? If we could focus the discussion, the problem is whether God's responses entail a denial of his meticulous sovereignty and his decree such that he could not have *first*

[97]See, for example, G. C. Berkouwer, *The Providence of God* (Grand Rapids: Eerdmans, 1952), and, for a non-Reformed approach, Luis de Molina, *On Divine Foreknowledge: Part IV of the Concordia*, trans. Alfred J. Freddoso (Ithaca, NY: Cornell University Press, 1988).
[98]In *Perspectives on the Doctrine of God: Four Views*, ed. Bruce Ware (Nashville: B&H Academic, 2008), 196–240. The open theist position is argued by John Sanders.
[99]Says Sanders, "The knowledgeable reader will note that most of the beliefs espoused by open theists are also affirmed by other free will theists such as the Eastern Orthodox and the Arminians. This is due to the family resemblance shared by proponents of free will theism when it comes to theologies of salvation, providence, anthropology, and impetratory prayer" (ibid., 199).
[100]Ibid., 200.
[101]Ibid.

determined or known that which motivated his responses. The problem, in other words, is whether we affirm that God controls "all things [τὰ πάντα] according to the counsel of his own will" (Eph. 1:11), or we affirm that God controls some things according to what we *first* determine to be the case.[102]

In that regard, we should note an important point from Paul Helm's response to Sanders. In one section of Sanders's defense of open theism, he marshals a number of biblical texts that he thinks support his openness view. However, as Helm points out, "Nowhere, as far as I can see, does he fairly and squarely address counterevidence; biblical statements of God's all encompassing knowledge and control, the election and predestination of the saints, the 'golden chain' of Romans 8, and so on."[103] This charge is serious enough, but it shouldn't surprise us by this point given that, as we have seen, both sides of the debate may tend to look, almost myopically, at their favorite biblical texts and passages (though the Reformed typically deal with both sides, as we have seen).

But a further critique from Helm underlines the context in which Sanders operates and explains why certain biblical texts must be thus construed by him. Helm rightly affirms that both compatibilism and theological determinism are, in their own ways, not a part of the biblical picture for a Reformed theology proper. If compatibilism is shown to be fatally flawed, that would not alter a Reformed understanding of God's relationship to the world or to us.

But this is not the case with free-will theism, whatever its particular variety (e.g., openness or Arminian). Not only is there a need to sublimate certain clear texts and passages of Scripture in order to bolster free-will theism, but the *reason* for such sublimation is that the foundation on which free-will theism stands is not itself drawn from Scripture. So, contrary to the Reformed view, for any variety of free-will theism,

> the philosophical doctrine *does* occupy center stage. Without such a doctrine
> the raison d'etre of free will theism disappears. . . . Libertarianism is . . . a philo-

---

[102]The "first" here may either be a logical or a temporal "first." So, for example, the latter option is thus explained: On the Molinist account, "God's foreknowledge is neither the effect nor the cause of our free actions." God's "foreknowledge should not be seen as in any sense the cause of that which is foreknown. . . . Hence, from a Molinist standpoint, we can indeed say with Molina that 'it is not because [God] knows that something is going to be that that thing is going to be. Just the opposite, it is because the thing will come to be from its causes that He knows that it is going to be'" (Thomas P. Flint, *Divine Providence: The Molinist Account*, Cornell Studies in the Philosophy of Religion [Ithaca, NY: Cornell University Press, 1998], 44–45). Though Roger Olson, for example, wants to distance his Arminianism from Molinism, we need not engage that debate here. Free-will theism, no matter the variety, is always libertarian.
[103]"Response to John Sanders," in Ware, *Perspectives on the Doctrine of God*, 242–43.

sophical doctrine derived from paganism but is now (in the case of Arminianism
and open theism) exalted to the status of a Christian doctrine. . . . Not only is
it essential that human beings are libertarian, it is also vital that God himself
is as well.[104]

But this is not simply Helm's view. Libertarians themselves have recognized
that the foundation of their theological system, with respect to God's sovereignty, his providence, and man's libertarian freedom, is simply a matter of a
supposed common set of beliefs. So, just to cite one example, Thomas Flint
recognizes the impetus behind the *scientia media* view of Molina.

> Molinism is most properly viewed as the philosophical development of *pre-
> philosophical beliefs which are widely shared both within the Christian com-
> munity and beyond it.* . . . Far more common, at least in my experience, is the
> reaction that Molinism is but an elaboration of a view which they have held
> implicitly all along.[105]

It seems the theoretical foundation for free-will theism (which Molinism
entails), including openness theism, is not Scripture, but "prephilosophical
beliefs which are widely shared," specifically including a belief that, in order
to be free, we must be in complete control of our decisions such that we could
have decided to the contrary. One does not have to look very far, however,
to recognize that "widely shared" prephilosophical beliefs and Christianity,
more often than not, make strange, if not mutually destructive, bedfellows.

Roger Olson, as well, admits that free-will theism is grounded on what is
beyond Scripture.

> Free will theists of all types point to experience to support their belief in libertar-
> ian free will. That we act freely at least some of the time is a matter of intuition.
> Determinism is counterintuitive. . . . However, just because free will theism
> uses intuition and reason to support itself does not mean it is based entirely or
> exhaustively on them. Classical Christian free will theists base their belief in
> libertarian freedom not on intuition or reason but on divine revelation. Every
> time Scripture says God repents or relents or changes his mind in response to
> human decisions or actions libertarian free will is taken for granted as divine
> determinism is denied.[106]

[104]Ibid., 244.
[105]Flint, *Divine Providence*, 76, my emphasis.
[106]Roger Olson, "The Classical Free Will Theist Model of God," in Ware, *Perspectives on the Doctrine of God*, 157–58.

This admission is illuminating, and it highlights again how pervasive and hegemonic the notion of libertarianism is in these systems. Given what we have discussed thus far, it should now be obvious that what is decidedly *not* taken for granted when Scripture says that God changes his mind is free-will theism. The crux of the problem, therefore, is that the free-will theist's *intuition* that freedom requires that God not be in control of our actions goes against all that we have set out thus far, from a biblical perspective, with respect to God's aseity and sovereignty, and how that aseity is related to God's covenantal character.[107] But it is worth underlining the fact that the libertarianism that controls all free-will theistic systems is simply assumed; it is prephilosophical or intuited, but it is not a part of biblical revelation in its descriptions of man or God.

The main headings of Sanders's chapter are instructive. They are meant to set out some of the central tenets of the open variety of free-will theism. Given our discussion throughout this book, it should be more obvious now which tenets are in agreement with a Reformed doctrine of God, and which are not.

Two main sections in Sanders's argument in particular highlight the need for our *Eimi*/*eikon*, essential/covenantal distinction. The first section is entitled "Biblical Support for Open Theism."[108] Sanders sees the four subsections/ propositions following this section to be inimical to "theological determinism." We should note, however, that the four propositions listed by Sanders have already been broached, in one form or another, in this book and have been shown to be compatible with a Reformed doctrine of God.

First, says Sanders, "The Bible portrays God as authentically responding to His people's petitions." We have already seen that there is no need to deny this tenet. For Sanders, however, this truth requires that God not have an eternal and immutable plan behind his response. Quoting John Goldingay, Sanders avers that "God does not operate from a blueprint." So, says Goldingay, "The First Testament story never talks about God having a plan for the world or a plan of salvation or a plan for people's individual lives, and the story it tells does not look like one that resulted from a plan."[109] The problematic notion, therefore, contrary to what Sanders lists, is *not* that God either responds (in free-will theism) or doesn't (in theological determinism); the problematic

---

[107]See also Linda Trinkaus Zagzebski, *The Dilemma of Freedom and Foreknowledge* (New York: Oxford University Press, USA, 1996), 34; and Olson's defense of free-will theism in Ware, *Perspectives on the Doctrine of God*, 148–72, esp. 157f.

[108]In John Sanders, "Divine Providence and the Openness of God," in Ware, *Perspectives on the Doctrine of God*, 214–24.

[109]Ibid., 215.

notion is that, in order for God "authentically" to respond, he cannot have had a predetermined plan.

Second, says Sanders, "The Bible portrays God as being affected by creatures and as sometimes being surprised by what they do." This, too, has been discussed in previous chapters. But, again, the problematic notion is *not* that God is affected, but what Sanders has to affirm in order for God's being affected to make sense: "Genesis 6:6 says that God was grieved because humans continually sinned. Why would God grieve if God always knew exactly what humans were going to do? It makes no sense to say that a timeless being experiences grief."[110] So, it is not God being affected that is the important point for Sanders; it is that God, in order to *be affected*, must not be eternal and must be less than fully and eternally omniscient (in the classical sense of that word).[111]

Third, "The Bible portrays God as testing people in order to discover what they will do." Sanders refers us to a passage with which we have dealt previously—Genesis 22:12 (he also references Ex. 33:5). Again, however, it is *not* the notion of God's discovering that is central. What is central to God's discovering is summed up in Sanders's rhetorical question: "Why test them if God eternally knew with certainty exactly how the people would respond?"[112]

Last (under this section), "The Bible portrays God as changing his mind as he relates to his creatures." As we would expect by now, it is not the affirmation of God's changing his mind that is problematic. What is problematic is that in order for God to change his mind in certain circumstances, those circumstances must be "open" to him; there can be no way in which such circumstances can be meticulously determined and controlled by God.

The problem in all of these biblical affirmations that Sanders lists is *not* the affirmation of such things,[113] but the assumption that affirming them implies that God cannot be in providential control of such things, since that would render incoherent any authenticity of God's reactions and responses in these circumstances.

---

[110]Ibid., 216.
[111]Sanders redefines omniscience as "dynamic" in order to say that he affirms omniscience. However, what he clearly does not affirm is the kind of exhaustive knowledge that we have discussed previously. So, he says, "It is questionable whether it is coherent to affirm both that God has always known of this event and that God now has changing emotions about that event" (ibid., 217).
[112]Ibid., 221.
[113]At least, given what I have argued thus far. Sanders is right to note that there have been those in the Reformed tradition who have misconstrued the clear teaching of Scripture in this area. Note his quote of Jonathan Edwards in this regard in ibid., 205.

So, God *does* "authentically respond" to us, he *is* "affected by us," he *does* test in order to discover something, and he *does* change his mind. But none of this requires, nor does it in any way entail, as we have seen, that God does not control all things by the counsel of his own will, or that he did not decree "whatsoever comes to pass."

The problem, again, centers on the relationship of necessity to contingency. For free-will theists, only that which is in no way necessarily caused or controlled can be free. But this construal fails to do justice to the dual mode of God's character. As one who is altogether necessary, he is, nevertheless, free.[114] As we have seen, that freedom relates to that which God determines *ad extra*. It is *not* a freedom that overrides or undermines his necessity. Thus, for example, God *necessarily* wills himself; to will himself *freely* would be to import contingency into his essential character.

Maybe an illustration from experiences can help us to make sense of how necessity and contingency might work. Anyone who has read a novel or watched a movie more than once has no doubt, likely unconsciously, lived within the convergence of necessity and contingency. The second run through the novel or movie, if we're honest, does not diminish the reactions that we have to that story. No one reading McMurtry's *Lonesome Dove* for a second time thinks that maybe Gus will make it to the end. Even when read the second time, the rescue of Lorie is no less dramatic. Yet in reading it a second or third or fourth time, the contingencies presented in that novel are not diminished; one does not read in a state of complete boredom, or with the assumption that the story is meaningless or without drama. Even so, everything that happens is "preplanned" and necessarily the case. And, even though we have read it once, knowing the end from the beginning does not keep us from fully engaging and living in the contingencies each time.

This illustration shows—over against, for example, the assertion of Olson above that "determinism is counterintuitive"—that a necessity in which the "story" is determined from first to last in no way destroys or negates the real contingency experienced in that story. What is "intuited" is not libertarian free will, but rather the right and biblical notion that there are real contingencies, and that we are responsible for what we choose to do. A biblical view of the decree and of providence does not negate that.

---

[114]If Roger Olson is correct that free-will theism demands that persons can do otherwise than they do, then, contrary to his argument that God is libertarianly free, he is not. God cannot choose to be essentially other than he is; he is constrained by his own nature. See Olson's discussion in "The Classical Free Will Theist Model of God," 150ff.

There is, therefore, a compatible, coherent, and consistent relationship in God between who he is necessarily and who he is freely (even if we are not able fully to explain that consistency). Not only so, but once God determines to condescend, those properties that he takes on are themselves compatible, coherent, and consistent with who he is essentially. Again, this does not mean that we can fully explain that consistency; it simply means that we affirm that there is no contradiction *in God*, even if the mysteries that are central and essential to the Christian faith may look contradictory at times. This means as well that the contingency that we and God experience is *real* and "literal," even though it has its source in God's immutable decree.

Perhaps it will help if we recall a previous illustration. When we affirm that God is everywhere, we are affirming that *all* of God is in, through, and with every *place*. Though it looks for all the world like the space that my desk currently occupies is filled by that desk, we nevertheless also affirm that the triune God is fully and completely there as well. This affirmation tells us, at least, that whatever "presence" *is* with respect to God's essential character, it is of a wholly different kind of presence than the presence of my desk. My desk is here, but so is God, and the "here-ness" of my desk is of a different kind than the "here-ness" of God. Presence, therefore, is analogical with respect to God and creation. There are continuities—in that God is certainly and unequivocally *here*—but there are radical discontinuities—in that his being here in no way violates the space that is taken up by my desk.

Suppose we now think of this with respect to the necessity that the plan and purposes of God impose on creation. We cannot deny that necessity; God's meticulous sovereignty and providence demand that all that is, is necessarily.[115] But the necessity that accrues to God's plan and providence is of a very different kind than the necessity that we experience in creation. Just as it is illegitimate to apply the concept of God's presence to the presence of my desk, so that either one or the other, but not both, can be "here," so also is it illegitimate to apply the necessity of God's eternal plan and providential control to all modes of behavior and actions in creation, such that either God's necessity or (for example) my contingent choice to type these words can apply, but not both.[116]

---

[115]For more on the relationship of necessity and contingency from a Reformed perspective, see K. Scott Oliphint, *Reasons for Faith: Philosophy in the Service of Theology* (Phillipsburg, NJ: P&R, 2006), chapter 16.

[116]The same is true with respect to the notion of causality. Whatever God's causality, it is of a wholly different kind than ours, such that it *establishes* rather than undermines the reality of our responsible actions as secondary causes.

We must recognize, in the first place, what I have been emphasizing all along, that whenever we are attempting to understand God's relationship to creation, we are always and everywhere in the midst of a unique and finally incomprehensible situation. As I have argued, this is nowhere more evident than in that quintessential relationship of God to creation as we have it in the person of Christ.

Consider that quintessentially intense moment of Christ's agony over the mission of the cross (Matt. 26:36–44; Mark 14:32–40; Luke 22:39–46). He goes to the garden of Gethsemane to pray. If free-will theists are correct, then Christ's prayer is genuine only because the cross was in no way eternally decreed. But clearly the cross was a central element of God's decree (cf. Eph. 1:4ff.; 1 Pet. 1:20ff.; Rev. 13:8ff.). How, then, could Christ's prayer make any difference? More pointedly, if he as the Son of God decreed (together with the Father and the Spirit) that he would accomplish his salvific work, why does he even pray? Why does he even *agonize* in prayer to his Father (cf. Heb. 5:7)?

He does so—and here is the point that seems never to have been properly grasped by free-will theists—*not* because the work he came to do was not decreed, but *because what was decreed was, as well, the utter contingency of the world to which he came.* That is, in the mind of Christ, a mind that is now theanthropic, there is no disharmony between what the triune God decreed, including that he controls what he has decreed, and the contingency that is required for the authenticity and coherence of prayer (and of human choices, more generally).[117] The agony that Jesus experiences in the garden is not the agony of an incoherence between his own necessity (as God) and contingency (as the God-man); it is the agony of the prospect of his separation from God.

Thus, from a biblical point of view, contingency (as is the case with everything) presupposes that God is, and is the *a se* and sovereign God who freely determines to create that which is, in its essence, contingent. And there is nothing in God's condescension to this contingent context that in any way negates its (hypothetical) necessity or violates its real and authentic contingency.[118]

---

[117]This is, in part, what the Westminster Confession means in 3.1: "God from all eternity, did, by the most wise and holy counsel of His own will, freely, and unchangeably ordain whatsoever comes to pass: yet so, as thereby neither is God the author of sin, nor is violence offered to the will of the creatures; nor is the liberty or contingency of second causes taken away, *but rather established*" (my emphasis).

[118]So, for example, Luke can say (Acts 2:23) that "this Jesus, delivered up according to the definite plan and foreknowledge of God, you crucified and killed by the hands of lawless men." The definite plan and foreknowledge of God did not negate or undermine the wickedness of those who put Christ to death.

The reality of this contingency can be seen, as well, just after Jesus's experience in the garden.

> Jesus said to him, "Friend, do what you came to do." Then they came up and laid hands on Jesus and seized him. And behold, one of those who were with Jesus stretched out his hand and drew his sword and struck the servant of the high priest and cut off his ear. Then Jesus said to him, "Put your sword back into its place. For all who take the sword will perish by the sword. Do you think that I cannot appeal to my Father, and he will at once send me more than twelve legions of angels? But how then should the Scriptures be fulfilled, that it must be so?" (Matt. 26:50–54)

In light of our current discussion, it is stunning what Jesus asks here. *Could* Jesus appeal to his Father so that what was decreed and prophesied in Scripture *would not* be fulfilled? In order that Scripture be fulfilled, Jesus does not appeal to his Father, but he *could* do so. Surely this highlights the clear and unambiguous affirmation that contingency is in no way undermined or negated by the necessity of God's decree and providence (including what Scripture says must be fulfilled). There is no hint in the life of Jesus that the necessity of God's decree and providence rendered him a robot or puppet. Those objections hold only if we (1) think univocally with respect to necessity (i.e., that it is the same thing relative to God and creation) or (2) fail to recognize the *compatibility* of necessity and contingency in the person of Christ, thus in all of God's dealings with creation. Compatibility, therefore, needs to be redefined according to biblical, rather than extrabiblical, models.

Just how these two *actually* go together is impossible for us to exhaust. But—and here is the challenge for free-will theism—once we affirm, as we must, that necessity and contingency come together in the Son of God with respect to his incarnation, and once we affirm, as we must, that the hypostatic union was indeed a union *in one person*, we ought easily to affirm that bringing together necessity and contingency into one consistent whole in creation is no large task for the triune God. If he can bring his own character together with creation (in the incarnation) without violating the essential properties of either aspect of that (now united) character, then his relationship to creation can be (and is) exhaustively marked by such a union.[119]

---

[119]This helps us to see as well that the free and sincere offer of the gospel is in no way a violation of the fact that God has chosen his own before the foundation of the world. Necessity and contingency co-inhere; the properties of both are maintained and not violated.

278   Things Secret and Revealed

The necessity that is foundational for God's character, and for his plan and purposes of the world, is gloriously (even if ultimately mysteriously) united to and with the contingency that permeates all that happens in this world. It is for this reason, at least, that Calvin and Turretin describe providence as "the secret nod of God."[120] It is a "nod"; it does bring to pass everything that is. But it is, in the end, a secret nod. We cannot plumb the depths of God's good and wise reasons for doing it just this way. This, however, should move us, not to an inquisitive anger, but to praise (Rom. 11:33–36).

E. Conclusion

It is past time to bring this chapter, and book, to a close. There is much more that could and should be pursued. We have not been able to broach in any serious way the difficult problem of sin and evil as it relates to the *Eimi/eikon* distinction.[121] I have not developed in detail a refutation of Molinism or Arminianism, as those systems, it seems, seek to do justice to real contingency by way of the supposed determined "restraint" of God. I have tried to set forth a strong argument as to why such systems fail and in the end truncate the richness of God's revelation to and relationship with us.

Specifically, it seems there may not be a strong argument left for free-will theism. If free-will theism is dependent on an intuition, or a prephilosophical notion, or a philosophical presupposition for the entirety of its system, and if such notions lose their strength in the face of an orthodox christology, then it is no long step to see that the *biblical* argument for compatibility with respect to God's relationship to creation renders free-will intuitions, or prephilosophical notions, or philosophical presuppositions weak and irrelevant. Put more simply, if the free-will theist's intuited notion of compatibility cannot apply to his christology, it cannot apply more generally to God's relationship to creation and to us. Necessity and contingency are happily united in God's covenant condescension; there is no need to let some supposed intuition undermine that compatibility.

One final point must be made, however, with respect to my general methodology and critique. Suppose it is argued, given what I have said, that since God takes on covenantal properties, some of which appear to undermine his aseity (e.g., his give-and-take responses to us), it is no stretch of mind to affirm that God also takes on the covenantal property of risk, in which he, though

---

[120] John Calvin, *Institutes of the Christian Religion*, 1.18.1, "arcano Dei nutu"; and Turretin, *Institutes*, 1:533 (6.8.12, "nutus Dei arcanus").
[121] For an attempt at a *Reformed* free-will defense, see Oliphint, *Reasons for Faith*.

essentially *a se*, determines to take a "hands off" approach in his relationship to us. Or, more radically, suppose someone wants to argue that God's taking on covenantal properties includes, for example, the *fact* that he does have a strong arm, and the like. The answer to these kinds of arguments must be the beacon that drives all of our discussions of this sort. The answer is that God's character and properties—whether essential or covenantal—cannot be driven by pure deduction. They must be understood only in the light of Holy Scripture.

If, for example, the Bible were unclear or absent affirmations of God's meticulous sovereignty and providence, then it might be possible for us to see him as a God who risks. But such is not the case. As we saw above, those who want to argue for free-will theism must do so (1) with extrabiblical pre-commitments firmly embedded and in control and (2) by either ignoring or misconstruing passages that explicitly affirm God as sovereign Lord. So, as with any other systematic theological tenet, it is only as strong and applicable as Scripture allows. It is never a license for pure logical deduction. For that reason, I have sought to ground our discussion, first, in that quintessential revelation of God in Christ, as that revelation informs and exegetes the rest of what Scripture tells us about God, and about "God with us."

My hope is that, from this, I have provided parameters within which further discussions of this sort may fruitfully continue.

Bibliography

Allert, Craig D. *A High View of Scripture? The Authority of the Bible and the Formation of the New Testament Canon*. Evangelical Ressourcement: Ancient Sources for the Church's Future. Grand Rapids: Baker Academic, 2007.

Anselm. *Proslogium; Monologium; an Appendix, in Behalf of the Fool, By Gaunilon; and Cur Deus Homo*. Translated by Sidney Norton Deane. Bellingham, WA: Logos Research Systems, 2009.

Aquinas, Thomas. *Summa contra Gentiles*. Translated by Charles J. O'Neil. 4 vols. Notre Dame: Notre Dame University Press, 1957.

———. *Summa theologica*. Translated by Fathers of the English Dominican Province.

Arminius, James. *The Works of James Arminius*. 3 vols. Christian Classics Ethereal Library.

Athanasius. *The Incarnation of the Word, Being the Treatise of St. Athanasius (De incarnatione verbi dei)*. Translated by Sister Penelope, CSMV London: Geoffrey Bles, Centenary, 1944.

Augustine. *City of God*. Translated by Marcus Dods. In *A Select Library of the Nicene and Post-Nicene Fathers of the Christian Church*. Series 1. Vol. 2. Edited by Philip Schaff. Grand Rapids: Eerdmans, 1988.

Barth, Karl. *Church Dogmatics*. 2nd ed. Translated by G. W. Bromiley. Edited by Thomas Forsyth Torrance and Geoffrey William Bromiley. Edinburgh: T&T Clark, 1975.

Bavinck, Herman. *The Philosophy of Revelation*. Grand Rapids: Baker, 1979.

———. *Reformed Dogmatics*. Vol. 2, *God and Creation*. Edited by John Bolt. Translated by John Vriend. Grand Rapids: Baker Academic, 2004.

———. *Reformed Dogmatics*. Vol. 3, *Sin and Salvation in Christ*. Edited by John Bolt. Translated by John Vriend. Grand Rapids: Baker Academic, 2006.

Beale, Gregory K. *The Erosion of Inerrancy in Evangelicalism: Responding to New Challenges to Biblical Authority*. Wheaton, IL: Crossway, 2008.

Beardslee, John W., III, ed. *Reformed Dogmatics: J. Wollebius, G. Voetius, F. Turretin.* A Library of Protestant Thought. New York: Oxford University Press, 1965.

Berkhof, Louis. *Systematic Theology.* Grand Rapids: Eerdmans, 1953.

Berkouwer, G. C. *The Providence of God.* Grand Rapids: Eerdmans, 1952.

Boethius. *Tractates, De consolatione philosophiae.* Translated by H. F. Stewart, E. K. Rand, and S. J. Tester. Loeb Classical Library. Cambridge, MA: Harvard University Press, 1978.

Borland, James A. *Christ in the Old Testament.* Chicago: Moody, 1978.

Boyd, Gregory A. *God of the Possible: A Biblical Introduction to the Open View of God.* Grand Rapids: Baker, 2000.

Brown, Raymond E. *The Gospel According to John I–XII.* Anchor Bible Series. Garden City, NY: Doubleday, 1966.

Bullinger, Ethelbert William. *Figures of Speech Used in the Bible.* New York: J. B. Yound, 1898.

Calvin, John. *The Comprehensive John Calvin Collection.* CD edition. The Ages Digital Library System, 2002.

———. *Institutes of the Christian Religion.* Translated by Ford Lewis Battles. Edited by John T. McNeill. 2 vols. The Library of Christian Classics. Philadelphia: Westminster Press, 1960.

Charnock, Stephen. *The Existence and Attributes of God.* 2 vols. Grand Rapids: Baker, 1979.

Childs, Brevard S. *The Book of Exodus: A Critical Theological Commentary.* Old Testament Library. Philadelphia: Westminster Press, 1974.

Clarke, W. Norris. "Charles Hartshorne's Philosophy of God: A Thomistic Critique." In *Charles Hartshorne's Concept of God: Philosophical and Theological Responses,* edited by Santiago Sia, 103–23. Dordrecht: Kluwer Academic, 1990.

Cobb, John B., Jr., and David Ray Griffin. *Process Theology.* Philadelphia: Westminster Press, 1976.

Cottrell, Jack W. "The Nature of Divine Sovereignty." In *The Grace of God, the Will of Man,* edited by Clark H. Pinnock, 97–119. Grand Rapids: Academie, 1989.

Craig, William L. "Middle Knowledge, A Calvinist-Arminian Rapprochement?" In *The Grace of God, the Will of Man,* edited by Clark H. Pinnock, 141–64. Grand Rapids: Academie, 1989.

———. *Time and Eternity: Exploring God's Relationship to Time.* Wheaton, IL: Crossway, 2001.

Davis, Stephen T. "Temporal Eternity." In *Philosophy of Religion: An Anthology,* edited by Louis P. Pojman, 209–16. Belmont, CA: Wadsworth/Thomson Learning, 2003.

de Molina, Luis. *On Divine Foreknowledge: Part IV of the* Concordia. Translated by Alfred J. Freddoso. Ithaca, NY: Cornell University Press, 1988.

Doolan, Gregory T. *Aquinas on the Divine Ideas as Exemplar Causes.* Washington, DC: Catholic University of America, 2008.

Drange, Theodore M. "Incompatible-Properties Arguments: A Survey." In *The Impossibility of God*, edited by Michael Martin, 185–97. Amherst, NY: Prometheus, 2003.

Durham, John I. *Word Biblical Commentary.* Vol. 3, *Exodus.* Nashville: Thomas Nelson, 1987.

Enns, Peter. *Inspiration and Incarnation.* Grand Rapids: Baker Academic, 2005.

Fee, Gordon D. *Paul's Letter to the Philippians.* The New International Commentary on the New Testament. Grand Rapids: Eerdmans, 1995.

Flint, Thomas P. *Divine Providence: The Molinist Account.* Cornell Studies in the Philosophy of Religion. Ithaca, NY: Cornell University Press, 1998.

Frame, John M. *The Doctrine of God.* Phillipsburg, NJ: P&R, 2002.

———. *No Other God: A Response to Open Theism.* Phillipsburg, NJ: P&R, 2001.

Freddoso, Alfred J. "God's General Concurrence with Secondary Causes: Why Conservation Is Not Enough." *Philosophical Perspectives* 5 (1991): 553–85.

Ganssle, Gregory E., and David M. Woodruff, eds. *God and Time: Essays on the Divine Nature.* Oxford: Oxford University Press, 2002.

Gathercole, Simon J. *The Preexistent Son: Recovering the Christologies of Matthew, Mark, and Luke.* Grand Rapids: Eerdmans, 2006.

Grillmeier, Alos, SJ. *Christ in Christian Tradition.* Vol. 1, *From the Apostolic Age to Chalcedon (451).* Translated by J. S. Bowden. New York: Sheed and Ward, 1965.

Helm, Paul. "Evil, Love and Silence." Unpublished manuscript, 2010.

———. "God and Spacelessness." In *Contemporary Philosophy of Religion*, edited by Stephen M. Cahn and David Shatz, 99–110. New York: Oxford University Press, 1982.

———. *John Calvin's Ideas.* Oxford: Oxford University Press, 2004.

Helm, Paul, and Terrance L. Tiessen. "Does Calvinism Have Room for Middle Knowledge? A Conversation." *Westminster Theological Journal* 71, no. 2 (2009): 437–54.

Henry, Matthew. *Matthew Henry's Commentary on the Whole Bible: Complete and Unabridged in One Volume.* Peabody, MA: Hendrickson, 1996.

Hickman, Edward, ed. *The Works of Jonathan Edwards.* 2 vols. Edinburgh: Banner of Truth, 1948.

Hodge, Charles. *Systematic Theology.* 3 vols. London: James Clarke, 1960.

Hughes, Christopher. *On a Complex Theory of a Simple God: An Investigation in Aquinas' Philosophical Theology*. Cornell Studies in the Philosophy of Religion. Ithaca, NY: Cornell University Press, 1989.

Immink, Frederik Gerrit. *Divine Simplicity = De Eenvoud Gods*. Kampen: Kok, 1987.

Jones, Douglas M. "Metaphor in Exile." In *Bound Only Once: The Failure of Open Theism*, edited by Douglas Wilson, 31–52. Moscow, ID: Canon, 2001.

Keil, C. F., and F. Delitzsch. *Commentary on the Old Testament in Ten Volumes*. Vol. 1, *The Pentateuch*. Translated by James Martin. Grand Rapids: Eerdmans, 1980.

Klauber, M. I., and Glenn S. Sunshine. "Jean-Alphonse Turrettini on Biblical Accommodation: Calvinist or Socinian?" *Calvin Theological Journal* 25 (1990): 7–27.

Köstenberger, Andreas J. *John*. Baker Exegetical Commentary on the New Testament. Grand Rapids: Baker Academic, 2004.

Leftow, Brian. "Aquinas, Divine Simplicity and Divine Freedom." In *Metaphysics and God: Essays in Honor of Eleonore Stump*, edited by Kevin Timpe, 21–38. New York: Routledge, 2009.

Leftow, Brian, and Brian Davies, eds. *Aquinas: Summa Theologiae, Questions on God*. Cambridge Texts in the History of Philosophy. Cambridge: Cambridge University Press, 2006.

Letham, Robert. *The Westminster Assembly: Reading Its Theology in Historical Context*. Phillipsburg, NJ: P&R, 2009.

Longman, Tremper, III, and Daniel G. Reid. *God Is a Warrior*. Grand Rapids: Zondervan, 1995.

MacDonald, Neil B. *Metaphysics and the God of Israel: Systematic Theology of the Old and New Testaments*. Grand Rapids: Baker Academic, 2007.

Martin, Michael, and Ricki Monnier. *The Impossibility of God*. Amherst, NY: Prometheus, 2003.

Maurer, Armand A. "James Ross on the Divine Ideas: A Reply." *American Catholic Philosophical Quarterly* 65 (1991): 213–20.

Mavrodes, George I. "How Does God Know the Things He Knows?" In *Divine and Human Action: Essays in the Metaphysics of Theism*, edited by Thomas V. Morris, 345–61. Ithaca, NY: Cornell University Press, 1988.

McCormack, Bruce. "Christ and the Decree: An Unsettled Question for the Reformed Churches Today." In *Reformed Theology in Contemporary Perspective*, edited by Lynn Quigley, 124–42. Edinburgh: Rutherford House, 2006.

———. "Grace and Being: The Role of Gracious Election in Karl Barth's Theological Ontology." In *The Cambridge Companion to Karl Barth*, edited by John Webster, 92–110. Cambridge: Cambridge University Press, 2000.

McGowan, A. T. B. *The Divine Authenticity of Scripture: Retrieving an Evangelical Heritage*. Downers Grove, IL: IVP Academic, 2008.

Moreland, J. P., and Scott Rae. *Body and Soul: Human Nature and the Crisis in Ethics*. Downers Grove, IL: InterVarsity, 2000.

Morris, Thomas V. *The Logic of God Incarnate*. Ithaca, NY: Cornell University Press, 1986.

Muller, Richard A. *After Calvin: Studies in the Development of a Theological Tradition*. Oxford: Oxford University Press, 2003.

———. *Christ and the Decree: Christology and Predestination in Reformed Theology from Calvin to Perkins*. Durham, NC: Labyrinth, 1986.

———. *Dictionary of Latin and Greek Theological Terms: Drawn Principally from Protestant Scholastic Theology*. Grand Rapids: Baker, 1985.

———. *Post-Reformation Reformed Dogmatics: The Rise and Development of Reformed Orthodoxy, ca. 1520 to ca. 1725*. Vol. 2, *Holy Scripture*. Grand Rapids: Baker, 2003.

———. *Post-Reformation Reformed Dogmatics: The Rise and Development of Reformed Orthodoxy, ca. 1520 to ca. 1725*. Vol. 3, *The Divine Essence and Attributes*. Grand Rapids: Baker, 2003.

———. *Post-Reformation Reformed Dogmatics: The Rise and Development of Reformed Orthodoxy, ca. 1520 to ca. 1725*. Vol. 4, *The Triunity of God*. Grand Rapids: Baker, 2003.

———. "The Priority of the Intellect in the Soteriology of Jacob Arminius." *Westminster Theological Journal* 55, no. 1 (1993): 55–72.

Murray, John. "Reviews: The Person and Work of Christ. By Benjamin Breckenridge Warfield." In *Collected Writings of John Murray*. Vol. 3, *Life, Sermons and Reviews*, 358–60. Carlisle, PA: Banner of Truth, 1982.

———. "The Study of the Bible." In *The Claims of Truth*, 3–8. Carlisle, PA: Banner of Truth, 1976.

Nicoll, W. Robertson, ed. *The Expositor's Greek New Testament*. Vol. 1. Grand Rapids: Eerdmans, 1970.

Oliphint, K. Scott. "Most Moved Mediator." *Themelios* 30, no. 1 (2004): 39–51.

———. *Reasons for Faith: Philosophy in the Service of Theology*. Phillipsburg, NJ: P&R, 2006.

———. "Something Much Too Plain to Say." In *Resurrection and Eschatology: Theology in Service of the Church*, edited by Lane G. Tipton and Jeffrey C. Waddington, 361–82. Phillipsburg, NJ: P&R, 2008.

Olson, Roger E. *Arminian Theology: Myths and Realities*. Downers Grove, IL: IVP Academic, 2006.

Owen, John. *The Works of John Owen.* Edited by W. H. Gould. Ages Digital Library CD edition. 16 vols. Edinburgh: Banner of Truth, 1977.

Peterson, Michael L. *Philosophy of Religion: Selected Readings.* Oxford: Oxford University Press, 1996.

Pictet, Benedict. *Christian Theology.* Translated by Frederick Reyroux. Oxford: Oxford University Press, 1834.

Pinnock, Clark H. "Between Classical and Process Theism." In *Process Theology,* edited by Ronald H. Nash, 309–27. Grand Rapids: Baker, 1987.

———. ed. *The Grace of God, the Will of Man.* Grand Rapids: Academie, 1989.

———. *Most Moved Mover: A Theology of God's Openness.* Didsbury Lectures, 2000. Grand Rapids: Baker Academic, 2001.

Pinnock, Clark H., et al. *The Openness of God: A Biblical Challenge to the Traditional Understanding of God.* Downers Grove, IL: InterVarsity, 1994.

Plantinga, Alvin. "Advice to Christian Philosophers." *Faith and Philosophy* 1, no. 3 (1984): 253–71.

———. "Divine Knowledge." In *Christian Perspectives on Religious Knowledge,* edited by C. Stephen Evans and Merold Westphal, 40–65. Grand Rapids: Eerdmans, 1993.

———. "Does God Have a Nature?" In *The Analytic Theist: An Alvin Plantinga Reader,* edited by James F. Sennett, 225–57. Grand Rapids: Eerdmans, 1998.

Pojman, Louis P., ed. *Philosophy of Religion: An Anthology.* Belmont, CA: Wadsworth, 1987.

Propp, William H. C. *Exodus 1–18.* The Anchor Yale Bible Commentaries. New Haven, CT: Yale University Press, 1999.

Rice, Richard. "Biblical Support for a New Perspective." In *The Openness of God: A Biblical Challenge to the Traditional Understanding of God,* by Clark H. Pinnock, et al., 11–58. Downers Grove, IL: InterVarsity, 1994.

———. "Process Theism and the Open View of God." In *Searching for an Adequate God: A Dialogue Between Process and Free Will Theists,* edited by John B. Cobb, and Clark H. Pinnock, 163–200. Grand Rapids: Eerdmans, 2000.

Ridderbos, Herman. *The Gospel of John: A Theological Commentary.* Translated by John Vriend. Grand Rapids: Eerdmans, 1997.

———. *Paul: An Outline of His Theology.* Translated by John Richard DeWitt. Grand Rapids: Eerdmans, 1975.

Ronning, John L. *The Jewish Targums and John's Logos Theology.* Peabody, MA: Hendrickson, 2009.

Ross, James F. "Aquinas's Exemplarism; Aquinas's Voluntarism." *American Catholic Philosophical Quarterly* 64 (1990): 171–98.

———. "God, Creator of Kinds and Possibilities: Requiescant Universalia Ante Res." In *Rationality, Religious Belief, and Moral Commitment*, edited by Robert Audi and William J. Wainwright. Ithaca, NY: Cornell University Press, 1986.

———. "Response to Maurer and Dewan." *American Catholic Philosophical Quarterly* 65 (1991): 235–43.

Rowe, William L., and William J. Wainwright, eds. *Philosophy of Religion: Selected Readings*. 3rd ed. Fort Worth, TX: Harcourt Brace, 1973.

Sanders, John. *The God Who Risks: A Theology of Providence*. Downers Grove, IL: InterVarsity, 1998.

———. "Historical Considerations." In *The Openness of God: A Biblical Challenge to the Traditional Understanding of God*, by Clark H. Pinnock, et al., 59–100. Downers Grove, IL: InterVarsity, 1994.

Schaff, Philip. *The Nicene and Post-Nicene Fathers*. Series 2. Vol. 10. Oak Harbor, WA: Logos Research Systems, 1997.

Sennett, James F. "Why Think There Are Any True Counterfactuals of Freedom?" *Philosophy of Religion* 32 (1992): 105–16.

Silva, Moisés. *Biblical Words and Their Meaning: An Introduction to Lexical Semantics*. Grand Rapids: Zondervan, 1983.

———. "The Case for Calvinistic Hermeneutics." In *Revelation and Reason: New Essays in Reformed Apologetics*, edited by K. Scott Oliphint and Lane G. Tipton, 74–94. Phillipsburg, NJ: P&R, 2007.

———. *Philippians*. The Wycliffe Exegetical Commentary. Chicago: Moody, 1988.

Sparks, Kenton L. *God's Word in Human Words: An Evangelical Appropriation of Critical Biblical Scholarship*. Baker Academic, 2008.

Stump, Eleonore. *Aquinas*. New York: Routledge, 2003.

———. "Aquinas' Metaphysics of the Incarnation." In *The Incarnation*, edited by Stephen T. Davis, Daniel Kendall, SJ, and Gerald O'Collins, SJ, 197–218. Oxford: Oxford University Press, 2002.

Stump, Eleonore, and Norman Kretzmann. "God's Knowledge and Its Causal Efficacy." In *The Rationality of Belief and the Plurality of Faith*, edited by Thomas D. Senor, 94–124. Ithaca, NY: Cornell University Press, 1995.

Taylor, Thomas. *Christ Revealed: Or, the Old Testament Explained. A Treatise of the Types and Shadows of Our Saviour Contained Throughout the Whole Scripture: All Opened and Made Usefull for the Benefit of God's Church*. 1635. Reprint, Delmar, NY: Scholar's Facsimiles and Reprints, 1979.

Tiessen, Terrance L. "Why Calvinists Should Believe in Divine Middle Knowledge, Although They Reject Molinism." *Westminster Theological Journal* 69, no. 2 (2007): 345–66.

Turretin, Francis. *Institutes of Elenctic Theology*. Translated by George Musgrave Giger. Edited by James T. Dennison Jr. 3 vols. Phillipsburg, NJ: P&R, 1992–1997.

van Asselt, Willem J. "The Fundamental Meaning of Theology: Archetypal and Ectypal Theology in Seventeenth-Century Reformed Thought." *Westminster Theological Journal* 64, no. 2 (2002): 319–36.

Van Dyke, Christina. "Not Properly a Person: The Rational Soul and 'Thomistic Substance Dualism.'" *Faith and Philosophy* 26, no. 2 (2009): 186–204.

Van Til, Cornelius. *Christianity and Barthianism*. Philadelphia: Presbyterian and Reformed, 1962.

———. *The Defense of the Faith*. 4th ed. Edited by K. Scott Oliphint. Phillipsburg, NJ: P&R, 2008.

———. *An Introduction to Systematic Theology*. 2nd ed. Edited by William Edgar. Phillipsburg, NJ: P&R, 2007.

———. *The New Modernism: An Appraisal of the Theology of Barth and Brunner*. Philadelphia: Presbyterian and Reformed, 1947.

Vos, Geerhardus. "The Doctrine of the Covenant in Reformed Theology." In *Redemptive History and Biblical Interpretation: The Shorter Writings of Geerhardus Vos*, edited by Richard B. Gaffin Jr., 234–67. Phillipsburg, NJ: Presbyterian and Reformed, 1980.

———. "The Idea of Biblical Theology." In *Redemptive History and Biblical Interpretation: The Shorter Writings of Geerhardus Vos*, edited by Richard B. Gaffin Jr., 3–24. Phillipsburg, NJ: Presbyterian and Reformed, 1980.

———. "The Range of the Logos-Title in the Prologue to the Fourth Gospel." *Princeton Theological Review* 11 (1913): 365–419. Also in *Redemptive History and Biblical Interpretation: The Shorter Writings of Geerhardus Vos*, edited by Richard B. Gaffin Jr., 59–90. Phillipsburg, NJ: Presbyterian and Reformed, 1980.

———. *The Self-Disclosure of Jesus: The Modern Debate About the Messianic Consciousness*. New York: Doran, 1926. Reprint, Phillipsburg, NJ: P&R, 2002.

Waltke, Bruce K. "Revisiting Inspiration and Incarnation." *Westminster Theological Journal* 71, no. 1 (2009): 83–128.

Waltke, Bruce K., and Charles Yu. *An Old Testament Theology: An Exegetical, Canonical, and Thematic Approach*. Grand Rapids: Zondervan, 2007.

Ware, Bruce, ed. *Perspectives on the Doctrine of God: Four Views*. Nashville: B&H Academic, 2008.

Warfield, Benjamin Breckinridge. *Calvin and Augustine*. Philadelphia: Presbyterian and Reformed, 1974.

———. "The Emotional Life of Our Lord." In *The Person and Work of Christ*, edited by Samuel G. Craig, 93–148. Philadelphia: Presbyterian and Reformed, 1950.

———. "Imitating the Incarnation." In *The Person and Work of Christ*, edited by Samuel G. Craig, 563–75. Philadelphia: Presbyterian and Reformed, 1950.

———. "The Person of Christ According to the New Testament." In *The Person and Work of Christ*, edited by Samuel G. Craig, 37–72. Philadelphia: Presbyterian and Reformed, 1950.

———. *The Works of Benjamin B. Warfield*. Vol. 5, *Calvin and Calvinism*. Bellingham, WA: Logos Research Systems, 2008.

Wolterstorff, Nicholas. "God Everlasting." In *God and the Good: Essays in Honor of Henry Stob*, edited by Henry Stob, Clifton Orlebeke, and Lewis B. Smedes. Grand Rapids: Eerdmans, 1975.

Wright, N. T. "Jesus' Self-Understanding." In *The Incarnation*, edited by Stephen T. Davis, Daniel Kendall, SJ, and Gerald O'Collins, SJ, 47–63. Oxford: Oxford University Press, 2002.

Zagzebski, Linda Trinkaus. *The Dilemma of Freedom and Foreknowledge*. New York: Oxford University Press, USA, 1996.

General Index

Abraham, Isaac, and Jacob, 57–59, 60, 112, 120, 124, 192
Abraham, sacrifice of Isaac, 192–93, 227–28
absolute necessity, 70
absolute power, 234
"accidental" union, hypostatic union as, 154–55
accommodation, 114, 121–28, 131. *See also* condescension of God
  as adoption or adaptation, 124–27, 131
action and patient, 86
actions of God, 217
actualistic ontology, 150–51
actuality, 105n41, 239, 242
Adonai, 53
affections, 212–18
Ainsworth, Henry, 30–31, 170n65
Alexander of Hales, 42n78
Ambrose, 172
analogical knowledge, 63, 131
analytic philosophy, 77
Angel of the covenant, 169–72
angel of the Lord, 56, 109, 124n88, 169–72, 182, 192
anger, of God, 189–91, 215, 216
anhypostatic, 142, 199
Anselm, 86n81
anthropomorphic language, 123, 124n87
anthropopathisms, 211–12, 218
antinomy, 36–38, 178–79, 208–9, 226
apophatic theology, 62, 68, 71
Aquinas. *See* Thomas Aquinas
archetype and ectype, 123, 127–28, 244

Arianism, 139
Aristotle, 91, 128, 151, 215
Arius, 65n33
Arminianism, 33n58, 44n79, 100n30, 101, 107, 188n9, 192, 199, 210n54, 217, 218n70, 225–26, 269–71, 278
Arminius, 32n57, 100n30
a se, 16, 19, 62, 64. *See also* God, aseity of
Asselt, Willem J. van, 244
assumptio carnis, 263–64, 265
atemporal causation, 34
Athanasian Creed, 41
Athanasius, 146
atheological arguments, 35
A-theory of time (process view), 74–75, 78
attributes of God, 12–19
attribution, 49–50
Augustine, 33n58, 81, 193–94, 209, 237, 238
autotheos, Son as, 175–76

Barth, Karl, 39, 83n78, 106n44, 149–51, 182n1, 256–67
Bavinck, Herman
  on anthropomorphisms, 123n85
  on aseity, 18–19
  on essences, 242–43
  on incarnation, 142n18, 148, 149, 267
  on Logos, 165n59, 169, 171
  on Mediator, 108–9, 197n27
  on names of God, 51
  on time and eternity, 249n51

Scripture Index

2:52—154, 228
9:22—145
10:21—149
12:41—149
22:39–46—276
24:26—109
24:27—207

John
book of—249n52
1:1—109, 110, 120, 145,
   266
1:1-2—157n45
1:1-3—111
1:1-5—158, 165
1:3—109, 158, 158nn47-
   48, 159
1:4—158, 158n47, 159,
   159n50, 160, 161, 163
1:4b—162
1:4-5—163
1:5—160, 161, 162, 163,
   165n60
1:6—161, 161n54
1:6-8—160, 161n54, 163,
   164
1:7-9—161n54
1:8—160, 161n54
1:9—161, 162, 163, 164,
   165
1:9-10—164
1:9-11—158
1:10—164, 165, 165n60,
   166, 166n60, 167
1:10c—167, 168, 168n62
1:10f.—162
1:11—164, 165, 166,
   166n60, 167
1:11c—167, 168, 168n62
1:12—168
1:14—120, 120n80,
   130n101
1:14-18—120n80
1:15—161, 161n54
1:30—161, 161n54
3:13—145
5:46—169
7:32-39—164
8:12—162

8:23—164
8:56—109
8:56ff.—172
8:57-59—170
8:58—109, 177n84
9:5—164
11:27—162, 164
11:33—149
11:35—149
11:38—149
12:48—164
14:6—109
14:8-10—173
15:16—112
15:18-19—164
17:3—5
17:4—106n46
17:5—164
17:12—233
17:18—106n46
17:24—105n42, 249

Acts
2:22-23—215
2:23—109, 276n118
2:36—177n84
4:12—109
4:28—109
7:30—170, 171n68
17:24—27n45
17:28—81n74
20:28—145

Romans
1:18ff.—27n45
1:20—22, 29, 82, 130
1:20-21—166n61
8—270
8:3—109
8:18-23—112
8:26-27—266
9:22-23—260n77
9:33—177
10:13—48
11:33ff.—42, 226
11:33-35—12
11:33-36—135, 209, 213,
   266, 278
14:11—177

1 Corinthians
2:8—145, 179

10:4—109
10:9—109
12:3—176
15:45ff.—138

2 Corinthians
4:4—138
5:19—31
6:16—60
8:9—109

Galatians
4:4—109, 266
4:4ff.—206

Ephesians
1:4—13n9, 105n42
1:4ff.—276
1:5-6—260n77
1:10—266
1:11—213, 270
1:20—13n9
1:22-23—81n74

Philippians
2—134, 139
2:1-10—266
2:3—118
2:4-8—197
2:5ff.—88n84, 266
2:5-7—136
2:5-8—87, 116–17
2:5-11—176
2:6—109, 138
2:8—119
2:9-11—176
2:11—177nn83–84

Colossians
1—139
1:15—116, 138, 199
1:19—116
2:8ff.—120, 221

1 Thessalonians
4:5—166n61

2 Thessalonians
1:8—166n61

1 Timothy
2:5—109

NOW AVAILABLE FROM CROSSWAY

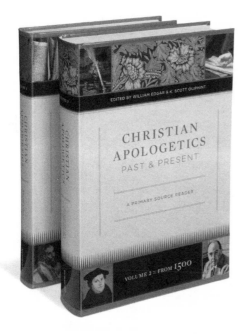

Christian Apologetics Past and Present
(Volume 1, To 1500)
978-1-58134-906-1

Christian Apologetics Past and Present
(Volume 2, From 1500)
978-1-58134-907-8

"Bill Edgar, one of evangelicalism's most valued scholars and apologists, has given us in this work with Scott Oliphint a classic destined to be used for generations. I highly recommend it to all who are called to defend the faith."
CHARLES COLSON, Founder, Prison Fellowship

"The texts here assembled are 'classics'—not in the sense that they answer all legitimate questions about Christianity, but that, when they were written, they made their readers think hard about the faith, and that they continue to do so today. This is a most worthy collection."
MARK A. NOLL, Francis A. McAnaney Professor of History, University of Notre Dame

"Understanding apologetics as explicating, affirming, and vindicating Christianity in the face of uncertainty and skepticism, Edgar and Oliphint have skillfully selected the best primary sources to introduce us to this ongoing task. Their work fills a gap in scholarly resources and highlights the strength, wisdom, and solidity of the prominent defenders of our faith."
J. I. PACKER, Board of Governors' Professor of Theology, Regent College; author, *Knowing God*

"This reader on the classical traditions of Christian apologetics is, to my knowledge, unmatched in basic compendia. It will equip and encourage thoughtful Christians to develop equally compelling defenses of the faith in our post-Enlightenment, post-Romantic, post-Postmodern era where global interdependencies plunge many into new varieties of suspicion, contempt, and hostility that demand reasonable and faith-filled encounter, dialogue, and debate."
MAX L. STACKHOUSE, De Vries Professor of Theology and Public Life Emeritus, Princeton Theological Seminary